Strive for a 5: Preparing for the Macroeconomics AP* Examination

D1383755

Strive for a 5:
Preparing for the Macroeconomics AP* Examination

to accompany

KRUGMAN'S

MACROECONOMICS for AP*

Margaret Ray and David Anderson

Margaret Ray

University of Mary Washington

David Mayer

Churchill High School

WORTH PUBLISHERS/BFW

Strive for a 5: Preparing for the Macroeconomics AP* Examination
by Margaret Ray and David Mayer
to accompany
Krugman's Macroeconomics for AP*

© 2011 by Worth Publishers

Printed in the United States of America

ISBN 10: 1-4292-6359-8
ISBN 13: 978-1-4292-6359-7

First Printing

Worth Publishers
41 Madison Avenue
New York, NY 10010
www.bfwpub.com/highschool

CONTENTS

Preface   *vii*

Section 1

Basic Economic Concepts   1

Module 1   The Study of Economics 2
Module 2   Introduction to Macroeconomics 7
Module 3   The Production Possibilities Model 11
Module 4   Comparative Advantage and Trade 14

Section 2

Supply and Demand   35

Module 5   Introduction and Demand 36
Module 6   Supply and Equilibrium 41
Module 7   Changes in Equilibrium 45
Module 8   Price Controls (Ceilings and Floors) 48
Module 9   Quantity Controls 51

Section 3

Measurement of Economic Performance   79

Module 10   The Circular Flow and Gross Domestic Product 80
Module 11   Interpreting Real Gross Domestic Product 85
Module 12   The Meaning and Calculation of Unemployment 88
Module 13   The Causes and Categories of Unemployment 91
Module 14   Inflation: An Overview 94
Module 15   The Measurement and Calculation of Inflation 97

Section 4

National Income and Price Determination   121

Module 16   Income and Expenditure 122
Module 17   Aggregate Demand: Introduction and Determinants 126
Module 18   Aggregate Supply: Introduction and Determinants 129
Module 19   Equilibrium in the Aggregate Demand-Aggregate Supply Model 132
Module 20   Economic Policy and the Aggregate Demand-Aggregate
               Supply Model 136
Module 21   Fiscal Policy and the Multiplier 139

Section 5

The Financial Sector   163

Module 22   Saving, Investment, and the Financial System 164
Module 23   The Definition and Measurement of Money 169
Module 24   The Time Value of Money 172
Module 25   Banking and Money Creation 174
Module 26   The Federal Reserve System: History and Structure 178
Module 27   The Federal Reserve System: Monetary Policy 181
Module 28   The Money Market 184
Module 29   The Market for Loanable Funds 187

Section 6

Inflation, Unemployment, and Stabilization Policies 213

Module 30 Long-run Implications of Fiscal Policy: Deficits and the Public Debt 214
Module 31 Monetary Policy and the Interest Rate 217
Module 32 Money, Output, and Prices in the Long Run 220
Module 33 Types of Inflation, Disinflation, and Deflation 223
Module 34 Inflation and Unemployment: The Phillips Curve 226
Module 35 History and Alternative Views of Macroeconomics 230
Module 36 The Modern Macroeconomic Consensus 234

Section 7

Economic Growth and Productivity 259

Module 37 Long-run Economic Growth 260
Module 38 Productivity and Growth 263
Module 39 Growth Policy: Why Economic Growth Rates Differ 266
Module 40 Economic Growth in Macroeconomic Models 269

Section 8

The Open Economy: International Trade and Finance 283

Module 41 Capital Flows and the Balance of Payments 284
Module 42 The Foreign Exchange Market 287
Module 43 Exchange Rate Policy 290
Module 44 Exchange Rates and Macroeconomic Policy 293
Module 45 Putting It All Together 295

Preparing for the AP Macroeconomics Exam 319

PREFACE

This book, *Strive for a 5: Preparing for the Macroeconomics AP* Examination,* is designed for use with *Krugman's Macroeconomics for AP** by Margaret Ray and David Anderson. It is intended to help you evaluate your understanding of the material covered in the textbook, reinforce the key concepts you need to learn, and prepare you to take the AP Macroeconomics exam. This book is divided into two sections: a study guide section and a test preparation section.

THE STUDY GUIDE SECTION

The study guide section is designed for you to use throughout your AP course. As each module is covered in your class, you can use the study guide to help you identify and learn the important economic models, concepts, and terms. After you read the modules in each section, this guide provides practice problems and review questions to help you master the material and verify your understanding before moving on to the next section.

For each **Section,** the study guide is organized as follows:

Overview: An overview of the section content that provides an orientation to the material covered in the section which will be broken down into the separate modules in the section.

Featured graph: Each section focuses on an important economic model. At the start of each section, the economic model that is developed in the section is identified and described.

Listing of modules: Each section is broken into 4–8 modules. This list identifies each of the modules within the section.

Module content: Each section includes a module-by-module presentation of the important content in the section.

Before You Take the Test:

- Draw the featured graph: For each section, a framework is provided to help you begin practicing drawing the featured graph.
- Complete the exercise: Each section includes an exercise designed to illustrate how to apply the economic content developed in the section.
- Problems: A set of comprehensive practice problems designed to help you learn to apply economic concepts.
- Review Questions: A set of multiple-choice questions that focus on the key concepts from the text that you should grasp after reading the Module. These questions are designed for quick exam preparation.
- Answer Key: Answers to all questions and problems in the study guide—along with thorough explanations. Students often use an answer section to simply check if they have gotten the "right" answer. I caution you to use the answer section accompanying each section with an eye to getting the highest possible value from the exercises provided. In economics, the reasoning used in coming to conclusions and correctly modeling the problems are as important as coming to an accurate answer. Explanations for each problem have been provided in order for you to check that your understanding of the concepts has been appropriately applied.

For each **Module,** the study guide is organized as follows:

Before You Read the Module: Use this section to gain a basic understanding of what you will be reading about and the learning objectives for the module BEFORE you start to read.

- Summary: an opening paragraph that provides a brief overview of the Module.
- Objectives: a list outlining and describing the material that you should have learned in the Module with a space to check as you master each one.

While You Read the Module: Use this section to be active as you read the module so that you begin to understand and remember what you read.

- Key Terms: a list of key terms with room to write definitions.
- Questions: space to note any questions that you have as you read the module.

After You Read the Module: Use this section to identify areas where you need to spend more time reading and studying the material in the module.

- Fill-in-the-blank questions designed to help identify important topics in the module.
- A module review that discusses common difficulties with the module material and providing tips for mastering the module content.

THE TEST PREPARATION SECTION

Preparing for the AP Macroeconomics Exam, the test preparation section of this guide, is written by David Mayer, an AP Economics teacher with a wealth of experience preparing students to successfully show their mastery of economic principles on the AP Macroeconomic exam. Use this guide to help you better understand how the exam is constructed and scored, how best to study for the exam, and how to make sure you highlight what you have learned when answering exam questions. While you focus on this guide as you complete your AP Macroeconomics course and begin to review for the AP Exam, it is a good idea to read through this guide early in the course so that you have a solid understanding of what you are preparing for from the start.

The study of economics has the potential of altering the way you evaluate and understand the world. I hope that your use of *Strive for a 5: Preparing for the Macroeconomics AP* Examination* will help you in your study of basic macroeconomics principles and will provide a jumping-off point for further study in the economics field.

Margaret A. Ray

David Mayer

Basic Economic Concepts

OVERVIEW

This section provides an introduction to the study of economics. It presents the definition of economics and the difference between the two main branches of the discipline, microeconomics and macroeconomics. In addition, it introduces the business cycle, a major focus of macroeconomics, and three important measures economists use when they study it: unemployment, inflation, and aggregate output. Finally, this section develops the production possibilities curve model and uses it to explain basic economic activity, including trade between countries. Because the study of economics relies heavily on graphical models, an appendix on the use of graphs follows this section.

Economics is a social science, and therefore, like history or geography, it is concerned with the study of people. However, learning the economic way of thinking can be different from learning about other social sciences. Often, the way you study math or statistics will be the best approach to studying economics. As you begin your study of economics, keep in mind that you need to adapt your approach to fit the unique nature of the discipline. Blend your approach to learning other social sciences with your approach to learning math or statistics.

FEATURED MODEL/GRAPH: THE PRODUCTION POSSIBILITIES CURVE

This section presents the first of many economic models in the course, the production possibilities curve, or PPC, which is also known as the production possibilities frontier, or PPF. The PPC is a basic macroeconomic model that illustrates the production choices (i.e., possibilities) from which an economy can choose. The model is used to illustrate the basic economic concepts presented in this section, as well as to introduce the use of models in economics.

MODULES IN THIS SECTION

Module 1: The Study of Economics

Module 2: Introduction to Macroeconomics

Module 3: The Production Possibilities Curve Model

Module 4: Comparative Advantage and Trade

Module ❶
The Study of Economics

Before You Read the MODULE

Summary

This module presents economics as the study of the production, distribution, and consumption of goods and services. It focuses on scarcity and the need to make choices, and the resulting importance of opportunity costs. The distinction between positive and normative economics and the two main branches of economics, micro and macro, are also explained.

Module Objectives

Review these objectives before you read the module. Place a "√" on the line when you understand each of the following:

_____**Objective 1.** Why **scarcity** is central to the study of economics

_____**Objective 2.** That the **opportunity cost** is what you must give up to get something

_____**Objective 3.** The difference between **positive** and **normative** economics

_____**Objective 4.** The two main branches of economics, **macroeconomics** and **microeconomics,** and what is studied in each

While You Read the MODULE

Key Terms

Define these key terms as you read the module.

Individual choice

Economy

Economics

Market economy

Resource

Land

Labor

Capital

Entrepreneurship

Scarce

Opportunity cost

Microeconomics

Macroeconomics

Economic aggregates

Positive economics

Normative economics

List questions from your initial reading of the module.

After You Read the MODULE

....

Fill-in-the-Blanks

Fill in the blanks to complete the following statements. Terms may be used more than once. If you find yourself having difficulties, please refer to the appropriate section in the text.

- You can say it isn't economics if it isn't about (1)_____.

- Individuals choose among a(n) (2)_____ number of alternatives.

  But they can't always get what they want because (3)_____ and

  _____ are limited.

- The activities that create the goods and services people want, and get them to the people

  who want them, form the system that we know as the (4)_____.

  The United States has a(n) (5)_____ economy, in which

production and consumption are the result of decentralized decisions made by many firms and individuals; there is no central authority telling people what to produce or where to ship it.

- A (6)_____ is anything that can be used to produce goods and services. Individuals must make choices because resources are (7)_____. A general list of resources would include (8)_____, _____, _____, and _____.

- Because economics is concerned with choices, it is important to consider what you must give up when you make a choice. This is known as the (9)_____ cost of a choice.

- Economics is divided into two main branches. Microeconomics studies the choices made by (10)_____, while macroeconomics focuses on data that summarize measures across many markets, called economic (11)_____.

- When economic analysis is used to answer questions about the way the world works that have definite right and wrong answers about the way the world works, it is known as (12)_____ economics. In contrast, economic analysis that involves saying how the world should work is known as (13)_____ economics. An economist who tells you that a certain policy is "good" or "bad" is engaging in (14)_____ economics.

Module Review

Studying Economics

John Maynard Keynes, considered by many to be the father of modern macroeconomics, wrote that "[Economics] is a method rather than a doctrine, an apparatus of the mind, a technique of thinking which helps its possessor to draw correct conclusions." Alfred Marshall, an influential microeconomist, describes economics as a study of the "ordinary business of life" and wrote that "[Economics] is not a body of concrete truth, but an engine for the discovery of concrete truth." Each of these important economists was pointing out that economics is a valuable way of thinking about the world rather than just an established body of knowledge.

You will be expected to solve new and varied problems by using this new "technique of think-ing," not by providing memorized definitions or explanations. Use the Problems and Review Questions below and in your textbook to determine if you have learned what you need to know.

At the beginning, try all of the sample questions, problems, and approaches you and your instructor can find, and determine which ones work best to help you master the material.

- The study of economics is cumulative. You should master each topic as it is presented because later topics build on earlier topics.

- Pay attention to new vocabulary and make sure you know, understand, and can apply these terms. You will be expected to do more than just define the terms: you must also be able to apply these terms in a meaningful manner.

- Plan to spend time every day studying economics. Review your lecture notes, review the vocabulary, work on the practice questions, and identify questions you have about the material. Once you identify your questions, seek out answers by returning to your text, your lecture notes, your classmates, or your teacher.

Module ❷
Introduction to Macroeconomics

Before You Read the MODULE

Summary

This module introduces the business cycle in an economy. It also presents three important related macroeconomic concepts: unemployment, inflation, and economic growth. Measures of employment, the price level, and aggregate output are used to evaluate the performance of the macroeconomy. The basic concepts are presented here and developed in greater detail in Section 3. These concepts will be used in the models we build throughout the course.

Module Objectives

Review these objectives before you read the module. Place a "√" on the line when you understand each of the following:

_____**Objective 1.** What **business cycles** are and why policy makers seek to diminish their severity

_____**Objective 2.** How **employment** and **unemployment** are measured, and how they change over the business cycle

_____**Objective 3.** What **aggregate output** is and how it changes over the business cycle

_____**Objective 4.** The meaning of **inflation** and **deflation,** and why **price stability** is preferred

_____**Objective 5.** How **long-run economic growth** determines a country's standard of living

_____**Objective 6.** The role of **models,** simplified representations of reality, in economics

While You Read the MODULE

Key Terms

Define these key terms as you read the module.

Business cycle

Short-run alternation between downturns, known as recessions, and economic upturns, known as expansions

Depression

a very deep & prolonged downturn

Recessions

are periods of economic downturns
when output & employment are falling

Expansions

recovery, period of economic upturn when
output & employment are rising

Employment

the number of people currently employed
in the economy

Unemployment

of people who are actually looking for
work but aren't currently employed

Labor force

equal to the sum of employment
& unemployment

Aggregate output

economy is total production of goods &
services for a given time period

Aggregate price level

Inflation

a rising of overall price level

Deflation

falling ut overall prize level

Price stability

the aggregate prize level is changing only slowly.

Long-run growth

an increase in the max possible output of an economy

Model

a simplified representation used to better understand a real-life situation.

Other things equal assumption (ceteris paribus)

means that all other relevant factors remain unchanged

List questions or difficulties from your initial reading of the module.

After You Read the MODULE

Fill-in-the-Blanks

Fill in the blanks to complete the following statements. Terms may be used more than once. If you find yourself having difficulties, please refer to the appropriate section in the text.

- The ups and downs in the macroeconomy are known as the

  (1) *business cycle*. Economic downturns are known as

  (2) *recessions*, and economic upturns are known as

  (3) *expansions*. During an economic downturn, employment and

aggregate output (4)___fall___ while unemployment

(5)___rises___.

- (6)___employment___ is the economic aggregate that measures the total number of people currently working for pay. Unemployment is the total number of people who are not currently employed but are actively (7)___looking for work___. A country's (8)___labor force___ is the sum of employment and unemployment.

- A rise in the overall price level is called (9)___inflation___.
(10)___reflection___ is a fall in the overall level of prices. Each of these creates problems in the economy, so economists work toward (11)___price stability___ as the desirable goal for the price level.

- A (12)___model___ is a simplified version of reality used to better understand real-life situations.

Module Review

Working with Models

A model is a simplified representation of reality used to better understand the world. An important part of economics is working with models. Very often, economic models use graphs to simplify reality and facilitate understanding. Graphs can make it much easier to understand verbal descriptions, numerical information, or ideas. An economist might say that a graph is worth a thousand words! To understand economics, you must learn how to interpret and manipulate graphs.

As you study economics, make sure that you are able not only to read and understand the graphs that you see, but also to construct and explain graphs of your own. The ability to represent an economic idea by drawing a graph is different from the ability to look at and understand an existing graph; you should be able to do both. The appendix to this section explains how graphs are constructed and interpreted, and how they are used in economics. The appendix, and lots of practice drawing, will help you to master graphs.

- Aggregation of data is at the heart of macroeconomics. This module briefly describes the meaning of aggregation and gives examples of aggregated measures like employment, real GDP, and the overall price level.

- To get used to the idea of drawing graphs in economics, begin by drawing your own graph of the business cycle. You can use the one in this module as a guide to the labels and information you will need on your graph.

- Many of the models you will encounter in this course make the other things equal assumption (also known as *ceteris paribus*), which means that the model considers only one change at a time while holding everything else constant. Make sure you understand this basic assumption before working with the models introduced in the module.

Module 3
The Production Possibilities Curve Model

Before You Read the MODULE

Summary

This module introduces the concept of model building by presenting the production possibility curve model. The PPC provides a simplified framework for discussing the concepts of opportunity cost, trade-offs, scarcity, efficiency, and (in the next module) gains from trade.

Module Objectives

Review these objectives before you read the module. Place a "√" on the line when you understand each of the following:

_____**Objective 1.** Why **trade-offs** are important in economic analysis

_____**Objective 2.** What a **production possibilities curve** illustrates and how it can be used to explain efficiency, opportunity cost, and economic growth

_____**Objective 3.** That the two sources of long-term economic growth (that shift the production possibilities curve outward) are **factors of production** and **technology**

While You Read the MODULE

Key Terms

Define these key terms as you read the module.

Trade-off

Production possibilities curve

Efficient

Factors of production
_____

Technology
_____

List questions or difficulties from your initial reading of the module.

After You Read the MODULE
....

Fill-in-the-Blanks

Fill in the blanks to complete the following statements. Terms may be used more than once. If you find yourself having difficulties, please refer to the appropriate section in the text.

- A graph that shows the trade-off between the production of two goods is called a

  (1)_____ curve. A production point is feasible if it lies

  (2)_____ or _____ this curve, but *not*

  feasible if it lies (3)_____ this curve. If a production point lies

  on this curve, there are no missed opportunities and production is

  (4)_____.

- If the PPC moves outward over time, the economy has experiencing

  (5)_____. This can be caused by an advance in

  (6)_____ or an increase in the economy's

  (7)_____.

- Because the PPC has a negative slope, producing more of one good means less of the other

  good can be produced. Therefore, a movement from one point on the PPC to another point

  on the PPC illustrates the concept of (8)_____ cost.

A First Economic Model

The production possibilities curve model is the first model presented in this book. It is important that you identify what the PPC model illustrates and how it is used to explain the choices facing any economy. The PPC model is a graphical representation of an economy that illustrates trade-offs, scarcity, opportunity cost, efficiency, and economic growth. You will need to understand how these concepts are illustrated on a PPC graph (i.e., movements along the curve, points on the curve, and shifts of the curve). You will also need to be able to draw a PPC graph and use it to illustrate and explain these concepts. Finally, you will need to understand these concepts with enough depth to answer questions in examples and contexts that you have not seen before. Achieving this level of understanding requires practice drawing and interpreting graphs, and applying the PPC model to different real-world and hypothetical examples. The ability to use economic models to analyze situations and answer questions is an essential part of mastering introductory economics.

- Economic models can be described verbally, but they can also be represented by graphs or equations. You will want to be comfortable working with all three types of representations. You may find it helpful to sketch graphs to illustrate the ideas you are analyzing. Practice making precise graphs using numbers, when they are provided, but also practice graphs that sketch the general relationship between variables without numbers.

- Opportunity cost can be measured using the production possibilities curve model. To do this calculation, pick a point on the PPC and identify how much of each good is being produced. Then, pick a second point on the PPC and identify the new levels of production. The opportunity cost is measured as the number of units of the good you must give up to get more of the other good.

- Make sure you understand the PPC model. In particular, make sure you can draw and understand what is shown by both a linear and a "bowed out" PPC. Know the assumption that leads to a linear or bowed out PPC. Make sure you can identify and indicate feasible and infeasible points, as well as efficient and inefficient points. Know what two factors can shift the PPC out in the future.

- Here is a useful method for calculating opportunity cost based on a linear PPC, which will be crucial when determining comparative advantage in the next module. First, construct the PPC and, since it is linear, calculate the slope. Use the slope measure to generate the opportunity cost you want: the opportunity cost of producing one more unit of the good measured on the x-axis is given by the slope, since the slope tells us the change in the y-variable divided by the change in the x-variable. Thus, if the slope of the PPC is -2, then the opportunity cost of producing an additional unit of good X is 2 units of good Y. To find the opportunity cost of the good produced on the y-axis, use the reciprocal of the slope. Thus, if the slope of the linear PPC is -2, then the opportunity cost of producing one more unit of good Y is ½ unit of good X, the amount of good X we must give up to get one more unit of good Y.

Module 4
Comparative Advantage and Trade

Before You Read the MODULE

Summary

This module introduces the concepts of comparative and absolute advantage, and explains the benefits of specialization and trade. It shows how the PPC model can be used to illustrate gains from trade based on comparative advantage, and presents the basic economic argument in favor of international trade by showing that total world output can be increased when countries specialize and trade.

Module Objectives

Review these objectives before you read the module. Place a "√" on the line when you understand each of the following:

_____**Objective 1.** How specialization and **trade** lead to gains for an individual or economy

_____**Objective 2.** The difference between **absolute advantage** and **comparative advantage,** and how to determine each using tables of data or PPC models for two countries

_____**Objective 3.** How comparative advantage leads to global gains from trade

While You Read the MODULE

Key Terms

Define these key terms as you read the module.

Trade

Gains from trade

Specialization
_____

Comparative advantage
_____

Absolute advantage
_____

List questions or difficulties from your initial reading of the module.

After You Read the MODULE

Fill-in-the-Blanks

Fill in the blanks to complete the following statements. Terms may be used more than once. If you find yourself having difficulties, please refer to the appropriate section in the text.

- When people divide tasks among themselves and each person provides a good or service
  that other people want in return for different goods and services that he or she wants, it is
  called (1)_____. This is a key to a much higher standard of
  living for everyone because it allows for a division of tasks, called
  (2)_____.

- If the opportunity cost of production is lower for one person (or country) than it is for
  other people (or countries), then that person (or country) has a(n)
  (3)_____ advantage. If an individual (or country) can produce
  more output with a given amount of input than another person (or country), then that
  person (or country) has a(n) (4)_____ advantage.
  (5)_____ advantage is the basis for mutual gains from trade.

- Consider a simple example with two goods, "A" and "B," and two countries, "X" and "Y." If country "X" has a comparative advantage in the production of good "A," we know that country "Y" will have a comparative advantage in the production of good

    (6)_____.

Module Review

Misunderstanding Comparative Advantage

Students do it, pundits do it, and politicians do it all the time: they confuse *comparative* advantage with *absolute* advantage. For example, back in the 1980s, when the U.S. economy seemed to be lagging behind that of Japan, commentators warned that if we didn't improve our productivity, we would soon have no comparative advantage in anything. What those commentators meant was that we would have no *absolute* advantage in anything—that there might come a time when the Japanese were better at everything than we were. And they had the idea that in that case we would no longer be able to benefit from trade with Japan. But just as Hank is able to benefit from trade with Tom (and vice versa) despite the fact that Tom is better at everything, nations can still gain from trade even if they are less productive in all industries than the countries with which they trade.

- Once you can calculate the opportunity cost of producing good X or good Y, as explained in the previous module, you can compare the opportunity costs faced by two countries. The model of comparative advantage illustrates that countries will benefit from trade when they specialize and produce the good that has the lower opportunity cost of production relative to the other country.

BEFORE YOU TAKE THE TEST: section

Draw the Featured Graph: Production Possibilities Curve

Graphing with numbers
Graph the PPC corresponding to the data provided in the table below.

y-axis label

Fish	Coconuts
0	8
2	6
4	4
6	2
8	0

x-axis label

Graphing relationships without numbers

Graph a PPC showing the trade-off between two goods, good "A" and good "B." Draw your PPC so that it illustrates increasing opportunity costs.

y-axis label

x-axis label

Complete the Exercise

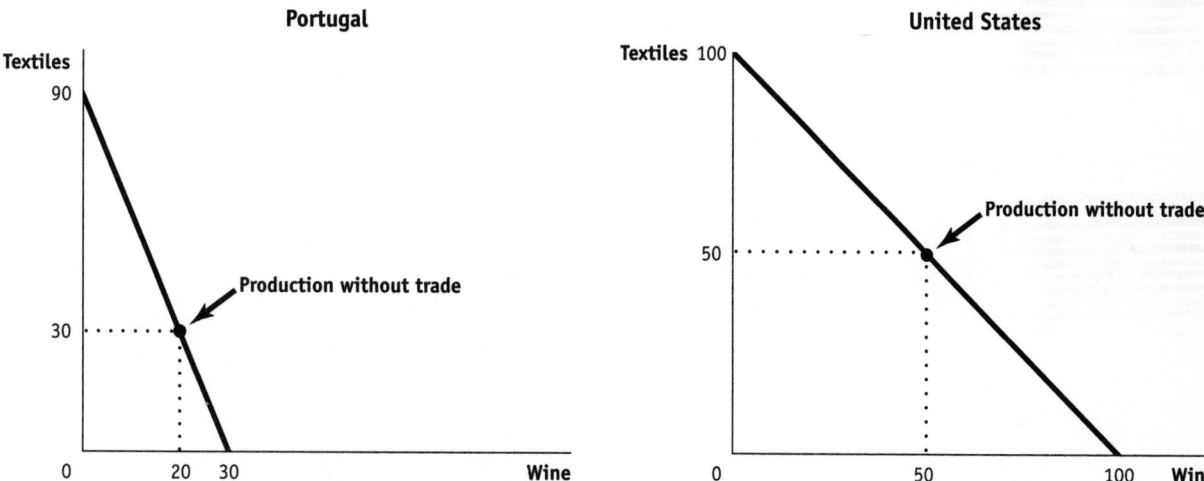

Use the information on the graphs above to fill in the blanks.

1. The opportunity cost of 1 unit of textiles in the United States is

    _____ and in Portugal is _____.

2. The opportunity cost of 1 unit of wine in the United States is

    _____ and in Portugal is _____.

3. Assuming the two countries have identical resources, the United States has an absolute ad-

    vantage in _____. Portugal has an absolute advantage in

    _____.

4. The United States has a comparative advantage in _____.

    Portugal has a comparative advantage in _____.

Fill in the table. Assume that with trade, each country specializes and exports ½ of its production.

	Without Trade		With Trade (Production)		With Trade (Consumption)	
	Wine	Textiles	Wine	Textiles	Wine	Textiles
Portugal						
United States						
Total						

5. What happens to total world output when countries specialize and trade?

6. What is this called?

7. Are the countries better off? Explain.

Problems

1. For each of the following situations, describe the opportunity cost of each decision.

   a. Sarah considers two options for Saturday night: she can attend a concert that costs $10 per ticket or she can see a free movie. She attends the concert.

   b. A new firm in town debates paying $20,000 for the prime location versus $10,000 for another location. The firm estimates that it will eventually serve the same number of customers in either location, but that it will take six months before the suboptimal location provides the same outcome as the prime location. The firm purchases the $10,000 property.

   c. Jamie can be either an unpaid intern at a company or he can earn $2,000 working as a camp counselor. He takes the internship.

2. The following table presents the possible combinations of study time available to Roberto this week as he prepares for his two midterms: economics and chemistry. Assume Roberto has 20 hours to study and that he will use all 20 hours studying economics and chemistry. Roberto currently plans to study 10 hours for economics and 10 hours for chemistry.

Hours of study time spent on economics	Hours of study time spent on chemistry	Grade in economics	Grade in chemistry
0	20	60	90
5	15	70	85
10	10	80	75
15	5	86	73
20	0	90	70

a. If he alters his plan and studies 15 hours for economics, what is his opportunity cost?

b. If he alters his plan and studies 15 hours for chemistry, what is his opportunity cost?

c. If he alters his plan and studies 20 hours for economics, what is his opportunity cost?

3. Decide whether each of the statements is a normative statement or a positive statement.
  a. The gasoline tax is projected to yield $10 million in tax revenue next year.

  b. If the gasoline tax were raised by 10 cents per gallon, tax revenue would increase by 4%.

  c. The state should raise the gasoline tax for the coming year. An increase in the tax will reduce congestion and smog, which is more important than the cost to commuters if they shift from private car transportation to public transportation.

d. Mandatory school enhances the work skills of students.

e. The age of mandatory school attendance should be extended.

f. An extension of mandatory school attendance will increase government education costs by $2 million for the state.

4. Economists sometimes disagree about positive economics, but more often they disagree about normative economics. Define both of these terms, and explain why economists do not always agree.

5. This section distinguishes between an economic expansion as part of the business cycle and long-run economic growth. Concisely explain the difference between these two terms.

6. In the beginning of 2008, suppose the population in Funland was 2 million people and the level of real GDP, or aggregate output, was $40 million. During 2008 population increased by 3%, while real GDP increased by 3%. During 2009 population increased by 4%, while real GDP increased by 3%. During 2010 population increased by 5%, while real GDP increased by 3%.

a. Fill in the following table using the given information. (Round to two decimal places.)

	Beginning of 2008	Beginning of 2009	Beginning of 2010	Beginning of 2011
Real GDP				
Population				
Real GDP/person				

b. What do you know about this country's standard of living between the beginning of 2008 and the end of 2010? Explain how you know.

7. The country of Utopia produces two goods from its available resources and technology. The only resource that Utopia has is labor. It takes 3 hours of labor to produce 2 widgets and 4 hours of labor to produce 1 gadget. For this question, assume that the PPC for Utopia is a straight line.

   a. Sketch the PPC for the country of Utopia. (Hint: Choose a relevant time period, e.g., 20 hours, as your labor constraint, and sketch your PPC based on this amount of time and labor.) Graph widgets on the y-axis and gadgets on the x-axis.

   b. What is the slope of your PPC?

   c. What is the opportunity cost of producing an additional widget in Utopia?

   d. What is the opportunity cost of producing an additional gadget in Utopia?

8. The country of Jonesville produces two goods from its available resources and technology. The only resource that Jonesville has is labor. It takes 2 hours of labor to produce a gadget and 5 hours of labor to produce a widget. For this question, assume that the PPC for Jonesville is linear.

   a. Suppose that you want to draw a PPC for Jonesville. What must you do first?

   b. Sketch the PPC for Jonesville assuming that it has 120 hours of labor available. Place gadgets on the x-axis and widgets on the y-axis.

   c. What is the slope of the PPC?

d. What is the opportunity cost of producing an additional gadget?

e. What is the opportunity cost of producing an additional widget?

f. Suppose that Jonesville has 240 hours of labor available instead of 120 hours of labor. Does this affect the opportunity cost of producing widgets or gadgets? Explain your answer.

9. The following table provides six possible production combinations that Smithtown can produce from its available resources and technology during this year. Assume that Smithtown produces only bicycles and tents from its available resources.

Combination	Bicycles	Tents
A	100	0
B	90	10
C	70	25
D	40	36
E	10	42
F	0	45

a. Sketch Smithtown's PPC. Measure bicycles along the x-axis and tents along the y-axis.

b. Suppose Smithtown is currently producing at combination C. If Smithtown chooses to produce at combination B, what is the opportunity cost of moving from combination C to B?

c. Suppose Smithtown is currently producing at combination C. If Smithtown chooses to produce at combination D, what is the opportunity cost of moving from combination C to D?

d. Smithtown's PPC is not linear. Explain why not.

10. There are two islands in the middle of the ocean, and these two islands produce fish and baskets. Big Island can produce either 100 fish per day and 0 baskets per day or 0 fish per day and 200 baskets per day. Big Island can also produce any combination of fish and baskets that lies on its linear PPC. Small Island can produce either 80 fish per day and 0 baskets per day or 0 fish per day and 80 baskets per day. Like Big Island, Small Island has a linear PPC.

   a. Sketch two graphs. Sketch Big Island's PPC on the first graph and Small Island's PPC on the second graph. Place fish/day on the *y*-axis and baskets/day on the *x*-axis.

   b. What is the slope of Big Island's PPC?

   c. What is the slope of Small Island's PPC?

   d. What is the opportunity cost of producing an additional basket on Big Island? What is the opportunity cost of producing an additional basket on Small Island? Which island can produce baskets at a lower opportunity cost?

   e. What is the opportunity cost of producing an additional fish on Big Island? What is the opportunity cost of producing an additional fish on Small Island? Which island can produce fish at a lower opportunity cost?

   f. What good should Big Island specialize in producing?

   g. What good should Small Island specialize in producing?

Review Questions

Circle the correct answer.

1. Scarcity of resources implies that

   A. people can do whatever they want and do not need to worry about making choices.
   B. life involves making choices about how to best use these scarce resources.
   C. societies need to invest time and money to discover more resources.
   D. only very wealthy individuals are not constrained by their resources.

2. Camillo is offered two jobs: one pays a salary of $30,000 per year and offers four weeks of vacation, and the other pays a salary of $32,000 per year and offers two weeks of vacation. What is the opportunity cost for Camillo of taking the job offering $32,000 per year?

   A. $2,000 plus two weeks of vacation per year
   B. $2,000 per year
   C. two weeks of vacation per year
   D. $30,000 plus two weeks of vacation per year

3. Which of the following statements is true about positive economics?
   I. Positive economics is about how the world should work.
   II. Positive economics is about how the world works.
   III. Positive economics is descriptive.

   A. Statements I, II, and III are all true.
   B. Statements I and III are true.
   C. Statements II and III are true.
   D. Statement II is true.

4. Which of the following statements is an example of normative economics?
   I. The United States should pass a value-added tax because this is a tax that will work best.
   II. A value-added tax will add $10 billion to the administrative costs of the U.S. tax system.
   III. A value-added tax will increase the economic burden of taxes on poor people by 15%.

   A. Statements I, II, and III
   B. Statements I and III
   C. Statements I and II
   D. Statement I

5. Macroeconomics, unlike microeconomics,

   A. considers the behavior of individual firms and markets.
   B. focuses on the production and consumption of particular goods.
   C. tries to explain increases in living standards over time.
   D. finds that the behavior of individuals is more important than its aggregate summation.

6. In a recession,

   A. unemployment increases, aggregate output decreases, and people enjoy higher living standards.
   B. unemployment increases while aggregate output and aggregate income decrease.
   C. aggregate output and aggregate income decrease, always leading to a depression.
   D. aggregate output must fall for at least three consecutive quarters.

7. Economic growth

   A. refers to increases in real GDP per capita over the long run.
   B. refers to short-term fluctuations in real GDP per capita.
   C. is best measured using the employment rate.
   D. is of little importance to economists.

8. Which of the following statements is true?

   A. An economy in a recession will have lower unemployment than during an expansion.
   B. In an economic expansion, the unemployment rate decreases while aggregate output increases.
   C. An economy's output level and employment rate move in opposite directions.
   D. Answers (b) and (c) are correct.

9. Inflation occurs when

   A. the aggregate level of output increases.
   B. the unemployment rate decreases.
   C. the aggregate price level rises over time.
   D. consumers' purchasing power increases over time.

10. An economic contraction

   A. is another term for an economic recession.
   B. indicates that the economy is experiencing a decrease in the level of employment.
   C. is part of the business cycle.
   D. Answers (a), (b), and (c) are all correct.

11. An economic expansion

   A. is another term for an economic recovery.
   B. indicates that the economy is experiencing a decrease in the level of unemployment.
   C. is that part of the business cycle between the trough and the peak.
   D. Answers (a), (b), and (c) are all correct.

12. Deflation occurs when

   A. economic production increases in the aggregate economy.
   B. the overall price level decreases in an economy.
   C. the overall level of employment decreases in the aggregate economy.
   D. both the overall price level and the overall level of employment in an economy decrease.

13. When the economy is in a recession,

   A. jobs are hard to find and the overall level of prices in the economy tends to rise.
   B. jobs are easy to find and the overall level of prices in the economy tends to rise.
   C. jobs are hard to find and the overall level of prices in the economy tends to fall.
   D. jobs are easy to find and the overall level of prices in the economy tends to fall.

14. Suppose Mike has a linear PPC in the production of potatoes and tomatoes. If he devotes all his time to the production of potatoes, he can produce 1,000 pounds of potatoes a year; if he devotes all his time to the production of tomatoes, he can produce 2,000 pounds of tomatoes a year. Which of the following combinations of potatoes and tomatoes is *not* feasible for Mike?

   A. 1,000 pounds of potatoes and 2,000 pounds of tomatoes per year
   B. 1,000 pounds of potatoes and 0 pounds of tomatoes per year
   C. 0 pounds of potatoes and 2,000 pounds of tomatoes per year
   D. 500 pounds of potatoes and 1,000 pounds of tomatoes per year

15. Utopia has a linear PPC in the production of widgets and gadgets. It can produce three gadgets per hour of labor time or four widgets per hour of labor time. What is the opportunity cost of producing one widget in Utopia?

   A. 3 gadgets   C. 0.75 gadget
   B. 4 widgets   D. 1.33 gadgets

16. (a) Jonesville produces widgets and gadgets, and its PPC is linear. It takes 5 hours of labor to produce a gadget and 10 hours of labor to produce a widget. Suppose that Jonesville has 100 hours of labor. What is the maximum number of widgets it can produce?

A. 10 widgets
B. 20 widgets
C. 1 widget
D. 100 widgets

(b) What is the maximum number of widgets and gadgets it can produce if it devotes half of its labor time to the production of gadgets and half of its labor time to the production of widgets?

A. 20 gadgets and 5 widgets
B. 10 gadgets and 5 widgets
C. 5 gadgets and 20 widgets
D. 5 gadgets and 10 widgets

(c) What happens to the opportunity cost of producing a widget if Jonesville's labor resource increases to 200 hours of labor? The opportunity cost of producing a widget

A. decreases.
B. increases.
C. does not change.
D. may increase, decrease, or remain unchanged, depending on the number of gadgets produced.

(d) If Jonesville has 100 units of labor, which of the following combinations of gadgets and widgets is *not* feasible for Jonesville?

A. 4 gadgets and 8 widgets
B. 7 gadgets and 7 widgets
C. 8 gadgets and 6 widgets
D. 0 gadgets and 10 widgets

17. Suburbia has a PPC bowed out from the origin of the two goods, guns and butter, that it produces from its available resources and technology. The following table describes six points that lie on Suburbia's PPC.

Combination	Number of guns	Pounds of butter
A	0	80
B	10	75
C	20	65
D	30	50
E	40	30
F	50	0

(a) Suppose Suburbia is initially producing at point *D*. What is the opportunity cost of moving to point *E*?

A. 10 guns
B. 40 guns
C. 20 pounds of butter
D. 30 pounds of butter

(b) Suppose Suburbia is initially producing at point *D*. What is the opportunity cost of moving to point *B*?

A. 25 pounds of butter
B. 20 guns
C. 10 guns
D. 75 pounds of butter

18. Suppose that two countries, Texia and Urbania, produce food and clothing, and currently do not trade. Both countries have linear PPCs. If Texia devotes all of its resources to food production, it can produce 1,000 units of food this year and 0 units of clothing. If it devotes all of its resources to clothing production, it can produce 500 units of clothing and 0 units of food. Urbania can produce either 500 units of food and 0 units of clothing or 200 units of clothing and 0 units of food. Which country has the absolute advantage in the production of clothing, and which has the absolute advantage in the production of food?

   A. Texia; Texia   C. Urbania; Texia
   B. Texia; Urbania   D. Urbania; Urbania

19. With regard to the two countries described in question 18, which country has the comparative advantage in the production of clothing, and which has the comparative advantage in the production of food.

   A. Texia; Texia   C. Urbania; Texia
   B. Texia; Urbania   D. Urbania; Urbania

20. Specialization and trade benefit

   A. usually only one of the trading partners.
   B. the wealthier country more than the poorer country.
   C. the poorer country more than the wealthier country.
   D. both countries if they specialize according to their comparative advantages.

ANSWER KEY

Fill-in-the-Blanks

Module 1: (1) choices; (2) unlimited; (3) time, income; (4) economy; (5) market; (6) resource; (7) scarce; (8) land, labor, capital, entrepreneurship; (9) opportunity; (10) individuals; (11) aggregate; (12) positive; (13) normative; (14) normative

Module 2: (1) business cycle, (2) recessions, (3) expansions (or recoveries), (4) fall, (5) rises, (6) employment, (7) looking for work, (8) labor force, (9) inflation, (10) deflation, (11) price stability, (12) model

Module 3: (1) production possibilities; (2) inside, on; (3) outside; (4) efficient; (5) economic growth, (6) technology; (7) factors of production; (8) opportunity cost

Module 4: (1) trade, (2) specialization, (3) comparative, (4) absolute, (5) comparative, (6) B

Featured Graph

Note: The vertical and horizontal axis labels can be switched in either graph.

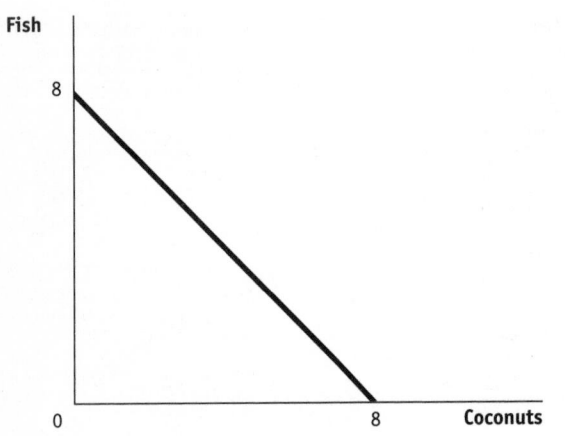
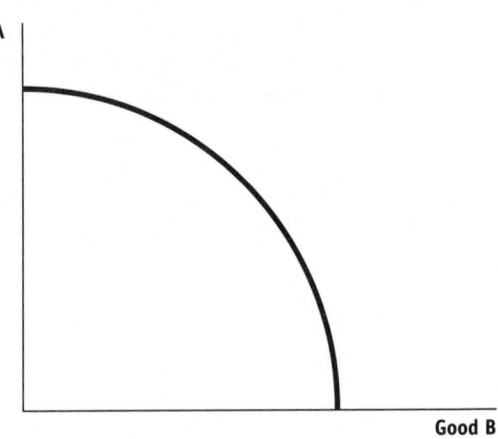

Exercise

1. 1 wine, 1/3 wine

2. 1 textiles, 3 textiles

3. wine and textiles, neither

4. wine, textiles

	Without Trade		With Trade (Production)		With Trade (Consumption)	
	Wine	Textiles	Wine	Textiles	Wine	Textiles
Portugal	20	30	0	90	50	45
United States	50	50	100	0	50	45
Total	70	80	100	90	100	90

5. it increases

6. comparative advantage

7. no, total consumption of textiles is lower for the United States

Answers to Problems

1. **a.** Sarah's decision to attend the concert has two opportunity costs: attending the concert means that she will be unable to attend the movie, and to attend the concert, she must pay $10 for a ticket. Her decision to attend the concert means that she is also giving up whatever she could have purchased with the $10.

   b. The firm gives up $10,000 to get the property, but this is not an opportunity cost since the firm must have a business location to exist. However, there is an opportunity cost to this decision: the firm gives up the additional business it would have gotten at the prime location during the first six months.

   c. When he decides to take the internship, Jamie incurs an opportunity cost of $2,000 because he is giving up his income to work in the intern position.

2. Remember that opportunity cost measures what is given up, so when Roberto studies more for his economics exam, he is giving up time he could devote to his chemistry exam. This decision will therefore affect his chemistry grade. Similarly, if Roberto devotes more time to studying for his chemistry exam, then he will be giving up points on his economics exam.

   a. The opportunity cost of studying 15 hours for the economics exam instead of 10 hours is 2 points on the chemistry exam.

   b. The opportunity cost of studying 15 hours for the chemistry exam instead of 10 hours is 10 points on the economics exam.

   c. The opportunity cost of studying 20 hours for the economics exam instead of 10 hours is 5 points on the chemistry exam.

3. **a.** Positive: this statement is a forecast of the tax revenue from the gasoline tax. It is verifiable and hence positive.

   b. Positive: this is also a forecast, and although it may be wrong, it can be verified through the data once they are available.

   c. Normative: this is a value statement that reflects one person's view of the way the world should work. It is not refutable because it reflects a person's opinion and not a set of facts.

   d. Positive: this statement can be tested for its accuracy.

   e. Normative: this statement reflects the opinions of the speaker.

   f. Positive: this is a forecast.

4. Positive economics is descriptive, whereas normative economics is prescriptive—that is, positive economics is objective and expresses how the world works, while normative economics is subjective and expresses how the world should work. Economists may differ because of positive economics: they may use different models with different assumptions that lead to different conclusions. Economists may also disagree over normative economics: economists may not share the same values and will therefore reach different conclusions about how the world should work. Economists can evaluate alternative policies in terms of their efficiency at reaching stated goals.

5. An economic expansion is a short-run increase in the level of aggregate output that may not be sustained indefinitely; long-run economic growth reflects a sustainable increase in an economy's ability to produce more goods and services.

6. a.

	Beginning of 2008	Beginning of 2009	Beginning of 2010	Beginning of 2011
Real GDP	$40 million	$41.20 million	$42.44 million	$43.71 million
Population	2 million	2.06 million	2.14 million	2.25 million
Real GDP/person	$20	$20	$19.83	$19.43

b. The standard of living in Funland between the beginning of 2008 and the end of 2010 is declining because the rate of population growth exceeds the rate of real GDP growth.

7. a. To draw the PPC, you must first identify the number of hours of labor that Utopia has available. Since it takes 3 hours of labor to produce 2 widgets (or 1.5 hours of labor to produce 1 widget) and 4 hours of labor to produce 1 gadget, you will find it helpful to select an amount of time that is divisible by both three and four. So, for instance, 12 hours would work, as would 120 hours, or 240 hours, or an infinite number of other numbers that are divisible by both three and four. For our sketch, let's suppose that there are 120 hours of labor available to Utopia and that its citizens can produce either widgets or gadgets, or some combination of the two goods. If they devote all of their labor time to widget production, they can produce 80 widgets, since (120 hours of labor/3 hours of labor) × (2 widgets) = 80 widgets. If they devote all of their labor time to gadget production, they can produce 30 gadgets, since (120 hours of labor/4 hours of labor) × (1 gadget) = 30 gadgets. The graph below illustrates Utopia's PPC.

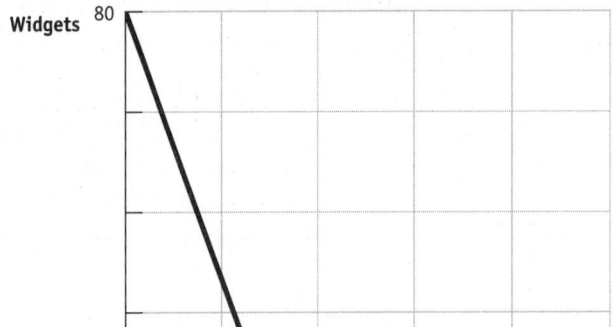

Utopia's Production Curve Frontier Based on 120 Hours of Labor

The values of your intercepts will be different, depending on the number of hours of labor you assume Utopia has, but the slope of the PPC should be the same as the one drawn above.

b. The slope of the PPC is –8/3.

c. The opportunity cost of producing an additional widget in Utopia is 3/8 gadget.

d. The opportunity cost of producing an additional gadget in Utopia is 8/3 widget.

8. a. You must first decide how much labor Jonesville has so that you can calculate the maximum number of widgets and gadgets it can produce. Since you know gadgets take 2 hours of labor and widgets take 5 hours of labor, you will want to pick a number of hours that is divisible by both 2 and 5. For example, 10 hours would work, or 100 hours, or 20 hours, or 2,000 hours—there is an infinite number of labor quantities that would work in constructing this PPC.

b.

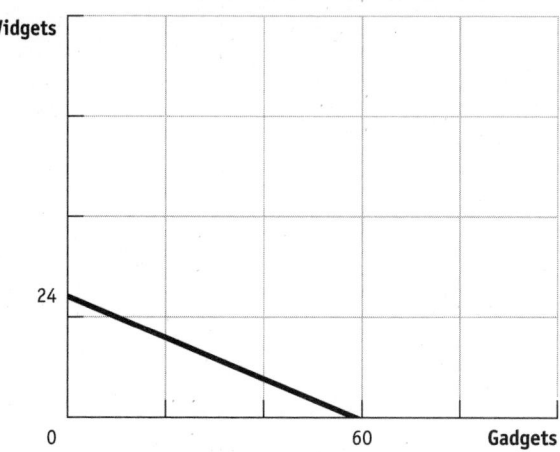

Production Curve Frontier for Jonesville Based on 120 Hours of Labor

c. The slope of the PPC is −24/60, or −4/10, or −0.4.

d. Recall that you can use the slope measure to quickly find the opportunity cost of producing one more unit of the good measured on the *x*-axis. To produce one more gadget, you must give up 0.4 widget; therefore, the opportunity cost of an additional gadget is 0.4 widget.

e. Recall that you can use the reciprocal of the slope measure to quickly find the opportunity cost of producing one more unit of the good measured on the *y*-axis. To produce one more widget, you must give up 1/0.4 gadgets, therefore the opportunity cost of an additional widget is 2.5 gadgets.

f. If Jonesville has an increase in the amount of labor available to use in producing gadgets and widgets, it can produce more gadgets and more widgets. That is, Jonesville's PPC will shift out from the origin. But the slope of the new PPC will be the same as the one drawn based upon 120 hours of labor, thus the opportunity cost of producing widgets or gadgets will not change for Jonesville.

9. a.

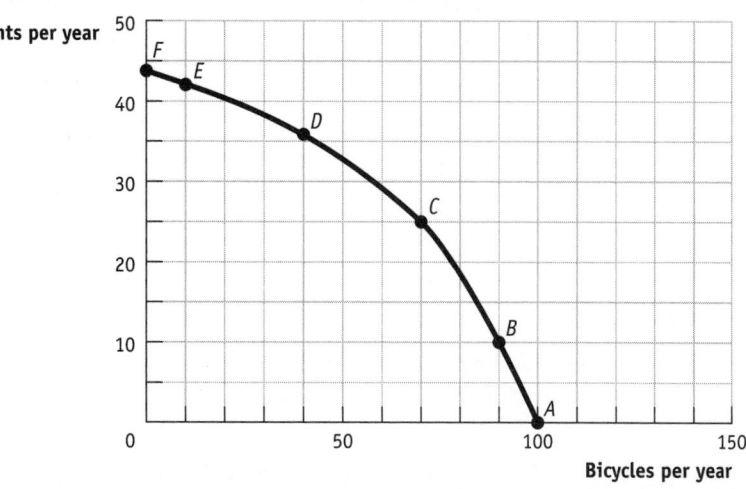

Production Curve Frontier for Smithtown

b. The opportunity cost of moving from point *C* to point *B* is measured in terms of the number of units of production you give up. In this case you give up 15 tents, so this is the opportunity cost.

c. The opportunity cost of moving from point *C* to point *D* is 30 bicycles.

d. Smithtown's resources are not equally well suited to producing bicycles and tents. If Smithtown initially devotes all of its resources to producing bicycles, then some of its resources currently going into the production of bicycles are not particularly productive at producing bicycles. Smithtown can move some of these resources away from bicycle production and into tent production without decreasing its bicycle production significantly. However, as Smithtown decides to produce more and more tents, this will eventually require moving resources that are well suited to bicycle production into tent production, where they are less productive. This specialization of resources results in a PPC that is bowed out from the origin.

10. a.

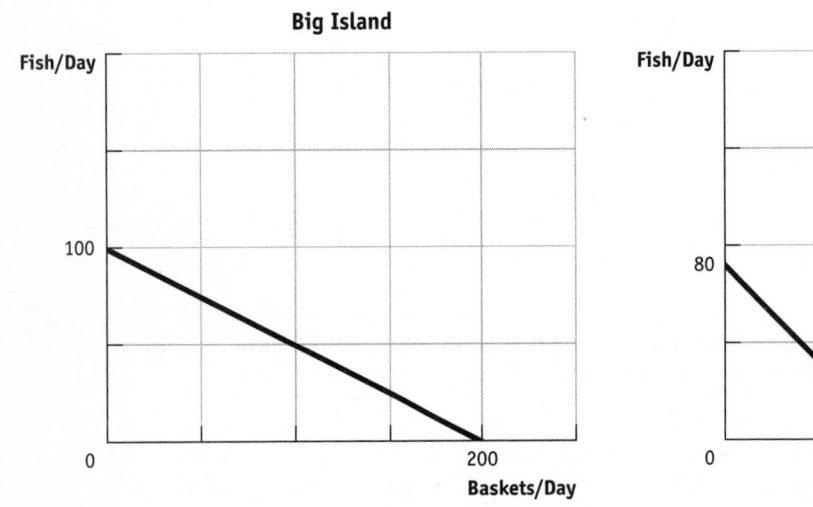
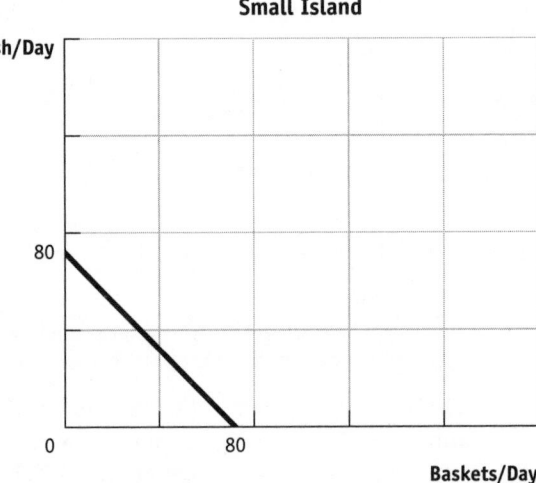

b. The slope of Big Island's PPC is −1/2.

c. The slope of Small Island's PPC is −1.

d. The opportunity cost of producing an additional basket for Big Island is ½ fish. The opportunity cost of producing an additional basket for Small Island is 1 fish. Big Island can produce an additional basket at a lower opportunity cost than can Small Island and therefore has a comparative advantage in baskets.

e. The opportunity cost of producing an additional fish for Big Island is 2 baskets. The opportunity cost of producing an additional fish for Small Island is 1 basket. Small Island can produce an additional fish at a lower opportunity cost than can Big Island and therefore has a comparative advantage in fish.

f. Big Island should specialize in producing baskets because it can produce baskets at a lower opportunity cost than can Small Island.

g. Small Island should specialize in producing fish because it can produce fish at a lower opportunity cost than can Big Island.

Answers to Review Questions

1. B. When resources are scarce, this implies that people and societies must make decisions about how to use those scarce resources because the scarcity of resources is a constraint on production and consumption.

2. C. The opportunity cost of taking the job includes what must be given up. In this case, Camillo is giving up two weeks of vacation because the other job offers four weeks of vacation instead of two. He is not giving up any salary when he selects the job paying $32,000.

3. C. Positive economics is objective, factual, and can be subject to proof. In contrast, normative economics is subjective and expresses what ought to happen or what should happen.

Statements II and III are both statements that describe positive economics because positive economics describes and analyzes how the world works.

4. **D.** Normative economics is subjective and value oriented. Both statements II and III are positive statements that can be evaluated as to their factual accuracy. Statement I is a normative statement since it expresses someone's subjective opinion and therefore cannot be proven true or false.

5. **C.** Macroeconomics studies the aggregate economy, not individual action; in studying the aggregate economy, macroeconomics seeks to explain the factors that determine a country's standard of living. In macroeconomics we are reminded that the aggregation of individual behavior often has a larger impact than just the sum of these individual behaviors.

6. **B.** A recession, by definition, occurs when both aggregate output and income decrease. As the economy produces a smaller level of output, employment of labor decreases because less labor is needed to produce the smaller level of output. Not all recessions turn into depressions, and there is no uniform agreement about the length of time aggregate output must decrease for the downturn in economic activity to be viewed as a depression.

7. **A.** Economic growth is measured as an increase in the level of real GDP in the economy. This increase refers to an increase over the long run, rather than a short-run economic expansion.

8. **B.** This question centers on the relationship between aggregate output and employment: as aggregate output increases, employment also increases and hence unemployment decreases.

9. **C.** Inflation is defined as the increase in the aggregate price level over time.

10. **D.** An economic contraction or recession is that part of the business cycle during which output and employment are falling.

11. **D.** An economic expansion, or recovery, is that part of the business cycle during which output and employment are increasing, and therefore unemployment is decreasing. The economic expansion occurs in that part of the business cycle between the business cycle trough and the business cycle peak, since this is the part of the business cycle when output and employment are increasing.

12. **B.** Deflation refers to a decrease in the overall level of prices in an economy and, although deflation may occur at the same time that employment in the economy decreases, the term refers only to the decrease in the overall price level.

13. **C.** In a recession, production is falling and that implies that fewer units of labor will be employed. This, in turn, implies that jobs will be difficult to find. In addition, as the level of production and employment fall, there is less demand for goods and services, and that leads to a general decrease in the overall level of prices in the economy.

14. **A.** Mike can produce 1,000 pounds of potatoes and 0 pounds of tomatoes a year, or he can produce 2,000 pounds of tomatoes and 0 pounds of potatoes a year. His resources do not allow him to produce a combination of 1,000 pounds of potatoes and 2,000 pounds of tomatoes in a year. Thus, answer (a) is not feasible, while answers (b) and (c) are feasible. Answer (d) is also feasible because if Mike devotes half of his resources this year to producing potatoes and half of his resources to producing tomatoes, he will be able to produce 500 pounds of potatoes and 1,000 pounds of tomatoes.

15. **C.** In Utopia 4 widgets can be produced in the same amount of labor time as 3 gadgets, 1 widget can be produced in the same amount of labor time as ¾ of a gadget. The opportunity cost of producing 1 widget is measured by the number of gadgets that must be given up, in this case ¾ of a gadget.

16. **(a) A.** Jonesville uses all of its labor to produce widgets. With 100 hours of labor, it can produce 10 widgets, since the production of each widget takes 10 hours of labor.

    (b) B. When Jonesville devotes 50 hours of labor to widget production, it can produce 5 widgets. When Jonesville devotes 50 hours of labor to gadget production, it can produce 10 gadgets. Thus, when Jonesville divides its labor evenly between widget and gadget production, the maximum number of gadgets it can produce is 10 while the maximum number of widgets it can produce is 5.

(c) C. Since the number of hours needed to produce each widget and each gadget has not changed in Jonesville, the opportunity cost of producing these goods does not change. Jonesville does see its linear PPC shift out due to the increase in the amount of available labor, but the new PPC has the same slope as the original PPC.

(d) B. A combination of gadgets and widgets is not feasible for Jonesville if that combination lies outside of its PPC. If gadgets are measured on the vertical axis and widgets are measured on the horizontal axis, then the PPC can be written as $G = 20 - 2W$, where G is the symbol for gadgets and W is the symbol for widgets. Answer (a) lies on the PPC because $G = 20 - 2(8) = 4$. Answer (c) lies on the PPC because $G = 20 - 2(6) = 8$. Answer (d) lies on the PPC because $G = 20 - 2(10) = 0$. Answer (b) does not lie on the production possibility frontier, nor does it lie inside the PPC: $G = 20 - 2(7) = 6$, but the answer in (b) has gadgets equal to 7, not 6. The combination of 7 widgets and 7 gadgets lies beyond the PPC for Jonestown.

17. **(a) C.** The opportunity cost of moving from point D to point E is measured by what Suburbia must give up when it makes this move. At point D, Suburbia has 50 pounds of butter, while at point E Suburbia has only 30 pounds of butter; thus, when moving from point D to point E, Suburbia must give up 20 pounds of butter. Notice that when measuring the opportunity cost of moving from one point on a PPC to another point on the PPC, it is important to provide the unit of measurement as well as the numerical value.

(b) B. The opportunity cost of moving from point D to point B is measured by what Suburbia must give up when it makes this move. In this case, Suburbia is giving up guns to get more butter. Moving from point D to point B, Suburbia gives up 20 guns.

18. **A.** Given the resources that Texia and Urbania have this year, Texia is able to produce more food and more clothing than Urbania this year.

19. **B.** For every unit of clothing that Texia produces, it must give up 2 units of food, while for Urbania the opportunity cost of producing 1 unit of clothing is 2.5 units of food. Thus, the opportunity cost of producing clothing is lower for Texia than it is for Urbania. Texia, therefore, has the comparative advantage in producing clothing, while Urbania has the comparative advantage in producing food.

20. **D.** Countries that elect to trade with one another do so because the trade is beneficial to them. As long as trade is a choice, then the decision to trade with one another must indicate that the trade is beneficial to both parties.

Notes

....

....

....

....

....

....

....

....

....

....

....

....

Supply and Demand

OVERVIEW

This section first lays out the pieces that make up the supply and demand model. Once each of the pieces has been presented, it puts them together and shows how the supply and demand model can be used to explain how many—but not all—markets behave. The fundamental approach outlined in this section provides the basis for most models and material that follow in later sections.

FEATURED MODEL/GRAPH: SUPPLY AND DEMAND

This section presents the supply and demand model, which is probably the best-known and perhaps the most important economic model. The basic supply and demand model provides the framework for the macroeconomic models presented in later sections. There are five key elements in this model: the demand curve; the supply curve; the set of factors that cause the demand curve to shift and the set of factors that cause the supply curve to shift; the market equilibrium, price, and quantity; and the way the market equilibrium changes when the supply curve or demand curve shifts. To explain the supply and demand model, we will examine each of these elements in turn.

MODULES IN THIS SECTION

Module 5: Supply and Demand: Introduction and Demand

Module 6: Supply and Demand: Supply and Equilibrium

Module 7: Supply and Demand: Changes in Equilibrium

Module 8: Supply and Demand: Price Controls (Floors and Ceilings)

Module 9: Supply and Demand: Quantity Controls

Module 5
Supply and Demand: Introduction and Demand

Before You Read the MODULE

Summary

This module introduces the supply and demand model, and presents the demand side of the model. It develops the concept of demand and presents demand schedules (tables) and curves. The module explains the difference between a change in demand and a change in quantity demanded, and presents the factors that will shift (increase or decrease) a demand curve.

Module Objectives

Review these objectives before you read the module. Place a "√" on the line when you understand each of the following:

_____**Objective 1.** What a **competitive market** is and how it is described by the supply and demand model

_____**Objective 2.** What a **demand curve** shows

_____**Objective 3.** The difference between a movement along and a shift of a demand curve

_____**Objective 4.** What factors will shift a demand curve

While You Read the MODULE

Key Terms

Define these key terms as you read the module.

Competitive market

Supply and demand model

Demand schedule

Quantity demanded

Demand curve

Law of demand

Change in demand

Movement along the demand curve

Substitutes

Complements

Normal good
_____

Inferior good
_____

Individual demand curve
_____

List questions or difficulties from your initial reading of the module.

After You Read the MODULE

Fill-in-the-Blanks

Fill in the blanks to complete the following statements. Terms may be used more than once. If you find yourself having difficulties, please refer to the appropriate section in the text.

- A competitive market is one in which there are (1)_____ buyers and sellers of the same good or service, but neither individual buyers nor individual sellers has a noticeable effect on market price.

- Demand is the relationship between the amount of a good consumers want to purchase and its (2)_____. According to the law of demand, people purchase more of a good or service when the price is (3)_____. As the price of a good or service increases, we say that there is a decrease in (4)_____. However, whenever something changes that causes consumers to want less at any price, we say that there has been a decrease in (5)_____.

- An increase in demand will shift the demand curve to the

  (6)_____. The five factors that will cause the demand curve to

  shift are (7)_____, _____,

  _____, _____, and

  _____.

- Goods that serve the same function in some way are called substitutes. When the price of

  one of these goods increases, its (8)_____ will decrease and the

  demand for the other good will (9)_____. Goods that are

  consumed together are called (10)_____. When the price of one

  of these goods increases, its quantity demanded will (11)_____

  while the demand for the other good will (12)_____.

- Inferior and normal goods are distinguished by how demand changes when there is a

  change in consumer income. If an increase in consumer income leads to a decrease in the

  demand for a good, it is a(n) (13)_____ good. If declining

  consumer income leads consumers to purchase less of a good at any possible price, that

  good is a(n) (14)_____ good.

Module Review

Demand Versus Quantity Demanded

When economists say "an increase in demand," they mean a rightward shift of the demand curve, and when they say "a decrease in demand," they mean a leftward shift of the demand curve—that is, when they're being careful. In ordinary speech most people, including professional economists, use the word "demand" casually. For example, an economist might say, "The demand for air travel has doubled over the past 15 years because of falling airfares," when he or she really means that the *quantity demanded* has doubled.

It's OK to be a bit sloppy in ordinary conversation. But when you're doing economic analysis, it's important to make the distinction between changes in the quantity demanded, which involve movements along a demand curve, and shifts of the demand curve. Sometimes students end up writing something like this: "If demand increases, the price will go up, but that will lead to a fall in demand, which pushes the price down . . ." and then go around in circles. If you make a clear distinction between changes in *demand*, which mean shifts of the demand curve, and changes in *quantity demanded*, you can avoid a lot of confusion.

- A full understanding of this chapter is critical for your study of economics. The model of supply and demand is used repeatedly in a variety of settings throughout this course.

- A demand curve illustrates the relationship between the price of the good and the quantity demanded at each specific price. Along a demand curve, the other determinants of demand are held constant; this constancy is referred to as the other things equal (or *ceteris paribus*) assumption. In the examples throughout the remainder of the course, we typically consider a single change in a situation while holding the other variables constant. Anytime you think "But what if . . . ," be careful, you may be violating this assumption!

- The demand for a good is affected by changes in these factors: income, tastes, expectations, the price of related goods, and the number of consumers. You will need to remember these factors, recognize them in examples, and know how they affect the demand curve.

- It can be easier to understand the concepts of substitutes and complements using examples.

- But remember that which goods are substitutes and which are complements for a particular individual depends on his or her preferences. Substitutes for me may not be substitutes for you! A possible example is soft drinks and popcorn. Two different brands of soft drinks are substitutes, while soft drinks and popcorn are complements. *Ceteris paribus,* if the price of Coke increases, you will buy less Coke and the demand for Pepsi will increase, since it is now relatively cheaper. In contrast, if the price of soft drinks increases, *ceteris paribus,* then the demand for popcorn will decrease. When soft drinks become more expensive, people buy fewer soft drinks. This leads to a decrease in the demand for popcorn people don't buy as much popcorn without soft drinks to go with it. Questions about substitutes and complements can be easier to understand using your own examples!

- It can also be easier to understand questions about normal and inferior goods if you think of specific examples. But don't let the terms "normal" and "inferior" mislead you. In economics, the opposite of normal is inferior (not abnormal) and the opposite of inferior is normal (not superior). Whether a good is normal or inferior for a particular individual depends on his or her preferences. A good that is normal for me might be inferior for you! A normal good is a good that you will choose to buy more of as your income increases (demand shifts to the right as income increases). For example, as your income increases, you may take more vacations. An inferior good is a good that you will buy less of as your income increases (demand shifts to the left as income increases). For example, as your income increases, you may buy fewer fast-food restaurant meals.

Module ⑥
Supply and Demand: Supply and Equilibrium

Before You Read the MODULE

Summary

This module develops the concepts of supply and equilibrium. It shows how supply can be represented using supply schedules (tables) and curves. The module explains the difference between a change in supply and a change in quantity supplied, and presents the factors that will shift (increase or decrease) a supply curve. It defines equilibrium and shows how to find equilibrium in the supply and demand model, and explains the forces that bring markets to equilibrium.

Module Objectives

Review these objectives before you read the module. Place a "√" on the line when you understand each of the following:

_____**Objective 1.** What a **supply curve** shows

_____**Objective 2.** The difference between a movement along and a shift of a supply curve

_____**Objective 3.** What factors will shift a supply curve

_____**Objective 4.** How **equilibrium price** and quantity are determined in a market

_____**Objective 5.** How **surpluses** and **shortages** move a market back to equilibrium

While You Read the MODULE

Key Terms

Define these key terms as you read the module.

Quantity supplied

Supply schedule

Supply curve

Law of supply

Change in supply

Shift of the supply curve

Movement along the supply curve

Input

Individual supply curve

Equilibrium

Equilibrium price

Market-clearing price
_____

Equilibrium quantity
_____

Surplus
_____

Shortage
_____

List questions or difficulties from your initial reading of the module.

After You Read the MODULE

Fill-in-the-Blanks

Fill in the blanks to complete the following statements. Terms may be used more than once. If you find yourself having difficulties, please refer to the appropriate section in the text.

- Supply is the relationship between the amount of a good producers are willing to sell and

  its (1)_____. As the price of a good or service increases, we say

  that there is a decrease in (2)_____. However, whenever

  something changes that causes producers to sell less at any price, we say that there has been

  a decrease in (3)_____.

- An increase in supply will shift the supply curve to the (4)_____.

  The five factors that will cause the supply curve to shift are

(5)_____, _____,

_____, _____, and

_____.

- Equilibrium in a competitive market occurs when quantity supplied equals

  (6)_____.

  At any price above equilibrium, there will be a (7)_____ and

  there will be pressure for price to (8)_____. At any price below

  equilibrium, there will be a (9)_____ and pressure for price

  to (10)_____.

Module Review

Bought and Sold?

We have been talking about the price at which a good or service is bought *and* sold, as if the two were the same. But shouldn't we make a distinction between the price received by sellers and the price paid by buyers? In principle, yes; but it is helpful at this point to sacrifice a bit of realism in the interest of simplicity—by assuming away the difference between the prices received by sellers and those paid by buyers. In reality, there is often a middleman—someone who brings buyers and sellers together—who buys from suppliers, then sells to consumers at a markup. However, the difference between the buying and selling price is quite small. So it's not a bad approximation to think of the price paid by buyers as being the *same* as the price received by sellers.

- A supply curve illustrates the relationship between the price of the good and the quantity supplied at each specific price. Along a supply curve, the other determinants of supply are held constant; this constancy is referred to as the other things equal (or *ceteris paribus*) assumption. In the examples throughout the remainder of the course, we typically consider a single change in a situation while holding the other variables constant. Any time you think "But what if . . . ," be careful, you may be violating this assumption!

- The supply of a good is affected by changes in each of the following factors: input prices, the price of related goods, technology, expectations, and the number of producers. You will need to remember these factors, recognize them in examples, and know how they affect the supply curve.

- Equilibrium occurs when there is balance. That is, opposing forces are equal and there is no tendency for change. Equilibrium is a general concept that appears in many different models. The concept is also used in most economic models. Learn the concept of equilibrium in general so you understand why it occurs at the intersection of the supply and demand curves, and so that it is easier to apply when you see it in later models. A competitive market is in equilibrium when quantity supplied equals quantity demanded. At this price there is balance between the quantity consumers want to buy and the quantity producers want to sell. If the price is above the equilibrium price, there is excess supply, or a surplus, in the market, and price tends to fall as producers try to sell the surplus. If the price is below equilibrium, there is excess demand, or a shortage, in the market, and price tends to rise as consumers compete to buy the good.

Module 7
Supply and Demand: Changes in Equilibrium

Before You Read the MODULE

Summary

This module uses the supply and demand model to determine how changes in a market will change the equilibrium price and quantity. You will learn how to use the supply and demand model to analyze how real-world and hypothetical changes affect a market.

Module Objectives

Review these objectives before you read the module. Place a "√" on the line when you understand each of the following:

_____**Objective 1.** How equilibrium price and quantity are affected when there is a change in either supply or demand

_____**Objective 2.** How equilibrium price and quantity are affected when there is a simultaneous change in both supply and demand

_____**Objective 3.** How to use the supply and demand model (i.e., draw supply and demand graphs) to analyze changes in markets

While You Read the MODULE

Key Questions

Answer these key questions as you read the module.

What happens to the demand curve and the equilibrium price and quantity when demand increases (decreases)?

What happens to the supply curve, and the equilibrium price and quantity when supply increases (decreases)?

What happens when supply and demand change simultaneously?

List questions or difficulties from your initial reading of the module.

After You Read the MODULE

Fill-in-the-Blanks

Fill in the blanks to complete the following statements. Terms may be used more than once. If you find yourself having difficulties, please refer to the appropriate section in the text.

- When demand increases, equilibrium price will (1)_____ and

  equilibrium quantity will (2)_____. When supply increases,

  equilibrium price will (3)_____ and equilibrium quantity will

  (4)_____. If there is a simultaneous increase in demand and

  supply, equilibrium (5)_____ will increase, but the effect on

  equilibrium (6)_____ can't be determined without knowing the

  relative size of the shifts.

- If demand increases at the same time supply decreases, equilibrium

  (7)_____ will increase but equilibrium

  (8)_____ can't be determined unless you know the relative size

  of the two shifts.

Which Curve Is It Anyway?

When the price of a good or service changes, in general, we can say that this reflects a change in either supply or demand. But it is easy to get confused about which one. A helpful clue is the direction of change in quantity. If the quantity sold changes in the *same* direction as the price—for example, if both the price and the quantity rise—this suggests that the demand curve has shifted. If the price and the quantity move in *opposite* directions, the likely cause is a shift of the supply curve.

- The main goal of this section is to learn how to use the supply and demand model to answer questions and solve problems. Memorizing definitions, rules, or lists won't get you very far; you must practice using the supply and demand model. Use the model to help you find answers to questions rather than guessing the answer and trying to make the model fit your preconceived notion.

- Often a quick sketch of a demand and supply curve is all that you need to answer questions about the effect of a change in the market on the equilibrium price or equilibrium quantity. Practice drawing a quick representation of the demand and supply curves as you do problems, recognizing that you do not always need a formal graph to find a solution. Use these sketches during your exams!

Module 8
Supply and Demand: Price Controls (Ceilings and Floors)

Before You Read the MODULE

Summary

This module looks at government intervention to affect the price in a market. Buyers would like to pay less, and sometimes they can make a strong moral or political case that they should pay lower prices. Sellers would like to receive more, and sometimes they can make a strong moral or political case that they should receive higher prices. This creates strong demands for governments to intervene in markets. When a government intervenes to regulate prices, we say that it imposes **price controls.** These controls take the form of either a **price ceiling** or a **price floor.** When a government tries to legislate prices, there are predictable side effects.

Module Objectives

Review these objectives before you read the module. Place a "√" on the line when you understand each of the following:

_____**Objective 1.** What a price control is

_____**Objective 2.** The effects of price controls and how they make a market inefficient

_____**Objective 3.** Why economists are skeptical of attempts to intervene in markets (like imposing price controls)

_____**Objective 4.** Who benefits and who loses from price controls, and why they are used

While You Read the MODULE

Key Terms

Define these key terms as you read the module.

Price controls

Price ceiling

Price floor

Black markets

Minimum wage

List questions or difficulties from your initial reading of the module.

After You Read the MODULE

Fill-in-the-Blanks

Fill in the blanks to complete the following statements. Terms may be used more than once. If you find yourself having difficulties, please refer to the appropriate section in the text.

- One way the government may try to affect markets is to use price controls to set either a

  minimum or maximum legal price in a market. A maximum legal price is called a price

  (1)_____, and a legal minimum price is called a price

  (2)_____.

- The government would impose a price ceiling if it believed the equilibrium price was too

  (3)_____. To be effective, the price ceiling would have to be set

  (4)_____ the equilibrium price. An effective price ceiling would

  lead to a (5)_____ in the market.

- The government would impose a price floor if it believed the equilibrium price was too

  (6)_____. To be effective, the price floor would have to be set

  (7)_____ the equilibrium price. An effective price floor would

  lead to a (8)_____ in the market.

Module Review

Ceilings, Floors, and Quantities

A price ceiling below the equilibrium price pushes the price of a good down. A price floor above the equilibrium price pushes the price of a good up. So it's easy to assume that the effects of a price floor are the opposite of the effects of a price ceiling. In particular, if a price ceiling reduces the quantity of a good bought and sold, doesn't a price floor increase the quantity? No, it doesn't. In fact, both floors and ceilings reduce the quantity bought and sold. Why? When the quantity of a good supplied isn't equal to the quantity demanded, the quantity sold is determined by the "short side" of the market, i.e., whichever quantity is less. If sellers don't want to sell as much as buyers want to buy, it's the sellers who determine the actual quantity sold because buyers can't force unwilling sellers to sell. If buyers don't want to buy as much as sellers want to sell, it's the buyers who determine the actual quantity sold because sellers can't force unwilling buyers to buy.

- A floor is a surface that you stand on and that is solid. Use this image to remember that a price floor is the lowest price that can be charged for a good. To be effective, a price floor must be set at a price that is above the equilibrium price. Otherwise, the floor will not prevent the market from going to equilibrium. An effective price floor results in a surplus of the good because at high prices, producers want to sell more but consumers want to buy less.

- A ceiling is a surface that you hope is solid and stays above your head. Use this image to remember that a price ceiling is the highest price that can be charged for a good. To be effective, a price ceiling must be set at a price that is below the equilibrium price. Otherwise, the ceiling will not prevent the market from going to equilibrium. An effective price ceiling results in a shortage of the good because at low prices consumers want to buy more but producers don't want to sell as much.

Module 9
Supply and Demand: Quantity Controls

Before You Read the MODULE

Summary

This module continues the discussion of government intervention in markets by looking at **quantity controls,** or **quotas.** Typically, the government limits quantity in a market by issuing **licenses.**

Module Objectives

Review these objectives before you read the module. Place a "√" on the line when you understand each of the following:

_____**Objective 1.** What a quantity control is

_____**Objective 2.** The effects of quantity controls and how they make a market inefficient

_____**Objective 3.** Who benefits and who loses from quantity controls, and why they are used

While You Read the MODULE

Key Terms

Define these key terms as you read the module.

Quantity control, or quota

License

Demand price

Supply price
_____

Wedge
_____

Quota rent
_____

Deadweight loss
_____

List questions or difficulties from your initial reading of the module.

After You Read the MODULE

Fill-in-the-Blanks

Fill in the blanks to complete the following statements. Terms may be used more than once. If you find yourself having difficulties, please refer to the appropriate section in the text.

- Whenever the government imposes a (1)_____, a limit on the amount that can be sold, or requires a (2)_____, which limits the number of goods supplied in the market, it affects not only the amount of the good sold in the market, but also the price.

- When the government imposes a quantity control, it drives a (3)_____ between the price that consumers are willing to pay for the quantity allowed of the good and the price at which producers are willing to offer that quantity. The price consumers are willing to pay for the legal market quantity is called the (4)_____ price, and the price at which producers are willing

to offer the legal market quantity is called the (5)_____ price.

- The price that consumers are willing to pay for the quantity allowed under a quota is

  higher than the price at which producers are willing to offer it. This difference is known as

  the quota (6)_____.

Module Review

Regulating Quantity Versus Regulating Price

In this module, we examine what happens when government intervention directly restricts the quantity of a good or service available in the market. There are similarities between this analysis of quantity controls and our previous analysis of price controls. When price is restricted through a price control, we draw a *horizontal* line on our supply and demand graph, at the level of the price ceiling or floor. When quantity is restricted, we draw a *vertical* line on our supply and demand graph at the maximum quantity permitted under the restriction—the quota limit. Note that we focus on maximum quantities (quotas) and do not talk about *minimum* quantities. In the case of a price control, the restricted price creates a difference between the quantity demanded and the quantity supplied. This leads to shortages or surpluses. In the case of a quantity control, the restriction creates a difference between the supply price and the demand price. This creates a wedge, or quota rent. While the terminology used to analyze quotas may be less familiar, the similarities with price controls can help you understand quantity controls. In each case, government intervention leads to market inefficiencies.

- A quota, or quantity control, is a policy implemented by the government to set a maximum amount of the good or service that can be sold in a market. A quota has no effect if it is set at a level greater than the equilibrium quantity; to be effective, a quota must be set at a level lower than the equilibrium quantity.

- With an effective quantity restriction, consumers are willing to pay more for each unit of the good, while suppliers are willing to supply the good for less. This difference is referred to as a wedge. This wedge corresponds to the quota rent the license holder of the good receives when the quantity control is imposed in a market.

Draw the Featured Graph: Supply and Demand

Graphing using data

Graph the supply and demand curves using the numbers in the table. Show equilibrium price and quantity on the axes.

P	Qd	Qs
0	8	0
2	6	6
4	4	12

y-axis label

x-axis label

Graphing relationships without numbers

Graph supply and demand curves and show equilibrium price and quantity on the axes.

y-axis label

x-axis label

Graphs like the ones you drew above serve as the starting point when using supply and demand analysis to determine the effects on price and quantity and when a determinant of supply or demand changes. Always start your analysis with one of these "starting point" graphs. Then follow these steps:

(1) Determine which side of the market is affected, supply or demand, using the lists of factors presented in previous modules, that affect supply and demand. Any single change will affect supply *or* demand, not both.

(2) Determine whether supply or demand increases or decreases.

(3) Shift the supply or demand curve to the left for a decrease or to the right for an increase. Draw the new equilibrium using the new curve to find your answer!

Complete the Exercises

Draw a correctly labeled graph showing the effect on equilibrium price and quantity in the market for oranges when, ceteris paribus, each of the following changes occurs. (Use the steps shown above.)

a. There is a freeze in Florida that kills many of the orange groves.

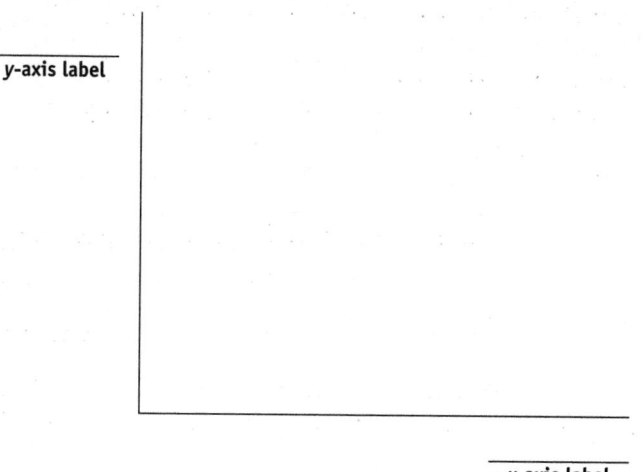

b. The wages of orange workers decrease.

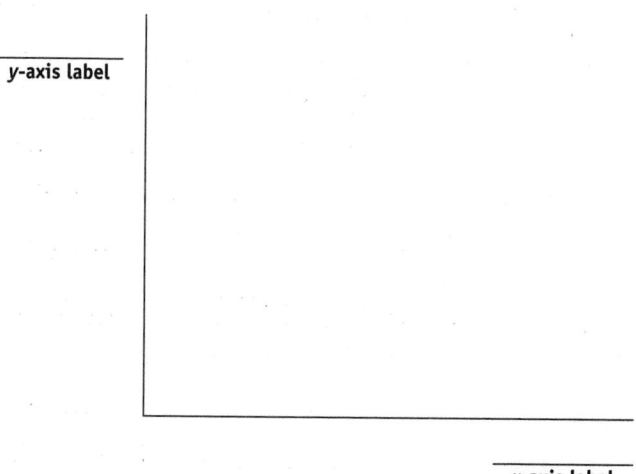

c. Research finds oranges have additional health benefits.

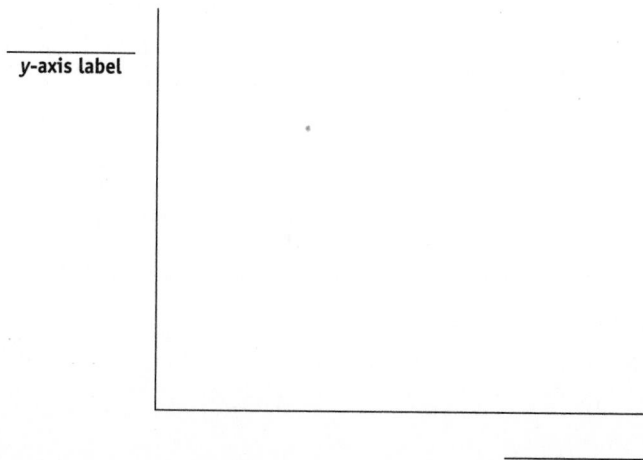

d. The price of tangerines decreases.

y-axis label

x-axis label

Problems

1. You are given the following information about quantity demanded in the competitive market for bicycles.

Price per bicycle	Quantity of bicycles demanded per week
$100	0
80	100
60	200
40	500
20	800
0	1,000

a. Graph this demand schedule.

b. Suppose the price is initially $40. If price rises by $20, what happens to the quantity demanded?

c. Suppose the price is initially $40. If price falls by $40, what happens to the quantity demanded?

2. For each of the following situations in the table below, fill in the missing information. First, determine whether the situation causes a shift of or a movement along the demand curve; then, if it causes a shift, determine whether the demand curve shifts to the right or to the left.

Situation	Specified market	Movement or shift	Rightward or leftward shift in demand
People's income increases.	Market for exotic vacations		
People's income decreases.	Market for goods sold in secondhand shops		
Price of bicycles increases.	Market for bicycles		
Price of tennis balls increases.	Market for tennis racquets		
Price of movie tickets decreases.	Popcorn at movie theatres		
Popularity of music-playing device increases.	Market for music-playing device		
Popularity of name-brand clothing items decreases.	Market for brand-name designer clothing		
Winter clothing is expected to go on sale next month.	Market for winter clothing		
Number of urban residents increases.	Market for apartments in urban areas		

3. The following graph represents the supply curve for the production of widgets in Town Center.

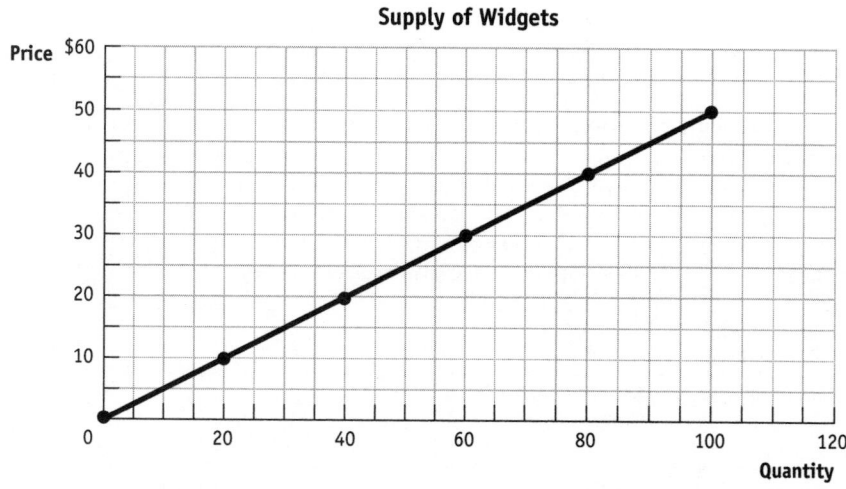

Supply of Widgets

a. At a price of $20, how many widgets are producers willing to supply?

b. At a price of $40, how many widgets are producers willing to supply?

c. Suppose there are ten widget producers in Town Center and the price of widgets is $50. If each producer produces the same number of widgets, how many widgets will each produce?

d. Suppose price is initially $30 but then falls to $20. What is the change in quantity supplied?

e. Suppose price is initially $30 but then rises to $50. What is the change in quantity supplied?

f. What price must suppliers receive in order to be willing to supply 80 widgets?

g. What price must suppliers receive in order to be willing to supply 40 widgets?

h. What does the slope of a supply curve imply about the relationship between price and quantity supplied?

4. For each of the following situations in the table below, fill in the missing information: first, determine whether the situation causes a shift or a movement along the supply curve; then, if it causes a shift, determine whether the supply curve shifts to the right or to the left.

Situation	Specified market	Movement or shift	Rightward or leftward shift in supply
Labor costs for air travel and cruise ships increase.	Market for exotic vacations		
Prices of office equipment and phone service rise by 40%.	Market for call center services		
Price of bicycles increases.	Market for bicycles		
Price of leather boots increases.	Market for beef products		
Price of leather boots increases.	Market for leather belts		
New technology for music-playing device revealed.	Market for music-playing devices		
Price of brand-name designer clothing increases.	Market for brand-name designer clothing		
Number of coffee shop owners in the metro area increases.	Market for coffee in the metro area		

5. The demand and supply schedules for Healthy Snacks, Inc., is provided in the table below.

Price	Quantity demanded	Quantity supplied
$0	1,000	0
10	800	125
20	600	275
30	400	400
40	200	550
50	0	675

a. Sketch the demand and supply curves for Healthy Snacks, Inc. Don't worry about drawing a precise graph. Focus on drawing the underlying relationships from the table. Your graph should be accurate with regard to x-intercepts and y-intercepts, and indicate equilibrium.

b. What are the equilibrium price and quantity in this market? Show these on your graph.

c. Fill in the following table based on the data given to you. Assume that for each row in the table the price is as given and you are calculating the excess demand or excess supply. (Hint: Some cells in the table are empty; e.g., if there is excess supply, there is no excess demand.)

Price	Excess demand	Excess supply
$0		
10		
20		
30		
40		
50		

d. Why is a situation of excess demand referred to as a shortage?.

e. Why is a situation of excess supply referred to as a surplus?.

6. For each of the following situations, sketch a graph of the initial market demand (D_1), supply (S_1), equilibrium price (P_1), and equilibrium quantity (Q_1). Then sketch any changes in the market demand (D_2) and/or supply (S_2) curves, and indicate the new equilibrium price (P_2) and quantity (Q_2).

a. The price of gasoline increases by 40 percent. What happens in the market for bicycles?

Market for Bicycles

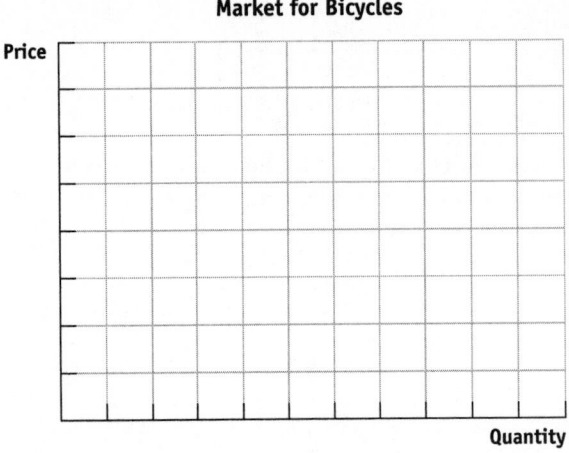

b. The price of gasoline increases by 40 percent. What happens in the market for fuel-inefficient SUVs?

Market for SUVs

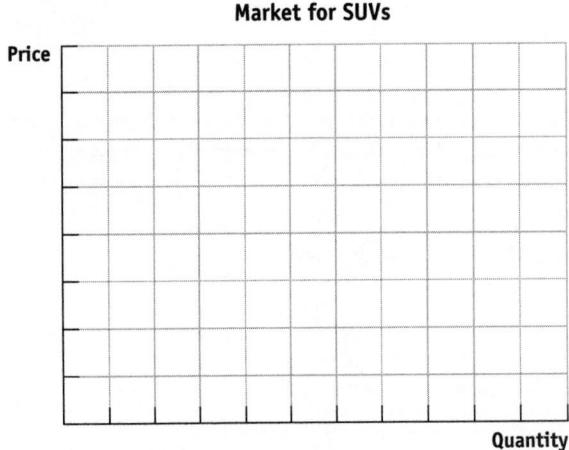

c. New technology for music-playing is developed. What happens in the market for the devices?

Market for Music-Playing Devices

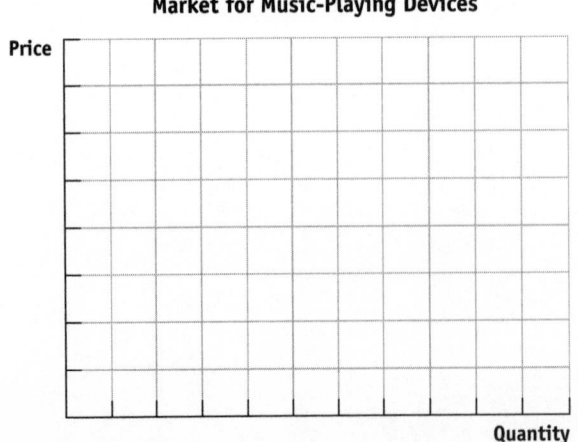

d. The price of labor decreases. What happens in the market for fast-food restaurants?

Market for Fast-Food Restaurants

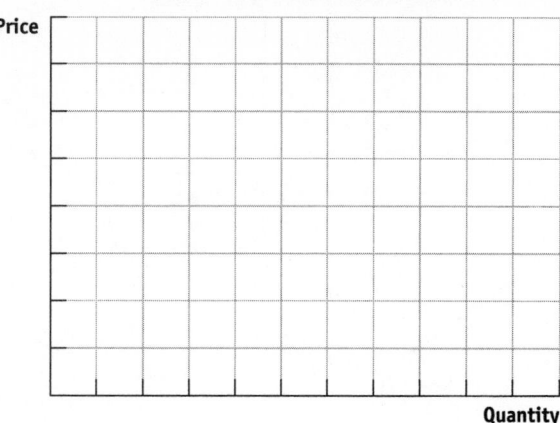

e. Income increases and good X is a normal good. What happens in the market for good X?

Market for Good X

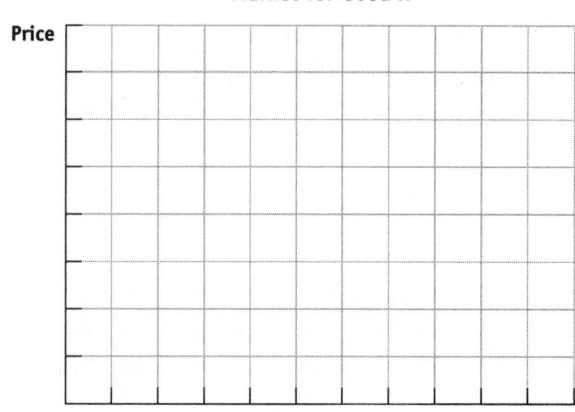

f. Income increases and good X is an inferior good. What happens in the market for good X?

Market for Good X

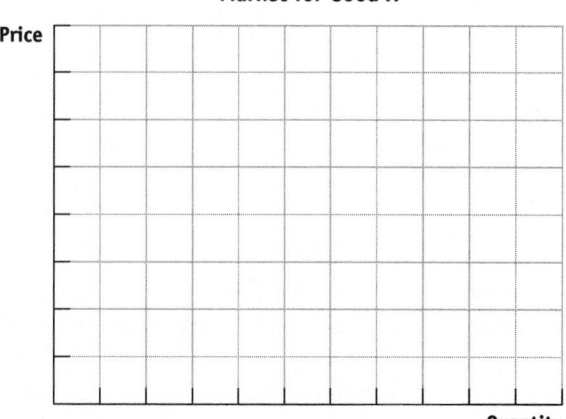

7. Use the graph below to answer the following questions:

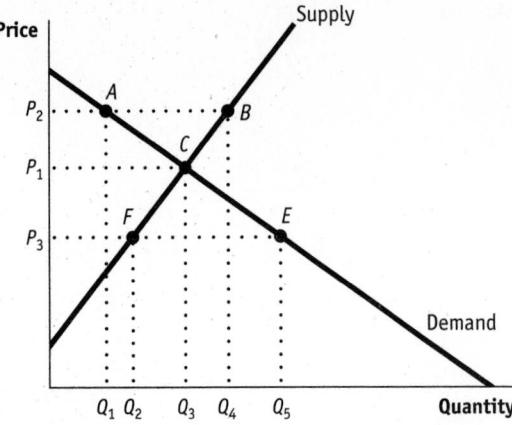

a. Identify the equilibrium price and the equilibrium quantity.

b. Suppose a price floor of P_3 is implemented by the government in this market. Describe what will happen to the price and quantity once this price floor is implemented.

c. Suppose a price floor of P_2 is implemented by the government in this market. Describe what will happen to the price and quantity once this price floor is implemented.

d. What must be true about a price floor in a market for a good or service in order for that price floor to be effective?

e. You are told that an effective price floor has been implemented in this market and that the resultant surplus is greater than $Q_4 - Q_1$. What do you know about the level of this price floor?

8. Use the graph below to answer the following questions.

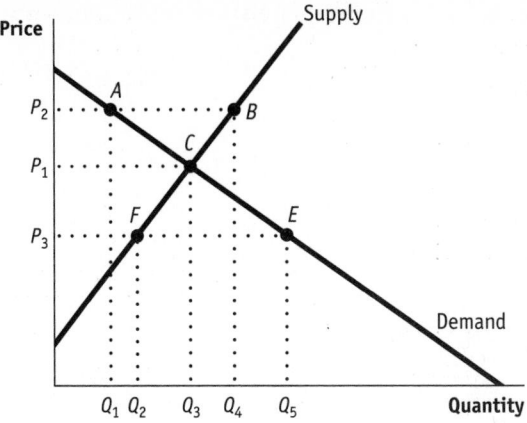

a. Identify the equilibrium price and the equilibrium quantity.

b. Suppose a price ceiling of P_2 is implemented by the government in this market. Describe what will happen to the price and quantity once this price ceiling is implemented.

c. Suppose a price ceiling of P_3 is implemented by the government in this market. Describe what will happen to the price and quantity once this price ceiling is implemented.

d. What must be true about a price ceiling in a market for a good or service for it to be effective?

e. You are told that an effective price ceiling has been implemented in this market and that the resultant shortage is smaller than $Q_5 - Q_2$. What do you know about the level of this price ceiling?

9. Consider the market for housing in Metropolitan City, where all housing units are exactly the same. Currently, the equilibrium price of housing is $2,000 a month and local residents consume 1,500 units of housing. The local residents argue that housing is too expensive and an effective price ceiling is implemented. When the price ceiling is implemented by the local government council, only 1,200 units of housing are supplied. Is this an efficient level of housing for Metropolitan City? Explain. To support your answer, provide two sketches:

in the first sketch, indicate the equilibrium quantity and price; in the second sketch, indicate the price ceiling and the quantity provided by the market. Is the price consumers are willing to pay for the last unit equal to the price suppliers must receive to supply the last unit? Explain.

10. The market for taxi rides in Metropolia this week is described in the following table. Assume that all taxi rides are the same in Metropolia.

Price of taxi rides	Quantity of taxi rides demanded per week	Quantity of taxi rides supplied per week
$1	200	40
2	180	60
3	160	80
4	140	100
5	120	120
6	100	140
7	80	160
8	60	180
9	40	200
10	20	220

a. What is the equilibrium price and quantity of taxi rides in Metropolia per week? Suppose the government of Metropolia institutes a medallion system that limits the number of taxi rides available in Metropolia per week to 80.

b. At what price will consumers want to purchase 80 taxi rides per week?

c. At what price will suppliers be willing to supply 80 taxi rides per week?

d. What price will a taxi medallion rent for in this market? Explain your answer.

e. Draw a graph of the taxi ride market in Metropolia. On this graph, indicate the quota limit, the demand price, the supply price, and the medallion's rental price.

f. What is the total value of the taxi medallions per week in Metropolia?

Review Questions

Circle the correct answer.

1. Competitive markets are characterized as having

   A. many buyers and a single seller.
   B. many buyers and a few sellers.
   C. many buyers and many sellers.
   D. a few buyers and many sellers.

2. Sue goes to the store to purchase a bottle of shampoo. When she gets to the store, she discovers her brand of shampoo is on sale for $4 a bottle. According to the law of demand, we can expect that

   A. Sue will purchase one bottle of shampoo.
   B. Sue will not purchase the shampoo.
   C. Sue will likely purchase more than one bottle of shampoo.
   D. Sue will substitute for her usual brand of shampoo with an alternative brand.

3. Consider the market for mangos. Suppose researchers discover that eating mangos generates significant health benefits. Which of the following statements is true? This discovery will

   A. not affect the market for mangos.
   B. cause the demand for mangos to shift to the right.
   C. cause the price of mangos to decrease due to a movement along the demand curve.
   D. cause a movement along the demand curve for mangos.

4. Consider the demand curve for automobiles. An increase in the price of automobiles due to a shift in the supply curve will

   A. cause a movement along the demand curve for automobiles.
   B. result in an increase in the quantity of automobiles demanded.
   C. have no effect on the quantity of automobiles demanded because the change was in supply.
   D. Answers (a) and (b) are both true statements.

5. Ham and turkey are considered to be substitutes in the diet of many people. Holding everything else constant, if the price of ham decreases, then the demand for

   A. turkey will shift to the left.
   B. turkey will shift to the right.
   C. ham will shift to the left.
   D. ham will shift to the right.

6. Consider two goods: good X and good Y. Holding everything else constant, the price of good Y increases and the demand for good X decreases. Good X and good Y are

   A. complements.
   B. substitutes.
   C. not related to one another.
   D. cannot be determined.

7. Consider a supply curve. An increase in the price of the good causes a movement along the supply curve, resulting in a greater

   A. supply of the good.
   B. quantity supplied.

8. Research and development result in the discovery of a new technology for electricity generation. Holding everything else constant, this discovery will

   A. increase the supply of electricity.
   B. increase the quantity supplied of electricity.
   C. decrease the supply of electricity.
   D. decrease the quantity supplied of electricity.

9. The sawmill industry expects lumber prices to rise next year due to growing demand for the construction of new homes. Holding everything else constant, this expectation will shift

   A. the supply curve for lumber this year to the left.
   B. the supply curve for lumber this year to the right.

10. Which of the following statements is true about equilibrium in a competitive market for a good?
    I. In equilibrium, the quantity demanded equals the quantity supplied.
    II. The equilibrium price and quantity are found where the demand and supply curves intersect.
    III. In equilibrium, every consumer who wishes to consume the product is satisfied.

    A. Statement I
    B. Statement II
    C. Statement III
    D. Statements I and II
    E. Statements I, II, and III

11. Consumers in Mayville consider houses and apartments to be substitutes. There is an increase in the price of houses at the same time three new apartment buildings are opened in Mayville. In the market for apartments there, the equilibrium

    A. price will rise relative to its level before these two events.
    B. price will fall relative to its level before these two events.
    C. quantity will rise relative to its level before these two events.
    D. quantity will fall relative to its level before these two events.

12. The implementation of an effective price floor

    A. decreases the price of the product.
    B. increases the price of the product.

13. Consider minimum-wage legislation requiring that all workers receive a wage payment greater than the equilibrium market wage. Which of the following groups is more likely to have advocated for this legislation?

    A. demanders of labor
    B. suppliers of labor

14. Use the information in the table below to answer the following two questions.

Price	Quantity demanded	Quantity supplied
$20	200	0
40	150	50
60	100	100
80	50	150
100	0	200

Suppose a price floor of $40 is implemented in this market. This results in

A. an excess demand of 100 units.
B. an excess supply of 100 units.
C. no effect in this market because the price floor is set below the equilibrium price.
D. no effect in this market because the price floor is set above the equilibrium price.

15. Suppose a price ceiling of $40 is implemented in this market. This results in

A. an excess demand of 100 units.
B. an excess supply of 100 units.
C. no effect in this market because the price ceiling is set below the equilibrium price.
D. a temporary shortage of the good while prices rise.

16. Black market or illegal activities increase with the imposition of price controls in markets. Black markets

A. improve the situation of all participants in the price-controlled market.
B. worsen the situation for those people who obey the rules imposed by the government.
C. have little or no real impact on price-controlled markets.
D. create greater respect in society for the need to obey all laws.

17. An effective quantity control, or quota,

A. limits the price that suppliers can charge for the good or service in the regulated market.
B. limits the price that consumers must pay for the good or service in the regulated market.
C. limits the amount of the good or service available in the regulated market.
D. increases the quantity of the good in the regulated market to a quantity above equilibrium.

18. A quota imposed on a market

A. restricts the amount of the good available in that market.
B. results in a payment being made by the government to the license holder.
C. places a lower limit on the amount of the good provided in the regulated market.
D. places an upper limit on the price of the good provided in the regulated market.

19. Which of the following statements is true? Quantity controls
    I. are inefficient because they prevent mutually beneficial transactions.
    II. result in too many resources being allocated to that market.
    III. result in a wedge: the demand price is less than the supply price for the last unit.

A. Statement I
B. Statement II
C. Statements I and III
D. Statements I, II, and III

20. Quantity controls

A. provide an incentive to engage in illegal activities.
B. result in underproduction of the good in the market with the quota limit.
C. result in a less efficient outcome than the market outcome.
D. Answers (a), (b), and (c) are all correct.

ANSWER KEY

Fill-in-the-Blanks

Module 5: (1) many; (2) price; (3) low(er); (4) quantity demanded; (5) demand; (6) right, (7) price of related goods, income, tastes, expectations, number of consumers; (8) quantity demanded; (9) increase; (10) complements; (11) decrease; (12) decrease; (13) inferior; (14) normal

Module 6: (1) price; (2) quantity supplied; (3) supply; (4) right; (5) input prices, price of related goods, technology, expectations, number of producers; (6) quantity demanded; (7) surplus; (8) decrease; (9) shortage; (10) increase

Module 7: (1) increase, (2) increase, (3) decrease, (4) increase, (5) quantity, (6) price, (7) price, (8) quantity

Module 8: (1) ceiling, (2) floor, (3) high, (4) below, (5) shortage, (6) low, (7) above, (8) surplus

Module 9: (1) quota, (2) license, (3) wedge, (4) demand, (5) supply, (6) rent

Featured Graph

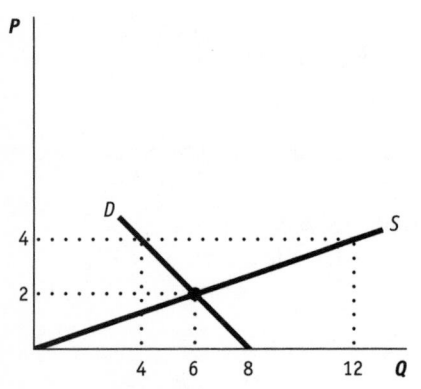

P	Qd	Qs
0	8	0
2	6	6
4	4	12

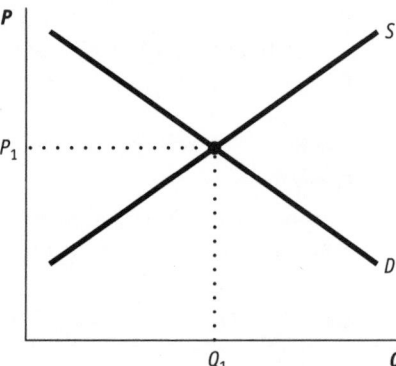

Exercises

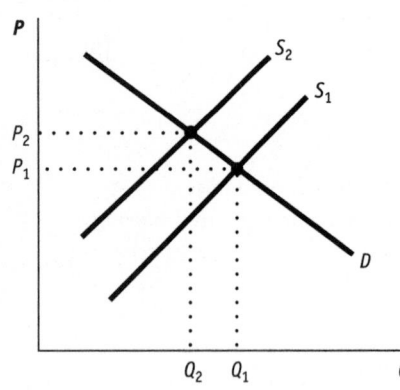

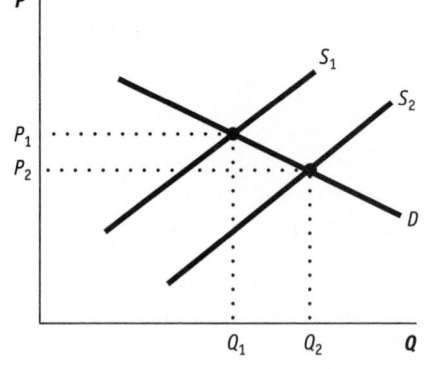

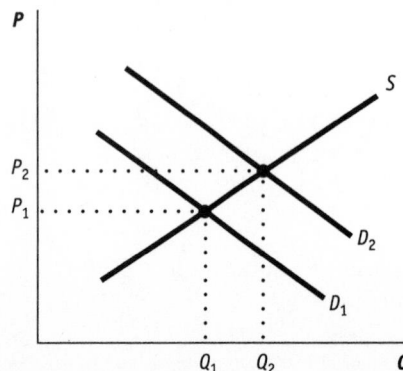

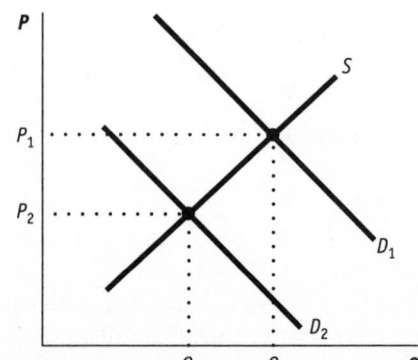

Answers to Problems

1. **a.**

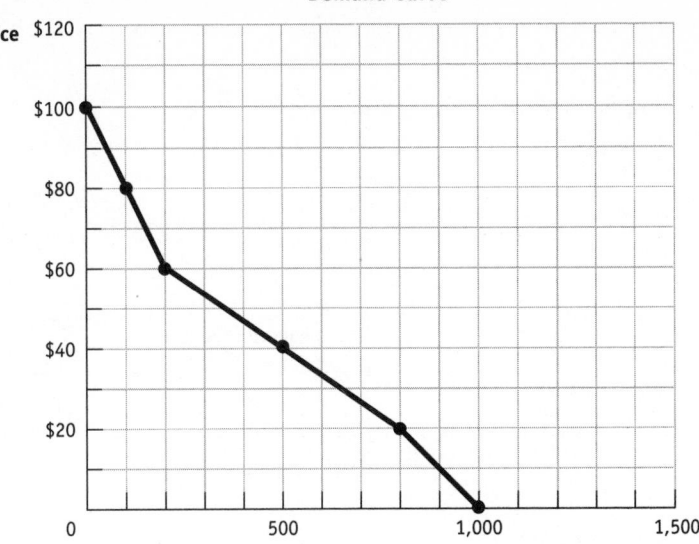

Demand Curve

b. If price rises to $60, the quantity demanded will fall by 300 units, from 500 to 200 bicycles.

c. If price falls to $0, the quantity demanded will increase by 500 units, from 500 to 1,000 bicycles.

2.

Situation	Specified market	Movement or shift	Rightward or leftward shift in demand
People's income increases.	Market for exotic vacations	Shift	Rightward
People's income decreases.	Market for goods sold in secondhand shops	Shift	Rightward
Price of bicycles increases.	Market for bicycles	Movement	
Price of tennis balls increases.	Market for tennis racquets	Shift	Leftward
Price of movie tickets decreases.	Popcorn at movie theatres	Shift	Rightward
Popularity of music-playing device increases.	Market for music-playing device	Shift	Rightward
Popularity of name-brand clothing items decreases.	Market for brand-name designer clothing	Shift	Leftward
Winter clothing is expected to go on sale next month.	Market for winter clothing	Shift	Leftward
Number of urban residents increases.	Market for apartments in urban areas	Shift	Rightward

3. **a.** At a price of $20, producers are willing to supply 40 units.

b. At a price of $40, producers are willing to supply 80 units.

c. At a price of $50, 100 widgets are supplied. Thus, if there are 10 producers producing exactly the same number of widgets, then each producer must produce 10 widgets.

d. When price falls from $30 to $20, the number of widgets supplied decreases by 20 widgets (from 60 widgets to 40 widgets).

e. When price rises from $30 to $50, the number of widgets supplied increases by 40 (from 60 to 100).

f. Suppliers are willing to supply 80 widgets if the price is $40.

g. Suppliers are willing to supply 40 widgets if the price is $20.

h. The typical supply curve is upward sloping: its slope is positive. This implies that quantity supplied increases when price increases and quantity supplied decreases when price decreases.

4.

Situation	Specified market	Movement or shift	Rightward or leftward shift in supply
Labor costs for air travel and cruise ships increase.	Market for exotic vacations	Shift	Leftward
Prices of office equipment and phone service rise by 40%.	Market for call center services	Shift	Leftward
Price of bicycles increases.	Market for bicycles	Movement	
Price of leather boots increases.	Market for beef products	Shift	Rightward
Price of leather boots increases.	Market for leather belts	Shift	Leftward
New technology for music-playing device revealed.	Market for music-playing devices	Shift	Rightward
Price of brand-name designer clothing increases.	Market for brand-name designer clothing	Movement	
Number of coffee shop owners in the metro area increases.	Market for coffee in the metro area	Shift	Rightward

5. a. and b. Equilibrium occurs at the price where quantity demanded equals quantity supplied. From the table we can see that this is at a price of $30. The equilibrium price is thus $30, and the equilibrium quantity is 400 units. This point is illustrated in the graph in part (d).

c.

Price	Excess demand	Excess supply
$0	1,000 units	
10	675 units	
20	325 units	
30	Equilibrium	Equilibrium
40		350 units
50		675 units

d. When there is excess demand, the quantity demanded is greater than the quantity supplied. For some reason the market does not provide an adequate amount of the good, and thus there is a shortage of the good. The figure below illustrates a shortage at a price of P_1. Note that at P_1, the quantity demanded is Q_1, the quantity supplied is Q_2, and the excess demand is equal to $Q_1 - Q_2$. When a market has excess demand, this implies that the current price is below equilibrium.

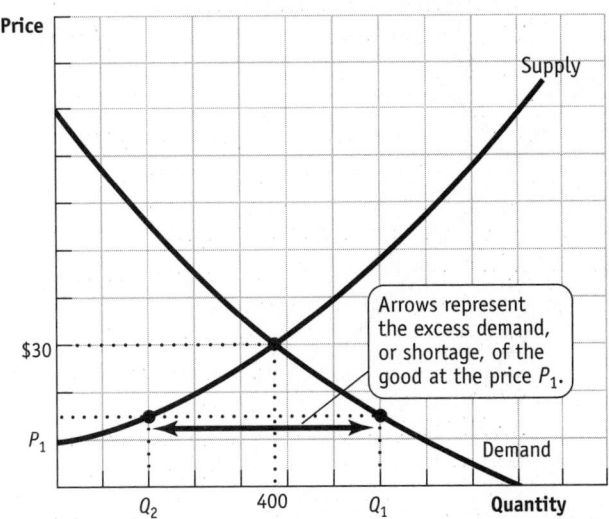

Illustration of a Situation of Excess Demand, or a Shortage

e. When there is excess supply, the quantity demanded is less than the quantity supplied. For some reason the market provides too much of the good, and thus there is a surplus of the good. The figure below illustrates a surplus at a price of P_1. Note that at P_1, the quantity demanded is Q_1, the quantity supplied is Q_2, and the excess supply is equal to $Q_2 - Q_1$. When a market has excess supply of a good, this implies that the current price is above equilibrium.

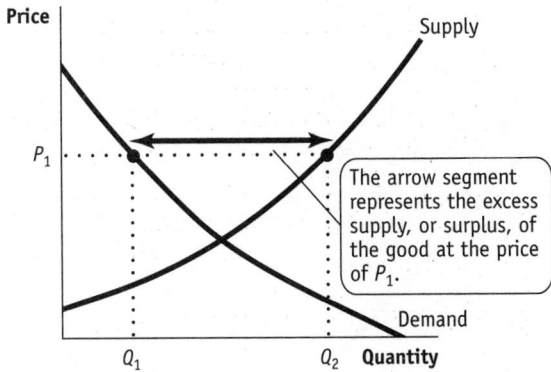

Illustration of a Situation of Excess Supply, or a Surplus

6. a. Gasoline and bicycles are substitutes for one another. When the price of gasoline rises, people substitute bicycle transportation for gasoline. This is illustrated in the graph below with the demand curve for bicycles shifting to the right, resulting in a higher

equilibrium price (P_2) and a higher equilibrium quantity (Q_2). Note that there is a shift in the demand curve and a movement along the supply curve.

Market for Bicycles

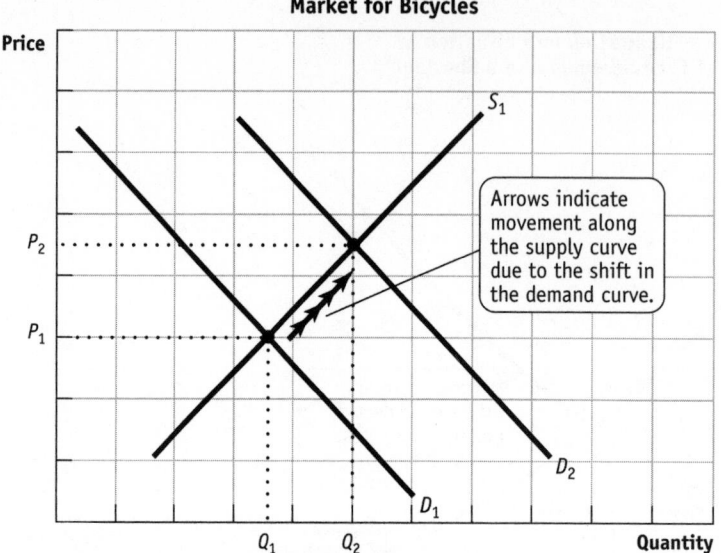

b. Gasoline and SUVs are complements for each other. When the price of gasoline rises, people find that driving SUVs is relatively more expensive and therefore decrease their demand for SUVs at every price. This is illustrated in the graph below with the demand curve for SUVs shifting to the left, resulting in a lower equilibrium price (P_2) and a lower equilibrium quantity (Q_2). Note that there is a shift in the demand curve and a movement along the supply curve.

Market for SUVs

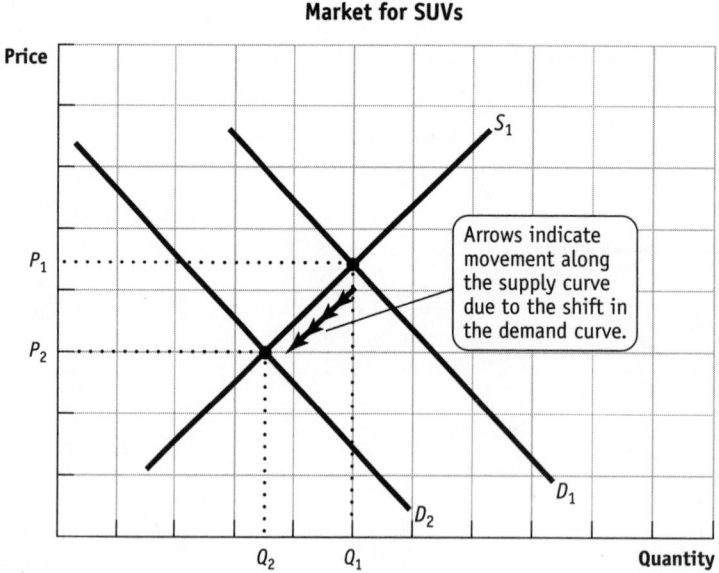

c. New technology shifts the supply curve to the right from S_1 to S_2. This causes a movement along the demand curve and results in a decrease in the equilibrium price and an increase in the equilibrium quantity. This is illustrated in the figure below.

Market for Music-Playing Devices

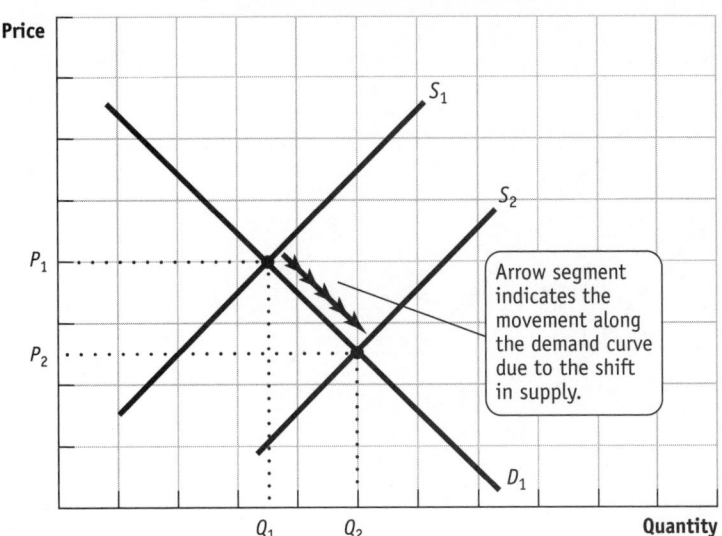

Arrow segment indicates the movement along the demand curve due to the shift in supply.

d. When the price of labor decreases, the supply of the good shifts to the right because labor is an input in the production of fast-food meals. This results in a movement along the demand curve, a decrease in the equilibrium price, and an increase in the equilibrium quantity as illustrated below.

Market for Fast-Food Restaurants

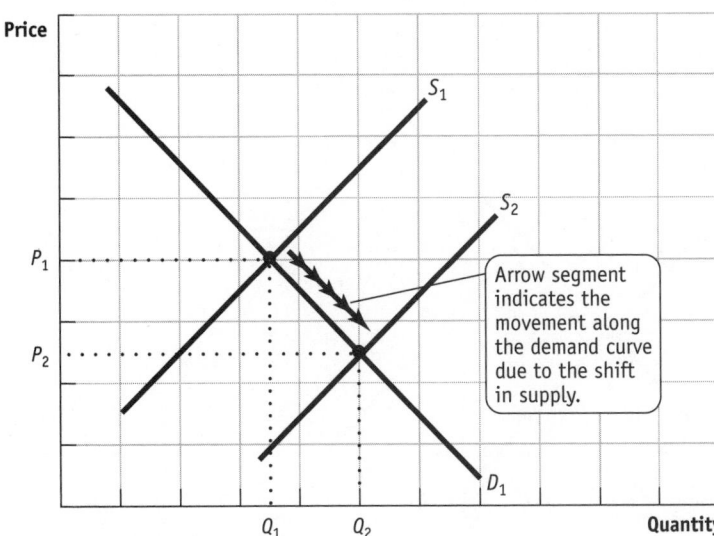

Arrow segment indicates the movement along the demand curve due to the shift in supply.

e. An increase in income shifts the demand curve to the right if the good is a normal good. This shift in demand causes a movement along the supply curve and an increase in both the equilibrium price and the equilibrium quantity as illustrated below.

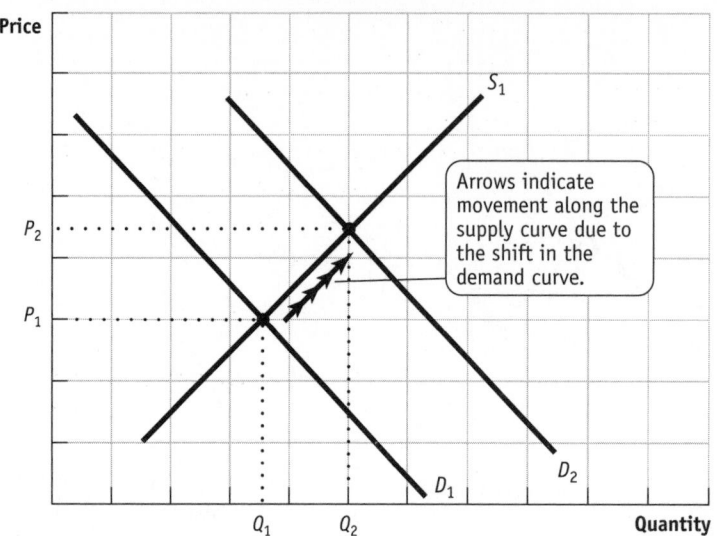

Market for Good X

f. An increase in income shifts the demand curve to the left if the good is an inferior good. This shift in demand causes a movement along the supply curve and a decrease in both the equilibrium price and the equilibrium quantity. The graph below illustrates this situation.

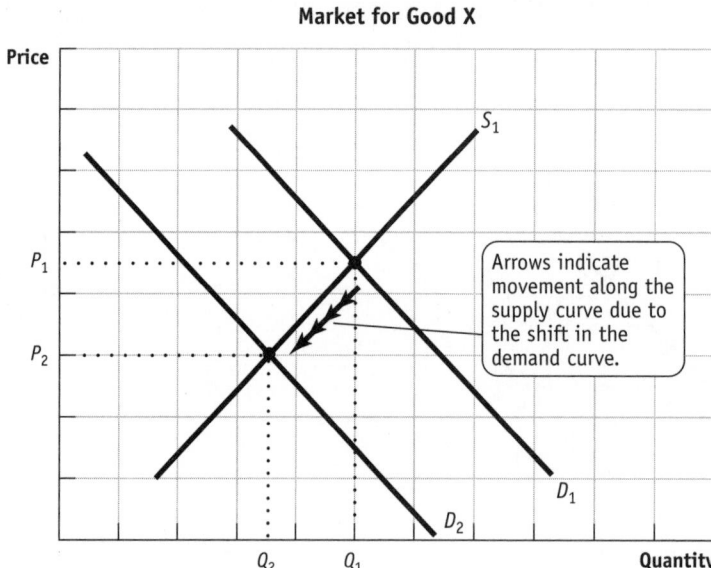

Market for Good X

7. a. The equilibrium price is P_1 and the equilibrium quantity is Q_3.

b. This is not an effective price floor because the price floor of P_3 is less than the equilibrium price. P_1. Because it is an ineffective price floor, the equilibrium price and quantity will not change.

c. This is an effective price floor because the price floor of P_2 is greater than the equilibrium price P_1. At P_2, Q_1 units of the good will be demanded and Q_4 units of the good will be supplied. This excess supply of $Q_4 - Q_1$ will not be eliminated by price decreases because the price is artificially set at P_2 by the government and is not allowed to decrease. An effective price floor creates a situation of excess supply, or a surplus, that is not eliminated by changes in the price of the good because the price has been set at a level greater than the market-clearing price.

d. For a price floor to have an effect on a market, the price floor must be set at a price greater than the equilibrium price.

e. The price floor must be set at a price greater than P_2 because we know from part (c) that the surplus in the market at P_2 equals $Q_4 - Q_1$.

8. a. The equilibrium price is P_1 and the equilibrium quantity is Q_3.

b. This is not an effective price ceiling because the price ceiling of P_2 is greater than the equilibrium price P_1. Since it is a nonbinding/ineffective price ceiling, the equilibrium price and quantity will not change.

c. This is an effective price ceiling because the price ceiling of P_3 is less than the equilibrium price P_1. At P_3, Q_5 units of the good will be demanded and Q_2 units of the good will be supplied. This excess demand of $Q_5 - Q_2$ will not be eliminated by price increases because the price is artificially set at P_3 by the government and is not allowed to increase. An effective price ceiling creates a situation of excess demand, or a shortage, that is not eliminated by changes in the price of the good because the price has been set at a level that is less than the market-clearing price.

d. For a price ceiling to have an effect on a market, the price ceiling must be set at a price that is less than the equilibrium price.

e. The price ceiling must be set at a price that is greater than P_3 but still less than the equilibrium price of P_1. We know this because when the price ceiling is set at P_3, the shortage is equal to $Q_5 - Q_2$ and the new price ceiling results in a smaller shortage than the shortage at price P_3.

9. The market is in equilibrium when there are 1,500 units of housing offered at the price of $2,000 per month, so 1,200 is not an efficient level of housing. The price ceiling forces consumers to reduce their consumption of the good from the efficient level. In the first sketch below, the housing market is represented and the equilibrium price and quantity are where the demand and supply curves intersect. In the second sketch, the price ceiling is imposed on the housing market and this results in suppliers reducing the number of apartments they supply in the market from 1,500 units to 1,200 units. Consumers are willing to pay more for the last unit than suppliers must receive in order to produce this last unit of housing. This indicates that the value to consumers of an additional unit of housing is greater than the cost to producers for providing this additional unit of housing: provision of more housing would lead to greater efficiency.

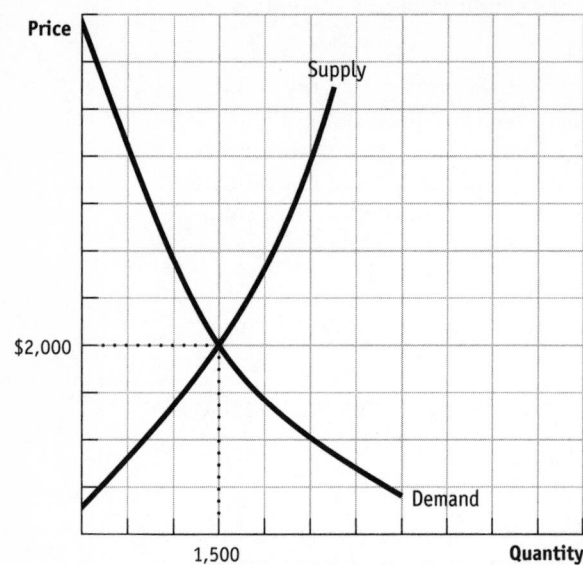

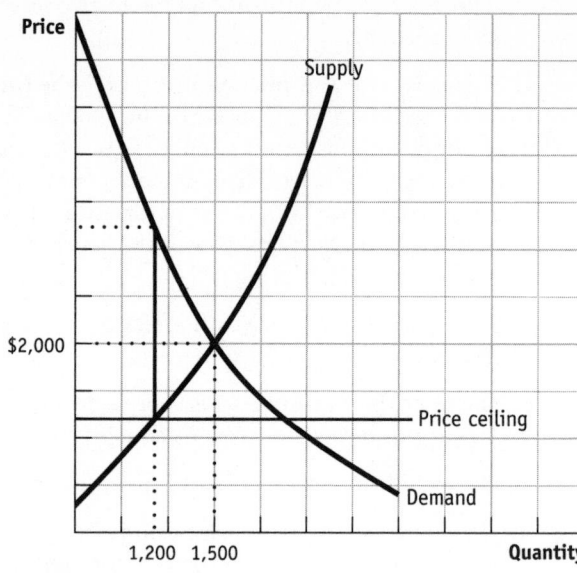

10. **a.** Equilibrium occurs when the quantity demanded equals the quantity supplied. According to the data in the table, the equilibrium price is $5 and the equilibrium quantity is 120 taxi rides per week.

b. Consumers will demand 80 taxi rides per week at a price of $7.

c. Suppliers are willing to supply 80 taxi rides per week for a price of $3.

d. The medallion will rent for $4 per taxi ride, or the difference between the demand price and the supply price when the quantity of taxi rides is limited to 80 per week.

e.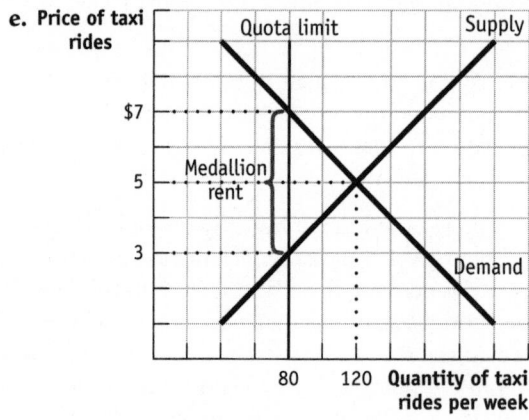

f. The taxi medallions are worth the product of the medallion rent per ride times the number of taxi rides per week or ($4 per ride)(80 rides), or $320.

Answers to Review Questions

1. **C.** This is a definitional statement.

2. **C.** The law of demand states that as the price of the good decreases, the quantity demanded of the good increases. Since the shampoo is on sale, its price has fallen and the law of demand suggests that the quantity demanded should increase.

3. **B.** This research finding is likely to result in an increase in preferences for mangos, which will cause the demand curve for mangos to shift to the right.

4. **A.** A shift in the supply curve holding everything else constant will cause the price of the good to increase. This increase in price will result in a movement along the demand curve because as the price increases, the quantity demanded of the good decreases.

5. **A.** Because ham and turkey are substitutes, when the price of ham decreases, this causes the quantity of ham demanded to increase. As more units of ham are demanded, fewer units of turkey are demanded at every price. The demand for turkey therefore shifts to the left.

6. **A.** As the price of good Y increases, this results in a decrease in the quantity demanded of good Y. Because the demand for good X decreases, this implies that good Y and good X are consumed together; thus good X and good Y are complements.

7. **B.** This question is asking you to recall that a change in the price of the good, holding everything else constant, results in a movement along the curve. This movement along the curve causes a change in the quantity supplied, not a change in the supply curve.

8. **A.** New technology causes the supply curve to shift to the right, resulting in an increase in the quantity supplied of the good at every price.

9. **A.** The sawmill industry will want to decrease the supply of lumber they provide to the market this year due to their expectation that next year's lumber prices will be higher. At every price the quantity of lumber supplied this year will decrease, and the supply curve for lumber this year will shift to the left.

10. **D.** The first two statements are fairly straightforward, but statement III may be somewhat appealing at first glance. At equilibrium, however, even though the quantity demanded equals the quantity supplied, this does not imply that every potential consumer of the good is consuming the good. Those consumers who would like to consume the good, but who are unwilling to pay the equilibrium price, will not consume the good.

11. **C.** The demand curve for apartments shifts to the right with the increase in the price of houses (houses and apartments are substitute goods for consumers in Mayville), while the supply curve for apartments also shifts to the right with the opening of the new apartment buildings. Since we do not know the magnitude of the shifts in the demand and supply curves, we know that the equilibrium quantity is now larger, but the equilibrium price may increase, decrease, or remain the same with these shifts in the demand and supply curves.

12. **B.** An effective price floor must be set above the equilibrium price in the market; thus, the effective price ceiling increases the price of the product in the market.

13. **B.** Suppliers of labor will receive this higher wage and therefore benefit from it. Consumers of labor will find this higher wage increases the cost of hiring labor, and they will not benefit from it.

14. **C.** A price floor of $40 in this market is an example of an ineffective price floor because a price floor of $40 is less than the equilibrium price of $60. This price floor would have no effect on the market.

15. **A.** A price ceiling of $40 results in 150 units being demanded and 50 units being supplied. This is therefore a situation of excess demand of 100 units.

16. **B.** Answers (a) and (b) are mutually exclusive: if one of these answers is correct, then the other must be incorrect. Reading answer (b) helps to identify a group that is hurt by black market activities; those individuals who decide not to engage in black market activities are left worse off because of their obedience to the rules imposed by the price-controlled market. Answer (c) is incorrect because price controls do affect markets when they are effective. Answer (d) is also incorrect because price-controlled markets generate black market activities, which are against the law.

17. **C.** A quota by definition is a limit on the number of units of the good that can be offered in the market. Answers (a) and (b) are both incorrect because they discuss price controls rather than quantity controls. Answer (d) is also incorrect because an effective quota results in reducing the amount of the good available rather than increasing the amount of the good available.

18. **A.** Answer (a) is the basic definition of a quota. Answer (b) is incorrect because there is no assumption of the government making a payment to the license holder when there is a quota. Answer (c) is incorrect because a quota represents the maximum amount of the good allowed in a market rather than the minimum amount. Answer (d) is incorrect because it focuses on price controls rather than quantity controls.

19. **A.** Statement I is correct because quantity controls restrict the amount of output to a level that is less than the equilibrium amount of output. They are inefficient because they prevent mutually beneficial trades from occurring. Because quantity controls restrict output, this implies that too few resources are devoted to the production of the good, so statement II is incorrect. Quantity controls do result in a wedge being created, but that wedge is the difference between the price consumers are willing to pay and the price producers must receive to provide the good, thus statement III is incorrect.

20. **D.** Quantity controls restrict output, result in too few resources being devoted to the production of the good, and create an incentive for black market activities as consumers seek out alternative methods for getting the scarce good.

Notes

Measurement of Economic Performance

OVERVIEW

This section focuses on economic aggregation and what aggregation means when measuring the level of production and prices in an economy. It presents a circular-flow model of the economy, introduces gross domestic product (GDP) and three ways of calculating GDP, and discusses the distinction between nominal and real GDP. In addition, this section presents the definition, calculation, causes, and categories of unemployment, and discusses inflation, including the calculation of price indexes as measures of the aggregate price level and how to calculate the inflation rate using a price index.

FEATURED MODEL/GRAPH: THE CIRCULAR-FLOW MODEL

This section presents the circular-flow model of the macroeconomy. This diagram represents the flow of payments through the economy and provides an illustration of the different ways to calculate aggregate production, or gross domestic product (GDP).

MODULES IN THIS SECTION

Module 10: The Circular Flow and Gross Domestic Product

Module 11: Interpreting Real Gross Domestic Product

Module 12: The Meaning and Calculation of Unemployment

Module 13: The Causes and Categories of Unemployment

Module 14: Inflation: An Overview

Module 15: The Measurement and Calculation of Inflation

Module 10
The Circular Flow and Gross Domestic Product

Before You Read the MODULE

Summary

This module presents the circular-flow model and introduces one of the most important macroeconomic measures: gross domestic product (GDP).

Module Objectives

Review these objectives before you read the module. Place a "√" on the line when you understand each of the following:

_____**Objective 1.** How **aggregate measures** are used to track the performance of the economy

_____**Objective 2.** How the circular-flow model represents the economy

_____**Objective 3.** The definition of **gross domestic product** (GDP)

_____**Objective 4.** The three ways to calculate GDP

While You Read the MODULE

Key Terms

Define these key terms as you read the module.

National income and product accounts

> keep track of money between
> sectors of the economy

Household

> A person or group of people who
> share income

Firm

> An organization that produces goods
> + services for sale

Product markets

Goods & services are bought & sold

Factor markets

When resources, especially capital & labor
are bought & sold

Consumer spending

household spending on goods & services

Stock

share in the ownership of a company held
by a shareholder

Bond

loan in the form of an IOU that
pay interest

Government transfers

payments that gov't makes individuals w/o
expecting a good or service in return

Disposable income

equal to income + gov't transfers minus taxes,
is total amt of household income available
to spend on consumption & to save.

Private savings

equal to disposable income minus consumer spending,
is disposable income that is not spent on
consumption

Financial markets

banking, stock, & bond markets which channel private
savings & foreign lending into investments spending, a
gov't borrowing, & foreign borrowing.

Government borrowing

amount of funds borrowed by the gov't in the financial market

Government purchases of goods and services

total expenditures on goods + services by federal, state, + local gov'ts.

Exports

goods + services sold to other countries

Imports

goods + services purchased from other countries.

Inventories

stocks of goods + raw materials held to facilitate business operations

Investment spending

Spending on new productive physical capital, such as machinery + structures, + on changes ~~structures~~ in inventories

Final goods and services

goods or services sold to final or end user

Intermediate goods and services

Goods + services bought from one firm by another firm to be used as inputs into the production of final goods + services.

Gross domestic product (GDP)

total value of all final goods + services produced in the economy during a given year

<u>Aggregate spending</u> total spending on domestically produced final goods + services in the economy is the sum of consumer spending, investment spending, gov't purchases of goods + services + exports minus imports.

<u>Value added</u>
producer is the value of its sales minus

<u>Net exports</u>

Difference between the value of exports + the value of imports.

List questions or difficulties from your initial reading of the module.

After You Read the MODULE

Fill-in-the-Blanks

Fill in the blanks to complete the following statements. Terms may be used more than once. If you find yourself having difficulties, please refer to the appropriate section in the text.

- A (1) __circular flow__ diagram of the economy focuses on money flows and illustrates the key concepts underlying the national accounts. Note that the flow of money into each market or sector must (2)__equal__ the flow of money out of each market or sector.

- The sum of consumer spending on goods and services, investment spending, government spending, and net exports is known as (3)__GDP__. It is equal to the total value of all (4)__final__ goods and services produced in an economy during a given time period. In the equation $GDP = C + I + G + X - IM$, the variables are (5)__consumption__, __investment__, __gov't__, __export__, and __imports__. GDP can also be measured as the sum of all

(6)_____*income*_____ earned by factors of production: this is the sum of
(7)_____*wages*_____, ____~~rent~~ *rent*____,
_____*interest*_____, and _____*profit*_____. The third method
of calculating GDP is to sum the (8)_____*value*_____ added by firms at
each stage of production.

Module Review

GDP—What's In and What's Out?

It's easy to confuse what is included and what isn't included in GDP. A likely source of confusion is the difference between investment spending and spending on inputs. Investment spending—spending on productive physical capital, construction of structures (residential or commercial), and changes to inventories—is included in GDP. But spending on inputs is not. Why? Recall the distinction between resources that are used up and those that are not used up in production. An input, such as steel, is used up in production. A metal-stamping machine, which is an investment good, is not. It will last for many years and will be used repeatedly to make many cars. Because spending on productive physical capital—investment goods—and construction of structures is not directly tied to current output, economists consider such spending to be spending on final goods.

Spending on changes in inventories is considered a part of investment spending, so it is also included in GDP. Why? Because, like a machine, additional inventory is an investment in future sales. And when a good is released for sale from inventories, its value is subtracted from the value of inventories and so from GDP. Used goods are not included in GDP because, as with inputs, to include them would be to double-count: counting them once when sold as new. Financial assets such as stocks and bonds are not included in GDP because they don't represent the production or sale of final goods and services. Rather, a bond represents a promise to repay with interest, and a stock represents ownership. And for obvious reasons, foreign-produced goods and services are not included in calculations of gross *domestic* product. Here are some important items to note are *not* included in GDP:

Intermediate goods and services   *Financial assets like stocks and bonds*
Inputs   *Foreign-produced goods and services*
Used goods   *Illegal goods and services*

- There are three methods for calculating GDP: (1) multiply the price of each final good and service produced in an economy during a given time period by the quantity produced and then add up the values; (2) add up the total expenditures in the domestic economy on final goods and services during a given time period by the sectors of the economy; households, government, firms, and the rest of the world $(C + I + G + X - IM)$; and (3) sum the value of factor payments in the domestic economy over the given time period. Each method yields the same value of GDP.

Module 11
Interpreting Real Gross Domestic Product

Before You Read the MODULE

Summary

This module presents the distinction between nominal GDP and real GDP, and discusses how they can be used to measure economic activity.

Module Objectives

Review these objectives before you read the module. Place a "√" on the line when you understand each of the following:

_____**Objective 1.** The difference between **real GDP** and **nominal GDP**

_____**Objective 2.** Why real GDP is the appropriate measure of real economic activity

While You Read the MODULE

Key Terms

Define these key terms as you read the module.

Aggregate output

Real GDP

Nominal GDP

Chain-linking
_____

GDP per capita
_____

List questions or difficulties from your initial reading of the module.

After You Read the MODULE
···

Fill-in-the-Blanks

Fill in the blanks to complete the following statements. Terms may be used more than once. If you find yourself having difficulties, please refer to the appropriate section in the text.

- GDP can increase over time because the economy is producing more or because the

    (1)_____ of the goods and services it produces have increased.

    (2)_____ GDP calculates the value of aggregate production dur-

    ing a given time period, using prices from some given base year. In contrast,

    (3)_____ GDP is the calculation of GDP using current prices.

    Real GDP measures allow one to compare growth in aggregate

    (4)_____ in an economy over time.

- When comparing GDP across countries, we can eliminate differences in population size by

    dividing each country's GDP by its population to get (5)_____

    GDP, which is the average GDP per person.

- Real GDP per capita is a measure of what an economy *can* do but it is not a sufficient goal

    in itself because it doesn't address how a country uses output to improve

    (6)_____.

Gross What?

Occasionally, you may see references to gross *national* product, or GNP. Is this just another name for the same thing? Not quite. If you look at the circular-flow diagram carefully, you may realize there's a possibility missing. According to the figure, all factor income goes to domestic households. That is, GDP defines a country as the people living within its borders, regardless of citizenship. But what happens when factor payments go to foreigners in the United States or U.S. citizens receive factor payments while overseas? GNP defines a country as its citizens, wherever they are located. Therefore, GNP is defined as the total factor income earned by citizens of a country. It excludes factor income earned by foreigners, for example, profits paid to foreign investors who own U.S. stocks and payments to foreigners who work temporarily in the United States. And it includes factor income earned abroad by U.S. citizens, for example, the profits of IBM's European operations that accrue to IBM's U.S. shareholders and the wages of U.S. citizens who work abroad temporarily.

In the early days of national income accounting, economists usually used GNP to measure the economy. They switched to GDP mainly because it's considered a better indicator of short-run movements in production and because data on international flows of factor income are considered unreliable. In practice, it doesn't make much difference which measure is used for large economies like that of the United States, where the flows of net factor income to other countries are relatively small. In 2007, the U.S. GNP was about 0.7% larger than the GDP, mainly because of the overseas profits of U.S. companies. For smaller countries, however, GDP and GNP can diverge significantly.

- Nominal GDP calculates GDP using current prices. Nominal GDP can change over time because the economy is producing more *or* because the prices of the goods and services it produces have increased. By contrast, real GDP calculates the value of aggregate production using prices from a base year, i.e., real GDP uses constant prices. Real GDP allows comparison of the growth in aggregate production in an economy over time without the effects of price increases.

- The distinction between real and nominal variables is important. Prices are used to measure the relative value of goods and services, but because prices are not constant it is important to measure economic variables that correct for price changes.

Module 12
The Meaning and Calculation of Unemployment

Before You Read the MODULE

Summary

This module explains in detail how unemployment is calculated and why the unemployment rate in an economy is significant. The module also explores the relationship between the unemployment rate and economic growth.

Module Objectives

Review these objectives before you read the module. Place a "√" on the line when you understand each of the following:

_____**Objective 1.** How **unemployment** is measured

_____**Objective 2.** The significance of the **unemployment rate** for the economy

_____**Objective 3.** The relationship between the unemployment rate and economic growth.

While You Read the MODULE

Key Terms

Define these key terms as you read the module.

Employed

Unemployed

Labor force

Labor force participation rate

Unemployment rate

Discouraged workers

Marginally attached workers

Underemployment

List questions or difficulties from your initial reading of the module.

After You Read the MODULE

Fill-in-the-Blanks

Fill in the blanks to complete the following statements. Terms may be used more than once. If you find yourself having difficulties, please refer to the appropriate section in the text.

- The (1)_____ is the sum of the number of employed workers

   and the number of unemployed workers. The unemployed category includes those who are not currently working, but who are (2)_____. The unemployed

category excludes (3)_____ workers, those who are not

employed and are not seeking work because they have given up hope of finding a job. The

(4)_____ rate is the percent of the labor force that is

unemployed. The (5)_____ rate is the percent of the population

that is employed or unemployed. The unemployment rate may

(6)_____ unemployment because it does not correct for the fact

that it takes time for someone looking for work to find a job. The unemployment rate may

(7)_____ unemployment because it excludes discouraged

workers. In general, there is a (8)_____ relationship between

growth in the economy and the rate of unemployment. That is, falling real GDP is

associated with a rising rate of unemployment.

Module Review

Unemployment Means More Than Not Working

The definition of employment is fairly straightforward. A person is employed if he or she has a job, either full time or part time. However, not having a job is not enough to be considered unemployed. To be considered unemployed, a person must be "jobless, looking for jobs, and available for work." An individual is considered unemployed only if he or she doesn't currently have a job but has been actively seeking a job during the past four weeks. So unemployment is defined as the total number of people who are actively looking for work but aren't currently employed. Many people don't have a job and are not actively seeking one. These people are considered neither employed nor unemployed. They are considered out of the labor force. A country's labor force is the sum of employment and unemployment. Be very careful to distinguish between those people who are unemployed and those who are out of the labor force. The key to distinguishing between people in these two groups is to identify whether or not an individual is actively seeking a job (that is, the individual is looking for jobs and is available for work).

- The unemployment rate provides a good indicator of current conditions in the labor market, but it is not a perfect measure. The unemployment rate overstates the difficulty of finding a job because it includes those individuals who are looking for a job and are confident that they will be employed once they identify a suitable position. The unemployment rate understates the difficulty of finding a job because it does not include discouraged workers, those jobless individuals who have given up searching for a job because there are no jobs available where they live. The unemployment rate also does not include the marginally attached workers, a group of individuals who are out of work and have recently looked for work, but who are currently not seeking employment. Lastly, the unemployment rate does not include those individuals who are currently working part-time jobs but who want to work full time; these underemployed workers are counted as employed rather than unemployed, even though they are unable to find full-time jobs .

- The unemployment rate never falls to zero. Jobs are constantly being created and eliminated because of structural changes in the economy and because the process of locating a job or the job search can take time.

Module ⑬
The Causes and Categories of Unemployment

Before You Read the MODULE

Summary

This module presents the three major categories of unemployment, which are distinguished by their causes. The module also develops the concept of the natural rate of unemployment.

Module Objectives

Review these objectives before you read the module. Place a "√" one the line when you understand each of the following:

_____**Objective 1.** The three different types of unemployment and their causes

_____**Objective 2.** The factors that determine the **natural rate of unemployment**

While You Read the MODULE

Key Terms

Define these key terms as you read the module.

Job search

Frictional unemployment

Structural unemployment

Efficiency wages

Natural rate of unemployment

Cyclical unemployment

List questions or difficulties from your initial reading of the module.

After You Read the MODULE

Fill-in-the-Blanks

Fill in the blanks to complete the following statements. Terms may be used more than once. If you find yourself having difficulties, please refer to the appropriate section in the text.

- (1)_____ unemployment occurs because of the constant process of job creation and job destruction, and because of the entry of new workers into the job market. (2)_____ unemployment exists when there are more people seeking jobs in a labor market than there are jobs available at the current wage rate. (3)_____ unemployment is the deviation of the actual rate of unemployment from the natural rate; that is, it is the difference between the actual and natural rates of unemployment. As the name suggests, cyclical unemployment is unemployment that arises from the (4)_____.

- Wages that employers set above the equilibrium wage rate as an incentive for their workers to deliver better performance are called (5)_____ wages.

- The (6)_____ rate of unemployment is the normal unemployment rate around which the actual unemployment rate fluctuates.

Module Review

Does It Matter *Why* a Person Is Unemployed?

We have presented three types of unemployment: frictional, structural, and cyclical. But if someone is unemployed, does it really matter *why* they are unemployed? Yes, if you want to create or evaluate policies to reduce unemployment. The reason a person is unemployed is key to determining how to change his or her employment status. For example, people looking for their first job may experience frictional unemployment. Frictional unemployment can be addressed by providing job search assistance and information. Workers in labor markets where there is an imbalance between supply and demand experience structural unemployment. For example, there may be more workers with a particular skill than there are jobs available requiring that skill, or there may be more workers in a particular geographic region than jobs available there. Structural unemployment can be addressed with job training or relocation assistance. Finally, a person may be cyclically unemployed due to an economic downturn. In this case, macroeconomic policies that promote production may help reduce unemployment.

- The natural rate of unemployment is not constant over time and may be affected by economic policies. The natural rate of unemployment changes with changes in the characteristics of the labor force, labor market institutions, government policies, and productivity.

Module **14**
Inflation: An Overview

Before You Read the MODULE

Summary

This module presents the economic costs of inflation and deflation, and how inflation and deflation create winners and losers. It also discusses why policy makers want to avoid inflation and deflation. Finally, the module explains the difference between real and nominal values.

Module Objectives

Review these objectives before you read the module. Place a "√" on the line when you understand each of the following:

_____**Objective 1.** The economic costs of inflation

_____**Objective 2.** How inflation creates winners and losers

_____**Objective 3.** Why policy makers try to maintain a stable **inflation rate**

_____**Objective 4.** The difference between real and nominal values

_____**Objective 5.** The distinction between deflation and **disinflation**

While You Read the MODULE

Key Terms

Define these key terms as you read the module.

Real wage

Real income

Inflation rate

Shoe-leather costs

Menu costs

Unit-of-account costs

Nominal interest rate

Real interest rate

Disinflation

List questions or difficulties from your initial reading of the module.

After You Read the MODULE

Fill-in-the-Blanks

Fill in the blanks to complete the following statements. Terms may be used more than once. If you find your-self having difficulties, please refer to the appropriate section in the text.

• If you cut a worker's wage in half, but also cut all prices in half, the worker's

(1)_____ (the wage rate divided by the price level), doesn't

change.

- Increased costs of transactions caused by inflation are known as

  (2)_____ costs. Changing a listed price has a real cost, called a

  (3)_____ cost. The (4)_____ costs of

  inflation are the costs arising from the way inflation makes money a less reliable unit of

  measurement.

- The (5)_____ interest rate is the interest rate in dollar terms—

  for example, the interest rate on a student loan. The (6)_____

  interest rate is the nominal interest rate minus the rate of inflation. For example, if a loan

  carries an interest rate of 8%, but there is 5% inflation, the real interest rate is 8% − 5% = 3%.

- Bringing the inflation rate down, a process called (7)_____, is

  very difficult and costly once a higher rate of inflation has become well established in the

  economy.

Module Review

Winning from Inflation

People often think of inflation as a universally bad thing. It can be difficult to understand how an individual can actually "win" from inflation. But, while the economy as a whole suffers inefficiency in the form of the three types of costs of inflation (shoe-leather costs, menu costs, and unit-of-account costs), some people in the economy actually do benefit from inflation.

Here is a simple example of how you, as a borrower, could "win" from inflation. Let's say that you get a loan from your local bank to buy a bicycle. The price of a bicycle is $100 and you get a $100 loan at an interest rate of 5% for one year. At the end of the year, you pay the bank back $105 the $100 you borrowed plus $5 in interest. So the bank has made 5% interest on the loan. Now assume that, over the course of the year you had your loan, the economy experienced inflation. Let's say that there was 7% inflation so the price of a bicycle is now $107. You borrowed $100 (a bicycle's worth of money) and then you paid back $105. At the end of your loan period, $105 is no longer enough to buy a bicycle. You borrowed a bicycle's worth of money and paid back *less than* a bicycle's worth of money. You gained by getting the money when it would still buy a bicycle! The bank received a nominal interest rate of 5%, but when you consider inflation, they received a real interest rate of −2% (5% nominal interest −7% inflation). The bank "lost" from inflation because it was paid back money that could not purchase as much as it could when the bank loaned it. If the bank had known that there would be 7% inflation, it would have increased its nominal interest rate. For instance, if the bank's goal was to earn a real interest rate of 5%, it should have charged a nominal interest rate of 5% + 7% = 12%.

Module 15
The Measurement and Calculation of Inflation

Before You Read the MODULE

Summary

This module explains how the inflation rate is calculated and how price indexes are used to measure and adjust for inflation and deflation in the economy.

Module Objectives

Review these objectives before you read the module. Place a "√" on the line when you understand each of the following:

_____**Objective 1.** How the inflation rate is measured

_____**Objective 2.** What a **price index** is and how it is calculated

_____**Objective 3.** The importance of the **consumer price index** and other price indexes

While You Read the MODULE

Key Terms

Define these key terms as you read the module.

Aggregate price level

Market basket

Price index

Consumer price index (CPI)

_____

Producer price index (PPI)

_____

GDP deflator

_____

List questions or difficulties from your initial reading of the module.

After You Read the MODULE
....

Fill-in-the-Blanks

Fill in the blanks to complete the following statements. Terms may be used more than once. If you find yourself having difficulties, please refer to the appropriate section in the text.

- Economists measure changes in the aggregate (1)_____ by

  tracking changes in the cost of buying a given market basket of goods. A price index

  measures the cost of purchasing a given market basket of goods in a given year, where that

  cost is normalized so that it is equal to 100 in the (2)_____ year.

  The (3)_____, measures the cost of a basket of goods typically

  purchased by consumers.

- The (4)_____ rate is the annual percent change in an official

  price index. The most widely used measure of prices in the United States is the

  (5)_____, often referred to simply as the CPI. It is calculated by

  surveying market prices for a (6)_____ that is constructed to represent the consumption of a typical family of four living in a typical U.S. city. There are two other price measures that are also widely used to track economy-wide price changes, the (7)_____, or PPI, which tracks the cost of a typical basket of goods and services purchased by producers and the (8)_____ for a given year, which is equal to 100 times the ratio of nominal GDP for that year to real GDP for that year expressed in prices of a selected base year.

Module Review

Inflating and Deflating Values Over Time

Over time, the price level changes and the economy experiences inflation or deflation. Because many of the economic measurements we use to track the macroeconomy are calculated in terms of dollars, changes in the price level (inflation or deflation) lead to changes in the measurements. Most often we are interested in changes in macroeconomic measurements that are due to changes in the economy *other than* changes in the price level. That is, we want to look at changes in real values separate from changes in the aggregate price level. For example, if nominal GDP increases over time, it could be due to increases in production or increases in the price level. We would like to know what part of the increase is due to changes in production in the economy. Because nominal GDP can increase due to either increases in production or an increase in the aggregate price level, it does not help us determine if production has increased. To isolate the changes in production, we convert nominal GDP to real GDP. Real GDP is GDP measured *as if prices had not changed*.

You might ask, "As if prices haven't changed *since when*?" To calculate real values, you must first determine the base year—the year you have picked as the "since when" year. If values have increased due to inflation since the base year, the increase is removed by calculating the values as if prices stayed the same as they were in the base year. If values were lower in the past because the price level was lower (that is, the period in the past was before there was inflation), then the lower values are "inflated" by calculating them as if the earlier time period had the higher prices in the base year. By using real values, that is calculating values as if prices had stayed the same as they were in a chosen base year, the real changes we are interested in can be separated from the changes in values that are due to inflation (or deflation).

- Economists measure changes in the aggregate price level by tracking changes in the cost of buying a given market basket of goods. A price index measures the cost of purchasing a given market basket of goods in a given year as if prices had stayed the same as they were in the base year. To calculate the cost of the market basket of goods, multiply the quantities of each good in the market basket times its price and then sum the values Then, use this information to calculate a price index by dividing the cost of the market basket for a particular time period by the cost of the market basket in the base year and then multiplying by 100. The price index for the base year is always equal to 100 because the prices in the base year are 100% of the prices in that year!

- An example of a price index is the consumer price index, or the CPI. The producer price index, or the PPI, (also known as the wholesale price index) is another price index that measures the cost of a basket of goods typically purchased by producers. The inflation rate between two years can be calculated using this formula: Inflation rate = [(price index in year 2) − (price index in year 1)/(price index in year 1)] × 100.

Draw the Featured Model: Circular-Flow Model

a. Fill in the labels for the simple circular-flow model.

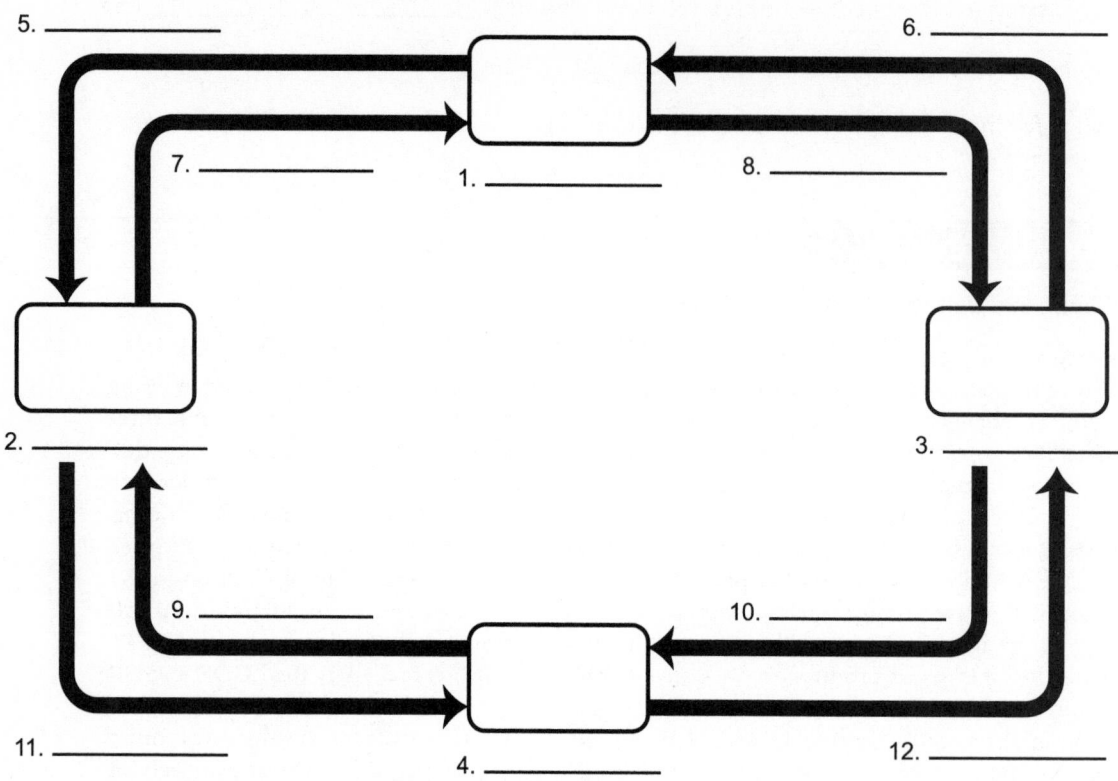

5. _____

6. _____

7. _____   1. _____   8. _____

2. _____

3. _____

9. _____   10. _____

11. _____   4. _____   12. _____

b. What three sectors of the economy are not included here?

Complete the Exercises

1. In Macro Space, the price index is based upon a market basket consisting of 10 apples, 2 pizzas, and 5 ice cream cones. You are given prices for these three items for 2010, 2011, and 2012 in the following table.

Year	Price of apples	Price of pizzas	Price of ice cream cones
2007	$0.50	$4.00	$1.00
2008	0.52	3.85	1.10
2009	0.49	3.90	1.30

a. Fill in the following table using year 2010 as your base year.

Year	Cost of market basket	Price index value
2010		
2011		
2012		

b. Use the information you computed in part (a) to calculate the rate of inflation between 2010 and 2011.

c. Use the information you calculated in part (a) to calculate the rate of inflation between 2011 and 2012.

d. Fill in the following table using year 2011 as your base year.

Year	Cost of market basket	Price index value
2010		
2011		
2012		

e. Use the information you calculated in part (d) to calculate the rate of inflation between 2010 and 2011

f. Use the information you calculated in part (d) to calculate the rate of inflation between 2011 and 2012?

g. Compare your answers in parts (b) and (c) to your answers in parts (e) and (f).

Problems

1. You are given the following information about Macronesia. During 2011, the government of Macronesia spent $200 million on goods and services as well as $20 million on transfer payments, while collecting $150 million in taxes. During 2011 households paid $150 million in taxes, purchased goods and services worth $400 million, and received $800 million in the form of wages, dividends, interest, and rent. Firms in 2011 had $100 million of investment spending, and they borrowed or had stock issues of $170 million from the financial markets. In 2011 exports to this economy equaled $150 million while imports to this economy equaled $50 million. In the financial markets, there was foreign borrowing of $50 million and foreign lending of $20 million.

   a. Sketch a circular-flow diagram of Macronesia's economy showing these flows.

   b. What is the GDP in 2011 in Macronesia?

   c. What is the value of disposable income in Macronesia in 2011?

   d. What is the value of household saving in Macronesia in 2011?

   e. Is the government running a balanced budget during 2011? Explain your answer.

   f. Compute the flows of money into the financial markets and the flows of money out of the financial markets. Are they equal?

g. Compute the flows of money into the market for goods and services and the flows of money out of the market for goods and services. Are they equal?

h. Compute the flows of money into the factor markets and the flows of money out of the factor markets. Are they equal?

2. Decide how each item affects the calculation of GDP for Macro States in 2011.

   a. A new house is constructed in Macro States during 2011.

   b. Jorge sells his house, built in 2001, in Macro States without the help of a realtor in January 2011.

   c. The government purchases new textbooks for the schools of Macro States during 2011.

   d. Macro States sells 100,000 pounds of beef to Neverlandia during 2011.

   e. Judy tutors Ellen's children in exchange for Ellen's driving the children's carpool three days a week throughout 2011.

   f. A candlemaker produces 500 candles during 2011 but sells only 200 candles that year; the other 300 candles are added to the candlemaker's inventories.

3. Suppose you are told that Finlandia produces three goods: tennis shoes, basketballs, and lawn mowers. The following table provides information about the prices and output for these three goods for the years 2010, 2011, and 2012.

Years	Price of tennis shoes	Quantity of tennis shoes	Price of basketballs	Quantity of basketballs	Price of lawn mowers	Quantity of lawn mowers
2010	$50	100	$10	200	$100	10
2011	52	108	10	205	100	12
2012	54	115	10	212	110	12

a. Use the previous information to fill in the following table.

Year	Nominal GDP
2010	
2011	
2012	

b. What was the percentage change in nominal GDP from 2010 to 2011?

c. What was the percentage change in nominal GDP from 2011 to 2012?

d. Use 2010 as the base year to fill in the following table.

Year	Nominal GDP
2010	
2011	
2012	

e. What was the percentage change in real GDP from 2010 to 2011?

f. What was the percentage change in real GDP from 2011 to 2012?

g. Use 2010 as the base year to fill in the following table.

Year	GDP deflator
2010	
2011	
2012	

4. The diagram below provides a circular-flow diagram for the economy of Littleton. You are also told the following about the economy of Littleton:

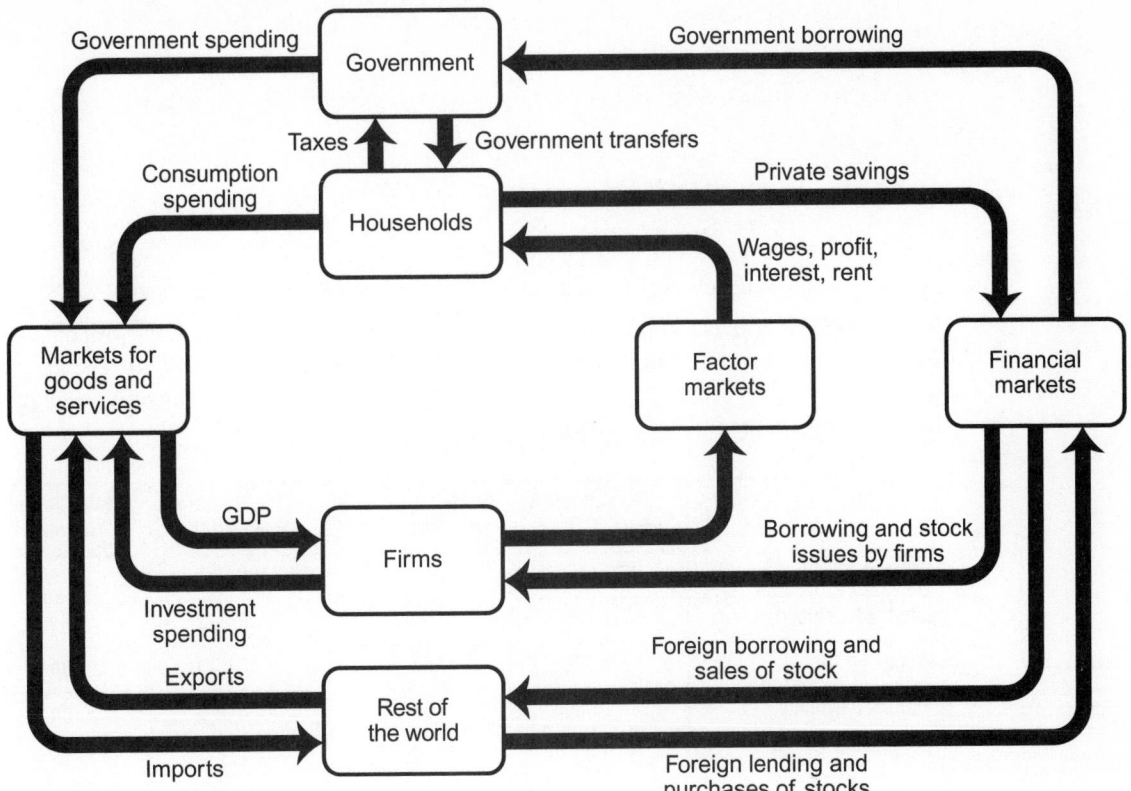

Consumer spending (C) = $200 million
Investment spending (I) = $50 million
Spending on exports (X) = $20 million
Wages + profit + interest + rent = $320 million
Government borrowing = $60 million
Taxes = $20 million
Transfers = $10 million

a. What is the GDP of Littleton? Explain how you found this value.

b. What is the value of government spending (G) in Littleton's economy? Explain.

c. What is the value of imports in Littleton's economy? Explain.

d. What is the value of private savings in Littleton's economy? Explain.

e. What is the level of firm borrowing and stock issues in this economy? Explain.

f. Is the rest of the world a net borrower or a net lender? Explain your answer.

5. You are given the following information about the small economy of Hyattville.

Hyattville's economy is composed of three firms: Hyattville Forest, Inc., which harvests trees used by Hyattville Lumber Products, Inc., to manufacture various lumber products used by Hyattville Houses, Inc., to produce houses. Assume lumber is the only raw material used to produce the houses in Hyattville.

	Hyattville Forest, Inc.	Hyattville Lumber Products, Inc.	Hyattville Houses, Inc.	Total Factor Income
Value of sales	$15,000	(a)	$100,000	
Intermediate goods	(b)	$15,000	40,000	
Wages	6,000	15,000	35,000	(g)
Interest payments	1,000	3,000	6,000	(h)
Rent	3,000	(d)	3,000	(i)
Profit	5,000	4,000	(f)	(j)
Total expenditures by firm	15,000	40,000	100,000	
Value added per firm	(c)	(e)	60,000	

a. Fill in the missing entries [(a)–(j)] in the above table (1) by measuring GDP as the value of the production of final goods and services in an economy as measured by the value added by each firm; (2) by measuring GDP as the sum of aggregate spending on domestically produced final goods and services in an economy; and (3) by measuring GDP as the sum of factor income earned by households in the economy.

b. Use the value-added approach to calculate the value of GDP? Explain.

c. Use the factor income approach to calculate the value of GDP? Explain.

d. Use the aggregate spending on domestically produced final goods and services approach to calculate the value of GDP? Explain.

6. Suppose there are 12,000 people living in Macroland. Of these 12,000 people, 1,000 are either too old or too young to work. Of the remaining individuals, 5,000 are employed full time; 3,000 are employed part time, but wish to work full time; 1,000 are underemployed, but working full time; 1,000 are currently not working, but are looking for work; and the remainder are discouraged workers.

   a. What is the size of the labor force in Macroland?

   b. What is the employment rate in Macroland?

   c. What is the unemployment rate in Macroland?

   d. What percentage of the population are discouraged workers?

   e. Suppose you are told that 100 people find jobs for every $10,000 increase in the level of aggregate output in Macroland. If you wanted the unemployment rate to equal 8%, what would the change in output need to be? Assume no changes in the number of young or old in the population, nor in the number of discouraged workers.

   f. Suppose the government department in Macroland responsible for compiling unemployment statistics redefines the employed as including only those with full-time jobs. How does this change the unemployment rate, given the initial information?

7. Suppose there are 10,000 adults in Finlandia and that 5,000 of these adults are employed, 2,000 are unemployed, 500 are discouraged workers, and the rest are not currently working and/or not seeking employment.

   a. What is the labor force equal to in Finlandia?

   b. What is the unemployment rate in Finlandia?

   c. What would the unemployment rate equal in Finlandia if discouraged workers were counted as unemployed workers?

   d. Currently, the Bureau of Labor Statistics does not count discouraged workers as unemployed workers. How does this decision affect the calculated value of the unemployment rate?

8. Sarah currently works for a firm in which her union has negotiated a cost-of-living adjustment that automatically adjusts her income to whatever the annual rate of inflation is for her community. Bob works for a firm that routinely grants its employees a 5% annual income increase. Milt is retired and receives two payments: a pension payment from his former employer that is fixed at $2,000 per month and a government-provided retirement payment the real value of which is $1,000 per month in the base year. The government-provided retirement payment is indexed to the inflation rate in the community.

   a. Suppose the rate of inflation is 8% this year. Describe the effect of this inflation on Sarah, Bob, and Milt in terms of their real purchasing power. Who is worse off with this inflation? Does anyone end up better off despite this inflation rate? Explain.

   b. Suppose the rate of inflation is 20% this year. Describe the effect of this inflation rate on Sarah, Bob, and Milt.

Review Questions

Circle the correct answer.

Use the information and the following table to answer the next three questions. The table represents data about an economy's performance during a year. And there are only three firms: American Racquet Co., which produces tennis racquets; American Metal Co., which produces the metals that go into racquet production; and American Ore Co., which mines the ores needed to manufacture the metal. This economy produces 100 racquets that sell for $50 each.

	American Racquet Co.	American Metal Co.	American One Co.	Total factor income
Value of sales	$5,000	$3,000	$500	
Intermediate goods	A	B		
Wages	3,000	1,000	100	C
Interest payments	100	50	20	D
Rent	500	100	50	E
Profit	200	750	130	F
Total expenditures by firm	5,000	3,000	500	
Value added per firm	G	H	I	

1. GDP for this hypothetical economy is equal to

   A. $5,000, or the value of sales for American Racquet Co.
   B. $8,500, or the sum of the value added for the three firms.
   C. $3,500, or the value of the intermediate goods used by the American Racquet Co.
   D. $980, or the sum of the profits for the three firms.

2. GDP can be measured using different methods. If you were using the factor payments approach, which entries would you combine to get a measure of GDP?

   A. *G*, *H* and *I*
   B. *A* and *B*
   C. *A*, *B*, *C*, and *D*
   D. *C*, *D*, *E*, and *F*

3. GDP can be measured using the value-added method. Using this method, which of the following values are correct for the missing entries in the table?

   A. $A = \$3,000, B = \$3,000, G = \$2,000, H = \$0, I = \$500$
   B. $A = \$3,000, B = \$500, G = \$2,000, H = \$2,500, I = \$500$
   C. $A = \$3,000, B = \$3,000, G = \$0, H = \$4,500, I = \$500$
   D. $A = \$3,000, B = \$500, G = \$0, H = \$4,500, I = \$500$

Use the information in the following table to answer the next three questions.

	Price in 2010	Price in 2011
Oranges	$0.50	$0.40
Apples	0.25	0.40
Bananas	0.40	0.50

Suppose 2010 is the base year and the market basket for purposes of constructing a price index consists of 200 oranges, 100 apples, and 100 bananas.

4. What is the value of the price index in 2010?

A. 1.15
B. 100
C. 165
D. 190

5. What is the value of the price index in 2011, using 2010 as the base year?

A. 0.97
B. 1
C. 100
D. 103

6. What is the rate of inflation between 2010 and 2011 in this economy?

A. 0%
B. 3%
C. 103%
D. 67% because two of the three prices increased between 2010 and 2011

7. In Macroland the GDP deflator for 2009 is 105, with 2008 as the base year. Real GDP in 2009 equals $210 billion. Nominal GDP in 2009 equals _____ and nominal GDP in 2008 equals _____.

A. $220.5 billion; $200 billion
B. $220.5 billion; $210 billion
C. $200 billion; $210 billion
D. $200 billion; $220.5 billion

8. $C + I + G + X - IM$ is

A. equal to an economy's GDP for a given period of time.
B. the value of all final goods and services produced in an economy during a given time period.
C. Answers (A) and (B) are both correct.
D. Neither (A) nor (B) is correct.

9. Which of the following is *not* included in the calculation of GDP?

A. Joey's Electronics manufactures CD players that individuals install.
B. Susy's Leather Goods manufactures leather pieces that are sold to manufacturers who use them to produce handbags and wallets.
C. Harry's Ice Cream Shoppe sells ice cream cones at the beach.
D. Monica's Hair Salon sells haircuts and manicures to the residents of Macroland.

10. The natural rate of unemployment is

A. a country's unemployment rate during a recession.
B. a country's unemployment rate during an expansion.
C. the sum of frictional and structural unemployment.
D. the sum of frictional and cyclical unemployment.

11. Which of the following statements is true?

A. Structural unemployment refers to the unemployment that occurs when there are more employers demanding labor than employees supplying labor.
B. Structural unemployment refers to a situation when the market wage rate is lower than the equilibrium wage rate.

C. Structural unemployment occurs when there is a surplus of labor at the current wage rate.

D. When there is structural unemployment, frictional unemployment equals zero.

12. The natural rate of unemployment is

  A. equal to 0% in every economy because this is the level of unemployment that every economy should naturally want to achieve.

  B. the sum of frictional and cyclical unemployment.

  C. equal to cyclical unemployment when the economy is producing at the full employment level of aggregate output.

  D. Answers (B) and (C) are correct.

  E. None of the above is correct.

13. Mary expects the inflation rate to be 5%, and she is willing to pay a real interest rate of 3%. Joe expects the inflation rate to be 5%, and he is willing to lend money if he receives a real interest rate of 3%. If the actual inflation rate is 6% and the loan contract specifies a nominal interest rate of 8%, then

  A. Joe is glad he lent out funds even though his real interest rate has fallen.

  B. Joe is sorry he lent out funds because his real interest rate is now 9%.

  C. Mary is glad she borrowed the funds because her real interest rate has fallen.

  D. Mary is sorry she borrowed funds because her real interest rate is now 9%.

14. Disinflation in an economy that has grown to expect inflation is

  A. easy to achieve and does not affect actual output.

  B. difficult to accomplish and results in an increase in the natural rate of unemployment.

  C. possible only if policy makers are willing to accept higher rates of unemployment and a lower level of aggregate output.

  D. Answers (A) and (C) are both correct.

  E. Answers (B) and (C) are both correct.

15. In a period of unexpected deflation,

  A. borrowers find that it is easier for them to make their loan payments because prices are falling.

  B. lenders benefit because more people are eager to borrow money during a period of deflation.

  C. lenders benefit because they are repaid dollars with greater real value than they anticipated when signing the loan contract.

  D. Answers (A), (B), and (C) are all correct.

16. Which of the following statements is true?

  I. The two principal goals of macroeconomic policy are price stability and low frictional unemployment.

  II. The primary goals of macroeconomic policy are price stability and low unemployment.

  III. In order to achieve the two primary goals of macroeconomic policy of price stability and low unemployment, it is necessary for policy makers to reduce the level of frictional unemployment.

  A. Statements I, II, and III

  B. Statements I and II

  C. Statements II and III

  D. Statement I

  E. Statement II

  F. Statement III

17. Which of the following statements is true? To be considered unemployed
    I. one must simply not have a job.
    II. one must not have a job and also must not be looking for a job.
    III. one must not have a job and also must be looking for a job.

    A. Statement I
    B. Statement II
    C. Statement III
    D. Statements I, II, and III are all false.

18. When the unemployment rate is high, this usually implies that it is

    A. easy to find a job.
    B. difficult to find a job.

19. Job search refers to the time workers spend looking for employment. Job search results in

    A. cyclical unemployment.
    B. structural unemployment.
    C. frictional unemployment.
    D. both structural and frictional unemployment.

20. The extra time and effort to make transactions due to inflation imposes

    A. shoe-leather costs.
    B. menu costs.
    C. unit-of-account costs.

ANSWER KEY

Fill-in-the-Blanks

Module 10: (1) circular flow; (2) equal; (3) gross domestic product; (4) final; (5) consumption; investment, government spending, exports, imports; (6) income; (7) wages, rent, interest, profit; (8) value

Module 11: (1) prices, (2) real, (3) nominal, (4) production, or output, (5) per capita, (6) living standards

Module 12: (1) labor force, (2) actively seeking employment, (3) discouraged, (4) unemployment, (5) labor force participation, (6) overstate, (7) understate, (8) negative

Module 13: (1) frictional, (2) structural, (3) cyclical, (4) business cycle, (5) efficiency, (6) natural

Module 14: (1) real wage, (2) shoe-leather, (3) menu, (4) unit-of-account, (5) nominal, (6) real, (7) disinflation

Module 15: (1) price level, (2) base, (3) consumer price index, (4) inflation, (5) consumer price index, (6) market basket, (7) producer price index, (8) GDP deflator

Featured Graph

1. **a.** (1) households, (2) markets for goods and services, (3) factor markets, (4) firms, (5) money, (6) money, (7) goods and services, (8) factors, (9) goods and services, (10) factors, (11) money, (12) money

   b. Rest of the world, government, financial markets

Exercises

1. **a.**

Year	Cost of market basket	Price index value
2010	(10)(0.5) + (2)(4) + (5)(1) = $18	(18/18) × 100 = 100
2011	(10)(0.52) + (2)(3.85) + (5)(1.1) = $18.4	(18.4/18) × 100 = 102.22
2012	(10)(0.40) + (2)(3.9) + (5)(1.3) = $19.2	(19.2/18) × 100 = 106.67

   b. 2.22%: [(102.22 − 100)/100] × 100 = 2.22%.

   c. 4.35%: [(106.67 − 102.22)/102.22] × 100 = 4.35%.

   d.

Year	Cost of market basket	Price index value
2010	(10)(0.5) + (2)(4) + (5)(1) = $18	(18/18.4) × 100 = 97.83
2011	(10)(0.52) + (2)(3.85) + (5)(1.1) = $18.4	(18.4/18.4) × 100 = 100
2012	(10)(0.40) + (2)(3.9) + (5)(1.3) = $19.2	(19.2/18.4) × 100 = 104.35

   e. 2.22%: [(100 − 97.83)/97.83] × 100 = 2.22%.

   f. 4.35%: [(104.35 − 100)/100] × 100 = 4.35%.

   g. Answers are the same. The choice of a base year will generate different values for the price index, but the rate of change in prices between years will be equal for any base year.

Answers to Problems

1. a.

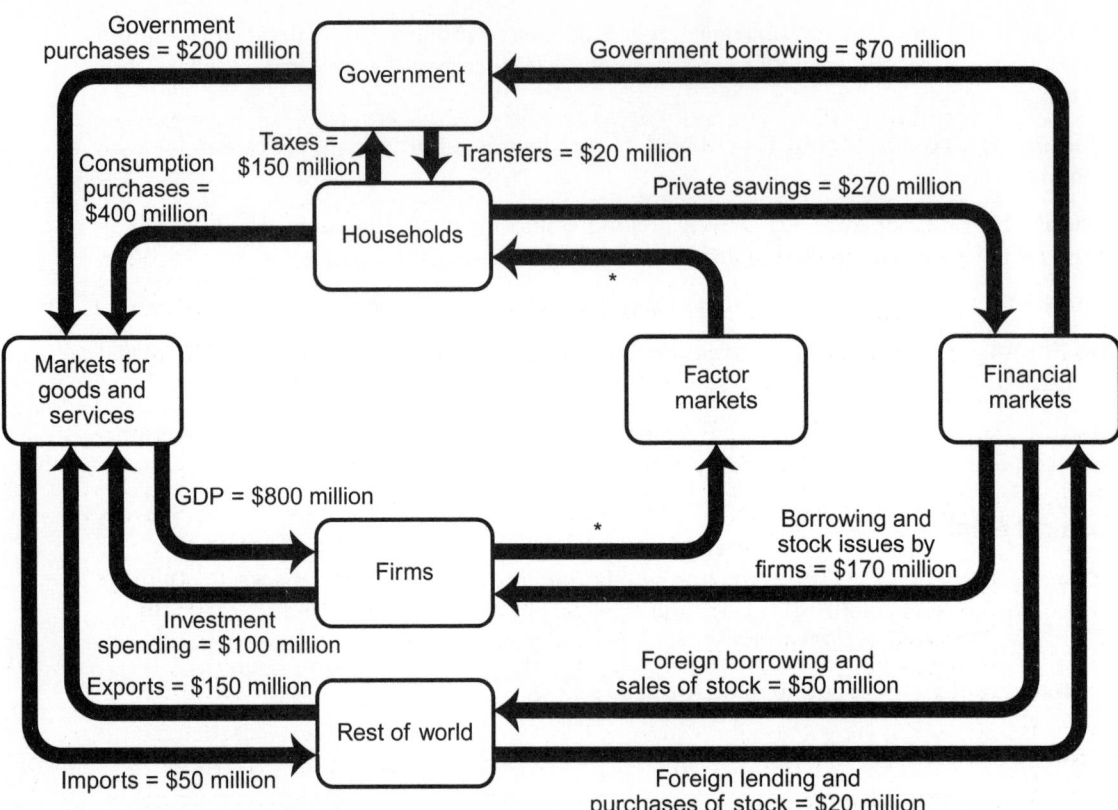

Government purchases = $200 million

Government borrowing = $70 million

Government

Taxes = $150 million

Transfers = $20 million

Consumption purchases = $400 million

Private savings = $270 million

Households

Markets for goods and services

Factor markets

Financial markets

GDP = $800 million

Borrowing and stock issues by firms = $170 million

Firms

Investment spending = $100 million

Exports = $150 million

Foreign borrowing and sales of stock = $50 million

Rest of world

Imports = $50 million

Foreign lending and purchases of stock = $20 million

*Wages, dividends, interest, and rent = $800 million

b. The value of GDP in 2009 in Macronesia is $800 million; this is equivalent to the sum of factor payments to households in the form of wages, dividends, interest, and rent. It is also equivalent to the sum of consumption spending, government spending, investment spending, and net exports.

c. Disposable income is income received by households minus taxes plus transfers. In this problem, disposable income equals $670 million.

d. Household saving equals household income minus taxes plus transfers minus consumption spending, or $270 million. Household saving is the amount households have left of their income once they pay their taxes and make their consumer purchases.

e. No. The government spends $200 million, and its net tax collections equal $130 million. To finance this level of spending without a change in taxes, the government will need to borrow $70 million from the financial markets.

f. The flow of money into the financial markets must equal the flow of money out of the financial markets in order for these markets to be in equilibrium. Borrowing in the financial markets equals the sum of government borrowing ($70 million) plus firm borrowing ($170 million) plus foreign borrowing ($50 million); lending in the financial market is equal to the sum of household saving ($270 million) plus foreign lending ($20 million).

g. The flow of money into the market for goods and services must equal the flow of money out of the market for goods and services. In this case, these flows equal $800 million. The flow of money into the market for goods and services includes government spending of $200 million, household purchases of $400 million, investment spending by firms of $100 million, and net exports of $100 million for a total of $800 million. The flow of money out of the market for goods and services equals GDP or the sum of wages, dividends, interest, and rent ($800 million).

h. The flow of money into the factor markets must equal the flow of money out of the factor markets. In this problem, these flows equal $800 million. The flow of money into the factor markets is equal to GDP ($800 million), while the flow of money out of the factor markets must equal the sum of wages, dividends, interest, and rent ($800 million).

2. a. New home construction is included in GDP as investment spending.

b. This is not included in GDP since the value of the house was counted in GDP the year the house was built.

c. Textbook purchases by the government are included in GDP as government spending.

d. Macro States exports beef and the value of these exports are included in the GDP of Macro States.

e. Although there is production occurring, Ellen and Judy do not exchange money, and therefore this transaction does not get included in GDP.

f. This increase in inventory is included in GDP as part of investment, since it represents new production in the economy of Macro States.

3. a.

Year	Nominal GDP
2010	$8,000
2011	8,866
2012	9,650

To calculate nominal GDP, multiply the price of each good times the quantity produced of that good and then sum together these products. For example, nominal GDP in 2010 = (price of tennis shoes) (quantity of tennis shoes) + (price of basketballs)(quantity of basketballs) + (price of lawn mowers)(quantity of lawn mowers) = $8,000.

b. The percentage change in nominal GDP from 2010 to 2011 was 10.83%: [(8,866 − 8,000)/8,000] × 10 × 0 = 10.83%.

c. The percentage change in nominal GDP from 2011 to 2012 was 8.84%: [(9,650 − 8,866)/8,866]100 = 8.84%.

d. To calculate real GDP, multiply the price of each good in the base year (2009) times the quantity of that good produced in a given year and then sum together the resulting values. The value of real GDP will equal nominal GDP in the base year. In 2010, real GDP can be calculated as the sum of the following: ($50 per pair of tennis shoes)(108 pairs) + ($10 per basketball)(205 basketballs) + ($100 per lawn mower)(12 lawn mowers).

e. The percentage change in real GDP from 2009 to 2010 was 8.13%: [(8,650 − 8,000)/8,000] × 100.

f. The percentage change in real GDP from 2010 to 2011 was 4.86%: [(9,070 − 8,650)/8,650] × 100.

g.

Year	GDP deflator
2010	(8,000/8,000) × 100 = 100
2011	(8,866/8,650) × 100 = 102.50
2012	(9,650/9,070) × 100 = 106.39

4. a. GDP in Littleton is equal to $320 million and can be found by recognizing that GDP can be expressed in two ways, given the above circular-flow diagram: (1) GDP is the sum of all the spending in Littleton's economy, or $GDP = C + I + G + X - IM$; and (2) GDP is the sum of the value of factor payments in the economy or GDP = wages + profit + interest + rents. You are given the value of these factor payments in the above information.

b. To find government spending (G), we can focus on the governmental sector of the economy and recognize that the flow of funds into that sector must equal the flow of funds out of that sector. This idea can be expressed in equation form as government borrowing + taxes = government spending + transfer payments. From the given information, we know government borrowing, taxes, and transfers. Thus, $60 million + $20 million = G + $10 million, or G = $70 million.

c. The value of imports (IM) in Littleton's economy is $20 million. To find this value, first recognize that $GDP = C + I + G + X - IM$. We know the value of GDP from answer (a), as well as the values of C, I, and X from the given information. In addition, answer (b) generated the value for G. So, $320 million = $200 million + $50 million + $70 million + $20 million − IM, or IM = $20 million.

d. To find the value of private savings, remember that the inflow of funds into the household sector must equal the outflow of funds from this sector. Households receive funds from their selling of factors of production and these funds are equal to the sum of wages, profit, interest, and rent, or $320 million in this example. In addition, households receive funds from the government in the form of transfer payments; in this example, transfer payments are $10 million. So, the total amount of funds flowing into the household sector is $320 million. The flow of funds out of the household sector is the sum of consumer spending, taxes, and private saving. Because consumer spending and taxes are given in the information ($220 million), this enables us to calculate private savings as $330 million − $220 million, or private savings = $110 million.

e. Recall that the flow of funds into the firm sector must equal the flow of funds out of the firm sector, or GDP + (borrowing and stock issues by firms) = (sum of wages, profits, interest, and rent) + investment spending. Because GDP is equal to the sum of wages, profits, interest, and rent, this implies that borrowing and stock issues by firms must equal investment spending, or $50 million.

f. To determine whether or not the rest of the world is a net borrower or a net lender, one needs to focus on the relationship between the flow of funds into and out of the rest of the world sector. The flow of funds into the rest of the world is equal to the sum of imports, foreign borrowing, and sales of stock while the flow of funds out of the rest of the world is the sum of exports, foreign lending, and purchases of stock. Or, $20 million + foreign borrowing and sales of stock = $20 million + foreign lending and purchases of stocks.

5. a.

	Hyattville Forest, Inc.	Hyattville Lumber Products, Inc.	Hyattville Houses, Inc.	Total Factor Income
Value of sales	$15,000	$40,000	$100,000	
Intermediate goods	0	15,000	40,000	
Wages	6,000	15,000	35,000	$56,000
Interest payments	1,000	3,000	6,000	10,000
Rent	3,000	3,000	3,000	9,000
Profit	5,000	4,000	16,000	25,000
Total expenditures by firm	15,000	40,000	100,000	
Value added per firm	15,000	25,000	60,000	

b. To find GDP using the value added approach requires summing the horizontal entries that are found in the row labeled "Value added per firm" in the above table. From your answer in part (a) you know that the sum of these entries is equal to $15,000 + $25,000 + $60,000 or $100,000.

   c. To find GDP using the factor income approach requires first summing horizontally the entries of the amount of wages paid, the amount of interest payments, the amount of rent, and the amount of profit, which corresponds to finding the values of (g), (h), (i), and (j) in the above table. Then, once these amounts have been calculated, these four values must be summed to find the total factor income in the economy; thus, from part (a) of this question we have $56,000 (the amount of total wages paid in the economy) + $10,000 (the total amount of interest payments in the economy) + $9,000 (the total amount of rent payments in this economy) + $25,000 (the total amount of profits in this economy) for a total of $100,000.

   d. To find GDP using the aggregate spending on domestically produced final goods and services approach, first recognize that Hyattville produces only one type of final good or service: houses. The value of the houses produced in Hyattville is $100,000.

6. a. The labor force is defined as the number of employed workers plus the number of unemployed workers. The number of employed workers equals the sum of full-time workers, part-time workers, and underemployed workers, or, in this example, 9,000 workers. The number of unemployed workers is the 1,000 workers who are currently not working, but who are actively looking for work. Thus, the labor force equals 10,000 workers.

   b. Employment rate = [employed/labor force] × 100 = (9,000/1,000) × 100 = 90%

   c. Unemployment rate = [unemployed/labor force] × 100 = (1,000/10,000) × 100 = 10%

   d. Percentage of discouraged workers in population = [(discouraged workers)/population] × 100 = (1,000/12,000) × 100 = 8.33%.

   e. The current unemployment rate is 10%. To reduce the unemployment rate to 8% requires that 200 of the currently unemployed workers find jobs. If output increases by $10,000 for every 100 people who find jobs, then output must increase by $20,000 for 200 people to find employment.

   f. Using the new definition of employment, the number of employed now is 6,000, and the unemployed would increase by 3,000 for a total of 4,000 unemployed. This change in definition results in a much higher unemployment rate (40%) and a much lower employment rate (60%). The definitions underlying calculations do matter.

7. a. The labor force is the sum of employed plus unemployed workers. In this case, the labor force is 5,000 + 2,000, or 7,000.

   b. To find the unemployment rate, use the formula unemployment rate = (unemployed/labor force) × 100. In this case, the unemployment rate equals (2,000/7,000) × 100, or 28.57%.

   c. If discouraged workers were counted as unemployed workers, the formula for calculating the unemployment rate would change to unemployment rate = [(unemployed + discouraged workers)/(labor force)] × 100. The unemployment rate would equal (2,500/7,500) × 100, or 33%.

   d. The decision by the Bureau of Labor Statistics to exclude discouraged workers from the calculation of the unemployment rate results in an understatement of the unemployment rate in the economy.

8. a. With an inflation rate of 8% for the year, Sarah finds that her income is automatically adjusted upward by that 8%; Sarah's real income has not changed because prices rose by 8% as did her income. Bob's income will rise by 5% even though the inflation rate was 8%; Bob is worse off because his nominal income rose but by an amount smaller than the amount needed to stay even with the inflation rate. Bob has less purchasing power than he did initially. Milt's situation is complicated: his pension from his former employer is fixed and does not adjust with the inflation rate. This implies that Milt will now have less purchasing power from his fixed pension of $2,000 per month than he did initially. Milt's government-provided retirement payment maintains its real value because it is adjusted with changes in the rate of inflation. Overall, Milt has less purchasing power than he did initially. No one in this example ends up better off.

    b. Again, Sarah's purchasing power is not affected because her nominal income is adjusted each year based upon the rate of inflation. Bob is much worse off this year because the overall price level rose 20% while his nominal income rose only 5%. Milt's fixed pension sees an even bigger erosion inits purchasing power than in part (a), while his government-provided retirement payment maintains its real value.

Answers to Review Questions

1. **A.** Because GDP is equal to the value of all final goods and services produced in an economy during a given time period, GDP for this economy can be found by multiplying the number of racquets produced during the given time period by their price. This yields $5,000. Alternatively, one could add up the total payments to factors of production: wages, interest payments, rent, and profit sum to $5,000.

2. **D.** To get the value of GDP using the factor payments approach, you would need to add up the sum of factor payments: wages, interest payments, rent, and profit, or cells C, D, E, and F.

3. **B.** The cost of intermediate goods in entry A is equal to the value of metal sales from American Metal Co., or $3,000. The cost of intermediate goods in entry B is equal to the value of ore sales from American Ore Co., or $500. The value added by American Racquet Co., or entry G, is equal to the value of sales by this company minus the value of intermediate goods used by this company ($5,000 − $3,000, or $2,000). The value added by American Metal Co., or entry H, is equal to the value of sales by this company minus the value of intermediate goods used by this company ($3,000 − $500, or $2,500); the value added by American Ore Co., or entry I, is equal to the value of sales by this company minus the value of intermediate goods used by this company ($500 − $0 or $500).

4. **B.** The value of a price index in the base year is always equal to 100. To calculate a price index in general, you need to calculate the ratio of the cost of the market basket in the current year to the cost of the market basket in the base year and then multiply this ratio by 100. In this question, the ratio is equal to 1 because the cost of the two market baskets is the same and thus the price index equals 100.

5. **D.** Calculate the value of the market basket in the base year: (200 oranges) ($0.5/orange) + (100 apples)($0.25/apple) + (100 bananas)($0.4/banana) = $165. Calculate the value of the market basket in 2009: (200 oranges)($0.4/orange) + (100 apples)($0.4/apple) + (100 bananas)($0.5/banana) = $170. Then put these two values into the following formula:

Price index = [(cost of market basket in current year)/(cost of market basket in base year)] × 100

Price index = [(170)/(165)] × 100 = 103

Note that the market basket stays fixed when calculating a price index.

6. **B.** To calculate the inflation rate between two time periods, you need the price index for each time period. Then, use the following formula:

Inflation rate = [(price index in period 2 − price index in period 1)/(price index in period 1)] × 100

In this case, Inflation rate = [(103 − 100)/100] × 100 = 3%.

7. **A.** To answer this question, it is helpful to first organize the information you are given in a table. We know that in the base year nominal GDP equals real GDP, but we still need to calculate this value. We can do so using the following formula:

Price index in 2009 = [(real GDP in 2009)/(real GDP in base year)] × 100

Or, in this case, 105 = [($210 billion)/(real GDP in base year)] × 100 or real GDP in base year = $200 billion.

To calculate nominal GDP in 2009, we use the formula for the GDP deflator:

Price index in 2009 = [(nominal GDP in 2009)/(real GDP in 2009)] × 100

Rearranging the formula, we have real GDP in 2009 = [(nominal GDP in 2009)/(price index in 2009)] × 100 or 210 billion = [(nominal GDP in 2009)/105] × 100 or nominal GDP in 2009 = $220.5 billion. Our completed table is below.

Year	GDP Deflator	Nominal GDP	Real GDP
2008	100	$200 billion	$200 billion
2008	105	$220.5 billion	$210 billion

8. **D.** The sum of consumer spending, investment spending, government spending, and net exports is equal to GDP. GDP provides a measure of the market value of the goods and services produced in an economy; this is the value of all final goods and services produced in the economy.

9. **B.** Answers (a), (c), and (d) are all included in GDP because they each represent a final good or service. Answer (b) is not included in GDP because the leather pieces are intermediate goods used to manufacture the final goods—handbags and wallets—included in GDP.

10. **C.** The natural unemployment rate is defined as the sum of frictional and structural unemployment. It is the unemployment rate that occurs when there is no cyclical unemployment, which is the unemployment directly tied to economic business cycles.

11. **C.** Structural unemployment occurs when there is an excess supply of labor in a labor market. This occurs when the wage rate is greater than the equilibrium wage rate in the market. Every economy has frictional unemployment due to job creation and job destruction, as well as the entry of new workers into the economy.

12. **E.** The natural rate of unemployment is equal to the sum of frictional and structural unemployment. It will always be greater than zero because there will always be new workers entering the job market and workers moving from one job to another. The cyclical unemployment rate is equal to zero when the economy produces at the full employment level of aggregate output, but at this level of output there is still frictional unemployment.

13. **C.** Both Mary and Joe would like to negotiate a contract in which the real interest rate is 3%, and they both anticipate the expected inflation rate will be 5%. Thus, the nominal rate in the contract will equal the desired real rate of interest plus the expected inflation rate, or 8%. When the actual rate of inflation is 6%, the dollars paid back have less purchasing power than anticipated. Mary will find this beneficial to her as the borrower, while Joe will find this hurts him because the dollars he receives in repayment of the loan have less purchasing power than the dollars he lent out.

14. **C.** Disinflation in an economy in which inflationary expectations are embedded requires policy makers to push the economy into a recession and thereby reduce inflationary expectations. This will necessarily result in an increase in the unemployment rate and a decrease in the level of aggregate output the economy produces. This policy does not affect the natural rate of unemployment.

15. **C.** In a period of unexpected deflation, borrowers will find that the real value of the loan payments they make has risen, so borrowers will be hurt by the unexpected deflation. Lenders will benefit because the loan payments they receive will have greater real value due to the deflation. Because of the increased economic burden of their debt, borrowers due to the increased economic burden of their debt, will typically reduce their overall spending and will choose, therefore, to borrow less during a period of deflation.

16. **E.** The two primary macroeconomic policy goals are low unemployment and price stability. To achieve low unemployment, the economy must produce at or near its potential output level: low unemployment necessitates reducing the level of cyclical unemployment. Economies always have some amount of frictional unemployment, and although policy makers can adopt policies that will lower the level of frictional unemployment, they cannot eliminate it.

17. **C.** To be considered unemployed, a person must not have a job and must be actively seeking a job. For example, the retired neither have jobs nor are they seeking employment; they are not part of the unemployed and they are not part of the labor force because they do not intend to work. The discouraged worker, although not working, is not considered unemployed because the discouraged worker has given up looking for a job.

18. **B.** The unemployment rate is a good indicator of how easy or difficult it is to find a job in the economy. When the economy's unemployment rate is high, this implies that many people are out of work and it will therefore be difficult to find employment. When the economy's unemployment rate is low, this implies that it will be relatively easy to find a job.

19. **C.** Frictional unemployment is considered unemployment because of the time workers spend in their job searches. Structural unemployment is the unemployment caused by the number of people seeking work exceeding the number of available jobs at the current wage rate. Cyclical unemployment is unemployment due to economic recession; cyclical unemployment is a result of business cycle fluctuations.

20. **A.** The transactions costs associated with high rates of inflation are referred to as shoe-leather costs. Menu costs refer to the cost associated with printing new menu and price lists due to the presence of inflation. Unit-of-account costs refer to the costs inflation imposes because of its effects on contracts that are stated in monetary, instead of real, terms.

Notes

National Income and Price Determination

OVERVIEW

This section further develops the aggregate supply and demand model (*AD–AS* model) of the macroeconomy. It introduces *multiplier analysis* and looks at aggregate demand, and its two most important components, consumer spending and investment spending. The section also introduces aggregate supply and explores how the relationship between the two curves—aggregate supply and aggregate demand—determines the equilibrium levels of aggregate output and aggregate prices in the economy. Here and in following sections, this model is used to evaluate the state of the economy and determine appropriate economic policies.

FEATURED MODEL/GRAPH: THE AGGREGATE DEMAND AND SUPPLY MODEL

This section presents the *AD–AS* model and shows how it is used to explain the behavior of the economy. The *AD–AS* model is the basic model we use to explain macroeconomic fluctuations.

MODULES IN THIS SECTION

Module 16: Income and Expenditure

Module 17: Aggregate Demand: Introduction and Determinants

Module 18: Aggregate Supply: Introduction and Determinants

Module 19: Equilibrium in the Aggregate Demand–Aggregate Supply Model

Module 20: Economic Policy and the Aggregate Demand–Aggregate Supply Model

Module 21: Fiscal Policy and the Multiplier

Module ⑯
Income and Expenditure

Before You Read the MODULE

Summary

This module introduces multiplier analysis and explains how an initial change in spending will multiply and contribute to business cycles.

Module Objectives

Review these objectives before you read the module. Place a "√" on the line when you understand each of the following:

_____**Objective 1.** What the multiplier is and why initial changes in spending lead to further changes

_____**Objective 2.** What the aggregate consumption function illustrates

_____**Objective 3.** How expected future income and aggregate wealth affect consumer spending

_____**Objective 4.** The determinants of investment spending and why investment spending is considered a leading indicator of the future state of the economy

While You Read the MODULE

Key Terms

Define these key terms as you read the module.

Marginal propensity to consume *(MPC)*

Marginal propensity to save *(MPS)*

Autonomous consumer spending

Autonomous change in aggregate spending

Multiplier

Consumption function

Aggregate consumption function

Planned investment spending

Inventories

Inventory investment

Unplanned inventory investment

Actual investment spending
_____

List questions or difficulties from your initial reading of the module.

After You Read the MODULE

Fill-in-the-Blanks

Fill in the blanks to complete the following statements. Terms may be used more than once. If you find your-self having difficulties, please refer to the appropriate section in the text.

- The marginal propensity to consume (*MPC*) is the additional consumer spending that

  results from a $1 change in disposable (1)_____. The

  additional savings that result from the same $1 change is called the

  (2)_____. An initial rise or fall in aggregate spending at a given

  level of GDP is known as (3)_____ spending. The final change

  in aggregate spending that results from an autonomous change in aggregate spending is

  (4)_____ than the initial change due to the "chain reaction"

  known as the (5)_____ effect.

- Stocks of goods held to satisfy future sales are known as (6)_____.

Module Review

How Can a Firm Invest Without Meaning To?

Part of managing a firm is planning for the future. This includes making decisions about when and how much to spend on capital investments, such as new equipment. The idea of planned investment spending is fairly intuitive. But how can a firm experience an "un-planned" investment in capital? Unplanned investment spending refers to unintended changes in a firm's inventories. A firm will determine the desired level of its inventories (i.e., the amount of output held in its warehouse). But because of miscalculations or changes in the economy, the firm may find that it has more or less than its desired level of output in inventories. If, for example, demand for the firm's output is lower than expected, inventories will build up in the warehouse. The additional inventories represent unplanned inventory investment. The firm has unintentionally invested in its own output (when no one else would buy it from the firm). On the other hand, if firms sell more than expected, then they will not be able to keep the desired inventories in the warehouse. Their output flies off the shelves! In this case, the firm has engaged in less investment spending than it had intended because it is reducing its level of inventories. Unplanned inventory investment signals firms to produce more or less. If inventories pile up, firms decrease production. If inventories decline, firms increase production.

- A thorough understanding of the aggregate consumption function and the variables that shift it is essential. Make sure you review the aggregate consumption function and understand the relationship between consumer spending and autonomous consumer spending, the marginal propensity to consume, and disposable income. The consumption function will shift upward with increases in wealth or expected future disposable income.

- An understanding of investment spending and its components is a critical aspect of this module. Make sure you can distinguish between planned investment spending and unplanned inventory investment.

- This module develops the concept of the multiplier, which is central to understanding the sections that follow. Review the definition of the multiplier and its calculation, and then practice using this concept in questions provided in the text and the study guide.

Module 17
Aggregate Demand: Introduction and Determinants

Before You Read the MODULE

Summary

This module begins the development of the aggregate demand–aggregate supply model by presenting the aggregate demand curve.

Module Objectives

Review these objectives before you read the module. Place a "√" on the line when you understand each of the following:

_____**Objective 1.** How the **aggregate demand curve** illustrates the relationship between the aggregate price level and the quantity of aggregate output demanded

_____**Objective 2.** How the wealth effect and interest rate effect explain the aggregate demand curve's negative slope

_____**Objective 3.** What factors can shift the aggregate demand curve

While You Read the MODULE

Key Terms

Define these key terms as you read the module.

Aggregate demand curve

Wealth effect of a change in the aggregate price level

Interest rate effect of a change in the aggregate price level

List questions or difficulties from your initial reading of the module.

After You Read the MODULE

Fill-in-the-Blanks

Fill in the blanks to complete the following statements. Terms may be used more than once. If you find yourself having difficulties, please refer to the appropriate section in the text.

- The aggregate demand curve has a negative slope, indicating that a higher aggregate price

  level is associated with a lower level of aggregate (1)_____.

  The aggregate demand curve has a negative slope due to two important effects, the

  (2)_____ effect and the (3)_____

  effect. That a rise in the aggregate price level reduces the purchasing power of many assets

  describes the (4)_____ effect. That a rise in the aggregate price

  level depresses investment and consumer spending through its effect on the purchasing

  power of money holdings describes the (5)_____ effect.

- A shift in the aggregate demand curve can be caused by changes in

  (6)_____, _____,

  _____, or _____.

Module Review

Changes in Wealth: A Movement Along Versus a Shift of the Aggregate Demand Curve

We explained that one reason the *AD* curve is downward sloping is due to the wealth effect of a change in the aggregate price level: a higher aggregate price level reduces the purchasing power of households' assets and leads to a fall in consumer spending, *C*. But we also explained that changes in wealth lead to a shift of the *AD* curve. Aren't those two explanations contradictory? Which one is it—does a change in wealth move the economy along the *AD* curve or does it shift the *AD* curve? The answer is both: it depends on the *source* of the change in wealth. A movement along the *AD* curve occurs when a change in the aggregate price level changes the purchasing power of consumers' existing wealth (the real value of their assets). This is the wealth effect of a change in the aggregate price level—a change in the aggregate price level is the source of the change in wealth. For example, a fall in the aggregate price level increases the purchasing power of consumers' assets and leads to a movement down the *AD* curve. In contrast, a change in wealth independent of a change in the aggregate price level shifts the *AD* curve. For example, a rise in the stock market or a rise in real estate values leads to an increase in the real value of consumers' assets at any given aggregate price level. In this case, the source of the change in wealth is a change in the values of assets without any change in the aggregate price level—that is, a change in asset values, holding the prices of all final goods and services constant.

- It is important to understand why the *AD* curve is downward sloping. Note that the inverse relationship between the aggregate price level and aggregate output are explained by the wealth and interest rate effects.

Module 18
Aggregate Supply: Introduction and Determinants

Before You Read the MODULE

Summary

This module continues developing the *AD–AS* model by presenting the aggregate supply curve.

Module Objectives

Review these objectives before you read the module. Place a "√" on the line when you understand each of the following:

_____ **Objective 1.** How the **aggregate supply curve** illustrates the relationship between the aggregate price level and the quantity of aggregate output supplied

_____ **Objective 2.** What factors can shift the aggregate supply curve

_____ **Objective 3.** Why the short-run and long-run aggregate supply curves are different

While You Read the MODULE

Key Terms

Define these key terms as you read the module.

Aggregate supply curve

Nominal wage

Sticky wages

Short-run aggregate supply curve

Long-run aggregate supply curve

Potential output

List questions or difficulties from your initial reading of the module.

After You Read the MODULE

Fill-in-the-Blanks

Fill in the blanks to complete the following statements. Terms may be used more than once. If you find yourself having difficulties, please refer to the appropriate section in the text.

- The aggregate supply curve shows the relationship between the aggregate price level and

  (1)_____ GDP. The short-run aggregate supply curve has a

  positive slope because nominal wages are (2)_____. The short-

  run aggregate supply curve will shift when there are changes in

  (3)_____, _____, or

  _____. The long-run supply curve is

  (4)_____ at the economy's (5)_____

output level because changes in the aggregate price level do not affect

(6)_____ in the long run. Potential output is the level of real

GDP the economy would produce if all prices and wages were fully

(7)_____. In the long run, the economy returns to potential

output through shifts in the (8)_____ curve.

Are We There Yet? What the Long Run Really Means

The long-run aggregate supply curve depicts the economy's potential output: the level of aggregate output that the economy would produce if all prices, including nominal wages, were fully flexible. Because the economy always tends to return to potential output in the long run, actual aggregate output fluctuates around potential output. As a result, the economy's rate of growth over long periods of time—say, decades—is very close to the rate of growth of potential output. And potential output growth is determined by long-run economic growth. So that means that the "long-run" of long-run economic growth and the "long-run" of the long-run aggregate supply curve coincide.

- It is important to distinguish between a movement along and a shift of the *AD* or *SRAS* curve. A change in the aggregate price level causes a movement along either curve. A change in commodity prices, nominal wages, or productivity shifts the *SRAS* curve; a change in expectations, wealth, physical capital, or fiscal or monetary policy shifts the *AD* curve.

- Make sure to distinguish between the short-run and the long-run *AS*. In the short run, wages are sticky; this stickiness results in a short-run *AS* curve (*SRAS*) that is upward sloping. In the long run, wages are fully flexible, leading the economy to always produce its long-run equilibrium at the potential output level of real GDP. This is the output level the economy produces when all wages and prices are fully flexible.

- The *LRAS* curve is vertical, and its position represents the economy's potential output when all resources are fully employed. It is important to understand why the *LRAS* curve is vertical, as well as the relevance of its position on the horizontal axis. Over time, if an economy experiences economic growth, the *LRAS* curve shifts to the right, indicating the economy's potential output has increased.

Module ⓳ Equilibrium in the Aggregate Demand–Aggregate Supply Model

Before You Read the MODULE

Summary

This module puts the aggregate supply curve and the aggregate demand curve together so we can use it to explain the behavior of the economy. The *AD–AS* model is the basic model we use to explain macroeconomic fluctuations; it will be expanded upon throughout future sections.

Module Objectives

Review these objectives before you read the module. Place a "√" on the line when you understand each of the following:

_____**Objective 1.** The difference between short-run and long-run **macroeconomic equilibrium**

_____**Objective 2.** The causes and effects of **demand shocks** and **supply shocks**

_____**Objective 3.** What **recessionary** and **inflationary gaps** are and how to calculate their size

While You Read the MODULE

Key Terms

Define these key terms as you read the module.

AD–AS model

Short-run macroeconomic equilibrium

Short-run equilibrium aggregate price level

Short-run equilibrium aggregate output

Demand shock

Supply shock

Stagflation

Long-run macroeconomic equilibrium

Recessionary gap

Inflationary gap

Output gap

Self-correcting

List questions or difficulties from your initial reading of the module.

After You Read the MODULE

Fill-in-the-Blanks

Fill in the blanks to complete the following statements. Terms may be used more than once. If you find yourself having difficulties, please refer to the appropriate section in the text.

• The short-run macroeconomic equilibrium is found where the aggregate demand curve

intersects the (1)_____ curve. An event that shifts the aggregate

demand/supply curve is called a demand/supply (2)_____.

When the aggregate demand/supply shift is to the left (a decrease), it is a

(3)_____ demand/supply shock. With a

(4)_____ shock, the effects on aggregate output and the

aggregate price level are in opposite directions (i.e., when aggregate output decreases, the

aggregate price level increases, and vice versa). A combination of decreasing aggregate

output and inflation is known as (5)_____.

• Long-run macroeconomic equilibrium occurs when the short-run macroeconomic

equilibrium occurs at a point on the (6)_____ curve. If short-run equilibrium occurs at an aggregate output level that is not on this curve, the economy is experiencing an output gap. If the short-run equilibrium output is below potential output, there is a(n) (7)_____ gap; if it is above it, there is a(n) (8)_____ gap.

Module Review

How Can There Be Two Equilibrium Points?

In the *AD–AS* model, we refer to both short-run macroeconomic equilibrium and long-run macroeconomic equilibrium. But how can there be two different equilibrium points? Short-run macroeconomic equilibrium occurs when the quantity of aggregate output demanded equals the quantity of aggregate output supplied in the short run. If this occurs at a level of aggregate output other than potential output, over time, wage adjustments in the labor market will return aggregate output back to potential output. Short-run macroeconomic equilibrium happens before nominal wages adjust and before the *SRAS* curve shifts. An economy reaches long-run macroeconomic equilibrium after nominal wages fully adjust and the *SRAS* curve shifts so that equilibrium aggregate output is equal to potential output. If the short-run equilibrium aggregate output is below potential output, unemployment will put downward pressure on nominal wages; if the short-run equilibrium aggregate output is above potential output, high employment will put upward pressure on nominal wages. While nominal wages are sticky in the short run, in the long run nominal wages adjust, shifting *SRAS* so that short-run macroeconomic equilibrium coincides with long-run macroeconomic equilibrium.

- Be sure you understand the difference between short-run and long-run macroeconomic equilibria and the relationship between these equilibria. In long-run macroeconomic equilibrium, aggregate output equals potential output and the economy's *AD* equals both its short-run and long-run *AS*. In the short–run, macroeconomic equilibrium aggregate output need not equal potential output, but the economy's *AD* must intersect the *SRAS*.

Module 20
Economic Policy and the Aggregate Demand–Aggregate Supply Model

Before You Read the MODULE

....

Summary

This module describes how stabilization policy can be used to improve the economy's performance.

Module Objectives

Review these objectives before you read the module. Place a "√" on the line when you understand each of the following:

_____**Objective 1.** How the *AD–AS* model is used to formulate macroeconomic policy

_____**Objective 2.** The rationale for **stabilization policy**

_____**Objective 3.** Why fiscal policy is an important tool for managing economic fluctuations

_____**Objective 4.** Which fiscal policies are **expansionary** and which are **contractionary**

While You Read the MODULE

....

Key Terms

Define these key terms as you read the module.

Stabilization policy

Social insurance

Expansionary fiscal policy

_____

Contractionary fiscal policy

_____

List questions or difficulties from your initial reading of the module.

After You Read the MODULE

....

Fill-in-the-Blanks

Fill in the blanks to complete the following statements. Terms may be used more than once. If you find your-self having difficulties, please refer to the appropriate section in the text.

- Government policy to reduce the severity of recessions and rein in excessively strong

  expansions is called (1)_____ policy. When there is a

  recessionary gap, the government can use (2)_____ fiscal policy

  to move equilibrium real GDP toward potential output through an increase in

  (3)_____ and/or a decrease in (4)_____.

  To eliminate an inflationary gap, the government can use (5)_____

  fiscal policy by decreasing (6)_____ and /or raising

  (7)_____. But economists caution against an extremely active

  stabilization policy, arguing that a government that tries too hard to stabilize the economy

  can end up making the economy less stable, especially because of time

  (8)_____.

Module Review

Why Would We Want to Decrease Real GDP?

From the beginning of our study of macroeconomics, we have recognized that increased aggregate output in the economy is a key macroeconomic goal. Why would we ever want to pursue a contractionary fiscal policy? Contractionary fiscal policy involves decreasing government spending, decreasing transfer payments, or raising taxes. Each of these actions works to shift the *AD* curve to the left, which results in a decrease in equilibrium aggregate output. When equilibrium aggregate output is above potential output, it creates inflationary pressures in the economy. The rising employment required to increase aggregate output above potential output leads to an increase in nominal wages that will eventually shift the *SRAS* curve leftward, which brings the economy back to potential output with a higher aggregate price level. So, the ultimate goal of contractionary fiscal policy is not to reduce aggregate output. Aggregate output will eventually decrease back to potential output in any case. The goal is to bring the economy back to potential output without a higher aggregate price level. The policy choice is not between higher and lower aggregate output in the long run, but between potential output with inflation and potential output without inflation.

Module ㉑ Fiscal Policy and the Multiplier

Before You Read the MODULE

Summary

This module applies the multiplier process to the use of fiscal policy to stabilize the economy.

Module Objectives

Review these objectives before you read the module. Place a "√" on the line when you understand each of the following:

_____**Objective 1.** Why fiscal policy has a multiplier effect

_____**Objective 2.** How the multiplier effect is influenced by **automatic stabilizers**

While You Read the MODULE

Key Terms

Define these key terms as you read the module.

Lump-sum taxes

Automatic stabilizers

Discretionary fiscal policy

List questions or difficulties from your initial reading of the module.

After You Read the MODULE

Fill-in-the-Blanks

Fill in the blanks to complete the following statements. Terms may be used more than once. If you find yourself having difficulties, please refer to the appropriate section in the text.

- Any increase in government spending will lead to a larger increase in total spending due to

  the (1)_____ effect. The key to the eventual size of this "chain

  reaction" is the additional consumer spending that happens at each stage of the reaction,

  which is measured by the (2)_____ or *MPC*. For example, if the

  MPC is .9, the initial effect of an autonomous increase in aggregate spending will be

  multiplied by (3)_____ (the value of the multiplier). The effect

  of changes in taxes and transfers would be (4)_____ than the

  effect of changes in government spending because households will

  (5)_____ part of the initial change in these.

- When the amount of a tax owed by households is independent of its income, the tax is

  known as a (6)_____ tax. Government spending and taxation

  rules that cause fiscal policy to be automatically expansionary when the economy contracts

  and automatically contractionary when the economy expands, without requiring any

  deliberate action by policy makers, are called (7)_____. When

  fiscal policy isn't automatic, it is known as (8)_____ fiscal policy.

Module Review

The Importance of the Multiplier Process

Suppose that a government decides to spend $50 billion building bridges and roads. The government's purchases of goods and services will directly increase total spending by $50 billion. But there will also be an indirect effect because the government's purchases will start a chain reaction throughout the economy. It is important to understand this chain reaction. When you buy something, the money you spend doesn't disappear. For example, it goes into a cash register and becomes income for the seller. The seller will then spend some part of that new income. That spending becomes someone else's income, and so on. The initial spending has a multiplier effect. How does this multiplier process affect fiscal policy? If any change in spending has a multiplier effect on income, that effect must be considered when determining the amount that G, T, or transfers are changed. If the multiplier process is not considered, then changes in G, T, or transfers will be too large and move the economy past potential output (creating a different problem).Make sure you are comfortable with the calculations associated with implementing the appropriate fiscal policy in hypothetical situations. Remember that the spending multiplier equals $1/(1 - MPC)$. Start any multiplier problem by finding your multiplier! Then use the equation:

Autonomous change in aggregate spending $\times$ multiplier = final change in real GDP

- Two multipliers are presented and used in this chapter: the multiplier for a change in government spending and the multiplier for a change in taxes. The multiplier for a change in government spending equals $1/(1 - MPC)$, while the multiplier for a change in taxes is smaller $[- MPC/(1 - MPC)]$. For example, if the MPC equals 0.8, then the multiplier for a change in government spending is 5, while the multiplier for a change in taxes is -4. Make sure you work some problems using these multipliers and that you understand why they do not have equivalent values. Also, spend time thinking about why the multiplier for government spending is positive while the multiplier for a change in taxes is negative.

- Understand the distinction between fiscal policy that is discretionary versus fiscal policy that reflects the impact of automatic stabilizers.

BEFORE YOU TAKE THE TEST: section 4

Draw the Featured Model: Aggregate Demand-Aggregate Supply Model

Draw an *AS–AD* graph showing long-run macroeconomic equilibrium. Label *AD, SRAS, LRAS,* potential output, equilibrium aggregate price level, and output. Note points on the horizontal axis indicating where aggregate output would be if there were a recessionary gap (label this Y_r) or an inflationary gap (label this Y_i).

Complete the Exercises

1. Consider an economy that is initially in long-run equilibrium as drawn in the following graph.

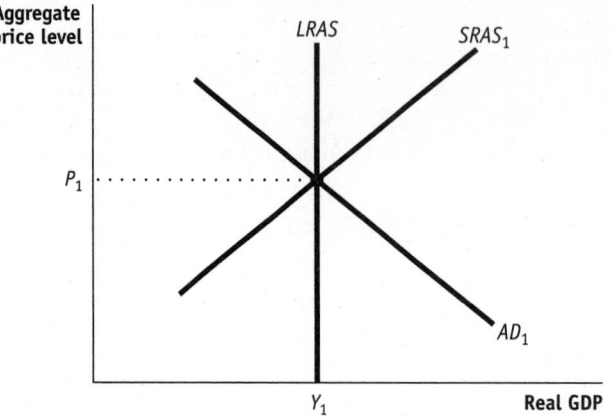

a. Draw a graph of the *AS–AD* model to show the effect of each of the following (*ceteris paribus*) changes.

(1) The economy's central bank decreases the money supply.

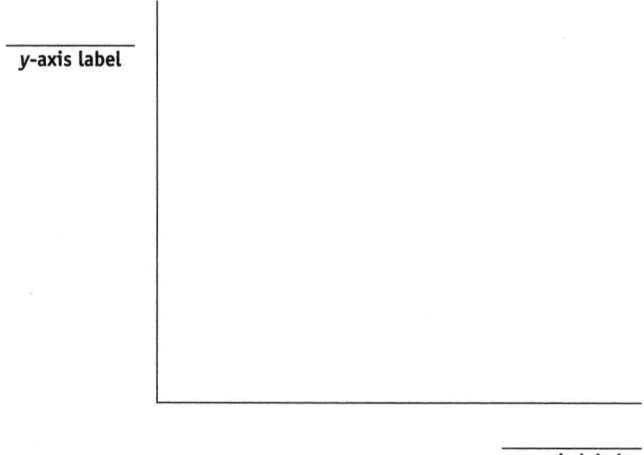

(2) Productivity decreases in the economy.

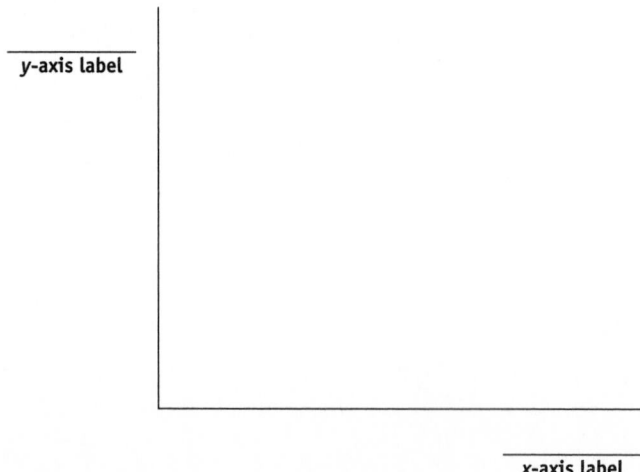

(3) Consumer confidence in the economy increases.

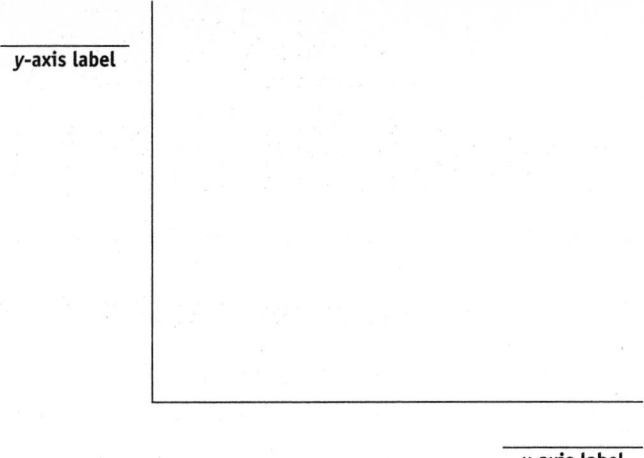

y-axis label

x-axis label

(4) Commodity prices fall dramatically.

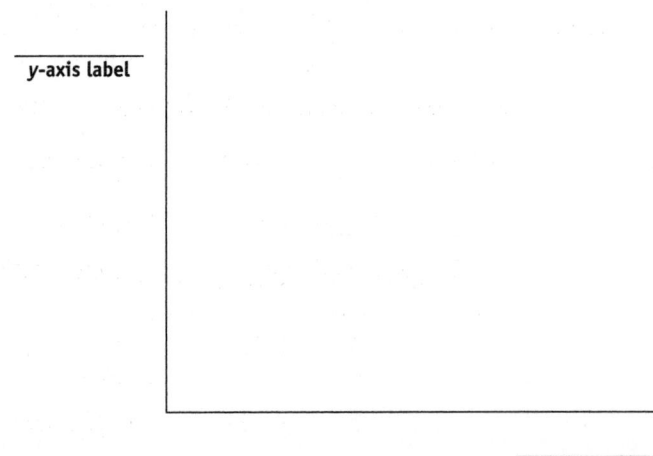

y-axis label

x-axis label

b. What happens to the aggregate output and price level relative to the initial long-run equilibrium in each case?

c. For each case, determine whether the economy faces a short-run recessionary gap or an inflationary gap.

d. For each case, what active stabilization policy can offset the particular shock?

e. For each case, what would happen in the long run to the aggregate price and output levels without an active stabilization policy?

Problems

1. In Mainland, a small, closed economy with no government sector, when disposable income is $800, consumer spending is $800. and when disposable income is $1,800, consumer spending is $1,600. Assume that the aggregate price level and the interest rate are fixed in Mainland.

   a. What is the value of autonomous consumer spending in Mainland?

   b. What is the value of the *MPC* in Mainland?

   c. What is the consumption function in Mainland?

2. Suppose you are given the following information about Macroland, a small, closed economy where *Y* is real GDP, *T* is taxes, *C* is consumption spending, and *I* is planned investment spending. Assume that government spending is currently $0, taxes are constant at $50, and the aggregate price level is originally fixed at $100.

Year	Y	T	C	I
1	$100	$50	$40	$50
2	150	50	80	50
3	300	50	200	50

   a. Fill in the following table, using the information given above.

Year	Disposable income
1	
2	
3	

   b. What is the *MPC* for this economy?

c. What is the *MPS* for this economy?

d. What is the value of the spending multiplier for this economy?

e. What is the consumption function for this economy?

f. Given the above information, what is the equilibrium output level for this economy?

3. Use a graph of the *AS–AD* model to illustrate long-run economic growth in an economy. Explain how your graph illustrates economic growth. Assume *AD* does *not* change over time.

4. Macroland is a small, closed economy that is currently operating at the long-run equilibrium level of output. It is therefore producing Y_p where Y_p is potential output. Its aggregate price level is P_1.

   a. Draw a graph of long-run equilibrium for Macroland depicting the *AD*, *SRAS*, and *LRAS* curves. Label both axes, and identify Y_p and P_1 on your graph.

b. Suppose that Macroland experiences a negative demand shock. Draw a new graph depicting the short-run changes in the original equilibrium that will occur because of this demand shock. On your graph, identify the new short-run equilibrium level of output Y_2 and the new short-run equilibrium aggregate price level P_2. Label any shifts in AD or AS clearly.

c. Given the change in part (b), draw a third graph illustrating the long-run adjustment to the negative demand shock. Label any shifting curves clearly, and identify the new long-run equilibrium level of aggregate output Y_3 and the new long-run aggregate price level P_3.

d. Given the change in part (b), suppose the government wishes to engage in activist fiscal policy in order to restore the economy to its initial equilibrium. Provide two fiscal policies that would accomplish this.

5. For each of the following, describe the effect on the AD, $SRAS$, and $LRAS$ curves, identify whether the effect causes a shift of or a movement along the curve, and identify the direction of the shift/movement.

   a. An increase in the money supply causes interest rates to fall.

   b. The price of commodities increases by 10% this year.

c. The price of oil falls.

d. Labor unions successfully negotiate an increase in nominal wages for their workers.

e. The supply of unsold houses in an economy increases by 20%.

f. There is an increase in labor productivity due to increases in human capital.

g. The government increases spending in order to finance a war.

6. For each of the following situations, identify whether it is an example of expansionary discretionary fiscal policy, contractionary discretionary fiscal policy, or an automatic stabilizer.

a. During 2006, tax revenue for Macrovia falls as the economy enters a recession.

b. During 2006, in light of projected deficiencies in *AD*, Macrovia's legislature authorizes an expenditure of $200 million to build a new hydroelectric dam.

c. In 2009, fearing a too rapidly expanding economy, Macrovia adopts a budget that calls for 10% spending cuts in all government departments for the following fiscal year.

d. In 2008, unemployment benefits rise 5% in response to rising unemployment in Macro via.

7. The following graph depicts the economy of Macroland's short-run aggregate supply curve (*SRAS*), its long-run aggregate supply curve (*LRAS*), and its aggregate demand curve (*AD*). Macroland is currently producing at point *E*.

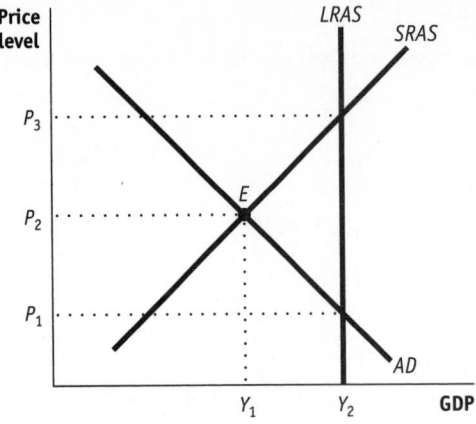

a. Is potential GDP for Macroland equal to Y_1 or Y_2? Describe Macroland's current production relative to its potential production.

b. Does Macroland have a recessionary gap or an inflationary gap? Explain your answer.

c. Holding everything else constant, which of the following policy initiatives might help Macroland produce at its potential output? Explain how each would help.
   i.   The government initiates policies that encourage private investment spending.
   ii. The government increases taxes on consumers and corporations.
   iii. The government authorizes new spending programs.

d. What is the current price level in Macroland? If Macroland engages in expansionary fiscal policy so that *AD* shifts and actual output equals potential output, what will happen to the price level?

8. Funlandia's economists estimate its potential output is $100 in year 1 and grows 5% per year. Assume Funlandia is a closed economy.

a. Fill in the following table for Funlandia, given the above information.

Year	Potential output
Year 1	$100
Year 2	
Year 3	
Year 4	

Suppose Funlandia's economists provide you with the following data. (All numbers are in dollars.)

Year	Potential output	Actual output	T	YD	C	I	G
Year 1	100		10	90	55	30	15
Year 2		104	10			30	17
Year 3		115	10			30	22.5
Year 4			10	108	64	30	24

b. What is the consumption function for this economy?

c. Fill in the missing values for the table, using the information you have been given or that you computed in parts (a) and (b).

d. Fill in the following table for Funlandia.

Year	Recessionary gap	Inflationary gap	Actual output equals potential output
Year 1	No	No	Yes
Year 2			
Year 3			
Year 4			

e. Suppose Funlandia maintains a policy of using discretionary fiscal policy to ensure that actual output equals potential output. Summarize the recommended discretionary fiscal policy necessary to achieve this goal in the following table.

Year	Discretionary fiscal policy
Year 1	
Year 2	
Year 3	
Year 4	

9. The *AS–AD* model is said to have a self-correcting mechanism. Explain what this means and how it works. Use a graph to illustrate your answer.

10. Explain why automatic stabilizers reduce the size of the multiplier. Provide several examples of automatic stabilizers and their effect on the economy during economic fluctuations.

Review Questions

Circle the correct answer.

1. Consumer spending is affected by changes in

   A. current disposable income.
   B. expected future disposable income.
   C. wealth.
   D. All of the above affect consumer spending.

2. Joe's disposable income increases by $500, and he finds that he spends $400 of it. Joe

   A. saves $100 and his *MPS* is equal to 0.8.
   B. saves $100 and his *MPC* is 0.8.
   C. saves 20% of any increase in his disposable income.
   D. Answers (a) and (c) are both correct.
   E. Answers (b) and (c) are both correct.

3. Suppose when Sue's disposable income is $10,000 she spends $8,000 and when her disposable income is $20,000 she spends $14,000. Sue's autonomous consumer spending is _____ and her *MPS* is _____.

   A. $0; 0.2
   B. $2,000; 0.2
   C. $0; 0.4
   D. $2,000; 0.4

4. Planned investment spending depends on the

    A. interest rate.
    B. expected future level of real GDP.
    C. current level of production capacity.
    D. Answers (a), (b), and (c) are all correct.
    E. Answers (a) and (c) are both correct.

5. When interest rates rise, this

    A. does not affect the profitability of investments financed through retained earnings.
    B. makes any given investment project more profitable.
    C. does not affect the opportunity cost of an investment financed through retained earnings.
    D. leads to a lower level of planned investment spending, holding everything else constant.

6. Nominal wages

    A. are often determined by contracts that were signed at some previous point in time.
    B. are slow to decrease in times of high unemployment because employers may be reluctant to alter wages as a response to economic conditions.
    C. are fully flexible in both the short run and the long run.
    D. Answers (a) and (b) are both correct.
    E. Answers (a), (b), (c), and (d) are all correct.

7. Which of the following statements is true? In the short run, holding everything else constant,

    A. as production costs increase, profit per unit decreases, and this causes suppliers to increase their production.
    B. as production costs increase, profit per unit decreases, and this causes suppliers to reduce their production.
    C. as production costs decrease, profit per unit increases, and this causes suppliers to reduce their production.
    D. the *AS* curve is unaffected by changes in production costs.

8. Which of the following will *not* make the *AS* curve shift to the left?

    A. an increase in the aggregate price level
    B. a decrease in commodity prices
    C. an increase in nominal wages
    D. None of the above.
    E. Answers (a) and (c) are both correct.
    F. Answers (b) and (c) are both correct.

9. Suppose the economy is in short-run equilibrium and the level of aggregate output is less than potential output. Then it must be true that

    A. unemployment in this economy is relatively low.
    B. over time, the short-run *AS* curve will shift to the left.
    C. over time, nominal wages will fall.
    D. the economy is also in long-run equilibrium.

10. Which of the following statements is true?

    A. In a recessionary gap, aggregate output exceeds potential output.
    B. In an inflationary gap, aggregate output exceeds potential output.
    C. A recessionary gap is a long-run phenomenon that requires government action to eliminate.
    D. Recessionary gaps and inflationary gaps, if they exist, will be eliminated in the short run by the natural workings of the economy.

11. An increase in the interest rate, holding everything else constant,

   A. reduces investment spending because the cost of borrowing is now higher.
   B. reduces consumer spending because households respond to higher interest rates by saving more.
   C. leads to a reduction in the level of aggregate demand for final goods and services.
   D. Answers (a), (b), and (c) are all correct.

12. Which of the following policies will shift the *AD* curve to the right?

   A. The government increases its level of taxation in the economy.
   B. The government decreases the money supply in the economy.
   C. The government decreases its level of taxation in the economy.
   D. The government decreases its level of spending in the economy.
   E. Answers (a) and (d) will both shift the *AD* curve to the right.
   F. Answers (c) and (d) will both shift the *AD* curve to the right.

13. Suppose an economy is currently in short-run equilibrium, during which the level of real GDP is less than potential output. Which of the following statements is true?

   A. In the long run, nominal wages will fall and the *SRAS* curve will shift to the left, restoring the economy to potential output.
   B. In the long run, nominal wages will fall and the *SRAS* curve will shift to the right, restoring the economy to potential output.
   C. In the long run, nominal wages will fall and the *AD* curve will shift to the left, restoring the economy to potential output.
   D. In the long run, nominal wages will fall and the *AD* curve will shift to the right, restoring the economy to potential output.

14. In the *AS–AD* model, a key feature that distinguishes the long run from the short run is

   A. wages and prices are sticky in the long run.
   B. wages and prices are sticky in the short run.

15. Suppose an economy is initially in long-run equilibrium. Then, holding everything else constant, there is an increase in people's wealth in this economy. If the government wishes to maintain the same aggregate price level and aggregate level of real GDP as it had initially, it should increase

   A. government spending.
   B. the money supply.
   C. the level of investment spending.
   D. the level of taxes.

16. Contractionary fiscal policy

   A. is most helpful for restoring an economy to the potential output level of production when there is a recessionary gap.
   B. shifts the *AD* curve to the right, restoring the equilibrium level of output to the potential output level for the economy.
   C. often causes inflation or an increase in the aggregate price level.
   D. if effective, shifts *AD* to the left, resulting in a reduction in the aggregate output and the aggregate price level for a given short-run aggregate supply curve (*SRAS*).

17. Which of the following statements is true?

   A. An economy can eliminate an inflationary gap by increasing government spending.
   B. Expansionary fiscal policy refers to an increase in taxes.
   C. When potential output is greater than actual aggregate output, the economy faces an inflationary gap.
   D. When *SRAS* intersects *AD* to the right of the long-run aggregate supply (*LRAS*) curve, the economy faces a recessionary gap.

18. Monetary and fiscal policy
    A. affect the economy in predictable ways and with relatively short time lags.
    B. involve significant time lags with regard to their implementation and effect on the economy.
    C. take so long to implement in the economy that they prove to be useless policies.
    D. when implemented, always worsen economic fluctuations because of the lags involved in their implementation.

19. Holding everything else constant, the multiplier effect for taxes or transfers
    A. is the same as the multiplier effect for changes in autonomous aggregate spending.
    B. is smaller than the multiplier effect for changes in autonomous aggregate spending.
    C. is larger than the multiplier effect for changes in autonomous aggregate spending.
    D. may be smaller than, larger than, or equal to the multiplier effect for changes in autonomous aggregate spending.

20. Which of the following statements is true?
    A. Automatic stabilizers act like expansionary fiscal policy when the economy is in a recession.
    B. Automatic stabilizers refer to government spending and taxation rules that cause fiscal policy to be expansionary when the economy expands and contractionary when the economy contracts.
    C. Automatic stabilizers reduce the size of the multiplier.
    D. Answers (a), (b), and (c) are all true.
    E. Answers (a) and (c) are both true.

ANSWER KEY

Fill-in-the-Blanks

Module 16: (1) income, (2) marginal propensity to save (*MPS*), (3) autonomous, (4) greater, (5) multiplier, (6) inventories

Module 17: (1) output, (2) wealth/interest rate, (3) wealth/interest rate, (4) wealth, (5) interest rate, (6) expectations, wealth, existing stock of capital, government policies

Module 18: (1) real; (2) sticky; (3) commodity prices, nominal wages, productivity; (4) vertical; (5) potential; (6) aggregate output or real GDP; (7) flexible; (8) aggregate supply

Module 19: (1) *SRAS*, (2) shock, (3) negative, (4) supply, (5) stagflation, (6) *LRAS*, (7) recessionary, (8) inflationary

Module 20: (1) stabilization, (2) expansionary, (3) government purchases/transfers, (4) taxes, (5) contractionary, (6) government spending, (7) taxes, (8) lags

Module 21: (1) multiplier, (2) marginal propensity to consume, (3) 10, (4) smaller, (5) save, (6) lump sum, (7) automatic stabilizers, (8) discretionary

Featured Model: The Aggregate Demand–Aggregate Supply Model

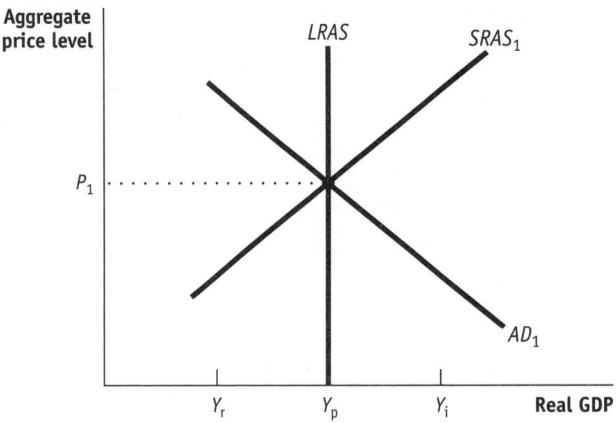

Exercises

1. a.

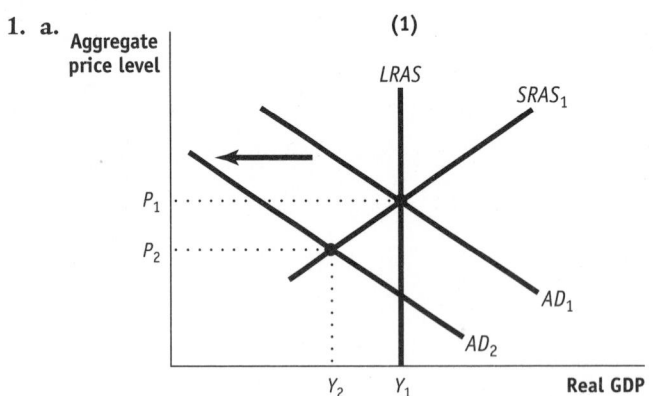

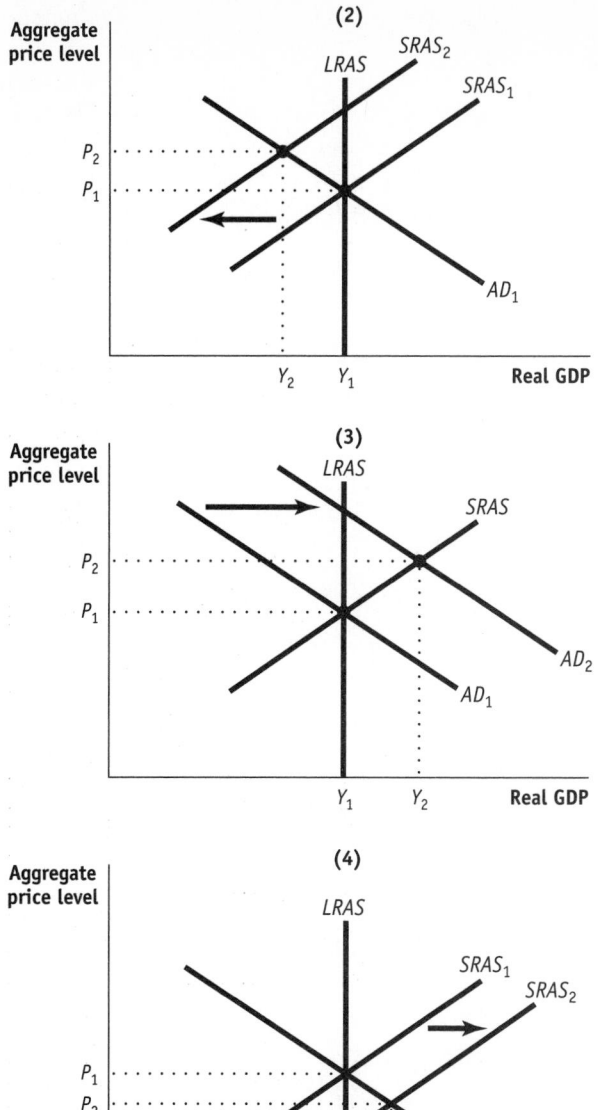

b. In scenario (1), the aggregate price level and the aggregate level of output both decrease relative to their initial levels. In scenario (2), the aggregate price level increases, while the aggregate level of output decreases relative to its initial levels. In scenario (3), the aggregate price level and the aggregate level of output both increase relative to their initial levels. In scenario (4), the aggregate price level falls, while the aggregate level of output increases relative to its initial levels.

c. A short-run recessionary gap is defined as a situation in which the economy produces at a level of output that is less than potential output: scenarios (1) and (2) illustrate this situation. Scenarios (3) and (4) represent inflationary gaps because the level of aggregate output is greater than potential output.

d. If there is no active stabilization policy implemented, then in scenario (1) the short-run *AS* curve will shift to the right as the nominal wage decreases in response to the recessionary gap. As the short-run *AS* curve shifts out, the economy will eventually reach long-run equilibrium during which the aggregate output level returns to potential output, Y_1, while the aggregate price level falls to a lower long-run aggregate price level than the initial long-run P_1. In scenario (2), the short-run AS curve will shift to the right, returning the economy back to its initial long-run macroeconomic equilibrium. In scenario (3), the short-run AS curve will shift to the left, restoring the economy to the original level of aggregate output but a higher aggregate price level than the initial long-run P_1. In scenario (4), the short-run AS curve will shift to the left, returning the economy to its initial equilibrium.

Answers to Problems

1. **a.** The value of autonomous consumer spending in Mainland is $160. To find this value, first recall that the consumption function can be written as $C = A + MPC \times YD$. Next, find the MPC, which is the change in consumer spending divided by the change in disposable income, or $800/1000 = 0.8$., substitute one of the consumer spending and disposable income combinations into the consumption function to find the value of autonomous consumer spending: thus, $C = A + 0.8 \times YD$ and $800 = A + (0.(8) \times (800)$ or $A = \$160$.

    b. The MPC is 0.8. See the explanation in part (a) of this problem.

    c. The consumption function is $C = 160 + 0.8 \times YD$. See the explanation in part (a).

2. **a.**

Year	Disposable income
1	$50
2	100
3	250

    b. The MPC is defined as the change in consumption spending divided by the change in disposable income. Using the information given to you and your calculations in part (a), you can calculate the MPC as 0.8 (since the change in consumption from year 1 to year 2 is 40 and the change in disposable income from year 1 to year 2 is 50).

    c. The MPS plus the MPC equals one. Since the MPC equals 0.8, the MPS equals 0.2.

    d. The value of the multiplier for this economy equals $[1/(1 - MPC)]$, or 5.

    e. The consumption function for this economy can be written as $C = A + MPC \times (Y - T)$. But, from part (b) you know the MPC is 0.8, and the taxes are constant at $50. Thus, $C = A + 0.8 (Y - 50)$. Using one of the disposable income and consumption pairs from the table, you can solve this equation for the value of A, the autonomous level of consumption spending. Thus, $40 = A + 0.8 (100 - 50)$, or $A = 0$. The consumption function is therefore $C = 0.8 \times (Y - Y)$.

    f. The equilibrium level of output is where planned aggregate expenditure equals production, or where planned AE equals Y. Planned AE is the sum of consumption spending and investment spending because there is no government spending nor foreign trade. Thus, $AE = 0.8 \times (Y - T) + 50$. Substituting 50 for taxes, we get $AE = 0.8 \times (Y - 50) + 50$ or $AE = 0.8Y + 10$. Recall that in equilibrium planned AE equals Y so $Y = AE = 0.8Y + 10$. Solving for Y, the equilibrium level of real GDP, we get Y equals 50.

3. Long-run economic growth is depicted in the AS–AD model as the long-run AS curve shifting to the right. Thus, your graph should depict several vertical AS curves, with each one farther to the right on the horizontal axis, representing the ability of the economy to reach even higher levels of potential output. For a given AD curve, the level of

aggregate output increases as the *LRAS* curve shifts to the right. The following graph illustrates this idea.

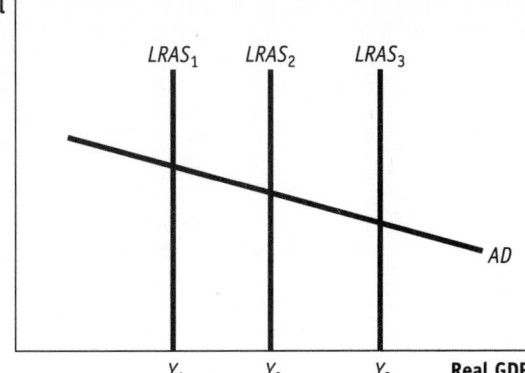

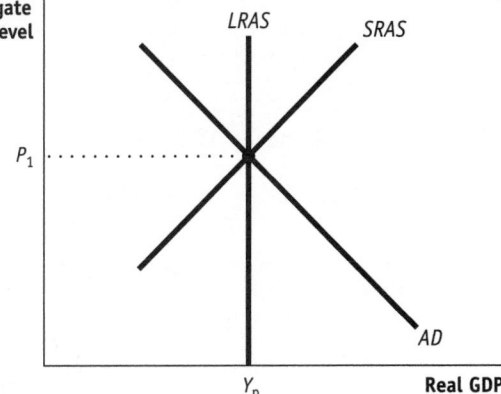

4. a.

b.

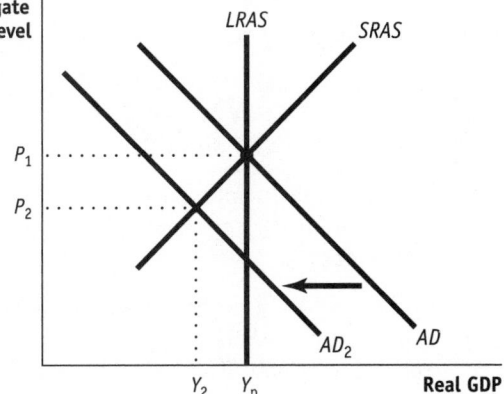

c.

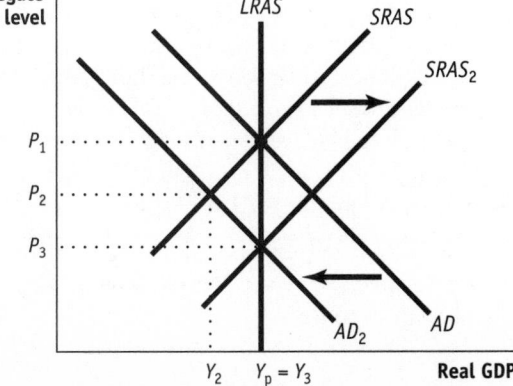

d. To offset a negative demand shock, the government needs to shift the *AD* curve to the right. Monetary policy that increases the money supply will shift the *AD* curve to the right and return the economy to P_1 and Y_p.

5. a. An increase in the money supply is an example of monetary policy: the *AD* curve shifts to the right and there is a movement upward along the *SRAS* curve. There will be no change in the *LRAS* curve.

b. When the price of commodities increases, this causes the *SRAS* curve to shift to the left. There will be a movement upward along the *AD* curve and no change in the *LRAS* curve.

c. When the price of oil decreases, this causes the *SRAS* curve to shift to the right and results in a downward movement along the *AD* curve. There is no change in the *LRAS* curve.

d. Successful labor union negotiations lead to higher wages, which leads to a leftward shift in the *SRAS* curve and an upward movement along the *AD* curve. There is no change in the *LRAS* curve.

e. When the inventory of unsold houses increases in an economy, this implies that the level of investment is high and there is therefore less incentive for firms to invest in this economy. As investment spending falls, this causes the *AD* curve to shift to the left, resulting in a downward movement along the *SRAS* curve. There is no change in the *LRAS* curve.

f. When labor productivity increases, this causes the *SRAS* curve to shift to the right, but it also causes the *LRAS* curve to shift to the right because the economy can now produce at a higher   potential output level. There is a downward movement along the *AD* curve.

g. When the government increases spending to finance a war, this causes the *AD* curve to shift to the right, resulting in a movement upward along the *SRAS* curve. There is no change in the *LRAS* curve.

6. a. This is an example of an automatic stabilizer: as GDP in Macrovia falls, this leads automatically to smaller tax collections for a given tax rate.

b. This is an example of expansionary discretionary fiscal policy: the additional government expenditure will increase *AD*.

c. This is an example of contractionary discretionary fiscal policy: Macrovia moves to cut government spending, which will reduce *AD* and slow down the economic expansion.

d. This is an example of an automatic stabilizer: as unemployment rises, this leads to lower *AD*. But the payment of unemployment benefits lessens this fall in aggregate spending and results in a smaller overall impact on *AD*.

7. a. The potential output level for Macroland is Y_2. Currently, Macroland is producing Y_1 at price level P_2: this is a recessionary gap because Macroland has the potential to produce a higher level of output than it is currently producing.

b. Macroland has a recessionary gap because its current level of production, Y_1, is less than its potential level of production, Y_2.

c. Any policy initiative that shifts *AD* to the right will help Macroland move toward its potential output level. Items (i) and (iii) will both shift *AD* to the right; government policies that stimulate private investment spending lead to higher levels of aggregate spending and a rightward shift in *AD*. New spending by government will also lead to higher levels of aggregate spending and a rightward shift in *AD*. Item (ii) will reduce disposable income and lead to lower levels of aggregate spending: *AD* will shift to the left.

d. The current price level in Macroland is P_2. If the government engages in fiscal policy that results in a shift of *AD* to the right, returning to the potential level of output, and leading to an increase in the price level from P_2 to P_3.

8. a.

Year	Potential output
Year 1	$100
Year 2	105
Year 3	110.25
Year 4	115.76

b. The consumption function can be written as $C = A + MPC (Y - T)$. From the table we can compute the MPC as the change in consumption divided by the change in disposable income, or 9/18, which equals 0.5. To find A, we need to use one of the consumption and disposable income combinations from the table. For example, when disposable income equals 90, consumption equals 55. So, $C = A + 0.5 (Y - T)$ can be rewritten as $55 = A + 0.5(90)$, and solving for A, we find A equals 10. Thus, the consumption function for this economy is $C = 10 + 0.5 (Y - T)$.

c.

Year	Potential output	Actual output	T	YD	C	I	G
Year 1	100	100	10	90	55	30	15
Year 2	105	104	10	94	57	30	17
Year 3	110.25	115	10	105	62.5	30	22.5
Year 4	115.76	118	10	108	64	30	24

d.

Year	Recessionary gap	Inflationary gap	Actual output equals potential output
Year 1	No	No	Yes
Year 2	Yes	No	No
Year 3	No	Yes	No
Year 4	No	Yes	No

e.

Year	Discretionary fiscal policy
Year 1	No policy necessary
Year 2	Increase government spending or decrease taxation
Year 3	Decrease government spending or increase taxation
Year 4	Decrease government spending or increase taxation

9. The *AS–AD* model is self-correcting; it will always return to long-run macroeconomic equilibrium if given a sufficient amount of time for the short-run *AS* curve to adjust to economic changes through changes in the nominal wage. This adjustment process comes from the short-run *AS* curve shifting due to changes in the nominal wage until that point at which *AD* intersects both the short-run and the long-run *AS* curves at potential output.

10. Automatic stabilizers act to moderate the effects of economic recessions or economic expansions. In the case of economic recessions, the automatic stabilizers provide a source of additional spending that occurs as the economy goes into the recession. For example, as production and spending slow in the economy, the amount of taxes people pay naturally decrease as their income levels decrease, and this moderates the fall in consumer spending. Or, as unemployment rates increase, the number of people receiving unemployment compensation rises, and this enables people to spend more than they would otherwise be able to spend. In the case of economic expansions, the automatic stabilizers slow down spending: as people's incomes rise, their taxes also rise, reducing the overall increase in consumer income, which moderates the economic expansion.

Answers to Review Questions

1. **D.** All three of these variables affect the level of consumer spending.

2. **E.** To calculate Joe's *MPC*, look at the ratio of the change in consumer spending divided by the change in disposable income: $400/$500 = 0.8. If Joe's *MPC* to 0.8, then his *MPS* is 0.2. When Joe's MPS is 0.2, this implies that he saves 20% of any increase in his disposable income, since 0.2 is equal to 20% when expressed as a percentage rather than a decimal.

3. **D.** To find Sue's autonomous consumer spending, it is helpful to write her consumption function, $C = MPC \times YD + A$. You know that two points on Sue's consumption function are ($10,000, $8,000) and ($20,000, $14,000) at which the variable measured on the *x*-axis is disposable income and the variable measured on the *y*-axis is consumer spending. The MPC can be calculated as (the change in consumer spending)/(the change in disposable income) or ($6,000)/($10,000) = 0.6. Thus, the MPS is 0.4. Using this information, Sue's consumption function can be written as $C = 0.6 \times YD + A$. Using one of the two known points from Sue's consumption function, you can solve for *A*, Sue's autonomous consumer spending, as $2,000.

4. **D.** Investment spending primarily depends on these three factors.

5. **D.** When interest rates rise, this makes any given investment project less profitable because the firm is either going to find that borrowed funds are now more expensive or that retained earnings used to finance the project will not be available to be invested in order to earn the higher rate of interest. When a firm finances an investment project through retained earnings, there is still an opportunity cost to using these funds for the project because the firm cannot invest the funds and earn the higher interest rate. Interest rates and the level of investment are inversely related to each other.

6. **D.** In the short run, nominal wages are sticky and take time to adjust to changes in economic conditions due to pre-existing contracts and employer reluctance to frequently alter wages. In the long run, nominal wages are fully flexible.

7. **B.** Production costs affect the level of aggregate production: as production costs increase, holding everything else constant, profit per unit decreases. Producers respond to this decrease in profit per unit by decreasing the quantity of goods and services they are willing to supply.

8. **A.** An increase in the aggregate price level results in a movement along the *AS* curve and not a shift of the curve. A decrease in commodity prices results in a rightward shift of the *AS* curve. An increase in nominal wages causes the *AS* curve to shift to the left.

9. **C.** Because the economy is producing at a level of aggregate output smaller than the level of potential output, the economy cannot be in long-run equilibrium. Since output is below potential output, we know that not all workers are being fully utilized; if all workers were fully employed, this would result in higher levels of production. Therefore, unemployment must be relatively high, and this will lead to decreases in the nominal wage over time because jobs are scarce and workers are abundant.

10. **B.** A recessionary gap is a situation in the short run during which aggregate output is less than potential output. A recessionary gap is eliminated in the long run as the short-run *AS* curve adjusts to return the economy to potential output and long-run equilibrium. An inflationary gap is a short-run situation during which aggregate output is greater than potential output. As the economy moves to a long-run equilibrium, the inflationary gap will be eliminated and aggregate output will return to potential output.

11. **D.** When the interest rate rises, borrowing becomes more expensive for firms and leads firms to reduce their level of investment spending. At the same time, a higher interest rate will provide households with an incentive to save more. Both of these effects will lead aggregate demand to fall when there is a rise in the interest rate: this is referred to as the interest rate effect.

12. **C.** When the *AD* curve shifts to the right, the level of aggregate demand is greater at any given aggregate price level than it was initially. When the government increases government spending, decreases taxes, or increases the money supply, this results in greater aggregate demand at every price level. When the government decreases government spending, increases taxes, or decreases the money supply, this results in less aggregate demand at every price level.

13. **B.** In the short run, this economy is producing a level of real GDP that is less than potential GDP. This implies that jobs are scarce and unemployment is high. Over time, workers will accept lower nominal wages in order to find employment. As the level of nominal wages falls, the *SRAS* curve shifts to the right, causing the level of real GDP to increase toward the potential output level.

14. **B.** In the short run, wages and prices are not perfectly flexible because of informal and formal agreements that limit the short-run flexibility of wages and prices. Ultimately, formal contracts and informal agreements can be renegotiated to take into account changed economic circumstances. In the long run, wages and prices are fully flexible.

15. **D.** An increase in wealth causes the *AD* curve to shift to the right, resulting in a higher aggregate price level and a higher level of real GDP. If the government wishes to restore the economy to the original aggregate price level and aggregate output level, it can accomplish this goal by reducing government spending, raising taxes, or decreasing the money supply.

16. **D.** Contractionary fiscal policy is a reduction in government spending or an increase in taxes aimed at shifting *AD* to the left. For a given *SRAS*, this leftward shift in *AD* will lead to a lower level of equilibrium aggregate output and a reduction in the aggregate price level. Contractionary fiscal policy is implemented when the economy produces a level of output in excess of potential output; contractionary fiscal policy is used to offset an inflationary gap.

17. **C.** When *SRAS* intersects *AD* to the right of *LRAS*, the economy faces an inflationary gap. This inflationary gap can be eliminated through a decrease in government spending or an increase in taxes, since either policy will cause *AD* to shift to the left, holding everything else equal. A decrease in government spending and an increase in taxes are examples of contractionary fiscal policy. By definition, when potential output is greater than actual aggregate output, the economy is operating with a recessionary gap.

18. **B.** There are significant lags involved in the implementation of fiscal and monetary policy. These lags can result in a situation during which the implemented policy actually worsens the economic situation (for example, using expansionary fiscal policy to counteract a recessionary gap that has turned into an inflationary gap by the time the fiscal policy takes effect).

19. **B.** In our simple model, the multiplier effect for changes in taxes or transfers equals (in absolute value) $MPC/(1 - MPC)$, while the multiplier effect for changes in autonomous aggregate spending equals $1/(1 - MPC)$. The multiplier effect of changes in taxes and transfers is smaller than the multiplier effect of changes in autonomous aggregate spending.

20. **E.** Automatic stabilizers act to automatically lessen the economic consequences of recessions and expansions. They do this by providing an automatic fiscal policy response that stimulates a contractionary economy and slows down, or contracts, an expansionary economy. This activity effectively lessens the multiplier process and therefore reduces the size of the multiplier.

Notes

The Financial Sector

OVERVIEW

This section presents the financial sector of the economy and explains how it facilitates economic activity. It discusses the various types of financial assets, such as savings and investment, and looks at the financial system. It also discusses institutions and policy, including banking and the Federal Reserve System. Finally, it explores the money and loanable funds markets.

FEATURED MODEL/GRAPH:
MONEY MARKET/LOANABLE FUNDS MARKET

This section presents two closely related markets: the money market and the market for loanable funds. Understanding these two markets, their similarities and their differences, is essential for understanding monetary policy.

MODULES IN THIS SECTION

Module 22: Saving, Investment, and the Financial System

Module 23: The Definition and Measurement of Money

Module 24: The Time Value of Money

Module 25: Banking and Money Creation

Module 26: The Federal Reserve System: History and Structure

Module 27: The Federal Reserve System: Monetary Policy

Module 28: The Money Market

Module 29: The Market for Loanable Funds

Module 22
Saving, Investment, and the Financial System

Before You Read the MODULE

Summary

This module explains how investment spending is financed through the relationship between savings and investment spending for the economy as a whole.

Module Objectives

Review these objectives before you read the module. Place a "√" on the line when you understand each of the following:

_____**Objective 1.** The relationship between savings and investment spending

_____**Objective 2.** The purpose of the four principal types of **financial assets**

_____**Objective 3.** How **financial intermediaries** help investors achieve **diversification**

While You Read the MODULE

Key Terms

Define these key terms as you read the module.

Interest rate

Savings–investment spending identity

Budget surplus

Budget deficit

Budget balance

National savings

Capital inflow

Wealth

Financial asset

Physical asset

Liability

Transaction costs

Financial risk

Diversification

Liquid

Illiquid

Loan

Default

Loan-backed securities

Financial intermediary

Mutual fund

Pension fund
_____

Life insurance company
_____

Bank deposit
_____

Bank
_____

List questions or difficulties from your initial reading of the module.

After You Read the MODULE

Fill-in-the-Blanks

Fill in the blanks to complete the following statements. Terms may be used more than once. If you find yourself having difficulties, please refer to the appropriate section in the text.

- It is an accounting fact that investment spending will always be equal to

  (1)_____. Governments, as well as individuals, can save. The

  government saves when its tax revenues exceed its spending; this difference is called a

  budget (2)_____. If government spending exceeds tax revenue, it

  is called a budget (3)_____. The term "budget balance" refers to

  both situations. The sum of private savings and the budget balance is called

  (4)_____.

- The savings of people who live in any one country can be used to finance investment spending that takes place in other countries; these flows of funds are known as (5)_____ flows.

- The three tasks of a financial system are to reduce (6)_____ and _____, and to provide (7)_____. An institution that transforms funds from many individuals into financial assets is called a(n) (8)_____.

Module Review

The Meaning of Investment

When macroeconomists use the term *investment spending*, they almost always mean "spending on new physical capital." This can be confusing because in ordinary life we often say that someone who buys stocks or purchases an existing building is "investing." The important point to keep in mind is that only spending that adds to the economy's stock of physical capital is "investment spending." In contrast, the act of purchasing an asset such as a share of stock, a bond, or existing real estate is "making an investment."

It's important to understand clearly the three different kinds of capital: physical capital, human capital, and financial capital. Physical capital consists of manufactured resources such as buildings and machines. Human capital is the improvement in the labor force generated by education and knowledge. Financial capital is funds from savings that are available for investment spending. So a country that has a positive capital inflow is experiencing a flow of funds from abroad that can be used for investment spending.

- It is important to understand that savings and investment spending are always equal whether the economy is open or closed. This is an accounting fact and is referred to as the savings–investment spending identity.

- It is good to have a basic idea of the definition of and differences between the types of financial assets. However, don't spend lots of time memorizing specific definitions and detailed distinctions. Strive to understand the categories of assets in the context of the macroeconomic models we are developing.

Module 23
The Definition and Measurement of Money

Before You Read the MODULE

....

Summary

This module explains what distinguishes money from other forms of wealth.

Module Objectives

Review these objectives before you read the module. Place a "√" on the line when you understand each of the following:

_____**Objective 1.** The definition and functions of **money**

_____**Objective 2.** The various roles money plays and the many forms it takes in the economy

_____**Objective 3.** How the amount of money in the economy is measured

While You Read the MODULE

....

Key Terms

Define these key terms as you read the module.

Money

Currency in circulation

Checkable bank deposits

Money supply
_____

Medium of exchange
_____

Store of value
_____

Unit of account
_____

Commodity money
_____

Commodity-backed money
_____

Fiat money
_____

Monetary aggregate
_____

Near-moneys
_____

List questions or difficulties from your initial reading of the module.

After You Read the MODULE

Fill-in-the-Blanks

Fill in the blanks to complete the following statements. Terms may be used more than once. If you find yourself having difficulties, please refer to the appropriate section in the text.

• Any asset that can easily be used to purchase goods and services is considered

(1)_____. Money serves three functions, it is a

(2)_____, _____, and

_____. Money whose value derives entirely from its official

status as a means of exchange is known as (3)_____ money. The

two most commonly cited monetary aggregates are known as

(4)_____ and _____. The narrowest,

most liquid form of money is (5)_____. Other types of less

liquid assets are known as (6)_____.

Module Review

What's Not in the Money Supply?

Are financial assets like stocks and bonds part of the money supply? No, not under any definition, because they're not liquid enough. M1 consists, roughly speaking, of assets you can use to buy groceries: currency, traveler's checks, and checkable deposits. M2 is broader: it includes things like savings accounts, which can easily and quickly be converted into M1. Normally, for example, you can switch funds between your savings and checking accounts with a click of a mouse or a call to an automated phone service. By contrast, converting a stock or a bond into cash requires selling the stock or bond—something that usually takes some time and also involves paying a broker's fee. That makes these assets much less liquid than bank deposits. So stocks and bonds, unlike bank deposits, aren't considered money.

• It is important to understand the distinction between assets and liabilities. Make sure you clearly understand what an asset and a liability are, and then recognize that any financial instrument represents both an asset and a liability. For example, a mortgage represents a liability for the borrower and an asset for the lender; a checking account deposit represents a liability for the bank providing the check service and an asset to the individual depositing the funds.

Module 24
The Time Value of Money

Before You Read the MODULE

Summary

This module explains how time is an issue in economic decision making.

Module Objectives

Review these objectives before you read the module. Place a "√" on the line when you understand each of the following:

_____**Objective 1.** How to make decisions when costs or benefits come in the future

_____**Objective 2.** How the concept of **present value** can help make decisions when time is a factor

While You Read the MODULE

Key Terms

Define these key terms as you read the module.

Present value

Net present value

List questions or difficulties from your initial reading of the module.

After You Read the MODULE

Fill-in-the-Blanks

Fill in the blanks to complete the following statements. Terms may be used more than once. If you find yourself having difficulties, please refer to the appropriate section in the text.

- Which is worth more, having one dollar today or having a dollar one year from today?

  Having a dollar (1)_____. The amount you would be willing

  to accept today, in exchange for $1 paid one year from today is known as

  (2)_____. The present value of $1 paid one year from today

  when the interest rate is "r" is equal to (3)_____. The present

  value of current and future benefits minus the present value of current and future costs is

  called (4)_____.

Module Review

Present Value

Understanding present value requires grasping two important points. First, a dollar today is worth more than a dollar in the future. If you receive a dollar today, you can either spend the dollar immediately (and enjoy the benefits of what you buy with it) *or* you can save the dollar (and earn interest on it until you decide to spend it in the future). In either case, spending now or saving for later, you gain more from having the dollar right away. Second, the interest rate determines the trade-off between receiving a dollar today and receiving it tomorrow. The interest rate is what borrowers are willing to pay to have a dollar to spend immediately and what lenders must receive in order to give up their dollar until a future date. Approach present value with this in mind and you will be better able to apply the concept to decision making when costs and/or benefits come in the future than if you try to memorize a formula without understanding its underlying principles.

Module 25
Banking and Money Creation

Before You Read the MODULE

Summary

This module presents the monetary role of banks.

Module Objectives

Review these objectives before you read the module. Place a "√" on the line when you understand each of the following:

_____**Objective 1.** The role of banks in the economy

_____**Objective 2.** The reasons for and types of banking regulation

_____**Objective 3.** How banks create money

While You Read the MODULE

Key Terms

Define these key terms as you read the module.

Bank reserves

T-account

Reserve ratio

Required reserve ratio
_____

Bank run
_____

Deposit insurance
_____

Reserve requirements
_____

Discount window
_____

Excess reserves
_____

Monetary base
_____

Money multiplier
_____

List questions or difficulties from your initial reading of the module.

After You Read the MODULE

Fill-in-the-Blanks

Fill in the blanks to complete the following statements. Terms may be used more than once. If you find yourself having difficulties, please refer to the appropriate section in the text.

- Currency in bank vaults and bank deposits held at the Federal Reserve are called

  (1)_____. The fraction of bank deposits that a bank holds as

  reserves is its (2)_____. When many of a bank's depositors try to

  withdraw their funds due to fears of a bank failure, it is known as a

  (3)_____. Banking regulation to prevent bank failures has three

  main features: (4)_____, _____, and

  _____. FDIC deposit insurance guarantees the first

  (5)_____ dollars of each bank account. Reserve requirements

  are set by the (6)_____, which also makes loans to banks

  through its (7)_____ window. Banks create money by lending

  out their (8)_____ reserves.

Module Review

Creating money

The idea that banks can "create" money can be difficult to understand unless you understand the definition of money and how it is measured. When we say that banks create money, we don't mean that they create it in the same way they did before the Civil War—by printing certificates that could be redeemed for silver coins on demand. We mean that banks are able to expand the money supply through lending.

Today, dollar bills are printed by the Treasury Department and issued into the economy by regional Federal Reserve banks. Banks no longer create currency. But recall that the supply of money in the economy consists of more than currency. The M1 definition of money includes currency in circulation, traveler's checks, and checkable bank deposits. It is through loans, which change the amount of checkable deposits, that banks create money. Because we have a fractional reserve banking system (banks are required to keep only a fraction of their deposits as cash in their vaults or on deposit at the Fed), when banks receive a new deposit, they can increase their loans. When they make a loan, they increase the amount of checkable deposits, therefore increasing the money supply.

- It is important to understand the definition and the distinction between the monetary base, the money supply, and reserves. The money supply is the value of financial assets in the economy that are considered money:this would include cash in the hands of the public, checkable bank deposits, and traveler's checks. Bank reserves are composed of the currency banks hold in their vaults plus their deposits at the Federal Reserve. The monetary base is the sum of currency in circulation and bank reserves. The monetary base is smaller than the money supply.

Module 26
The Federal Reserve System: History and Structure

Before You Read the MODULE

Summary

This module introduces the Federal Reserve System, the U. S. central bank. It explains how central banks oversee and regulate the banking system, and control the monetary base.

Module Objectives

Review these objectives before you read the module. Place a "√" on the line when you understand each of the following:

_____**Objective 1.** The history of the Federal Reserve System

_____**Objective 2.** The structure of the Federal Reserve System

_____**Objective 3.** How the Federal Reserve has responded to major financial crises

While You Read the MODULE

Key Terms

Define these key terms as you read the module.

Central bank

Commercial bank

Investment bank

Savings and loan (thrift)

Leverage

Balance sheet effect

Vicious cycle of deleveraging

Subprime lending

Securitization

List questions or difficulties from your initial reading of the module.

After You Read the MODULE

Fill-in-the-Blanks

Fill in the blanks to complete the following statements. Terms may be used more than once. If you find yourself having difficulties, please refer to the appropriate section in the text.

- The (1)_____ is the central bank of the United States. It is

  overseen by the (2)_____, which is part of the federal

  government, and its services are provided by the (3)_____

  regional reserve banks. There are (4)_____ governors appointed

  to the Board of Governors for (5)_____-year terms. The New

  York Federal Reserve bank carries out the most important function of monetary policy,

  conducting (6)_____.

- The Glass-Steagall Act of 1933 separated banks into two categories:

  (7)_____ and (8)_____ banks.

Module Review

When Is a Central Bank *Not* a Central Bank?
When It's 12 Banks (a Board of Governors, and an FOMC).

The central bank of the United States is more than a single bank—it is a multi-part system. When the Fed was created in 1913, its creation was influenced by the politics and geography of the country at that time (for example, look at the locations of the 12 regional Federal Reserve Banks). The Federal Reserve System has both public and private elements, as well as regional banks spread across the country. The important parts of the Federal Reserve System are summarized below.

The Board of Governors is a government agency located in Washington, DC. It oversees the Federal Reserve System. The board has 7 members, appointed by the President and approved by the Senate for 14-year terms. Because governors can be appointed to complete the terms of a governor who did not complete his or her 14-year term (and then serve their own 14-year term), some governors serve more than 14 years. The Chairman of the Board of Governors is appointed every 4 years.

The 12 Federal Reserve Banks are privately owned. They are owned by the member commercial banks in their district and are overseen by boards of directors, who appoint their presidents. Federal Reserve Banks are nonprofit—their operating budgets come from fees charged to the commercial banks they serve. If regional Federal Reserve Bank revenues exceed their expenses, the difference is given to the Treasury. Fed banks are not government agencies and are not funded by taxes.

The Federal Open Market Committee (FOMC) makes decisions about monetary policy. The FOMC has 12 voting members at any given time. It is made up of the 7 members of the Board of Governors, the president of the New York Federal Reserve Bank, and the other 11 regional Federal Reserve Bank presidents. Only 4 of the other 11 regional Federal Reserve Bank presidents vote at any given time. Voting seats are rotated among the 11 other regional Federal Reserve Bank presidents.

Module 27
The Federal Reserve System: Monetary Policy

Before You Read the MODULE

Summary

This module presents the functions of the Federal Reserve System and how it serves them.

Module Objectives

Review these objectives before you read the module. Place a "√" on the line when you understand each of the following:

_____**Objective 1.** The functions of the Federal Reserve System

_____**Objective 2.** The major tools the Federal Reserve uses to serve its functions

While You Read the MODULE

Key Terms

Define these key terms as you read the module.

Federal funds market

Federal funds rate

Discount rate

List questions or difficulties from your initial reading of the module.

After You Read the MODULE

Fill-in-the-Blanks

Fill in the blanks to complete the following statements. Terms may be used more than once. If you find yourself having difficulties, please refer to the appropriate section in the text.

- The Fed provides financial services to (1)_____ banks. It also

  supervises and regulates the nation's banking system, and maintains the integrity of the

  financial system. Perhaps the most important function of the Fed is to conduct

  (2)_____ policy. The Fed has three main tools it can use to

  conduct policy: (3)_____, _____,

  and _____.

- When banks need to borrow additional reserves from other banks, they do so through the

  (4)_____ market. When banks need to borrow reserves from the

  Fed, they may do so by paying the (5)_____ rate.

  (6)_____ operations occur when the Fed buys or sells U.S.

  Treasury bills through a transaction with commercial banks.

Module Review

Open-Market Operations: Buying and Selling Treasury Bills, Notes, and Bonds

The term "open-market operations" refers to buying and selling United States Treasury securities (Treasury bills, notes, and bonds). Treasury securities are bought and sold through auctions held by the Federal Reserve Bank of New York—that is, they are sold on the "open market." Treasury securities are sold both to finance the federal government debt and to implement monetary policy. The U.S. Treasury Department must regularly borrow to finance the federal government's debt. Approximately one-half of the national debt is held in Treasury securities. The Treasury Department sells many of these securities through auctions held at the Federal Reserve Bank of New York. Most Treasury securities sold through Federal Reserve auctions are bought by primary dealers. Primary dealers are financial institutions that buy and sell large quantities of government securities and have established business relationships with the New York Federal Reserve bank. Currently, there are approximately 19 primary dealers. Others can purchase Treasury bills, notes, and bonds from banks or brokers in the secondary market.

In addition to selling securities to finance the federal debt, the New York Fed's Open Market Desk buys and sells Treasury bills, notes, and bonds to carry out the monetary policy designated by the FOMC. The Open Market Desk adds reserves to the banking system when it buys Treasury securities; it drains reserves when it sells Treasury securities.

- Remember that when the Fed purchases Treasury bills, it injects reserves into the banking system, increasing the money supply, and that when the Fed sells Treasury bills, it removes reserves from the banking system, decreasing the money supply.

Module 28
The Money Market

Before You Read the MODULE

Summary

This module examines what determines *how much* money individuals and firms want to hold at any given time.

Module Objectives

Review these objectives before you read the module. Place a "√" on the line when you understand each of the following:

_____ **Objective 1.** What the **money demand curve** is

_____ **Objective 2.** Why the **liquidity preference model** determines the interest rate in the short run

While You Read the MODULE

Key Terms

Define these key terms as you read the module.

Short-term interest rates

Long-term interest rates

Money demand curve

Liquidity preference model of the interest rate

_____

Money supply curve

_____

List questions or difficulties from your initial reading of the module.

After You Read the MODULE

Fill-in-the-Blanks

Fill in the blanks to complete the following statements. Terms may be used more than once. If you find your-self having difficulties, please refer to the appropriate section in the text.

*   The opportunity cost of holding money is equal to the (1)_____

    rate. The relationship between the interest rate and the quantity of money demanded by

    the public is illustrated by the (2)_____ curve. This curve will

    shift as a result of changes in (3)_____,

    _____, _____, or

    _____. The money supply curve is

    (4)_____, and its location is determined by

    (5)_____. This model of interest rates is known as the liquidity

    preference model. Another important model of interest rates is the market for

    (6)_____ funds.

Which Interest Rate?

There are many different interest rates in the economy. For example, there are mortgage interest rates, automobile loan interest rates, credit card interest rates, and the prime interest rate. The different interest rates tend to move in the same general direction, moving together like a "web" of interest rates. It is important that you are able to distinguish between two important interest rates in our macroeconomic models, the federal funds rate and the discount rate. The federal funds rate is the interest rate banks charge each other for overnight loans. It is set in the federal funds market, but is targeted by the Fed. Other interest rates tend to follow the federal funds rate, rising when it rises and falling when it falls. The other interest rate in our macroeconomic models is the discount rate. The discount rate is the interest rate the Fed charges banks to borrow. The discount rate is set directly by the Fed.

You will sometimes hear people say that interest rates do not reflect the supply and demand for money since the Fed sets the interest rate. In fact, the federal funds rate is determined by the supply and demand for money in the money market. The only difference is that the Fed adjusts the supply of money to achieve its target interest rate.

Module 29
The Market for Loanable Funds

Before You Read the MODULE

Summary

This module explains how savers and borrowers are brought together in the loanable funds market.

Module Objectives

Review these objectives before you read the module. Place a "√" on the line when you understand each of the following:

_____**Objective 1.** How the **loanable funds market** matches savers and investors

_____**Objective 2.** The determinants of supply and demand in the loanable funds market

_____**Objective 3.** How the two models of interest rates can be reconciled

While You Read the MODULE

Key Terms

Define these key terms as you read the module.

Loanable funds market

Rate of return

Crowding out

List questions or difficulties from your initial reading of the module.

After You Read the MODULE

Fill-in-the-Blanks

Fill in the blanks to complete the following statements. Terms may be used more than once. If you find your-self having difficulties, please refer to the appropriate section in the text.

- A market that brings together those who want to lend money (savers) and those who want

   to borrow (firms with investment spending projects) is called the

   (1)_____ market. The demand for loanable funds depends on

   the interest rate and the (2)_____ businesses earn on projects.

   The demand for loanable funds will shift in response to changes in

   (3)_____ or (4)_____. The negative

   effect of government budget deficits on investment spending is called

   (5)_____. The supply of loanable funds will shift in response to

   changes in (6)_____ or (7)_____.

   The most important factor affecting interest rates over time is expectations about the

   future rate of (8)_____.

Module Review

Which Model?

To discuss monetary policy and interest rates, we have used both the liquidity preference model (the money market) and the loanable funds model. In this module we have shown how these two models are related. So how do you know which model to use if you are asked to explain how monetary policy will affect the macroeconomy? You must understand both models and be prepared to discuss either one. Pay particular attention to the labels on the axes and curves, and the slope of the supply curve in each graph. Since the Federal Reserve determines the supply of money in the economy, the equilibrium quantity of money is not affected by the interest rate—therefore the money supply curve is vertical in the money market. As the interest rate rises, the quantity of loanable funds supplied increases—the incentive to save is higher when interest rates are higher. Therefore, the supply curve for loanable funds has a positive slope. You may be asked specifically to use one or the other of these models to explain your answer to questions dealing with monetary policy.

When you are not asked specifically to use one model or the other, remember that the money market determines the interest rate in the short run and the loanable funds market determines the interest rate in the long run. Use the money market to discuss short-run changes and the loanable funds market to discuss changes in the long run. However, in some cases it is possible to explain a situation using either model. In these cases, just be certain that your explanation is consistent and correct for the model you choose.

BEFORE YOU TAKE THE TEST: section 5

Draw The Featured Model: Money Market/Loanable Funds Market

Show the equilibrium interest rate and quantity in each market. (Hint: What is the slope of the supply curve in each market?)

Money Market

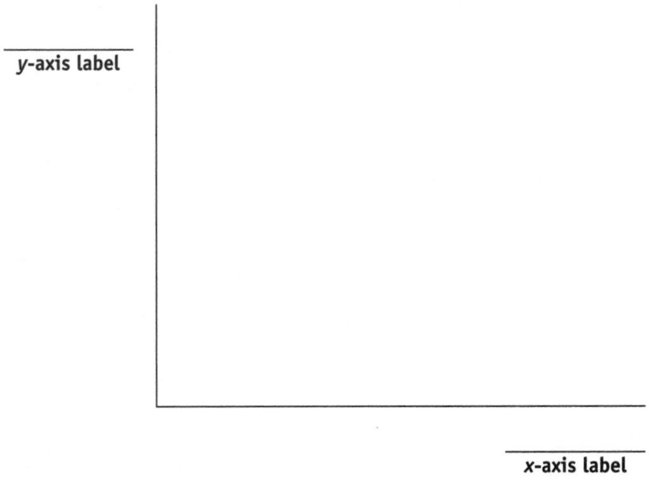

y-axis label

x-axis label

Loanable Funds Market

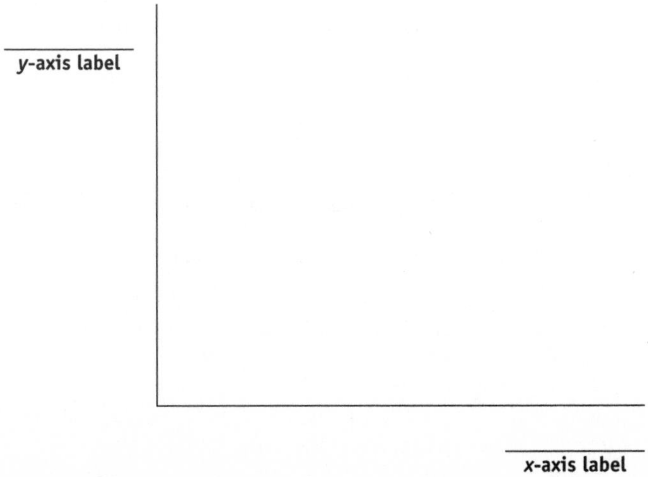

y-axis label

x-axis label

Complete the Exercises

1. Use the *AS–AD* model to complete this exercise.

   The economy of Macroland is initially in long-run equilibrium. Then the FOMC of Macroland decides to reduce interest rates through an open-market operation.

   a. Draw a graph representing the initial situation in Macroland. On your graph, be sure to include the short-run aggregate supply curve (*SRAS*), the long-run aggregate supply curve (*LRAS*), and the aggregate demand curve (*AD*). On your graph, mark the equilibrium aggregate price level and the aggregate output level as well as potential output.

   b. Draw a graph of the money market depicting Macroland's initial situation before the FOMC engages in monetary policy, as well as the effect of the FOMC's monetary policy actions. Be sure to indicate the initial equilibrium, as well as the equilibrium after the monetary policy.

   c. How does this monetary policy action affect the aggregate economy in the short run? Explain your answer verbally while also including a graph of the *AS–AD* model to illustrate your answer.

   d. How does this monetary policy action affect the aggregate economy in the long run?

Problems

1. You have won the lottery and can receive your winnings as a single payment of $2 million in cash now or you can receive a payment of $500,000 a year for five years starting now. The interest rate is constant at 10% per year. Which payment plan do you prefer?

2. Suppose Fantasia has a single bank that initially has $10,000 of deposits, reserves of $2,000, and loans of $8,000. To simplify our example, we will assume that bank capital is zero. Furthermore, Fantasia's central bank has a required reserve of 10% of deposits. All monetary transactions are made by check; no one in Fantasia uses currency.

   a. Construct a T-account depicting the initial situation in Fantasia. In your T-account, make sure you differentiate between required and excess reserves and that your T-account's assets equal its liabilities.

   b. Explain how you calculated the level of excess reserves in Fantasia.

   c. Suppose the bank in Fantasia lends these excess reserves [the amount of excess reserves you calculated in part (b)] until it reaches the point at which its excess reserves equal zero. How does this change the T-account?

   d. Did the money supply in Fantasia change when the bank loaned out the excess reserves? Explain your answer.

   e. What is the value of the money multiplier in Fantasia? Using the money multiplier, compute the change in deposits.

3. You are provided the following T-accounts for the central bank of Economia and the only commercial bank in Economia. In Economia, all financial transactions occur within the banking system; no one holds currency. The required reserve ratio imposed by the central bank is 20% of deposits. Suppose the central bank in Economia purchases $2,000 of Treasury bills from the commercial bank.

Central Bank of Economia

Assets		Liabilities	
Treasury bills	$20,000	Reserves	$20,000
Total assets	$20,000	Total liabilities	$20,000

Commercial Bank of Economia

Assets		Liabilities	
Required reserves	$20,000	Deposits	$100,000
Loans	$70,000	Capital	$20,000
Treasury bills	$30,000		
Total assets	$120,000	Total liabilities and capital	$120,000

a. Provide a T-account for both the central bank and the commercial bank showing the immediate effect of this transaction. Be sure to differentiate between required and excess reserves for the commercial bank.

b. Provide a T-account for the commercial bank once the commercial bank lends out its excess reserves and all adjustments have been made through the money multiplier process.

c. What happens to the money supply when the central bank purchases $2,000 of Treasury bills from the commercial bank?

d. Relate the change in the money supply to the money multiplier.

e. What was the monetary base initially?

f. What is the monetary base after all adjustments to the central bank's monetary policy have taken effect?

4. Use the following information about Macroland to answer these questions.

Bank deposits at the central bank	$100 million
Currency in bank vaults	$50 million
Currency held by the public	75 million
Checkable deposits	600 million
Traveler's checks	5 million

a. What are bank reserves equal to in Macroland?

b. Suppose banks hold no excess reserves in Macroland. What is the required reserve ratio, given the information in this table?

c. If the public does not change its currency holdings, what will happen to the level of checkable deposits in Macroland, relative to their initial level, if the central bank of Macroland purchases $10 million worth of Treasury bills in the open market? Explain your answer and provide a numerical answer.

d. If the public does not change its currency holdings, what will happen to the level of checkable deposits in Macroland, relative to their initial level, if the central bank of Macroland sells $5 million in Treasury bills on the open market? Explain your answer.

5. Use the following table to answer this question.

Change	Effect on nominal money demand	Effect on real money demand
Decrease in aggregate price level		
Increase in interest rate		
Change in regulation so that interest is now allowed on checking accounts		

    a. In the table above, enter how each scenario will affect nominal money demand and real money demand.

    b. Explain why a change in the aggregate price level affects the nominal demand curve differently from the way it affects the real money demand curve.

6. Use the following figure of the nominal money demand and money supply curves to answer these questions. Assume this market is initially in equilibrium with the nominal quantity of money equal to M_1 and the interest rate equal to r_1.

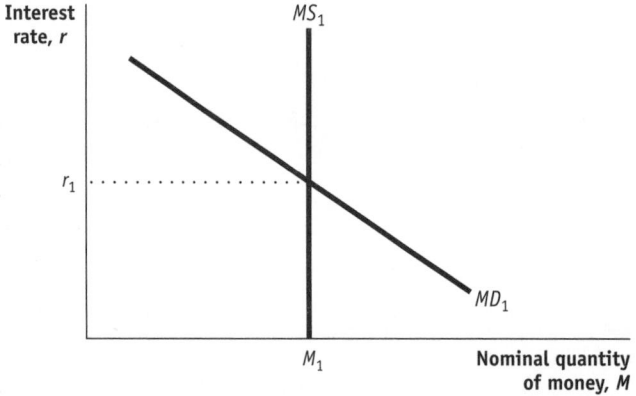

    a. Suppose the FOMC engages in an open-market purchase of Treasury bills. Holding everything else constant, what happens to the equilibrium quantity of money and the equilibrium interest rate? Sketch a graph illustrating these changes.

b. Suppose the FOMC engages in an open-market sale of Treasury bills. Holding everything else constant, what happens to the equilibrium quantity of money and the equilibrium interest rate? Sketch a graph illustrating these changes.

c. Suppose the aggregate price level increases. Holding everything else constant, what happens to the equilibrium quantity of money and the equilibrium interest rate? Sketch a graph illustrating these changes.

7. Use the *AS–AD* model to answer these questions.

The economy of Macroland is initially in long-run equilibrium. Then the central bank of Macroland decides to purchase Treasury bills on the open market.

a. Draw a graph representing the initial situation in Macroland. In your graph, be sure to include the short-run aggregate supply curve (*SRAS*), the long-run aggregate supply curve (*LRAS*), and the aggregate demand curve (*AD*). On your graph, mark the equilibrium aggregate price level and the aggregate output level, as well as potential output.

b. Draw a graph of the money market depicting Macroland's initial situation before the purchase of Treasury bills, as well as the effect of the purchase. Be sure to indicate the initial equilibrium as well as the final equilibrium.

c. How does the purchase of Treasury bills affect the aggregate economy in the short run?

d. How does the purchase of Treasury bills affect the aggregate economy in the long run?

8. Suppose that when the FOMC reduces the interest rate by 1 percentage point, it increases the level of investment spending by $500 million in Macroland. If the marginal propensity to save equals 0.25, what will be the total rise in real GDP, assuming the aggregate price level is held constant? Explain your answer.

9. For each of the following situations, determine the appropriate central bank monetary response.

a. The central bank adopts an interest rate target of 5%. Currently the interest rate in the economy is at 8%.

b. The central bank adopts an inflation target of 3%. Currently the inflation rate is 4%.

c. The central bank adopts an inflation target of 4%. Current inflation is 4%. However, this quarter the central bank expects data to reveal that the economy is entering a recession and has a projected negative output gap.

d. Current unemployment is greater than the natural rate of unemployment.

10. For each of the following situations, state the effect on the equilibrium interest rate and the equilibrium quantity of loanable funds. In your answer, make reference to how the demand and supply curves in the loanable funds market are affected. Hold everything else constant.

   a. Capital inflows into a country increase.

   b. The government reduces the government deficit.

   c. There is an increase in the expected inflation rate. Comment on the real interest rate as well as the nominal interest rate in your answer to this question.

   d. Private savings increase.

   e. Perceived business opportunities decrease.

Review Questions

Circle the correct answer.

1. Financial markets are beneficial
   A. to savers because they provide interest payments for the use of savers' funds.
   B. to borrowers because they provide a source of funds for productive investments.
   C. to the government because they provide both a use for surplus government funds and a source of funds should the government run a deficit.
   D. Answers (A), (B), and (C) are all correct.

2. Investment spending includes all of the following *except*
   A. the construction of a new residence during the current year.
   B. the purchase of a new piece of equipment at a factory during the current year.
   C. the purchase of a home, built 20 years ago, during the current year.
   D. the acquisition of new computers for a business during the current year.

3. Sources of funds for investment spending include

   A. domestic savings.
   B. foreign savings.
   C. the Federal Reserve Bank.
   D. Answers (A), (B), and (C) are all correct.
   E. Answers (A) and (B) are both correct.

4. When government spending is greater than net taxes,

   A. government savings is positive.
   B. there is a budget surplus.
   C. there is a positive surplus.
   D. there is a budget deficit.

5. Suppose a country exports goods and services worth $50 million, while it imports goods and services worth $60 million. This country

   A. has a positive capital inflow.
   B. lends funds to foreigners.
   C. has a negative capital inflow.
   D. Answers (A) and (B) are both correct.
   E. Answers (B) and (C) are both correct.

6. Given this T-account and assuming the bank holds no excess reserves, what is the required reserve ratio?

Assets		Liabilities	
Required reserves	$100	Deposits	$1,000
Loans	$400		
Treasury bills	$800		

   A. 10%   **B.** 40%   **C.** 80%   **D.** 1%

7. Given the T-account above, how much capital does this bank currently hold?

   A. zero
   B. $300
   C. $400
   D. $500
   E. $1,300

8. Refer to the T-account above. Suppose this is the only bank in the banking system. Furthermore, suppose all money is held in this bank and the bank holds no excess reserves. If the Fed makes an open-market sale of $50 worth of T-bills to this bank, what will happen to the money supply after all adjustments are made?

   A. The money supply will increase by $50.
   B. The money supply will decrease by $50.
   C. The money supply will increase by $500.
   D. The money supply will decrease by $500.

9. The monetary base consists of

   A. currency in circulation plus bank deposits.
   B. bank deposits plus bank reserves.
   C. bank deposits, bank reserves, and currency in circulation.
   D. currency in circulation plus bank reserves.

10. In a simple banking system, where banks hold no excess reserves and all funds are kept as bank deposits, then

  A. the money multiplier equals 1 divided by the required reserve ratio.
  B. total deposits will equal reserves multiplied by the reciprocal of the required reserve ratio.
  C. $1 increase in excess reserves will increase deposits by an amount equal to 1 divided by the required reserve ratio.
  D. Answers (A), (B), and (C) are all correct.

11. The three primary policy tools available to the Federal Reserve include

  A. reserve requirements, the ability to tax banks, and the discount rate.
  B. reserve requirements, the discount rate, and open-market operations.
  C. reserve requirements, the ability to tax banks, and open-market operations.
  D. the ability to tax banks, the discount rate, and open-market operations.

12. When banks borrow from one another, the rate of interest they pay for this loan is called the

  A. discount rate.   **B.** federal funds rate.

13. Suppose a hypothetical economy that uses a checkable-deposits-only monetary system has a required reserve ratio of 10%. When the central bank in this economy sells $10 million worth of Treasury bills, this will

  A. decrease the money supply by 10%.
  B. decrease the money supply by $10 million.
  C. decrease the money supply by $100 million.
  D. decrease the money supply by $1 million.

14. The opportunity cost of holding money

  A. is always greater than the short-term interest rate.
  B. is the difference between the interest rate on assets that are not money and the interest rate on assets that are money.
  C. is the long-term interest rate.
  D. is always zero because it costs you nothing to hold money.

15. Which of the following statements is true?

  A. The real quantity of money is the nominal amount of money divided by the aggregate price level.
  B. The real quantity of money measures the purchasing power of the nominal quantity of money.
  C. The real quantity of money is proportional to the nominal quantity of money for any given interest rate.
  D. All of the above statements are true.
  E. Answers (A) and (B) are both true.
  F. Answers (A) and (C) are both true.
  G. Answers (B) and (C) are both true.

16. If the price level doubles, holding everything else constant, we know that

  A. the nominal quantity of money demanded also doubled.
  B. the real quantity of money demanded also doubled.
  C. the interest rate also doubled.
  D. Answers (A) and (B) are both correct.

17. The Federal Open Market Committee sets a target interest rate and achieves it through

    A. open-market purchases, if the federal funds rate is initially less than the target rate.
    B. open-market sales, if the federal funds rate is initially less than the target rate.
    C. legislative action by Congress that decrees the level of the discount rate and thus the federal funds rate.
    D. stimulating the demand for money, if the initial interest rate is less than the target rate.

18. The liquidity preference model of interest rate determination states that

    A. interest rates are determined solely by the Federal Open Market Committee.
    B. interest rates are determined by the supply of and demand for money.
    C. people always prefer liquidity and do not consider the opportunity cost of holding money when they decide how much money they wish to hold at any given time.
    D. interest rates are determined in the market for nonmonetary assets and not the market for money.

19. The money supply curve in the liquidity preference model is drawn as a vertical line because

    A. there is only one level of money supply that will enable an economy to produce at the full employment level of output and the appropriate aggregate price level.
    B. Congress sets by law the level of the money supply in the economy.
    C. the Fed can control the level of the money supply through its open-market operations.
    D. the money supply curve is unimportant in determining the equilibrium level of interest rates in the liquidity preference model.

20. The money supply curve shifts to the left. The most likely cause for this shift is the FOMC's open-market

    A. purchase of Treasury bills.
    B. sale of Treasury bills.

21. The money demand curve shifts to the right. The most likely cause for this shift is

    A. an increase in the interest rate.
    B. a decrease in the interest rate.
    C. a change in bank institutions that allows banks to pay even higher rates of interest on checking account funds.
    D. Answers (B) and (C) are both correct.

22. Expansionary monetary policy will, holding everything else constant,

    A. lower the interest rate and cause *AD* to shift to the right.
    B. lower the interest rate and cause *AD* to shift to the left.
    C. raise the interest rate and cause *AD* to shift to the right.
    D. raise the interest rate and cause *AD* to shift to the left.

23. Suppose in the short run the level of aggregate output in an economy decreases at the same time the aggregate price level decreases. This is most likely due to a

    A. leftward shift in the short-run aggregate supply curve, holding everything else constant.
    B. rightward shift in the short-run aggregate supply curve, holding everything else constant.
    C. leftward shift in the aggregate demand curve, holding everything else constant.
    D. rightward shift in the aggregate demand curve, holding everything else constant.

24. When the economy is currently producing at a short-run level of aggregate output that is less than potential output, it is most likely that the Fed will engage in open-market

    A. purchases of Treasury bills.
    B. sales of Treasury bills.

25. The Taylor rule for monetary policy provides guidance for setting the federal funds rate and states that this rate should be set by considering

   A. both the inflation rate and the output gap.
   B. both the inflation rate and the level of unemployment.
   C. both the output gap and the level of unemployment.
   D. the inflation rate, the output gap, and the level of unemployment.

26. Inflation targeting means that

   A. the central bank adheres to maintaining a very strict interest rate target.
   B. the central bank announces the inflation rate it is trying to achieve and then uses monetary policy to achieve it.
   C. there may be a range of acceptable inflation rates or a specific inflation rate that the central bank hopes to achieve through monetary policy.
   D. Answers (A), (B), and (C) are all correct.
   E. Answers (B) and (C) are both correct.

27. The loanable funds market

   A. provides a market where savers and borrowers can make mutually beneficial transactions.
   B. uses supply and demand to determine an equilibrium price or interest rate.
   C. interest rate is the return a lender receives for allowing borrowers the use of one dollar for one year.
   D. Answers (A), (B), and (C) are all correct.

28. When the government runs a deficit, this shifts the

   A. supply of loanable funds curve to the right.
   B. supply of loanable funds curve to the left.
   C. demand for loanable funds curve to the right.
   D. demand for loanable funds curve to the left.

29. In the loanable funds market, which of the following statements is true?

   A. Savers are best represented by the demand for loanable funds curve.
   B. Borrowers are best represented by the demand for loanable funds curve.
   C. The equilibrium interest rate equates the quantity of loanable funds supplied to the quantity of loanable funds demanded.
   D. Answers (A), (B), and (C) are all true.
   E. Answers (A) and (B) are both true.
   F. Answers (B) and (C) are both true.
   G. Answers (A) and (C) are both true.

30. In the short run, money is

   A. neutral because it can have no real effect on aggregate output.
   B. not neutral because changes in the money supply can cause real aggregate output to change.

ANSWER KEY

Fill-in-the-Blanks

Module 22: (1) savings; (2) surplus; (3) deficit; (4) national savings; (5) capital; (6) transactions costs, risk; (7) liquidity; (8) financial intermediary

Module 23: (1) money; (2) medium of exchange, unit of account, store of value; (3) fiat; (4) M1, M2; (5) M1; (6) near-moneys

Module 24: (1) today, (2) present value, (3) $1/(1+r)$, (4) net present value

Module 25: (1) bank reserves; (2) reserve ratio; (3) bank run; (4) deposit insurance, capital requirements, reserve requirements; (5) 250,000; (6) Federal Reserve; (7) discount; (8) excess

Module 26: (1) Federal Reserve, (2) Board of Governors, (3)12, (4) 7, (5)14, (6) open-market operations, (7) commercial, (8) investment

Module 27: (1) commercial; (2) monetary; (3) discount rate, reserve requirement, open-market operations; (4) federal funds, (5) discount, (6) Open-market

Module 28: (1) interest; (2) money demand; (3) aggregate price level, real GDP, technology, institutions; (4) vertical; (5) Fed; (6) loanable

Module 29: (1) loanable funds, (2) rate of return, (3) perceived business opportunities, (4) government borrowing, (5) crowding out, (6) private saving, (7) capital inflows, (8) inflation

Featured Graph

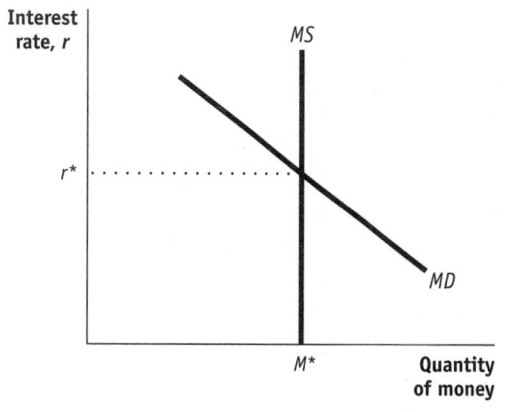

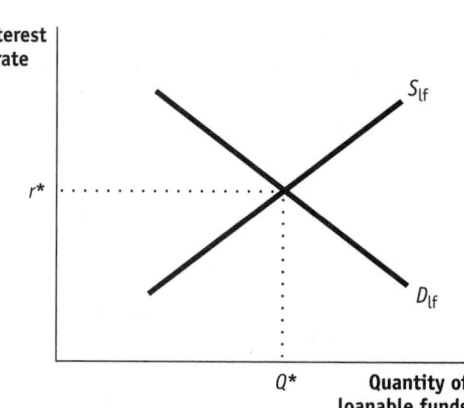

Exercise

a.

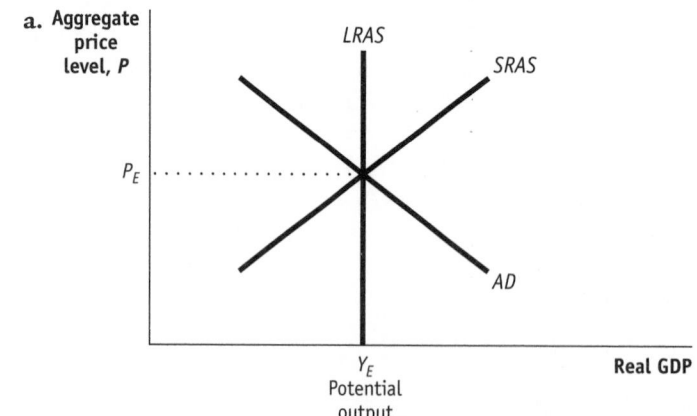

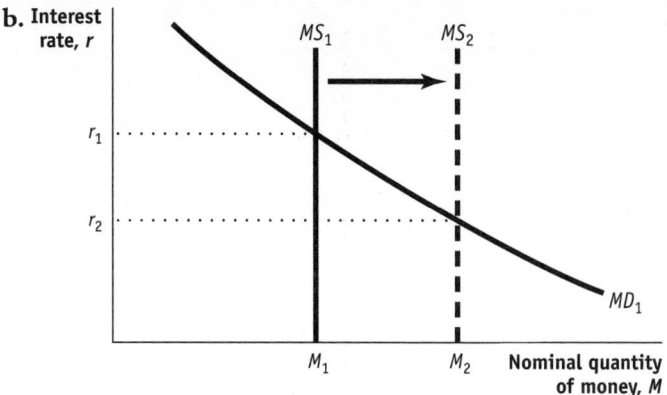

b.

c. When the FOMC reduces interest rates through an open-market purchase of Treasury bills, this increases aggregate demand and causes the *AD* curve to shift to the right, to AD_2. In the short run, this causes aggregate real output to increase to Y_2 and the aggregate price level to increase to P_2. This is illustrated in the following figure.

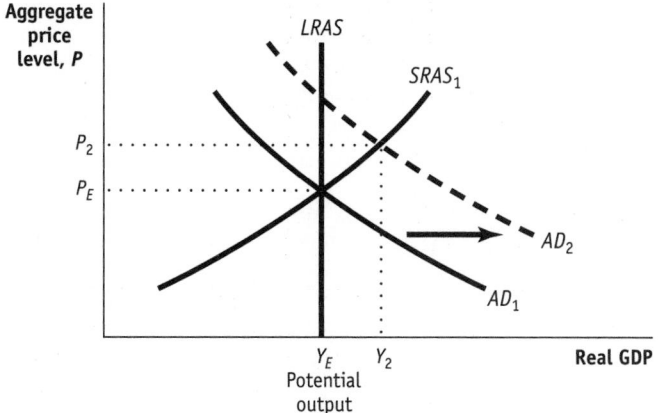

d. In the long run, the economy must return to producing its potential output, Y_E. This economic adjustment will occur as the *SRAS* curve shifts to the left as nominal wages rise. As the *SRAS* curve shifts back to $SRAS_3$, this will eliminate the inflationary gap, restore the economy to its potential output level, and lead to an even higher aggregate price level, P_3. The following figure illustrates this long-run adjustment.

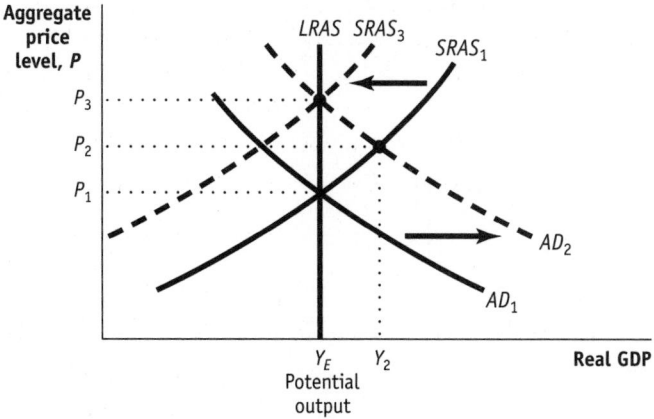

Answers to Problems

1. Compare the present value of the future payments to the single payment now. The present value is $\$500,000 + (\$500,000)/(1.1) + (\$500,000)/(1.1)^2 + (\$500,000)/(1.1)3 + (\$500,000)/(1.1)4 = \$2,086,164$, which is greater than \$2 million.

2. a.

Assets		Liabilities	
Required reserves	$1,000	Deposits	$10,000
Excess reserves	$1,000		
Loans	$8,000		
Total assets	$10,000	Total liabilities	$10,000

b. Excess reserves are equal to total reserves minus required reserves, or $1,000. To find required reserves, multiply deposits by the required reserve ratio [($10,000)(0.1) = $1,000].

c.

Assets		Liabilities	
Required reserves	$2,000	Deposits	$20,000
Excess reserves	0		
Loans	$18,000		
Total assets	$20,000	Total liabilities	$20,000

d. Yes, because the money supply is defined as bank deposits plus currency in circulation. Because Fantasia has no currency in circulation, we need to consider only what happens to bank deposits. Initially, bank deposits equaled $10,000, and after the lending out of all the excess reserves, bank deposits equaled $20,000. Thus, the money supply increased by $10,000.

e. The money multiplier is $1/rr$, or 10 in this example, since no one holds currency and the bank does not hold excess reserves. The change in deposits equals the money multiplier times the change in reserves or, in this case, the change in deposits equals $(1/.1)($1,000)$ or $10,000.

3. a.

Central Bank of Economia

Assets		Liabilities	
Treasury bills	$22,000	Reserves	$22,000
Total assets	$22,000	Total liabilities	$22,000

Commercial Bank of Economia

Assets		Liabilities	
Required reserves	$20,000	Deposits	$100,000
Excess reserves	$2,000	Capital	$20,000
Loans	$70,000		
Treasury bills	$28,000		
Total assets	$120,000	Total liabilities and capital	$120,000

b.

Commercial Bank of Economia

Assets		Liabilities	
Required reserves	$22,000	Deposits	$110,000
Loans	$80,000	Capital	$20,000
Treasury bills	$28,000		
Total assets	$130,000	Total liabilities	$130,000

c. The money supply increases from $100,000 to $110,000. Recall that the money supply equals checkable deposits plus currency in circulation; because Economia has no currency in circulation, the money supply equals the level of deposits.

d. The change in the money supply equals the money multiplier times the change in the monetary base. In this problem, the money multiplier is 5, and the change in the monetary base is the $2,000 increase in reserves that occurs when the central bank purchases the Treasury bills.

e. The monetary base equals reserves plus currency in circulation. In Economia, currency in circulation is zero, so the monetary base is equivalent to reserves. Initially, the monetary base was $20,000.

f. The monetary base increases to $22,000.

4. a. Bank reserves equal currency in bank vaults plus bank deposits at the central bank, or $150 million.

b. We can calculate the required reserve ratio, rr, as the ratio of required reserves to checkable deposits. Because there are no excess reserves in Macroland, the bank reserves calculated in part (a) equal the required reserves:thus, $150 million/$600 million equals a required reserve ratio of 0.25.

c. When the central bank of Macroland purchases $10 million in Treasury bills, the level of reserves in the banking system increases by $10 million. This increase in reserves starts the multiplier process; the change in the money supply is calculated as the increase in reserves times the money multiplier, or ($10 million)(4) = $40 million. Thus, the money supply increases by $40 million when the Central Bank purchases Treasury bills on the open market.

d. Using the concept explained in part (c), this sale of Treasury bills by the central bank will decrease the money supply by $20 million. We can see this by recalling that the change in the money supply equals the change in reserves times the money multiplier or (–$5 million)(4), or –$20 million.

5. a.

Change	Effect on nominal money demand	Effect on real money demand
Decrease in aggregate price level	Shifts the nominal money demand curve to the left	Has no effect
Increase in interest rate	Causes a movement along the nominal money demand curve	Causes a movement along the real money demand curve
Change in regulation so that interest is now allowed on checking accounts	Shifts the nominal money demand curve to the right	Shifts the real money demand curve to the right

b. When the aggregate price level changes, the nominal money demand curve does not automatically take into account the effect of this change in prices on the nominal demand for money. For example, as the aggregate price level rises, people will find that, due to the increase in the aggregate price level, they need to hold greater amounts of money in order to make their transactions. This causes the nominal money demand curve to shift to the right; people demand a greater quantity of nominal money at every interest rate. In contrast, the real money demand curve automatically takes into account any change in the aggregate price level; a change in the aggregate price level requires a proportionately equal change in the nominal quantity of money in order that the real quantity of money is unchanged.

6. a. When the Fed increases the money supply through an open-market purchase of Treasury bills, the money supply curve shifts from MS_1 to MS_2, resulting in a decrease in the equilibrium interest rate from r_1 to r_2 and an increase in the equilibrium quantity of money from M_1 to M_2. The following figure illustrates these changes.

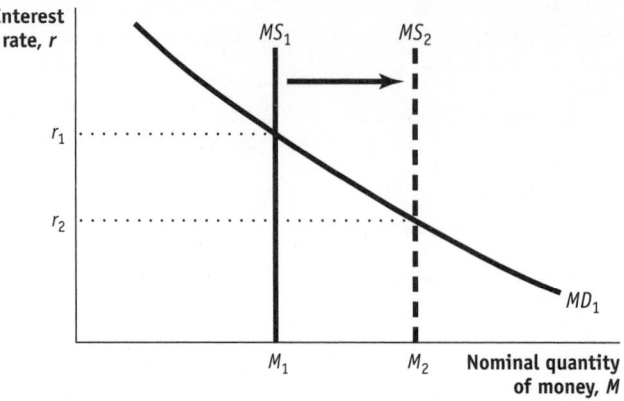

b. When the FOMC decreases the money supply through an open-market sale of Treasury bills, the money supply curve shifts from MS_1 to MS_2. This causes the equilibrium interest rate to increase from r_1 to r_2, while the equilibrium quantity of money decreases from M_1 to M_2. These changes are illustrated in the following figure.

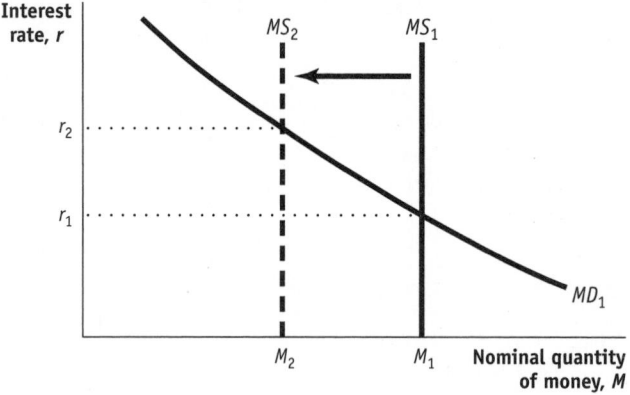

c. An increase in the aggregate price level shifts the nominal money demand curve to the right, from MD_1 to MD_2. This causes the equilibrium interest rate to increase from r_1 to r_2, while the equilibrium quantity of money is unchanged. The following figure illustrates this situation.

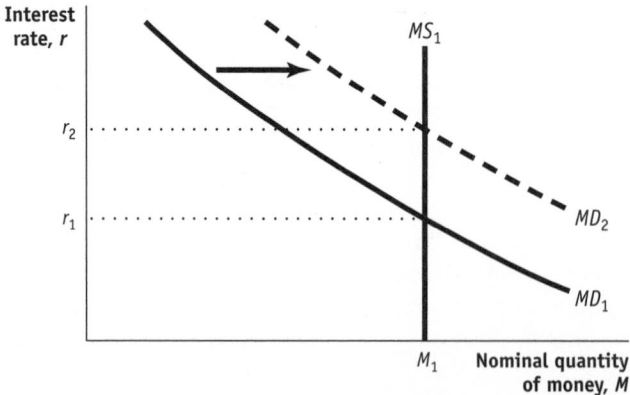

7. a. Aggregate price level, P

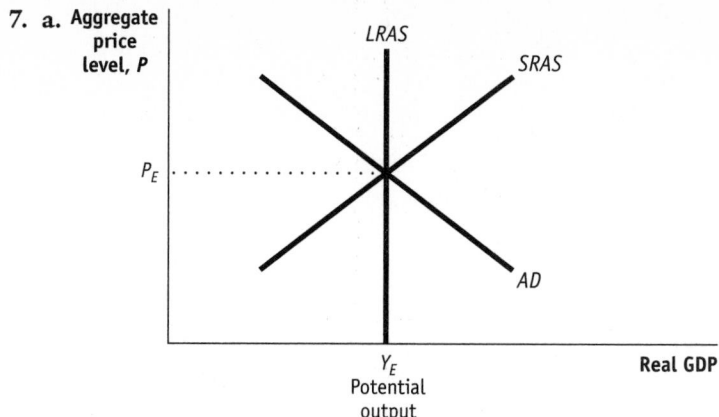

b. Interest rate, r

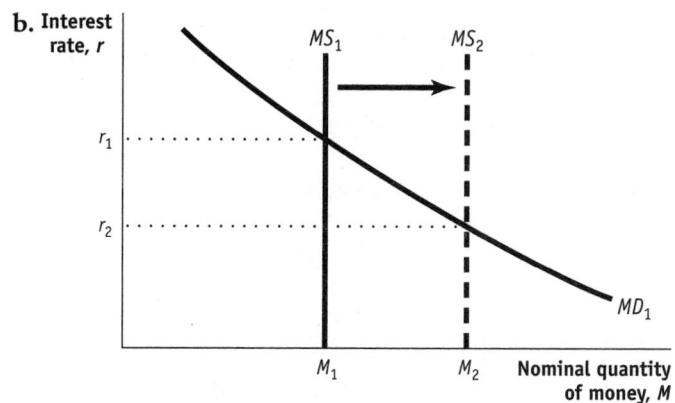

c. When the FOMC reduces interest rates through an open-market purchase of Treasury bills, aggregate demand increases and causes the AD curve to shift to the right, to AD_2. In the short run, this causes aggregate real output to increase to Y_2 and the aggregate price level to increase to P_2.

d. In the long run, the economy must return to producing its potential output, Y_E. This economic adjustment will occur as the $SRAS$ curve shifts to the left as nominal wages rise. As the $SRAS$ curve shifts back to $SRAS_3$, this will eliminate the inflationary gap, restore the economy to its potential output level, and lead to an even higher aggregate price level, P_3.

8. The action by the FOMC effectively creates a change in autonomous investment spending of $500 million. This change in autonomous investment spending will cause real GDP to increase by a larger, multiplied amount due to the multiplier process. Since the multiplier equals $1/(1 - MPC)$ or, in this case, 4, we can compute the total change in real GDP as 4($500 million), or $2 billion.

9. a. The central bank will want to decrease the interest rate. It can accomplish this goal by engaging in open-market purchases of Treasury bills.

b. The central bank wants to reduce the inflation rate. It can do this by increasing the interest rate because this will slow the economy and result in a smaller output gap, which will help to pull the interest rate and, therefore, the rate of inflation down in the economy. The central bank should engage in open-market sales of Treasury bills.

c. Because the central bank anticipates a slowdown in the economy, it also anticipates downward pressure on the aggregate price level as the level of spending in the economy falls. The central bank can stabilize the aggregate price level by engaging in expansionary monetary policy; the central bank should engage in open-market purchases of Treasury bills.

d. Because the current rate of unemployment is greater than the potential rate of unemployment, the economy is in a recession. The central bank will want to engage in expansionary monetary policy unless it is actively seeking to reduce the targeted rate of inflation and the actual rate of inflation in the economy.

10. a. An increase in capital inflows into a country will shift the supply of loanable funds curve to the right, which will cause the equilibrium interest rate to decrease and the equilibrium quantity of loanable funds to increase.

   b. When the government reduces its deficit level, the demand for loanable funds from the government has diminished. This will cause the demand for loanable funds curve to shift to the left and result in a decrease in both the equilibrium interest rate and the total equilibrium quantity of loanable funds. But, because the interest rate is now lower, the quantity of funds for private investment spending will increase.

   c. Both the demand and the supply curves for loanable funds will shift due to the change in expected inflation. The demand curve will shift to the right, reflecting the fact that borrowers are willing to borrow just as much as they did at the original nominal interest rate as they are now willing to borrow at the higher nominal interest rate. (Remember that the real interest rate is the nominal interest rate minus the inflation rate.) The supply curve will shift to the left because lenders now are willing to lend the same amount of funds only if the nominal interest rate they receive reflects the new higher expected inflation rate. Both curves shift, resulting in the nominal interest rate rising by the amount of the change in the expected inflation rate; there is no change in the equilibrium quantity of loanable funds.

   d. An increase in private savings will cause the supply of loanable funds curve to shift to the right, resulting in a decrease in the equilibrium interest rate and an increase in the equilibrium quantity of loanable funds.

   e. When there is a decrease in perceived business opportunities, the demand for loanable funds curve will shift to the left, which will result in both the equilibrium interest rate and the equilibrium quantity of loanable funds decreasing.

Answers to Review Questions

1. **D.** Financial markets provide funds for those who need to borrow funds, as well as a means of earning interest for those with surplus funds.

2. **C.** Investment spending refers to spending on the economy's stock of physical capital. It includes spending on physical equipment, inventories, and new construction. It does not include the selling of a pre-existing structure because this represents a change of ownership rather than new productive capacity.

3. **E.** The Federal Reserve Bank is not a source of funds for investment spending, while domestic and foreign savings do provide funds for investment spending.

4. **D.** If the government spends more than its net revenue, it runs a budget deficit or a negative surplus. This implies that government saving is negative.

5. **A.** Capital inflow is defined as imports minus exports. In this case, capital inflow is positive. When capital inflow is positive, the country spends more on imports than it earns from exports and must therefore borrow the difference from foreigners.

6. **A.** The required reserve ratio is equal to the required reserves divided by checkable deposits. In this example, the bank holds 10% of its checkable deposits as required reserves.

7. **B.** The bank's capital is the difference between its total assets and total liabilities. In this case, the bank's assets are $1,300 while the liabilities total $1,000. The difference, $300, is the bank's capital.

8. **D.** When the Fed sells $50 worth of T-bills, it debits the reserve account of the bank that sells them. This results in the bank having insufficient reserves to support its current level of deposits. The bank will contract the loans it holds until the deposits in the bank are the amount that can be supported by the new level of reserves. The new reserves in this problem equal $50 (the initial $100 minus the $50 spent on the T-bills). The $50 in reserves can support $500 in deposits when the required reserve ratio is 10. So the money supply will decrease from $1,000 to $500, or $500.

9. **D.** The monetary base consists of currency in circulation and bank reserves, while the money supply equals currency in circulation plus bank deposits.

10. **D.** All of the statements restate the relationship between excess reserves and the required reserve ratio and their impact on the level of bank deposits. We can write this relationship as the change in bank deposits equals excess reserves times $(1/rr)$. Recall that $1/rr$ is simply the reciprocal of the required reserve ratio.

11. **B.** The Federal Reserve can affect the money supply by engaging in open-market operations in which it either purchases or sells Treasury bills. The Fed can also affect the money supply by changing the reserve requirements. When the reserve requirement increases, the money supply decreases; when the Fed reduces the reserve requirement, the money supply increases. Finally, the Fed can affect the money supply by changing the discount rate. When the discount rate falls relative to the federal funds rate, it is relatively cheaper to borrow from the Fed, which leads to increases in the money supply.

12. **B.** The interest rate charged for loans from one bank to another is called the federal funds rate. The interest rate charged for a loan to a bank from the Fed is called the discount rate.

13. **C.** When the required reserve ratio is 10%, the money multiplier is 10 in a checkable-deposits-only monetary system. Thus, an open-market sale of $10 million worth of Treasury bills will result in a $100 million decrease in the money supply.

14. **B.** The opportunity cost of holding money is measured by what is given up when money is held. This is calculated as the difference between the rate of return you could earn by holding nonmonetary assets minus the rate of return on monetary assets.

15. **E.** The first two statements are true by definition. The real quantity of money is not proportional to the nominal quantity of money. However, the nominal quantity of money demanded is proportional to the aggregate price level.

16. **A.** To maintain the initial level of purchasing power, when the aggregate price level doubles, the nominal quantity of money demanded will also double. However, a doubling of prices will have no effect on the real quantity of money demanded because the real money demand is, by definition, the amount of money that holds purchasing power constant. Holding everything else constant, assumes that a doubling of the price level will have no impact on the interest rate.

17. **B.** If the target interest rate is greater than the federal funds rate, then the Fed needs to engage in monetary policy that will shift the money supply curve to the left, resulting in an increase in interest rates for a given money demand curve. The FOMC, therefore, will engage in open-market sales of Treasury bills. Congress does not set the discount rate, and the Fed's monetary policy affects the money supply curve, not the money demand curve.

18. **B.** The liquidity preference model uses the interaction between the demand for money and the supply of money to determine interest rates. Interest rates are impacted by Federal Reserve policy and its effect on the money supply curve. People consider the opportunity cost of holding money when making decisions about the amount of money they wish to hold.

One can model interest rate determination in the framework of either money demand and supply or the demand and supply of loanable funds.

19. **C.** The Fed controls the money supply through open-market operations. We know that the determination of interest rates depends not only on the demand for money but also on the supply of money. Congress does not have the authority to determine the country's money supply. Different levels of money supply are compatible with the full-employment level of output because interest rate determination depends on both the money supply and the money demand.

20. **B.** When the FOMC engages in open-market sales of Treasury bills, it sells Treasury bills to the public and receive dollars for those Treasury bills. The FOMC effectively removes reserves from the banking system with the sale of Treasury bills, which reduces the quantity of money supplied at every interest rate; the supply of money curve shifts to the left.

21. **C.** A change in the interest rate, whether an increase or a decrease, causes a movement along the money demand curve. An increase in the amount of interest banks can pay on checking account funds reduces the opportunity cost of holding funds in a checking account rather than in an interest-bearing asset; people will increase the quantity of money they demand at every interest rate with this change, which will result in the money demand curve shifting to the right.

22. **A.** Expansionary monetary policy is an increase in the money supply. When the money supply increases, the supply of money curve shifts to the right, causing the interest rate to fall. A fall in the interest rate results in higher investment spending and consumption spending, which causes the *AD* curve to shift to the right.

23. **C.** If there is only one shift in either the short-run *AS* curve or the *AD* curve, then a fall in both the aggregate output level and the aggregate price level is only possible with a leftward shift of the *AD* curve.

24. **A.** When the current level of aggregate output is less than potential output, the Fed will likely engage in expansionary monetary policy to stimulate the economy to return to the potential output level. Expansionary monetary policy implies that the Fed is increasing the money supply; hence, the Fed is purchasing Treasury bills in the open market.

25. **A.** The original Taylor rule for setting the federal funds rate is given by the following equation: federal funds rate = 1 + (1.5 × inflation rate) + (0.5 × output gap). Although there is a relationship between the level of output and the unemployment rate, the Taylor rule does not explicitly include the unemployment rate.

26. **E.** Inflation targeting involves having the central bank announce the inflation rate or range for the inflation rate it is trying to achieve and then using its monetary policy to achieve this announced goal. Monetary policy to achieve a stated inflation goal will necessarily imply the loss of interest rate control because the interest rate will need to vary in order for the central bank to achieve its inflation target.

27. **D.** The loanable funds market is a hypothetical market in which savers can lend money or supply funds to borrowers. The price for borrowing funds is the interest rate, or the return the lender of funds receives for loaning out one dollar for one year.

28. **C.** When the government runs a deficit, it becomes a borrower in the loanable funds market and the demand curve for loanable funds shifts to the right at any given interest rate.

29. **F.** The demand for loanable funds curve represents borrowers who enter this market in order to demand funds for investment spending. The supply of loanable funds curve repre-

sents savers who provide excess funds to this market in order to supply these excess funds to those individuals who want to borrow funds. The equilibrium interest rate equates the supply of funds with the demand for funds.

30. **B.** In the short run money is not neutral. When the central bank changes the money supply, the *AD* curve shifts and, in the short run, this shift will cause the economy to either contract or expand. In the long run, the short-run aggregate supply curve shifts, returning the aggregate economy to its potential output level. In the long run, money is neutral because it cannot alter the level of aggregate real output.

Notes

Inflation, Unemployment, and Stabilization Policies

OVERVIEW

This section uses the models introduced in Sections 4 and 5 to further develop our understanding of stabilization policies (both fiscal and monetary), including their long-run effects on the economy. In addition, we introduce the Phillips curve to investigate the role of expectations in the economy. The section ends with a brief summary of the history of macroeconomic thought and how the modern consensus view of stabilization policy has developed.

FEATURED MODEL/GRAPH: THE PHILLIPS CURVE

This section presents the Phillips curve, which shows the relationship between unexpected inflation and unemployment.

MODULES IN THIS SECTION

Module 30: Long-run Implications of Fiscal Policy: Deficits and the Public Debt

Module 31: Monetary Policy and the Interest Rate

Module 32: Money, Output, and Prices in the Long Run

Module 33: Types of Inflation, Disinflation, and Deflation

Module 34: Inflation and Unemployment: The Phillips Curve

Module 35: History and Alternative Views of Macroeconomics

Module 36: The Modern Macroeconomic Consensus

Module 30

Long-Run Implications of Fiscal Policy: Deficits and the Public Debt

Before You Read the MODULE

Summary

This module presents some of the long-term effects of fiscal policy, including budget balance, debt, and liabilities.

Module Objectives

Review these objectives before you read the module. Place a "√" on the line when you understand each of the following:

_____**Objective 1.** Why governments calculate the **cyclically adjusted budget balance**

_____**Objective 2.** Why a large **public debt** may be a cause for concern

_____**Objective 3.** Why **implicit liabilities** of the government are also a cause for concern

While You Read the MODULE

Key Terms

Define these key terms as you read the module.

Cyclically adjusted budget balance

Fiscal year

Public debt

Debt–GDP ratio

Implicit liabilities

List questions or difficulties from your initial reading of the module.

After You Read the MODULE

Fill-in-the-Blanks

Fill in the blanks to complete the following statements. Terms may be used more than once. If you find yourself having difficulties, please refer to the appropriate section in the text.

- The budget balance, also known as savings by government, is defined by the

    equation (1)_____. The budget balance is reduced

    by (2)_____ fiscal policies, while it is increased by

    (3)_____ fiscal policies.

- When the government spends more than it receives in tax revenue, it results in a

    budget (4)_____. In these situations, the government

    must borrow money and over time that borrowing increases the national

    (5)_____, which is clearly affected by the business cycle.

    An estimate of what the budget balance would be if real GDP were exactly equal to

    potential output (i.e., there is no recession or expansion) is known as the

    (6)_____ budget balance.

- The (7)_____ ratio is used to assess the ability of governments to pay their debt. But the financial situation of a country can be worse than it appears because of (8)_____, which are spending promises made by governments that are effectively a debt, despite the fact that they are not included in the usual debt statistics.

The Deficit or the Debt?

One common mistake—it happens all the time in newspaper reports—is to confuse *deficits* with *debt*. A *deficit* is the difference between the amount of money a government spends and the amount it receives in taxes over a given period—usually, though not always, a year. Deficit numbers always come with a statement about the time period to which they apply, as in "the U.S. budget deficit in *fiscal 2008* was $410 billion." A *debt* is the sum of money a government owes at a particular point in time. Debt numbers usually come with a specific date, as in "U.S. public debt *at the end of fiscal 2008* was $5.8 trillion." Deficits and debt are linked, because government debt grows when governments run deficits. But they aren't the same thing, and they can even tell different stories. For example, at the end of fiscal 2008, U.S. *debt* as a percentage of GDP was fairly low by historical standards, but the *deficit* during fiscal 2008 was considered quite high.

- You will want to understand what the cyclically adjusted budget balance is and how it relates to the budget balance and to potential GDP. The cyclically adjusted budget balance is an estimate of what the budget balance would be if real GDP were exactly equal to potential GDP. This measure takes into account the extra tax revenue the government would receive and the smaller level of transfer payments the government would make if the recessionary gap were eliminated or the tax revenue the government would lose and the extra transfer payments the government would make if the inflationary gap were eliminated. The cyclically adjusted budget balance fluctuates less than the actual budget deficit, because years with a large budget deficit are typically associated with large recessionary gaps.

Module ③① Monetary Policy and the Interest Rate

Before You Read the MODULE

....

Summary

This module shows how to use the money market and the loanable funds market to explain how the Federal Reserve can use monetary policy to stabilize the economy in the short run.

Module Objectives

Review these objectives before you read the module. Place a "√" on the line when you understand each of the following:

_____**Objective 1.** How the Federal Reserve implements monetary policy, moving the interest rate to affect aggregate output

_____**Objective 2.** Why monetary policy is the main tool for stabilizing the economy

While You Read the MODULE

....

Key Terms

Define these key terms as you read the module.

Target federal funds rate
_____

Expansionary monetary policy
_____

Contractionary monetary policy
_____

Taylor rule for monetary policy
_____

Inflation targeting
_____

List questions or difficulties from your initial reading of the module.

After You Read the MODULE

Fill-in-the-Blanks

Fill in the blanks to complete the following statements. Terms may be used more than once. If you find your-self having difficulties, please refer to the appropriate section in the text.

- At each FOMC meeting, the Federal Reserve sets the target

  (1)_____ rate. The target is enforced by the Open Market Desk

  of the Federal Reserve Bank of (2)_____. If the rate needs to be

  lowered, the Open Market Desk will (3)_____ Treasury bills to

  (4)_____ the money supply so that the rate will fall.

- If the Fed pursues contractionary monetary policy, it (5)_____

  the money supply so that the interest rate will (6)_____. The

  new interest rate will result in (7)_____ investment spending

  and (8)_____ real GDP.

Module Review

The Fed's Target

Over the years, the Federal Reserve has changed how it makes monetary policy. In the late 1970s and early 1980s, it set a target level for the money supply and altered the monetary base to achieve it. Under this policy, the federal funds rate fluctuated freely. Today the Fed does the reverse, it sets a target for the federal funds rate and allows the money supply to fluctuate to achieve the target. A common mistake is to believe these changes in the way the Federal Reserve operates alter the way the money market works. People will sometimes say that the interest rate does not reflect the supply and demand for money because the Fed sets it. In fact, the money market works the same way as always: the interest rate is determined by the supply and demand for money. The only difference is that now the Fed adjusts the supply of money to achieve its target interest rate. It's important not to confuse a change in the Fed's operating procedure with a change in the way the economy works.

Module 32
Money, Output, and Prices in the Long Run

Before You Read the MODULE

Summary

This module analyzes how a counter-productive action by a central bank can actually destabilize the economy in the short run.

Module Objectives

Review these objectives before you read the module. Place a "√" on the line when you understand each of the following:

_____**Objective 1.** How a counter-productive monetary policy action can destabilize the economy

_____**Objective 2.** Why economists believe in **monetary neutrality**—that monetary policy affects only the price level, not aggregate output, in the long run

While You Read the MODULE

Key Term

Define this key term as you read the module.

Monetary neutrality

List questions or difficulties from your initial reading of the module.

After You Read the MODULE

Fill-in-the-Blanks

Fill in the blanks to complete the following statements. Terms may be used more than once. If you find yourself having difficulties, please refer to the appropriate section in the text.

- Monetary policy can be destabilizing if the Fed pursues (1)_____

  policies during a recession or (2)_____ policies when there

  is inflation.

- Attempts to move the economy to a point above or below potential output in the long run

  will not work because the economy will adjust through a shift in the aggregate supply

  curve caused by a change in (3)_____.

- In the long run, the only effect of an increase in the money supply is to raise the aggregate

  price level by an equal percentage. This describes the concept known as money

  (4)_____.

Module Review

The Fed and Inflation

In the long run, changes in the quantity of money affect the aggregate price level, but they do not change real aggregate output or the interest rate. Therefore, in the long run, the Federal Reserve can affect only the aggregate price level. So, while short-run stabilization policy is an important function of monetary policy, the Federal Reserve keeps a close eye on the aggregate price level to ensure that monetary policy prevents inflation or deflation in the long run. Because the aggregate price level is the only variable monetary policy can affect in the long run, it is a primary focus of the Fed. Achieving stable prices in the long run is the best way for the Fed to promote a stable, growing economy.

We noted in the previous module that the Federal Reserve does not have an explicit inflation target for the U.S. economy. However, we know that the Fed is very careful to avoid deflation—which, in practical terms, means accepting a very low level of inflation. Trying to achieve an inflation rate of zero is too difficult and runs the risk of allowing deflation in the economy. As we have said, it is widely believed to prefer inflation at around 2% per year. But the Fed does not have an explicitly stated target for inflation. Rather, the Federal Open Market Committee sets a target federal funds rate. Can an implicit inflation target lead to price stability in the long run? If people believe, as many do, that the Fed will keep inflation at around 2%, then 2% will serve as an anchor for inflationary expectations. That is, if people believe that inflation will be kept at 2%, then they build 2% inflation into their decisions for the future. Wages, prices, and interest rates. are all determined with the expectation that there will be 2% inflation. If there is, in fact, 2% inflation, then inflation has no effect on real values in the economy. Nominal values are adjusted upwards by the 2% inflation that everyone expects and real values stay the same. By providing an anchor for expectations, an implicit inflation target can serve to stabilize the economy as long as people believe the implicit target will be met. And one important key to maintaining the belief that the implicit target will be met is for the Fed to meet the implicit target!

The fact that over recent years (or decades) inflation has been low and stable and that people have little fear (or even awareness) of inflation levels indicates that an implicit inflation target met by the central bank (or even accidental price stability) can anchor expectations and further price stability in the economy.

- It is important to distinguish between the short-run and long-run effects of monetary policy. In the short run, monetary policy can be used to stimulate *AD* and shift it to the right, resulting in an increase in aggregate real output, or monetary policy can be used to contract *AD*, thereby shifting it to the left and leading to a decrease in the level of aggregate real output. In the long run, monetary policy has no effect on aggregate real output because aggregate real output in the long run will always equal potential output. Economists refer to this as monetary neutrality:money is neutral in its effect on aggregate real output in the long run, since it cannot affect the level of aggregate real output.

Module 33
Types of Inflation, Disinflation, and Deflation

Before You Read the MODULE

....

Summary

This module discusses two phenomena that involve monetary policy: inflation and deflation.

Module Objectives

Review these objectives before you read the module. Place a "√" on the line when you understand each of the following:

_____**Objective 1.** The **classical model of the price level**

_____**Objective 2.** Why efforts to collect an **inflation tax** by printing money can lead to high rates of inflation

_____**Objective 3.** The types of inflation: **cost-push** and **demand-pull**

While You Read the MODULE

....

Key Terms

Define these key terms as you read the module.

Classical model of the price level

Inflation tax

Cost-push inflation

_____

Demand-pull inflation

_____

List questions or difficulties from your initial reading of the module.

After You Read the MODULE

Fill-in-the-Blanks

Fill in the blanks to complete the following statements. Terms may be used more than once. If you find your-self having difficulties, please refer to the appropriate section in the text.

- Inflation caused by significant increases in input prices is known as

  (1)_____ inflation. Inflation caused by increases in aggregate

  demand is known as (2)_____ inflation. The idea that people

  who hold money end up "paying for" inflation through a reduction in the purchasing

  power of their money holdings is known as an (3)_____ tax.

- When actual aggregate output equals potential output, the actual unemployment rate is

  (4)_____ the natural rate of unemployment. When the output

  gap is positive (an inflationary gap), the unemployment rate is

  (5)_____ the natural rate. When there is a

  (6)_____ gap, the unemployment rate is *above* the natural rate.

Nominal Versus Real Money Supply

We have already seen the difference between nominal and real values in a variety of situations. In this module, we consider nominal versus real money supply. The general concept of nominal values versus real values still applies here. Nominal money supply refers to the dollar value of the money supply in the economy (for example, the size of M1). Real money supply refers to the value of the nominal money supply, adjusted for changes in the aggregate price level, that is, the value of the money supply taking inflation into account. When the aggregate price level rises (that is, there is inflation in the economy), then a given quantity of money will not purchase as much. The real money supply has fallen because the purchasing power of money has gone down. The real money supply is the nominal money supply divided by the aggregate price level. That is, the real quantity of money is M/P.

- Deflation refers to a fall in the aggregate price level; disinflation refers to a decrease in the inflation rate. Disinflation reflects policy makers' decision that the economy's built-in inflationary expectations need to be reduced.

Module 34
Inflation and Unemployment: The Phillips Curve

Before You Read the MODULE

Summary

This module discusses the short-run trade-off between unemployment and inflation—lower unemployment tends to lead to higher inflation, and vice versa. This trade-off is represented by the Phillips curve.

Module Objectives

Review these objectives before you read the module. Place a "√" on the line when you understand each of the following:

_____**Objective 1.** What the **Phillips curve** is and the nature of the short-run trade-off between inflation and unemployment

_____**Objective 2.** Why there is no long-run trade-off between inflation and unemployment

_____**Objective 3.** Why expansionary policies are limited due to the effects of expected inflation

_____**Objective 4.** Why even moderate levels of inflation can be hard to end

_____**Objective 5.** Why deflation is a problem for economic policy and leads policy makers to prefer a low but positive inflation rate

While You Read the MODULE

Key Terms

Define these key terms as you read the module.

Short-run Phillips curve

Nonaccelerating inflation rate of unemployment (NAIRU)

Long-run Phillips curve

Debt deflation

Zero bound

Liquidity trap

List questions or difficulties from your initial reading of the module.

After You Read the MODULE

Fill-in-the-Blanks

Fill in the blanks to complete the following statements. Terms may be used more than once. If you find yourself having difficulties, please refer to the appropriate section in the text.

- The short-run Phillips curve shows a (1)_____ short-run

  relationship between the (2)_____ rate and the

  (3)_____ rate. A shift in the short-run Phillips curve is caused

  by a change in the expected rate of (4)_____.

- The unemployment rate at which inflation does not change over time is known as the

  (5)_____, or NAIRU. Most economists believe there is a NAIRU and that, in the long run, the Phillips curve is a (6)_____ line at the natural rate of unemployment.

- The effect of deflation in reducing aggregate demand is known as

  (7)_____ deflation.

- The nominal interest rate can't go below zero. This is known as the zero

  (8)_____.

Module Review

The Phillips Curve

In this module, we introduce a new concept—the Phillips curve. Since we have already used several important models and graphs, it is important to keep them straight and to understand how they relate to each other. When you work with the Phillips curve, keep in mind the labels on the axes. This graph looks at the relationship between the inflation rate and the unemployment rate. You may have gotten used to looking at the aggregate price level and the level of real GDP when working with aggregate demand and supply graphs. Recall that the Phillips curve was created when A.W.H. Phillips looked at data for unemployment and inflation rates, and saw a negative relationship between the two. It was Phillips's interest in these two important macroeconomic variables (inflation and unemployment) that led to the development of this concept. Once you have the two key variables in the front of your mind, it will be easier to correctly draw and understand Phillips curve graphs.

To relate Phillips curve analysis to analysis in the aggregate demand and supply model, remember that the NAIRU, the natural rate of unemployment, and the level of potential output are all related. When the economy is operating at full employment, it reaches its potential output and this is where the NAIRU is found. The vertical axes in both models can be used to measure increases in the aggregate price level (inflation), but the horizontal axes measure unemployment in the Phillips curve model and aggregate output in the *AD/AS* model. Remember, aggregate output and unemployment are inversely related. When output goes up, it means more people are employed producing output and unemployment falls. When output falls, fewer workers are needed and unemployment rises. A rightward shift of the *LRAS* curve represents an increase in potential output and a decrease in the natural rate of unemployment. This corresponds to a leftward shift of the long-run Phillips curve (showing a decrease in the NAIRU).

- You should fully understand the concept of the nonaccelerating inflation rate of unemployment, or the NAIRU. The NAIRU provides a measure of the unemployment rate that corresponds to the economy operating at its potential output level without any inflationary pressures. Economies that adopt policies in order to reduce their unemployment rate below this natural rate will experience inflation; persistent adoption of these policies will generate accelerating inflation.

- It is important to understand the short-run Phillips curve (*SRPC*) and how the expected inflation rate affects it, as well as why the long-run Phillips curve (*LRPC*) is a vertical line at the NAIRU. The *SRPC* illustrates the negative relationship between the inflation rate and the unemployment rate. The *SRPC* is drawn with a given level of expected inflation. If expected inflation increases, the *SRPC* will shift upward by the change in the expected inflation rate. In the long run, the economy—no matter what the expected inflation rate—will settle at an unemployment rate equal to the NAIRU.

- Debt deflation refers to a situation in which deflation makes existent loan contracts more costly for borrowers: as the real burden of their debt increases, borrowers will decrease their spending. This reduction in aggregate spending is referred to as debt deflation.

- You should review the concept of the liquidity trap and the zero bound for nominal interest rates. The zero bound refers to the lower limit for the nominal interest rate: nominal interest rates cannot fall below zero percent. When an economy finds that its nominal interest rate has fallen to zero, it will no longer be able to use monetary policy to stimulate the economy; monetary policy will be unable to stimulate aggregate spending through decreases in the nominal interest rate. This situation is referred to as a liquidity trap: increasing the money supply, an increase in liquidity, does nothing for the economy since the economy is "trapped" by the inability of the nominal interest rate to fall further.

Module 35
History and Alternative Views of Macroeconomics

Before You Read the MODULE

Summary

This module presents a brief overview of the history of macroeconomics.

Module Objectives

Review these objectives before you read the module. Place a "√" on the line when you understand each of the following:

_____**Objective 1.** Why classical macroeconomics wasn't adequate for the problems posed by the Great Depression

_____**Objective 2.** How Keynes and the experience of the Great Depression legitimized **macroeconomic policy activism**

_____**Objective 3.** What **monetarism** is and its views about the limits of **discretionary monetary policy**

_____**Objective 4.** How challenges led to a revision of Keynesian ideas and the emergence of the **new classical macroeconomics**

While You Read the MODULE

Key Terms

Define these key terms as you read the module.

Macroeconomic policy activism

Monetarism

Discretionary monetary policy

Monetary policy rule

Quantity Theory of Money

Velocity of money

Natural rate hypothesis

Political business cycle

New classical macroeconomics

Rational expectations

New Keynesian economics

List questions or difficulties from your initial reading of the module.

After You Read the MODULE

Fill-in-the-Blanks

Fill in the blanks to complete the following statements. Terms may be used more than once. If you find yourself having difficulties, please refer to the appropriate section in the text.

- During the 1930s, economists had an incentive to develop theories to guide

  macroeconomic policy-making as a result of (1)_____.

  Monetary policy activism was legitimized by the work of

  (2)_____. But that work was later challenged by Milton

  Friedman, who led a movement known as (3)_____. Underlying

  the movement was the Quantity Theory of Money, which is based on the equation

  (4)_____. Friedman also proposed the

  (5)_____ hypothesis, which said that, because inflation is

  eventually embedded into expectations, to avoid accelerating inflation over time, the

  unemployment rate must be high enough that the actual inflation rate equals the

  (6)_____ rate of inflation. That is, attempts to keep the

  unemployment rate below the natural rate leads to an ever-rising inflation rate.

Module Review

The Goal of Macroeconomics

This module takes an historical view of macroeconomics, presenting an overview of how modern macroeconomics developed and the issues and events that triggered changes in economists' understanding of the macroeconomy. The module presents alternative macroeconomic theories that have developed over the past 70 years. This module is important because it provides historical background for the economic theories we study today and it presents important alternative economic theories (some of which are still supported by a significant number of economists today). But the material in this module is perhaps even more important because understanding how modern macroeconomic theory has developed and what differences of opinion remain is crucial to truly understanding the current state of the discipline. Up to this point, the current macroeconomic consensus has been the main focus of this book (and it is summarized in the next module).

To differentiate between generally accepted macroeconomic theory and areas about which economists still have significant differences of opinion, return to the distinction between positive and normative economics. Positive economics answers questions about the way the world works and relies heavily on models. For example, "Can expansionary fiscal policy result in an increase in aggregate demand?" The answer to this question can be modeled and tested. Economists have come to a consensus regarding many of the important positive questions in macroeconomics. Normative economics, on the other hand, involves prescription. That is, answering questions about how the economy *should* work. For example, "Should expansionary fiscal policy be used to alleviate recessions?" Here we find considerably more disagreement among economists and no way to determine a "right" or "wrong" answer.

Recall from our earlier discussion of positive versus normative economics that we identified several sources of the differences between economists regarding normative questions. First, economics is unavoidably tied up in politics. Individuals and groups have political opinions, and they have an incentive to try to support their political views with the opinions of economists. A second source of differences is individual values. In any diverse group of individuals, reasonable people can differ. This certainly applies to economists. Finally, differences arise from economic modeling. Recall that economic models are simplifications of reality that require assumptions about how the world works. Economists may legitimately disagree about which models and which simplifying assumptions are appropriate, and therefore they arrive at different conclusions.

The goal of an introductory course in macroeconomics (as opposed to political science or philosophy) is to understand how the economy works. Your focus should be on the economic models presented. To fully understand the economic models presented, you also need to understand their simplifying assumptions and how those assumptions affect the model. Given this goal, questions and answers in introductory economics courses will not focus on history, politics, or values. Rather, they will focus on understanding and applying macroeconomic models. This module should help you to understand differences in important macroeconomic models and their effect on our understanding of how the economy works.

Module 36
The Modern Macroeconomic Concensus

Before You Read the MODULE

Summary

This module explains how the intense debates about macroeconomics in the 1960s, 1970s, and 1980s have led to a broad consensus about several crucial macroeconomic issues.

Module Objective

Review this objective before you read the module. Place a "√" on the line when you understand the following:

_____**Objective 1.** The elements of the modern consensus and the main remaining disputes

While You Read the MODULE

List questions or difficulties from your initial reading of the module.

After You Read the MODULE

Fill-in-the-Blanks

Fill in the blanks to complete the following statements. Terms may be used more than once. If you find yourself having difficulties, please refer to the appropriate section in the text.

- (1)_____ economists generally believed that expansionary

  monetary policy was ineffective or even harmful in fighting recessions. In the early years,

  (2)_____ economists tended to believe that monetary policy was

  of doubtful effectiveness. (3)_____ convinced economists that

  monetary policy is effective after all.

- Today, most economists agree that (4)_____ policy should play

  the main role in stabilization policy. But there is disagreement regarding how a central

  bank should set its policy. A formal guideline for what the inflation rate should be is

  known as an inflation (5)_____. And while the Fed does not

  have a formal policy, it is widely believed to want an inflation rate around

  (6)_____ %.

Module Review

Consensus and Disagreement

The material presented in this module is not meant to imply that there is complete agreement among economists. As we have seen, economists often disagree. Over time, economists have reached a general consensus (though not complete agreement) regarding the way the economy works. Over the past 70 years, the economics discipline has grown and developed. Economic theories have been developed, tested, discarded, and refined. While there is still much to learn and the economy is ever-changing, the economics discipline has developed a considerable understanding of the macroeconomy and has reached a modern macroeconomic consensus. This consensus should be the focus of your initial study of macroeconomics.

Disagreements between economists most often arise with regard to normative questions that involve value judgments or political beliefs. Of course, you have your own values and political opinions, and these will factor into your answers to normative questions. However, the focus in an introductory macroeconomic course is on positive questions and understanding how the economy works. Questions and answers will focus on understanding models and their underlying assumptions rather than history, politics, or philosophies. Once you understand the basics, you will be in a better position to form your own position with regard to normative questions.

BEFORE YOU TAKE THE TEST: section 6

Draw the Featured Model: The Phillips Curve

Draw a short-run Phillips curve for an expected rate of inflation of 0, a short-run Phillips curve with an expected rate of inflation of 2% and the long-run Phillips curve. Note: Why is there a negative portion of the horizontal axis on this graph?

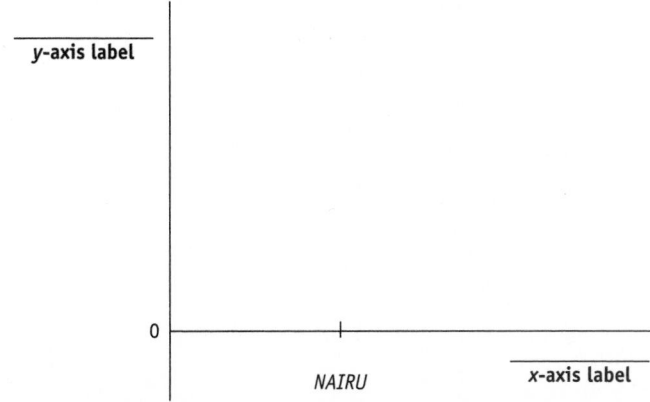

Complete the Exercise

Assume the economy is in long-run equilibrium with an expected inflation rate of 3 percent and an unemployment rate of 8 percent.

a. Draw the short-run and long-run Phillips curves, and show the long-run equilibrium.

b. Suppose expected inflation rises to 4%. Show on your graph, and explain what will happen to the short-run Phillips curve and the long-run equilibrium.

Problems

1. Uplandia is concerned about its debt–GDP ratio and the projections about this ratio over the next five years. The following table gives data about Uplandia's real GDP for this year (year 1) and its projected real GDP for the next five years. Real GDP is projected to grow 3% per year over the next five years as is the government deficit.

a. Fill in the missing cells in the table.

Year	Real GDP (millions of dollars)	Debt (millions of dollars)	Budget deficit (millions of dollars)	Debt (percentage of real GDP)	Budget deficit (percentage of real GDP)
Year 1	$800	$200	$20	25%	2.5%
Year 2					
Year 3					
Year 4					
Year 5					
Year 6					

b. Describe in words what is happening to the government's debt–GDP ratio and deficit–GDP ratio when real GDP and the government deficit grow at the same rate.

Suppose Uplandia decides to reduce government spending over the next five years. This results in the government deficit growing 1% per year over the next five years while real GDP continues to grow 3% per year.

c. Fill in the table below based on these projections.

Year	Real GDP (millions of dollars)	Debt (millions of dollars)	Budget deficit (millions of dollars)	Debt (percentage of real GDP)	Budget deficit (percentage of real GDP)
Year 1	$800	$200	$20	25%	2.5%
Year 2					
Year 3					
Year 4					
Year 5					
Year 6					

d. Describe in words what is happening to the government's debt–GDP ratio and deficit–GDP ratio when real GDP grows at 3% per year while the deficit grows at 1% per year.

Suppose Uplandia, buoyed by its projected real GDP growth rate, passes legislation reducing its taxes while simultaneously deciding to go to war. Its economists project real GDP will continue to grow at 3% per year but now, due to these policy decisions, the government deficit is projected to grow at 10% per year. The results of these changes are shown in the following table.

Year	Real GDP (millions of dollars)	Debt (millions of dollars)	Budget deficit (millions of dollars)	Debt (percentage of real GDP)	Budget deficit (percentage of real GDP)
Year 1	$800	$200	$20	25%	2.5%
Year 2	824	222	22	26.94	2.67
Year 3	848.72	246.2	24.2	29.01	2.85
Year 4	874.18	272.82	26.62	31.21	3.05
Year 5	900.41	302.10	29.38	33.55	3.25
Year 6	927.42	334.30	32.2	36.05	3.47

e. Describe in words what is happening to the government's debt–GDP ratio and deficit–GDP ratio when real GDP grows at 3% per year while the deficit grows at 10% per year.

f. Can you generalize your findings from this exercise? What general principles does this exercise present?

2. Explain why automatic stabilizers reduce the size of the multiplier. Provide several examples of automatic stabilizers and their effect on the economy during economic fluctuations.

3. Suppose that the government currently operates with a deficit that grows by 4% a year. Furthermore, suppose that this economy initially had zero debt until the government started operating with a deficit. The economy's annual economic growth rate is 5% a year. What will happen to this economy's debt–GDP ratio over time, given this information? Explain your answer fully.

4. Use the *AS-AD* model to answer this question. The economy of Macroland is initially in long-run equilibrium. Then the FOMC of Macroland decides to reduce interest rates through an open-market operation.

   a. Draw a graph representing the initial situation in Macroland. In your graph, be sure to include the short-run aggregate supply curve (*SRAS*), the long-run aggregate supply curve (*LRAS*), and the aggregate demand curve (*AD*). On your graph, mark the equilibrium aggregate price and aggregate output levels, as well as potential output.

   b. Draw a graph of the money market depicting Macroland's initial situation before the FOMC engages in monetary policy, as well as the effect of the FOMC's monetary policy actions. Be sure to indicate the initial equilibrium as well as the equilibrium after the monetary policy.

c. How does this monetary policy action affect the aggregate economy in the short run? Explain your answer verbally while also including a graph of the *AS-AD* model to illustrate your answer.

d. How does this monetary policy action affect the aggregate economy in the long run?

5. In your own words, explain how the Fed's actions can affect the economy. Be sure to include an explanation about how the Fed can affect the economy when it is in recession or when it is producing at an aggregate output level that is greater than the potential output level.

6. Joe lends Mary $1,000 for the year. They agree that Mary will repay the full $1,000 at the end of the year and in addition, they agree that Mary will pay Joe $50 in interest payments.

a. What is the nominal interest rate that Mary and Joe have agreed to in this contract?

b. If Joe and Mary both anticipate that inflation will be 3% for the year, what real interest rate is each of them trying to achieve in their loan contract?

c. Suppose the actual inflation rate for the year is 2%. Who benefits more from this inflation rate, and why do you think they benefit more? Explain your answer.

d. Suppose the actual inflation rate for the year is 4%. Who benefits more from this inflation rate, and why do you think they benefit more? Explain your answer.

e. If the actual inflation rate equals the nominal interest rate, how does this affect the outcome of this loan contract?

f. If you knew what the actual inflation rate was going to be, and it happened to equal the nominal interest rate, would you be willing to be a lender? Why or why not? Explain your answer.

7. Suppose that both borrowers and lenders anticipate correctly that the inflation rate will increase by 5 percentage points over the next year.

a. What do you know will happen to the real interest rate?

b. What do you know will happen to the nominal interest rate?

c. Describe the effects of this anticipated inflation on the demand for loanable funds curve and the supply of loanable funds curve. Use the following graph to illustrate your answer.

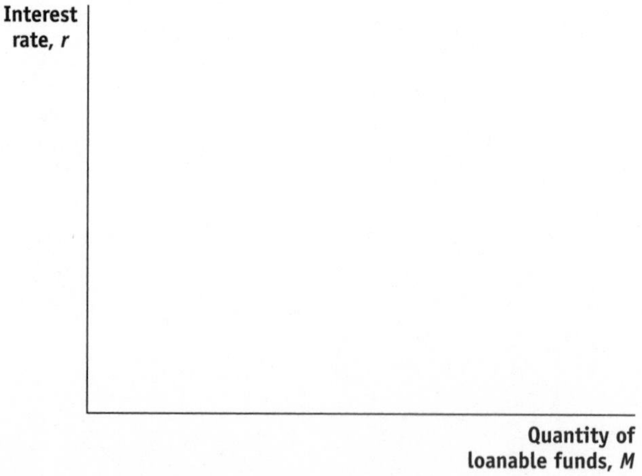

Interest
rate, *r*

Quantity of
loanable funds, *M*

8. Expansionary monetary policy typically reduces the nominal interest rate, and this in turn acts as a stimulus for aggregate demand. Why does this not work in the case of a liquidity trap? In your answer, make sure you identify what a liquidity trap is and why it prevents monetary policy from stimulating the economy. Use the following graph to illustrate your answer.

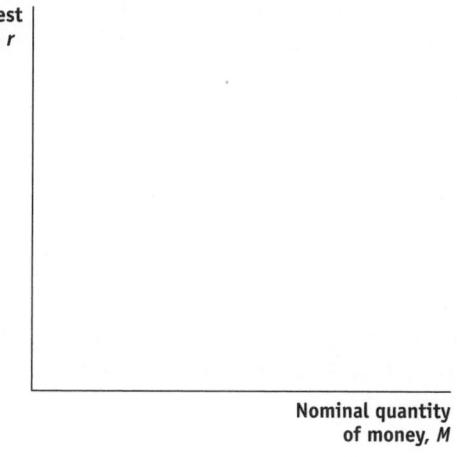

9. Explain why during a period of deflation the debt burden increases and how this relates to debt deflation.

10. Suppose you are given the following information about the economy of Funland.

Unemployment rate	Inflation rate	Expected inflation rate
1%	6%	2%
2	5	2
3	4	2
4	3	2

a. Draw a graph with the unemployment rate on the horizontal axis and the inflation rate on the vertical axis. On this graph, represent the above short-run Phillips curve ($SRPC$) based on expected inflation of 2%. Label this $SRPC_1$. Assume this curve is linear.

b. Given $SRPC_1$, at what rate of unemployment will inflation equal 0% for this economy? If expected inflation is 2%, then how will this economy adjust over time to this expected inflation rate? Illustrate this short-run adjustment on a graph and then explain your answer.

c. If policy makers could effectively change inflationary expectations such that people expected inflation to be 0%, then what would be this country's NAIRU? Illustrate this on a graph, labeling all new information clearly. Explain your answer.

d. For the economy of Funland, what will the long-run Phillips curve (*LRPC*) look like and where will it be located? Use a graph to explain and illustrate your answer.

Review Questions

Circle your answer.

1. Holding everything else constant, the government's budget balance

   A. tends to increase during a recession.
   B. tends to increase during an expansion.
   C. will increase if the government pursues expansionary fiscal policy.
   D. Answers (A) and (C) are both correct.
   E. Answers (B) and (C) are both correct.

2. When a government decides to spend more than it collects in tax revenue,

   A. it usually borrows the necessary funds.
   B. the budget balance increases.
   C. it runs a budget deficit but reduces its overall level of government debt.
   D. it is forced to sell valuable assets to finance its spending.

3. The government debt is

   A. an alternative but equivalent term for the government deficit.
   B. the difference between the amount of money government spends and the amount of tax revenue the government collects during a given period of time.
   C. the amount of money the government owes at a particular point in time.
   D. best measured over a given period of time.

4. Suppose the government of Macroland repeatedly finds itself running a deficit. This may

   A. result in less private investment spending as government borrowing crowds out this spending.
   B. result in lower long-run economic growth if the deficit reduces private investment spending.
   C. cause the government of Macroland to have less budgetary flexibility in the future due to the diversion of tax revenue to pay interest on the debt.
   D. Answers (A), (B), and (C) are all possible effects of repeatedly running a deficit.

5. The debt–GDP ratio

   A. provides a measure of government debt as a percentage of GDP.
   B. provides a measure of government debt relative to the potential ability of the government to collect taxes to cover that debt.
   C. can fall, even if the level of government debt is rising, provided GDP grows faster than debt.
   D. Answers (A), (B), and (C) are all correct.

6. Which of the following statements is true?

   A. In the long run, an increase in the nominal money supply increases the potential output level.
   B. In the long run, an increase in the nominal money supply will have no effect on real variables, including the aggregate price level.
   C. In the long run, an increase in the nominal money supply will lead to a proportionate increase in the aggregate price level.
   D. Answers (A) and (B) are both true.
   E. Answers (A), (B), and (C) are all true.

7. Suppose that an economy experiences an increase in the aggregate output level. Assuming that the central bank does not engage in monetary policy, which of the following statements is true?

   A. The interest rate in this economy will increase.
   B. The interest rate in this economy will decrease.
   C. The interest rate in this economy will be unaffected by this change in aggregate output.
   D. This change in aggregate output will cause a movement along the money demand curve.

8. The money supply curve shifts to the left. The most likely cause for this shift is the FOMC's open-market

   A. purchase of Treasury bills.
   B. sale of Treasury bills.

9. Expansionary monetary policy will, holding everything else constant,

    A. lower the interest rate and cause *AD* to shift to the right.
    B. lower the interest rate and cause *AD* to shift to the left.
    C. raise the interest rate and cause *AD* to shift to the right.
    D. raise the interest rate and cause *AD* to shift to the left.

10. When the economy is currently producing at a short-run level of aggregate output that is less than potential output, it is most likely that the Fed will engage in open-market

    A. purchases of Treasury bills.
    B. sales of Treasury bills.

11. Inflation targeting means that

    A. the central bank adheres to maintaining a very strict interest rate target.
    B. the central bank announces the inflation rate that it is trying to achieve and then uses monetary policy to achieve this inflation rate.
    C. there may be a range of acceptable inflation rates or a specific inflation rate that the central bank hopes to achieve through monetary policy.
    D. Answers (A), (B), and (C) are all correct.
    E. Answers (B) and (C) are both correct.

12. Suppose the aggregate economy in the short run is operating at an aggregate output level that is greater than the potential output level. Holding everything else constant, what do you anticipate will happen to nominal wages in the long run given this information?

    A. Nominal wages will decrease.
    B. Nominal wages will remain constant.
    C. Nominal wages will increase.

13. In the short run, money is

    A. neutral because it can have no effect on real aggregate output.
    B. not neutral because changes in the money supply can cause real aggregate output to change.

14. In periods of high inflation, the short-run *AS* curve

    A. adjusts quickly by shifting to the right.
    B. adjusts slowly, if at all, and will eventually shift to the left.
    C. is insensitive to it and is therefore unaffected by it.
    D. adjusts swiftly and shifts to the left due to rising nominal wages.
    E. None of the above statements is true.

15. When there is unexpected inflation in an economy, then

    A. real GDP will decrease in the economy in the long run.
    B. real income will decrease in the economy in the long run.
    C. borrowers benefit while lenders lose.
    D. lenders benefit while borrowers lose.
    E. Answers (A), (B), and (C) are all correct.
    F. Answers (A), (B), and (D) are all correct.

16. The relationship between changes in the output gap and changes in the unemployment rate is less than one-to-one because

    A. companies often meet changes in the demand for their product by changing the number of hours their current workers work.
    B. the availability of jobs affects the number of people who are looking for jobs.
    C. the rate of growth in labor productivity tends to accelerate during times of economic prosperity and decelerate during times of economic adversity.
    D. Answers (A), (B), and (C) are all correct.

17. Which of the following statements is true?

    A. Moderate inflation may be the result of politicians pursuing too low an unemployment rate for the economy prior to an election.

    B. Moderate inflation may be the result of an aggregate supply shock to the economy.

    C. Moderate inflation is easily brought under control through a process called disinflation.

    D. Answers (A), (B), and (C) are all true.

    E. Answers (A) and (B) are both true.

    F. Answers (A) and (C) are both true.

    G. Answers (B) and (C) are both true.

18. Which of the following statements is true?

    A. The short-run Phillips curve is a vertical line with the horizontal intercept equaling the NAIRU.

    B. The short-run Phillips curve depicts the negative relationship between the unemployment rate and the inflation rate.

    C. An economy with a low rate of unemployment is an economy that has a shortage of labor and other resources, which leads to falling prices.

    D. Answers (A) and (C) are both true.

    E. Answers (B) and (C) are both true.

19. When the central bank finds that it cannot use monetary policy to reduce the nominal interest rate, it must be the case that

    A. the economy is operating in a liquidity trap.

    B. the central bank has reached the zero bound.

    C. the money market is in disequilibrium.

    D. Answers (A), (B), and (C) are all correct.

    E. Answers (A) and (B) are both correct.

    F. Answers (A) and (C) are both correct.

    G. Answers (B) and (C) are both correct.

20. Expected inflation

    A. does not impact the short-run or the long-run Phillips curve.

    B. is the rate of inflation that workers and employers expect in the near future.

    C. and the unemployment rate are the most significant factors affecting the rate of inflation in an economy.

    D. Answers (A), (B), and (C) are all correct.

    E. Answers (B) and (C) are both correct.

Use the following graph to answer the next three questions. In this graph $SRPC_1$ is the short-run Phillips curve for this economy when the expected inflation rate equals 0%.

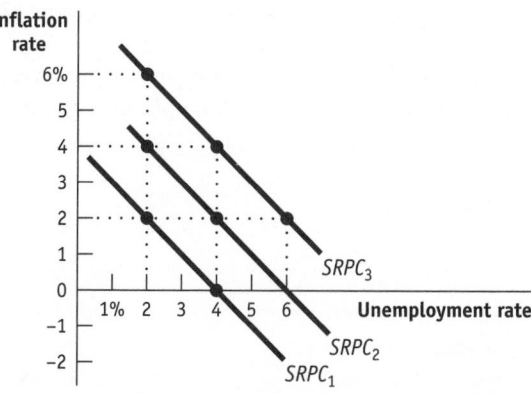

21. Using the above graph, we know that the short-run Phillips curve (*SRPC*) equals *SRPC*$_2$ when the expected inflation rate equals

    A. 0%.   **B.** 2%.   **C.** 4%.   **D.** 6%.

22. Suppose the inflation rate is 4% and this economy finds that its unemployment rate equals 3%. What is the NAIRU for this economy, given this information?

    A. 0%   **B.** 2%   **C.** 4%   **D.** 6%

23. Suppose the policy makers for the economy depicted in the above graph decide to pursue an unemployment rate of 2%. This will

    A. cause accelerating inflation in the long run.
    B. lead to rightward shifts in the *SRPC*, with each shift reflecting the expected inflation rate.
    C. cause equilibrium wage rates to fall.
    D. Answers (A), (B), and (C) are all correct.
    E. Answers (A) and (B) are both correct.

24. Governments that run large deficits can

    A. reduce the size of the deficit by raising taxes.
    B. reduce the size of the deficit by reducing spending.
    C. finance the deficit by printing money.
    D. Answers (A), (B), and (C) are all correct.

25. A positive output gap implies an unemployment rate

    A. above the natural rate of unemployment.
    B. below the natural rate of unemployment.

26. A negative supply shock will, holding everything else constant, cause the aggregate price level to

    A. increase and the aggregate level of real GDP to decrease in the short run.
    B. decrease and the aggregate level of real GDP to decrease in the short run.
    C. increase and the aggregate level of real GDP to increase in the short run.
    D. decrease and the aggregate level of real GDP to increase in the short run.

27. Disinflation in an economy is

    A. easy to accomplish and relatively painless for people living and working in this economy.
    B. difficult to accomplish and typically results in reduced real GDP and high rates of unemployment.

28. Which of the following statements is true for the modern consensus in macroeconomics?
    I. Prices are flexible in the long run but likely to be sticky in the short run.
    II. Inadequate spending can cause short-run decreases in the aggregate output level.
    III. In the long run the macroeconomy will produce at the full employment level of output.

    A. Statements I, II, and III are all true.
    B. Statements I and II are both true.
    C. Statements II and III are both true.
    D. Statements I and III are both true.

29. When the central bank pursues a formula that determines its actions, this is called

    A. monetarism.

    B. a monetary policy rule.

    C. discretionary monetary policy.

    D. discretionary fiscal policy.

30. The NAIRU

    A. is equivalent to the natural rate of unemployment.

    B. hypothesis states that inflation eventually gets built into expectations, so that any attempt to keep the unemployment rate above the natural rate will lead to an ever-rising inflation rate.

    C. states that once inflation is embedded in the public's expectations, it would continue even in the face of high unemployment.

    D. Answers (A), (B), and (C) are all correct.

    E. Answers (A) and (B) are both correct.

    F. Answers (A) and (C) are both correct.

    G. Answers (B) and (C) are both correct.

ANSWER KEY

Fill-in-the-Blanks

Module 30: (1) $S = T - G - TR$, (2) expansionary, (3) contractionary, (4) deficit, (5) debt, (6) cyclically adjusted, (7) debt–GDP, (8) implicit liabilities

Module 31: (1) federal funds, (2) New York, (3) purchase, (4) increase, (5) decreases, (6) rise, (7) lower, (8) lower

Module 32: (1) contractionary, (2) expansionary, (3) nominal wages, (4) neutrality

Module 33: (1) cost-push, (2) demand-pull, (3) inflation, (4) equal to, (5) below, (6) recessionary

Module 34: (1) negative, (2) inflation/unemployment, (3) inflation/unemployment, (4) inflation, (5) nonaccelerating inflation rate of unemployment, (6) vertical, (7) debt, (8) bound

Module 35: (1) the Great Depression, (2) Keynes, (3) monetarism, (4) $MV = PQ$, (5) natural rate, (6) expected

Module 36: (1) Classical, (2) Keynesian, (3) Monetarist, (4) monetary, (5) target, (6) **2**

Featured Graph

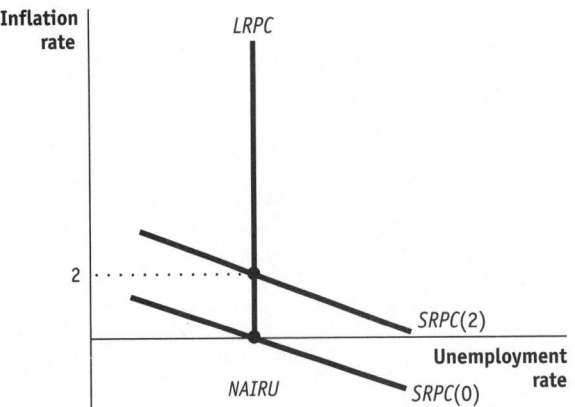

The horizontal axis has a negative portion because the economy could experience deflation.

Exercise

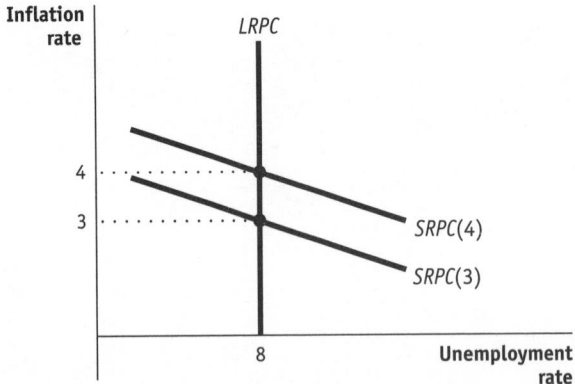

The higher inflation rate will be incorporated into expectations and the SRPC will shift upward. The economy will readjust to a new long-run equilibrium with an actual inflation rate of 4%.

Answers to Problems

1. a.

Year	Real GDP (millions of dollars)	Debt (millions of dollars)	Budget deficit (millions of dollars)	Debt (percentage of real GDP)	Budget deficit (percentage of real GDP)
Year 1	$800	$200	$20	25%	2.5%
Year 2	824	220.6	20.6	26.77	2.5
Year 3	848.72	241.82	21.22	28.49	2.5
Year 4	874.18	263.68	21.86	30.16	2.5
Year 5	900.41	286.2	22.52	31.79	2.5
Year 6	927.42	309.4	23.2	33.36	2.5

b. When the real GDP and the government deficit grow at the same rate, the deficit–GDP ratio stays constant at 2.5%, while the debt–GDP ratio increases from 25% to 33.36% in five years.

c.

Year	Real GDP (millions of dollars)	Debt (millions of dollars)	Budget deficit (millions of dollars)	Debt (percentage of real GDP)	Budget deficit (percentage of real GDP)
Year 1	$800	$200	$20	25%	2.5%
Year 2	824	220.2	20.2	26.72	2.45
Year 3	848.72	240.6	20.4	28.35	2.40
Year 4	874.18	261.2	20.6	29.88	2.36
Year 5	900.41	282.0	20.8	31.32	2.31
Year 6	927.42	303.0	21	32.67	2.26

d. When the real GDP grows at 3% per year and the government deficit grows at 1% per year, the deficit–GDP ratio falls from 2.5% to 2.26% in five years, while the debt–GDP ratio increases from 25% to 32.67% in five years.

e. When real GDP grows at 3% per year and the deficit grows at 10% per year, the deficit–GDP ratio increases from 2.5% to 3.47% over five years while the debt–GDP ratio increases from 25% to 36.05% over five years.

f. The rate of growth of both real GDP and the deficit each year are important when considering what happens to the debt–GDP ratio and the deficit–GDP ratio. If GDP grows at a faster rate than the deficit, the deficit–GDP ratio will decline while the debt–GDP ratio may continue to increase, but at a slower rate than would occur if the deficit and GDP grew at the same rate.

2. Automatic stabilizers act to moderate the effects of economic recessions or economic expansions. In the case of economic recessions, the automatic stabilizers provide a source of additional spending that occurs as the economy goes into the recession. For example, as production and spending slow in the economy, the amo and this moderates the fall in consumer spending. Or, as unemployment rates increase, the number of people receiving unemployment compensation rises, and this enables people to spend more than they would otherwise be able to spend. In the case of economic expansions, the automatic stabilizers slow down spending: as people's incomes rise, their taxes also rise, reducing the overall increase in consumer income, and this moderates the economic expansion. (Students may provide different examples of automatic stabilizers.)

3. The government will operate with a deficit each year and, therefore, the government debt will grow over time. But, because the economy is growing at a faster rate than the growth rate of the deficit, the debt–GDP ratio will fall over time.

4. **a.**

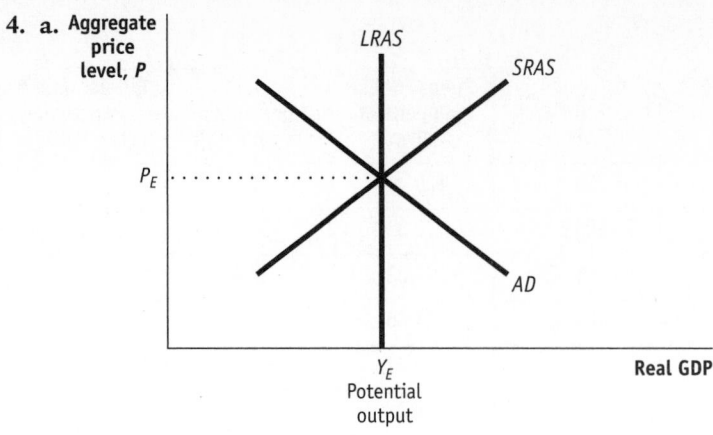

b.

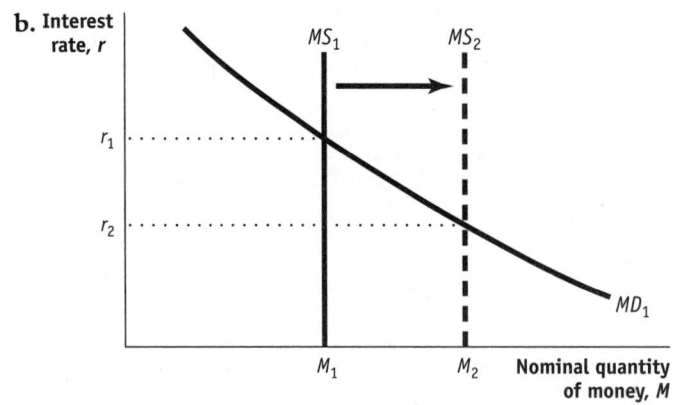

c. When the FOMC reduces interest rates through an open-market purchase of Treasury bills, aggregate demand increases and causes the *AD* curve to shift to the right, to AD_2. In the short run, aggregate real output increases to Y_2 and the aggregate price level increases to P_2. This is illustrated in the following figure.

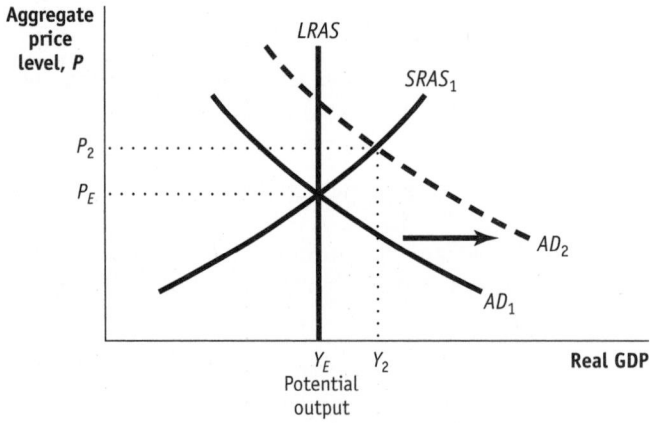

d. In the long run, the economy must return to producing its potential output, Y_E. This economic adjustment will occur as the *SRAS* curve shifts to the left and nominal wages rise. As the *SRAS* curve shifts back to $SRAS_3$, this will eliminate the inflationary gap, restore the economy to its potential output level, and lead to an even higher aggregate price level, P_3. The following figure illustrates this long-run adjustment.

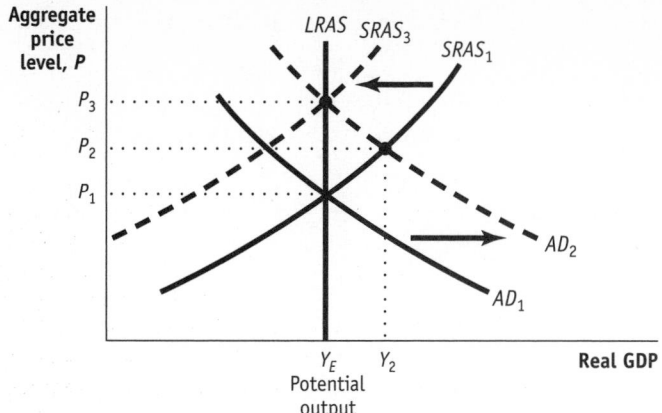

5. The Fed can affect the economy through its open-market operations. When the Fed expands the money supply by purchasing Treasury bills, the interest rate falls, holding everything else constant. As the interest rate declines, this acts as a stimulus to investment and consumer spending and, therefore, as a stimulus to aggregate demand. Thus, open-market purchases typically are used to stimulate the economy; when the economy is producing below the potential output level (i.e., the economy is in a recession), the Fed has the potential to alter this output level via active monetary policy. Conversely, when the economy is producing at a level greater than the potential output level, the Fed can engage in open-market sales that will effectively lead to higher interest rates and lower investment and consumer spending, thereby causing the level of aggregate demand to fall, holding everything else constant.

6. a. The nominal interest rate that Mary and Joe have agreed to in this contract is 5%, since the $50 interest payment represents 5% of the $1,000 loan.

b. We can calculate the real interest rate as the nominal interest rate minus the expected inflation rate; in this case, the nominal interest rate is 5% and the expected inflation rate is 3%, giving us a real interest rate of 2%.

c. If the actual inflation rate is 2%, then the real rate of interest paid on the loan is 3%, which is higher than the real interest rate that Mary and Joe thought they were agreeing to when they signed their loan contract. For Joe, the lender, this means that he is earning more than he anticipated from the loan. For Mary, the borrower, this means that she is paying back more dollars in real terms than she had planned on when she signed the contract.

d. If the actual inflation rate is 4%, then the real rate of interest paid on the loan is 1%, which is lower than the real interest rate that Mary and Joe thought they were agreeing to when they signed their loan contract. For Joe, the lender, this means that he is earning less than he anticipated from the loan. For Mary, the borrower, this means that she is paying back fewer dollars in real terms than she had planned on when she signed the contract.

e. If the actual inflation rate equals the nominal rate of interest, then the real interest rate is zero. When the real rate of interest is zero, the lender earns no real return on the money he or she has lent out, while the borrower is paying no real cost for the use of the money. The borrower wins, while the lender is hurt under this scenario.

f. No, if you knew what the actual inflation rate was going to be and it equaled the nominal interest rate for the loan, you would refuse to be a lender since the real return you would earn on the loan would be zero. If you made the loan, you would be giving up the use of your funds for the period of the loan without receiving any real compensation for the use of those funds.

7. a. The real interest rate will be unaffected by this anticipated inflation rate because both consumers and suppliers in the loanable funds market will take this anticipated inflation into account.

b. The nominal interest rate will increase by 5 percentage points due to the increase in the anticipated rate of inflation of 5 percentage points.

c. Both the demand and the supply curves in the loanable funds market will shift upward (demand will shift to the right and supply will shift to the left) by the amount of the anticipated inflation rate, leaving the equilibrium quantity of loanable funds unchanged in the market while increasing the nominal interest rate by the amount of the anticipated inflation.

8. In the case of a liquidity trap, the nominal interest rate initially is zero and thus cannot fall any lower despite expansionary monetary policy. The following graph illustrates a liquidity trap, in which *MS* is the nominal money supply, *MD* is the nominal money demand, and *r* is the nominal interest rate.

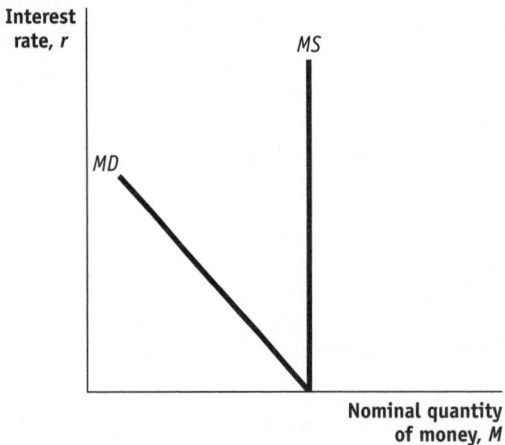

In the graph, when the central bank pursues expansionary monetary policy to shift the *MS* to the right, it will have no effect on the nominal interest rate because it is already at its minimal level of zero. Monetary policy cannot be used to stimulate the economy if the economy faces a liquidity trap.

9. When there is deflation, prices in an economy fall. The effect of this fall in prices is to increase the economic burden of any preexisting debt, since the borrower's payments are not adjusted downward to reflect the deflation. Borrowers lose from deflation due to the increased real burden of their debt; this increased debt burden may lead them to be short of cash and force them to cut their spending sharply when their debt burden rises. Thus, deflation reduces aggregate demand, which deepens the economic slump that may, in turn, lead to further deflation. This reduction in aggregate demand due to the effect of deflation is referred to as debt deflation.

10. a.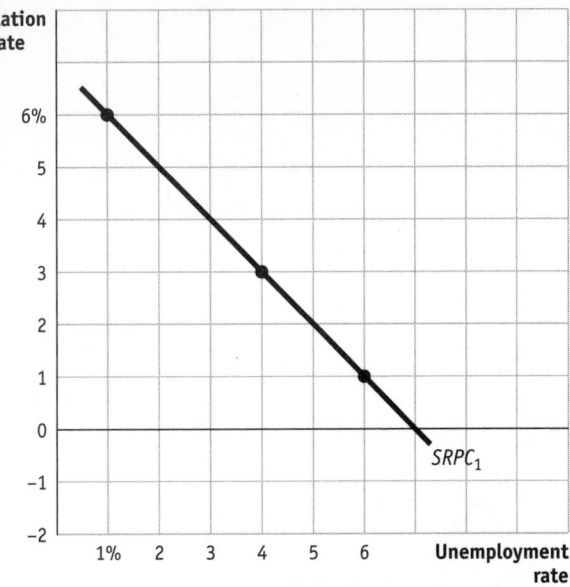

b. Given $SRPC_1$, inflation is 0% when the unemployment rate is 7%. Over time, people will come to expect inflation of 2%, causing the $SRPC$ to shift up by this amount and people's expectations of inflation to rise to 4%. The new $SRPC$ will be $SRPC_2$, as illustrated in the following graph.

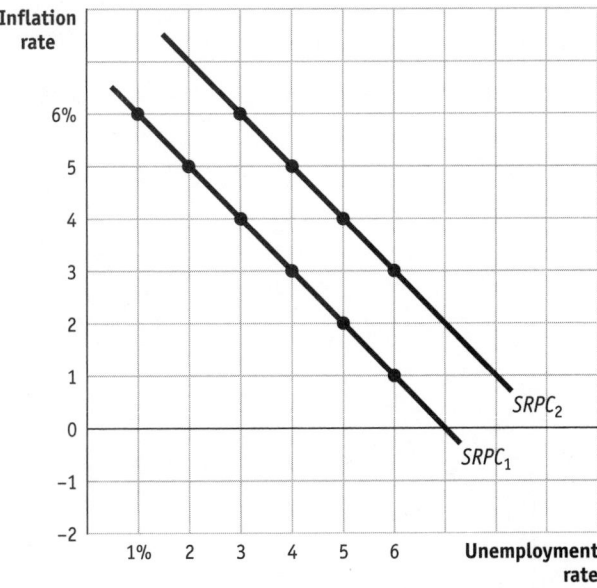

Of course, over time this will cause $SRPC_2$ to shift up reflecting higher inflationary expectations.

c. This country's NAIRU would be 5%. Effectively, we are looking for the *SRPC* that has inflationary expectations of 0%, which we can illustrate as a downward shift of $SRPC_1$ where at any given unemployment rate, the inflation rate is reduced by 2%. We can illustrate this in the following figure as $SRPC_0$.

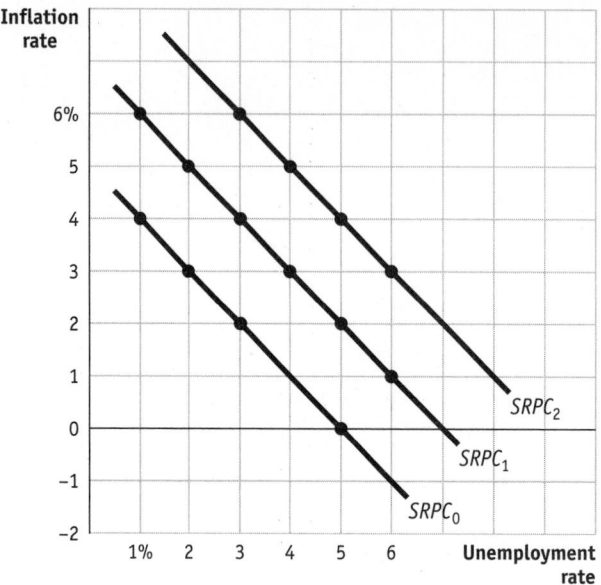

Remember that the expected inflation rate for $SRPC_2$ is 4%, the expected inflation rate for $SRPC_1$ is 2%, and the expected inflation rate for $SRPC_0$ is 0%.

d. For Funland the *LRPC* will be a vertical line at a 5% unemployment rate, as illustrated in the following figure.

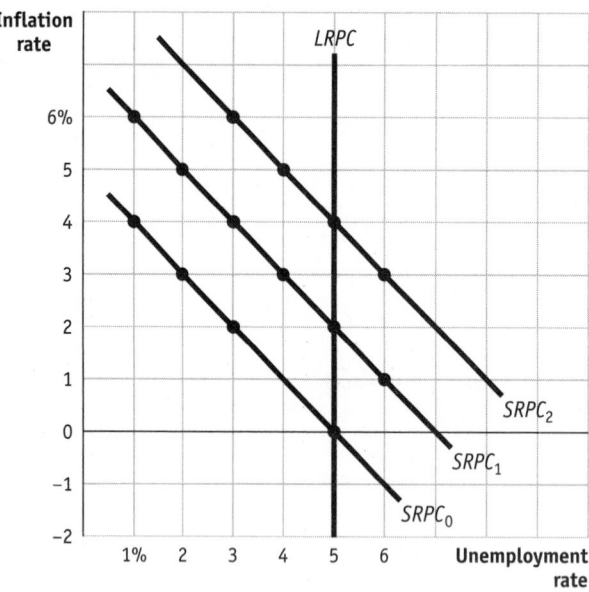

Answers to Review Questions

1. B. The budget balance, $S_{Government}$, is defined by the equation $S_{Government} = T - G - TR$. In an expansion, tax revenue increases and transfers decrease (both of these changes are the result of automatic stabilizers); for a given level of government spending, the budget balance increases. If the government pursues expansionary fiscal policy while holding everything else constant, the budget balance will decrease.

2. **A.** When the government spends more than it collects in tax revenue, it runs a deficit and must acquire additional funds; typically, it does this by borrowing the necessary funds. When the government's deficit increases, this adds to the value of the government debt. It is unusual for governments to sell valuable assets to finance their spending programs. When the government spends more than it collects in tax revenue, the budget balance decreases. (Recall the budget balance is defined in equation form as $S_{Government} = T - G - TR$.)

3. **C.** The government debt is not the same as the government deficit. The government deficit is the difference between the amount of money a government spends and the amount of money it collects in tax revenue during a given period of time. The government debt, in contrast, is the total amount of money a government owes at a particular point in time.

4. **D.** Answers (A), (B), and (C) are all possibilities. When the government runs a deficit, it will typically borrow funds. When the government borrows funds, it competes with firms in the financial markets for those funds. This competition may crowd out private investment spending and therefore lead to lower long-run rates of economic growth. In addition, as the deficits persist, the government will find that increasing amounts of its tax revenue must be dedicated to paying the interest expense of the debt; the government must either reduce its spending in other areas or raise more revenue from taxes.

5. **D.** The debt–GDP ratio provides a measure of the size of the government debt relative to the size of the economy; this is a helpful comparison because the size of the economy provides a measure of the potential tax revenue that can be raised by the government. If the government debt is increasing at the same time that GDP is also increasing, it is possible that the debt–GDP ratio is actually falling, provided that GDP is growing at a faster rate than debt.

6. **C.** In the long run, the economy will operate at the potential output level; any increase in the money supply will not affect the real value of aggregate output, but will lead to a proportionate increase in the aggregate price level.

7. **A.** When aggregate real output increases in an economy, the demand for money shifts to the right. For a given money supply curve (remember the central bank is not engaging in monetary policy), the interest rate will increase.

8. **B.** When the FOMC engages in open-market sales of Treasury bills, it sells Treasury bills to the public and receives dollars for those Treasury bills. The FOMC effectively removes reserves from the banking system with the sale of Treasury bills, which reduces the quantity of money supplied at every interest rate; the supply of money curve shifts to the left.

9. **A.** Expansionary monetary policy is an increase in the money supply. When the money supply increases, the supply of money curve shifts to the right, causing the interest rate to fall. A fall in the interest rate results in higher investment spending and consumption spending, this causing the *AD* curve to shift to the right.

10. **A.** When the current level of aggregate output is less than potential output, the Fed will likely engage in expansionary monetary policy to stimulate the economy to return to the potential output level. Expansionary monetary policy implies that the Fed is increasing the money supply; hence, the Fed is purchasing Treasury bills on the open market.

11. **E.** Inflation targeting involves having the central bank announce the inflation rate or range for the inflation rate it is trying to achieve and then using its monetary policy to achieve this announced goal. Monetary policy to achieve a stated inflation goal will necessarily imply the loss of interest rate control because the interest rate will need to vary in order for the central bank to achieve its inflation target.

12. **C.** When the economy operates in the short run at an aggregate output level greater than the potential level of output, unemployment is below the natural rate of unemployment. As the economy moves to the long run, nominal wages will increase due to labor market pressures arising from this lower-than-natural level of unemployment. The nominal wage will continue to increase until the short-run *AS* curve shifts far enough to the left to return this economy to its potential output level.

13. **B.** Money in the short run is not neutral; when the central bank changes the money supply, the *AD* curve shifts and in the short run this shift will cause the economy to either contract or expand. In the long run, the short-run aggregate supply curve shifts, returning the aggregate economy to its potential output level. In the long run, money is neutral because it cannot alter the level of aggregate real output.

14. **D.** In periods of high inflation, the short-run *AS* curve adjusts quickly through wage and price adjustment; this causes the short-run *AS* curve to shift to the left due to the higher nominal costs associated with the high inflation in order to move the economy toward its long-run equilibrium.

15. **C.** Unexpected inflation has no effect on real GDP and real income in the long run; the economy will return to its potential output level. However, the unexpected inflation will hurt some people while benefiting others:borrowers will find that they are paying back dollars with less purchasing power. Hence, borrowers will benefit from the unexpected inflation while lenders will be hurt.

16. **D.** The relationship between changes in the output gap and changes in the unemployment rate is that rise in the output gap of 1 percentage point reduces the unemployment rate by about one-half of a percentage point. The reasons for this being less than a one-to-one relationship relate to how firms react to changes in the demand for their product, how workers respond to changes in economic conditions, and how the growth rate of labor productivity is affected by economic conditions. The text reviews each of these factors and its effect on the relationship between changes in the output gap and changes in the unemployment rate.

17. **E.** Moderate inflation may be caused by politicians pursuing too low an unemployment rate due to using a target rate of unemployment that is lower than the natural rate of unemployment or because of aggregate supply shocks to the economy. Eliminating moderate inflation through disinflation is a costly procedure because it requires accepting a higher than normal unemployment rate in order to reduce inflationary expectations.

18. **B.** The short-run Phillips curve is downward sloping and depicts the relationship between the unemployment rate and the inflation rate. It is not vertical; the long-run Phillips curve is vertical and intersects the horizontal axis at the NAIRU. An economy that has a low unemployment rate will typically see rising prices in the short run due to shortages of labor and other resources.

19. **E.** When the central bank cannot effectively use monetary policy to stimulate the economy, it must be at the zero bound, or the nominal interest rate must equal zero. When the nominal interest rate is at zero, then the economy is operating in a liquidity trap—a situation in which monetary policy is ineffective. The money market can still be in equilibrium, even though monetary policy cannot be used to stimulate the economy.

20. **E.** Expected inflation and the unemployment rate are the most significant factors affecting the inflation rate in an economy. Expected inflation is that rate of inflation that workers and employers expect in the near future. Changes in expected inflation cause the short-run Phillips curve to shift; increases in the expected inflation rate cause the short-run Phillips curve to shift up, while decreases in the expected inflation rate cause the short-run Phillips curve to shift down.

21. **B.** $SRPC_2$ reflects a short-run Phillips curve drawn with an expected inflation rate of 2%. We know this because this curve has shifted up by 2% at every unemployment rate from the short-run Phillips curve drawn with an expected inflation rate of 0% ($SRPC_{(1)}$.

22. **D.** The NAIRU is the nonaccelerating inflation rate of unemployment for the economy, or that level of unemployment where the inflation rate matches inflationary expectations. An unemployment rate below 4% requires ever-accelerating inflation.

23. **E.** The unemployment rate of 2% is below the unemployment rate that this economy can maintain while still avoiding inflation. If this economy tries to pursue an unemployment rate of 2%, this unemployment rate will be initially accompanied by 2% inflation. This inflation

rate will then be built into inflationary expectations and the *SRPC* will shift to the right. But, again, if policy makers persist in trying to achieve 2% unemployment, this will cause even higher inflationary expectations to be built into the *SRPC*, shifting the *SRPC* further to the right. Thus, trying to achieve an unemployment level of 2% for this economy will lead to accelerating inflation in the long run along with shifts in the *SRPC* in the short run. We can expect wages to rise with expectations of higher inflation and with higher actual inflation rates.

24. **D.** Governments run deficits whenever their spending is greater than their revenue. They can reduce the size of the deficit by increasing the revenue they collect or by reducing the level of spending or by doing a combination of both of these options. When a government is unwilling to increase taxes or cut spending, it is forced to finance any deficit spending it incurs by printing money to cover its budget deficit.

25. **B.** When the output gap is positive, actual aggregate output is greater than potential output. When actual aggregate output exceeds potential output, the unemployment rate is below the natural rate because the level of production is greater than the potential output level.

26. **A.** A negative supply shock will cause the short-run *AS* curve to shift to the left. For a given *AD* curve, this will cause the short-run aggregate price level to increase and the short-run aggregate level of real GDP to decrease.

27. **B.** Disinflation involves eliminating inflation and inflationary expectations from an economy. Once an economy has developed inflationary expectations, the only way to reduce these expectations is to throw the economy into a major recession. Such a recession results in reductions in production as well as increases in the unemployment rate.

28. **A.** All three of these statements are part of the modern macroeconomic consensus. The text discusses this consensus in detail.

29. **B.** A monetary policy rule describes the use of a formula by the central bank to determine its actions.

30. **F.** The NAIRU is the same as the natural rate of unemployment, and the NAIRU hypothesis says that once inflation is built into expectations, any attempt to keep the unemployment rate below the natural rate will lead to accelerating inflation. Thus, once inflation is embedded in the public's expectations, then that inflation will continue even if the unemployment rate is high.

Notes

Economic Growth and Productivity

OVERVIEW

This section presents some facts about long-run growth, the factors that economists believe determine the pace at which long-run growth takes place, and how government policies can help or hinder growth. It also addresses the environmental sustainability of long-run growth.

FEATURED MODEL/GRAPH

Rather than present a new graph, this section reiterates how economic growth is represented in models we have already developed, the PPC and the *AS/AD* models.

MODULES IN THIS SECTION

Module 37: Long-run Economic Growth

Module 38: Productivity and Growth

Module 39: Growth Policy: Why Economic Growth Rates Differ

Module 40: Economic Growth in Macroeconomic Models

Module 37
Long-run Economic Growth

Before You Read the MODULE

Summary

This module analyzes the sources of long-run economic growth and presents data illustrating how much the U.S. economy has grown over time. It also discusses how large the gaps are between wealthy countries like the United States and countries that have yet to achieve comparable growth.

Module Objectives

Review these objectives before you read the module. Place a "√" on the line when you understand each of the following:

_____**Objective 1.** How we measure long-run economic growth

_____**Objective 2.** How real GDP has changed over time

_____**Objective 3.** How real GDP varies across countries

_____**Objective 4.** The sources of long-run economic growth

_____**Objective 5.** How productivity is driven by physical capital, human capital, and progress in technology

While You Read the MODULE

Key Terms

Define these key terms as you read the module.

Rule of 70

Labor productivity, or productivity

Physical capital
_____

Human capital
_____

Technology
_____

List questions or difficulties from your initial reading of the module.

After You Read the MODULE

Fill-in-the-Blanks

Fill in the blanks to complete the following statements. Terms may be used more than once. If you find yourself having difficulties, please refer to the appropriate section in the text.

- The total value of an economy's production of final goods and services in a given year is its

  (1)_____. When we calculate the value of production in *real*

  terms, we exclude the effect of changes in the (2)_____ level.

  And when we want to account for changes in population over time, we use

  (3)_____, the key statistic used to track economic growth.

- The mathematical formula that tells us how long it takes real GDP per capita, or any other

  variable that grows gradually over time, to double is called the rule of

  (4)_____.

- There has been an increase in (5)_____ in an economy when the

  amount of output produced by the average worker increases. Productivity is calculated as

  (6)_____.

Module Review

The Level Versus the Rate of Change

When studying economic growth, it's vitally important to understand the difference between a change in level and a rate of change. When we say that real GDP "grew," we mean that the level of real GDP increased. For example, we might say that U.S. real GDP grew during 2007 by $229 billion.

If we knew the level of U.S. real GDP in 2006, we could also represent the amount of 2007 growth in terms of a rate of change. For example, if U.S. real GDP in 2006 was $11,295 billion, then U.S. real GDP in 2007 was $11,295 billion + $229 billion = $11,524 billion. We could calculate the rate of change, or the growth rate, of U.S. real GDP during 2007 as: [($11,524 billion − $11,295 billion)/$11,295 billion] × 100 = ($229 billion/$11,295 billion) × 100 = 2.03%. Statements about economic growth over a period of years almost always refer to changes in the growth rate.

When talking about growth or growth rates, economists often use phrases that appear to mix the two concepts, and that can be confusing. For example, when we say that "U.S. growth fell during the 1970s," we are really saying that the U.S. growth rate of real GDP was lower in the 1970s compared to in the 1960s. When we say that "growth accelerated during the early 1990s," we are saying that the growth rate increased year after year in the early 1990s—for example, going from 3% to 3.5% to 4%.

- Real GDP per capita is a key statistic for measuring economic growth. Real GDP, not nominal GDP, is used to measure economic growth because real GDP focuses on the increase in the quantity of goods and services being produced and not on the effects of an increase in the aggregate price level. Real GDP per capita provides a measure of the average standard of living in a country.

- It is important to understand and know the sources of long-run economic growth. Economic growth arises because of increases in productivity, or output per worker. This increase in productivity is due to increases in human capital per worker, physical capital per worker, and/or technological advance. Economic growth is enhanced by high levels of saving and investment spending, a strong educational system, adequate infrastructure, well-supported research and development, political stability, and appropriate levels of government intervention in the economy.

- Productivity increases when physical capital per worker or human capital per worker increases, or technology advances. Increases in productivity are the primary source of economic growth over time. It is important to understand what productivity is and how an economy's productivity can be improved. Make sure you understand what an aggregate production function is and how it illustrates the relationship between productivity and the variables that determine productivity.

Module 38
Productivity and Growth

Before You Read the MODULE

Summary

This module shows how an aggregate production function can be used to analyze economic growth. It also presents the convergence hypothesis.

Module Objectives

Review these objectives before you read the module. Place a "√" on the line when you understand each of the following:

_____**Objective 1.** How changes in productivity are illustrated using an **aggregate production function**

_____**Objective 2.** How growth has varied among regions of the world and why the **convergence hypothesis** applies to economically advanced countries

While You Read the MODULE

Key Terms

Define these key terms as you read the module.

Aggregate production function

Diminishing returns to physical capital

Growth accounting

Total factor productivity

_____

Convergence hypothesis

_____

List questions or difficulties from your initial reading of the module.

After You Read the MODULE

....

Fill-in-the-Blanks

Fill in the blanks to complete the following statements. Terms may be used more than once. If you find yourself having difficulties, please refer to the appropriate section in the text.

- There are three main reasons why U.S. worker productivity has increased over time. First,

  workers have more equipment and machinery, or (1)_____

  capital, with which to work. Second, workers are better educated and so possess more

  (2)_____ capital. Finally, modern firms have the advantage of a

  century's accumulation of technical advancements, reflecting

  (3)_____.

- The aggregate (4)_____ shows how productivity depends on the

  quantities of physical capital per worker and human capital per worker, as well as the state

  of technology. Typically, when the amount of human capital per worker and the state of

  technology are held fixed, each successive increase in the amount of physical capital per

  worker leads to a smaller increase in productivity. This phenomenon is known as

  (5)_____ to physical capital.

- The amount of output that can be produced with a given number of factor inputs is

  known as (6)_____ productivity.

It May Be Diminished . . . but It's Still Positive

We have seen that diminishing returns to physical capital is an "other things equal" statement. That is, holding the amount of human capital per worker and the technology fixed, each successive increase in the amount of physical capital per worker results in a smaller increase in real GDP per worker. But this doesn't mean that real GDP per worker eventually falls as more and more physical capital is added. Rather, the *increase* in real GDP per worker gets smaller and smaller, albeit remaining at or above zero. So an increase in physical capital per worker will never reduce productivity. But due to diminishing returns, at some point increasing the amount of physical capital per worker no longer produces an economic payoff. At some point the increase in output is so small that it is not worth the cost of the additional physical capital.

- The concept of diminishing returns to physical capital is important. Holding everything else constant, an increase in physical capital per worker will eventually lead to smaller increases in productivity. Adding more physical capital to a fixed level of labor and technology initially increases output at an increasing rate, but eventually, each successive addition to physical capital per worker produces a smaller increase in output per worker.

Module 39
Growth Policy:
Why Economic Growth
Rates Differ

Before You Read the MODULE

Summary

This module investigates why growth rates differ across countries and across periods of time.

Module Objectives

Review these objectives before you read the module. Place a "√" on the line when you understand each of the following:

_____ **Objective 1.** The factors that explain why long-run growth rates differ so much among countries

_____ **Objective 2.** The challenges to growth posed by scarcity of natural resources and environmental degradation, and efforts to make growth **sustainable**

While You Read the MODULE

Key Terms

Define these key terms as you read the module.

Research and development (R & D)

Infrastructure

Sustainable

List questions or difficulties from your initial reading of the module.

After You Read the MODULE

Fill-in-the-Blanks

Fill in the blanks to complete the following statements. Terms may be used more than once. If you find yourself having difficulties, please refer to the appropriate section in the text.

- Economies grow when they increase their physical capital stock through

  (1)_____ spending, add to their

  (2)_____ capital through education, or benefit from scientific

  advances that lead to (3)_____ progress. Spending to create new

  technologies and implement their use is known as (4)_____

  spending.

- Governments can spur economic growth by spending on the parts of the economy's

  physical capital that provide an underpinning for economic activity, known as

  (5)_____. The government can also spur private investment

  spending by providing an efficient (6)_____ system that links

  savers with investors. Finally, governments facilitate economic growth through spending

  on education to develop the economy's (7)_____ capital and by

  providing political stability and (8)_____ rights.

Module Review

Growth and the Environment

In the United States during the 1960s, increased awareness of declining environmental quality led to the start of a growing environmental movement often associated with the creation of the first Earth Day in 1970. Before this time, neither the economics discipline nor the country was very focused on environmental issues. But the growing environmental movement has led both the economic discipline and the country to think more about the environment in recent decades.

Early in the environmental movement, many assumed that there was a trade-off between economic growth and environmental quality. According to this view, you could draw a production possibility curve with a trade-off between environmental quality and other goods and services. If this were true, the only way to protect the environment would be to restrict economic growth.

However, since that time, economists have come to realize that there is not a strictly negative relationship between economic growth and environmental quality. It is possible to continue long-run economic growth while protecting the environment through technological progress and market-based incentives.

Module 40
Economic Growth in Macroeconomic Models

Before You Read the MODULE

Summary

This module explains how to evaluate the effects of long-run growth policies, using the production possibilities curve and the aggregate demand and supply model.

Module Objectives

Review these objectives before you read the module. Place a "√" on the line when you understand each of the following:

_____**Objective 1.** How long-run economic growth is represented in macroeconomic models

_____**Objective 2.** How to model the effects of economic growth policies

While You Read the MODULE

Key Term

Define this key term as you read the module.

Depreciation

List questions or difficulties from your initial reading of the module.

After You Read the MODULE

Fill-in-the-Blanks

Fill in the blanks to complete the following statements. Terms may be used more than once. If you find your-self having difficulties, please refer to the appropriate section in the text.

- On a production possibilities curve graph, economic growth is shown by an

  (1)_____ shift of the PPC. This shift will result from an increase

  in physical or human (2)_____, or

  (3)_____ progress. Over time, physical capital will wear out.

  This is known as (4)_____, and it will shift the PPC inward.

- In the aggregate supply and aggregate demand model, economic growth is shown as a

  rightward shift of the (5)_____ curve. This shift represents an

  increase in the economy's level of (6)_____ output.

Module Review

Long-run Growth Versus Short-run Fluctuations

It is important to distinguish long-run changes from short-run fluctuations due to the business cycle. Both the production possibilities curve and the aggregate demand and aggregate supply model can help us do this. In the production possibilities curve model, if the economy experiences a macroeconomic fluctuation due to the business cycle, for example, unemployment due to a recession, production falls to a point inside the production possibilities curve. On the other hand, long-run growth will appear as an outward shift of the production possibilities curve.

In the aggregate demand and aggregate supply model, fluctuations of actual aggregate output around potential output are illustrated by shifts of the short-run aggregate supply curve. In the case of short-run fluctuations due to the business cycle, adjustments in nominal wages will eventually bring the actual level of real GDP back to the potential level. Long-run economic growth is represented by a rightward shift of the long-run aggregate supply curve and corresponds to an increase in the economy's level of potential output.

- Investment spending determines the level of physical capital available to workers. It plays a vital role in determining an economy's rate of economic growth and can be funded through domestic saving or through the borrowing of foreign saving.

Draw the Featured Model

Show economic growth in the PPC and *AS/AD* graphs below.

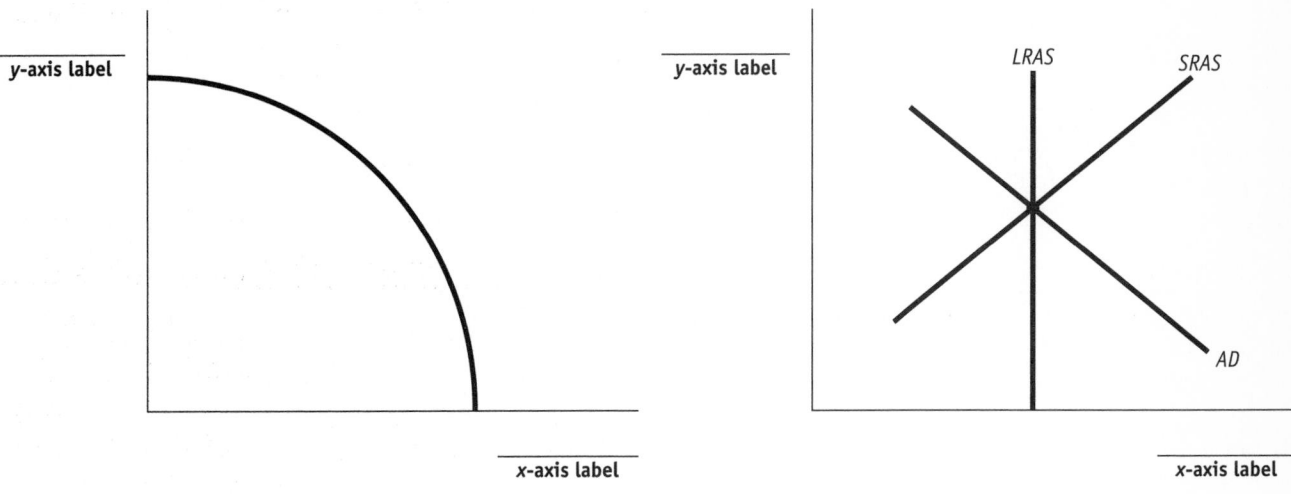

Complete the Exercise

1. How will each of the following changes shift the PPC and the *LRAS* (→, ←, or not at all)?

	PPC	LRAS

   a. The economy's physical capital stock decreases due to depreciation.
   b. Government education programs lead to increases in human capital.
   c. Research and development spending lead to technological progress.
   d. A war reduces a country's political instability.

Problems

1. You are given the following information about the country of Macronesia.

Year	Nominal GDP	CPI	Real GDP	Population
2009	$10 billion	100		1.0 million
2010	10.5 billion	105		1.05 million
2011	11.0 billion	108		1.08 million

   a. What is the base year for the economy represented in the previous table? How did you identify the base year?

   b. Calculate the missing values in the table, and then round to the nearest billion: e.g., 14,829,000,000 would be rounded to 14.8 billion.

c. Use the completed table from part (b) to calculate the missing values in the following table. You will find it helpful to define real GDP in millions (for example, 14.8 billion is 14,800 million) because population is expressed in millions.

Year	Real GDP per capita
2009	
2010	
2011	

d. Let's compare the percentage changes in some of the variables we are working with in this problem. Use the following table to organize your calculations.

Year	Percentage change in nominal GDP	Percentage change in real GDP	Percentage change in population	Percentage change in real GDP per capita
2009				
2010				
2011				

e. In order for real GDP per capita to increase over time, what must be true about the relationship between the percentage change in real GDP and the percentage change in population?

f. Why do we focus on computing real GDP per capita instead of nominal GDP per capita?

2. Suppose real GDP per capita in Fun Land is $10,000 in 2009. Economists there predict steady increases in real GDP of 7% a year for the foreseeable future.

Year	Real GDP per capita
2009	$10,000
2010	
2011	
2012	
2013	
2014	
2015	
2016	
2017	
2018	
2019	

a. According to the Rule of 70, how many years will it take for Fun Land's real GDP per capita to double?

b. To verify your answer in part (a), compute the values for real GDP per capita in the table above.

c. Is your value for real GDP per capita for 2019 equal to $20,000? If it differs, does this surprise you? Explain your answer.

3. The economy of Macro States estimates its aggregate production function as $Y/L = 50(K/L)^{1/2}$ when technology and human capital per worker are held constant. In the equation Y is real GDP, L is the number of workers, and K is the quantity of physical capital. Macro States has 500 workers.

a. Calculate real GDP per worker (Y/L) and physical capital per worker (K/L) for the given levels of physical capital in the following table. Round (K/L) to the nearest hundredth and (Y/L) to the nearest whole number.

K	K/L	Y/L
$0		
20		
40		
60		
80		
100		
200		
400		

b. Plot Macro States's aggregate production function on a graph. Physical capital per worker is measured on the x-axis and real GDP per worker is measured on the y-axis.

c. As physical capital per worker increases, what happens to real GDP per worker?

4. Suppose that Macro States increases its level of technology and human capital per worker relative to its economic condition in Problem 3. Now, Macro States economists estimate that the aggregate production function is given by the equation $Y/L = 60(K/L)^{1/2}$.

a. Relative to the aggregate production function you plotted in Problem 3b, what do you anticipate will happen to Macro States's aggregate production function as a result of this increase in human capital per worker and technology?

b. Compare productivity in Macro States in the initial situation to its new situation, assuming that Macro States has $100 in physical capital.

c. Why are increases in productivity important?

5. Suppose there are two countries, Macroland and Pacifica, that currently have real GDP per capita of $10,000 and $15,000, respectively. Furthermore, suppose Macroland's economy has an average annual growth rate of 2%, while Pacifica's has an average annual growth rate of 1.4%.

a. Compute real GDP per capita for both Macroland and Pacifica 50 years from now.

b. Compute real GDP per capita for both Macroland and Pacifica 100 years from now.

c. Initially, Macroland's real GDP per capita is 67% of Pacifica's real GDP per capita. After 50 years, what is the relationship of Macroland's real GDP per capita to Pacifica's real GDP per capita in percentage terms? What is this relationship after 100 years?

6. Many people worry that the world may run out of important resources, such as oil, and that this depletion of a vital resource will bring an end to economic growth. Why do many economists *not* believe in this particular perspective?

7. Economists argue that the problems presented by widespread climate destruction can be resolved only through government intervention, as well as cooperation among different governments. Why do they hold this view?

Review Questions

Circle the correct answer.

1. Real GDP per capita is
   A. the value of real GDP divided by the number of units of capital in an economy in a given time period.
   B. always increasing over time for any given economy.
   C. the value of real GDP divided by population for a given country.
   D. Answers (B) and (C) are both correct.

2. Suppose real GDP for Macronesia is $200 million in 2011. Furthermore, suppose the population of Macronesia is 100,000 in 2011. If population increases to 105,000 in 2012 while GDP increases by 5%, then it must be true that real GDP per capita in Macronesia in 2012
   A. increased.
   B. decreased.
   C. stayed constant.
   D. may have increased, decreased, or remained constant.

3. Which of the following statements is true?
   A. Other things being equal, an increase in population raises the average standard of living in an economy.
   B. In 1907, the U.S. economy produced only 16% as much per person as it did in 2007.
   C. The median American household income in the United States in 2007 was $50,000.
   D. Answers (A), (B), and (C) are all true.
   E. Answers (B) and (C) are both true.

4. Suppose that real GDP per capita grows at 2% per year. For real GDP per capita to approximately double, it will take
   A. 70 years because of the Rule of 70.
   B. 140 years because the Rule of 70 states that a variable will double in 70 years if the variable has an annual growth rate of 1%; therefore, a variable growing at 2% will take twice as long to double.
   C. 35 years because the Rule of 70 states that the number of years it takes for a variable to double is equal to 70 divided by the annual growth rate of the variable.
   D. 50 years because at 2% per year it takes 50 years to reach 100% more than the initial real GDP per capita.

5. Which of the following has been most important in driving long-run economic growth?

    A. rising labor productivity or output per worker
    B. putting more people to work
    C. being a relatively rich country initially
    D. the availability of abundant natural resources

6. Productivity increases can be attributed to

    A. increases in physical capital or the amount of machinery and office space available to workers.
    B. increases in human capital or the level of workers' education.
    C. technological advances.
    D. Answers (A), (B), and (C) are all correct.

7. Which of the following statements is true?

    A. An aggregate production function indicates how output per worker depends on the level of physical capital per worker, human capital per worker, and the state of technology.
    B. Holding everything else constant, an increase in human capital per worker reduces the level of output per worker.
    C. Holding everything else constant, a decrease in physical capital per worker increases the level of output per worker.
    D. Answers (A), (B), and (C) are all true.

8. Suppose the amount of human capital per worker and the state of technology are held constant. As physical capital per worker increases, each additional increase in physical capital per worker leads to

    A. greater increases in output per worker.
    B. greater decreases in output per worker.
    C. smaller increases in output per worker.
    D. smaller decreases in output per worker.

9. An economy increases its level of physical capital per worker by increasing the level of investment spending. This can be achieved by

    A. having domestic residents spend more of their income on consumption.
    B. having domestic residents spend less of their income on consumption while increasing their domestic saving.
    C. borrowing foreign savings from residents of other countries.
    D. Answers (A) and (C) are both correct.
    E. Answers (B) and (C) are both correct.

10. Which of the following statements is true?

    A. Between 1907 and 2007, U.S. real GDP per capita increased by approximately 620%.
    B. Despite dramatic economic growth in China and India over the past thirty years, as of 2007 China and India were still poorer than the U.S. was in 1907.
    C. Today more than 50% of the world's population lives in countries that are poorer than the U.S. was a century ago.
    D. Answers (A), (B), and (C) are all true.

11. Suppose real GDP in Macroland was $400 billion in 2011 and $450 billion in 2012. Then the growth rate of real GDP between 2011 and 2012 was

    A. 50%.
    B. 5%.
    C. 125%.
    D. 12.5%

12. Which of the following statements is true?

    A. Countries with low levels of infrastructure typically experience low rates of economic growth.
    B. Infrastructure is primarily provided by private companies.
    C. Basic public health measures, like clean water, are not considered part of an economy's infrastructure.
    D. Answers (A), (B), and (C) are all true.

13. Long-run economic growth requires

    A. the imposition of bureaucratic restrictions on business and household activity.
    B. political stability and respect for property rights.
    C. extensive government intervention in markets in the form of import restrictions, government subsidies, and protection of firms from competitive economic pressures.
    D. Answers (A), (B) and (C) are all correct.

14. Which of the following statements is true?

    A. Today there is approximately $130,000 worth of physical capital per average U.S. private-sector worker.
    B. The U.S. population today is more highly educated than it was 50 years ago.
    C. Modest innovations can result in large technological gains for an economy.
    D. Answers (A), (B), and (C) are all true.
    E. Answers (A) and (B) are both true.

15. Holding human capital per worker, the number of workers, and the level of technology constant, suppose an economy increases the amount of physical capital per worker. In this economy, output per worker will

    A. initially increase at a diminishing rate but will eventually increase at an increasing rate as the economy uses greater amounts of physical capital per worker.
    B. eventually lead to output per worker increasing at a diminishing rate.
    C. eventually lead to output per worker increasing at an increasing rate.
    D. eventually lead to output per worker staying constant at the potential output level for the economy.

ANSWER KEY

Fill-in-the-Blanks

Module 37: (1) GDP, (2) price, (3) real GDP per capita, (4) 70, (5) productivity, (6) real GDP/number of workers

Module 38: (1) physical, (2) human, (3) technological progress, (4) production function, (5) diminishing returns, (6) total factor

Module 39: (1) investment, (2) human, (3) technological, (4) research and development, (5) infrastructure, (6) financial, (7) human, (8) property

Module 40: (1) outward, (2) capital, (3) technological, (4) depreciation, (5) *LRAS*, (6) potential

Featured Graph

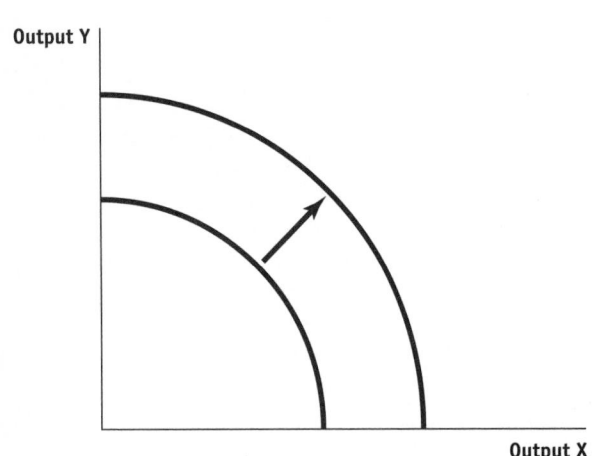

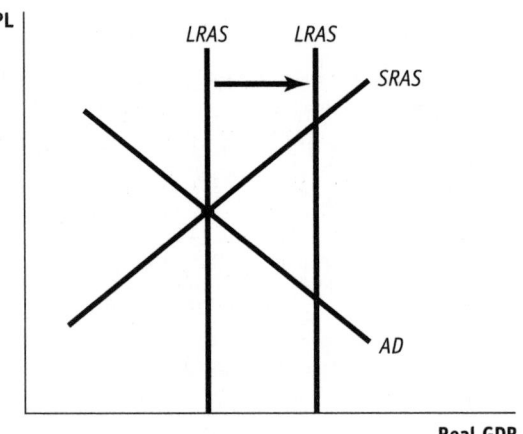

Exercise

a. ←

b. →

c. →

d. ←

Answers to Problems

1. **a.** 2007. The base year is that year with the CPI value of 100.

b.

Year	Nominal GDP	CPI	Real GDP	Population
2009	$10 billion	100	$10 billion	1.0 million
2010	10.5 billion	105	10 billion	1.05 million
2011	11.0 billion	108	10.19 billion	1.08 million

c.

Year	Real GDP per capita
2009	$10,000
2010	9,524
2011	9,435

d.

Year	Percentage change in nominal GDP	Percentage change in real GDP	Percentage change in population	Percentage change in real GDP per capita
2009	—	—	—	—
2010	5%	0%	5%	−4.8%
2011	4.8	1.9	2.9	−0.93

e. The percentage change in real GDP must be greater than the percentage change in population for real GDP per capita to increase over time.

f. Real GDP per capita allows us to track the increase in the quantity of goods and services available in our economy rather than just the effects of a rising price level.

2. a. Ten years because the Rule of 70 says the number of years it takes for a variable to double is approximately equal to 70 divided by the annual growth rate of the variable.

b.

Year	Real GDP per capita
2009	$10,000
2010	10,700
2011	11,449
2012	12,250
2013	13,108
2014	14,026
2015	15,007
2016	16,058
2017	17,182
2018	18,385
2019	19,672

c. The value of real GDP per capita for 2019 is $19,672, which is less than the estimated $20,000. This is not surprising because the Rule of 70 is an estimation of the number of years it takes a variable to double rather than a numerically precise calculation.

3. a.

K	K/L	Y/L
$0	$0	$0
20	0.04	10
40	0.08	14
60	0.12	17
80	0.16	20
100	0.2	22
200	0.4	32
400	0.8	45

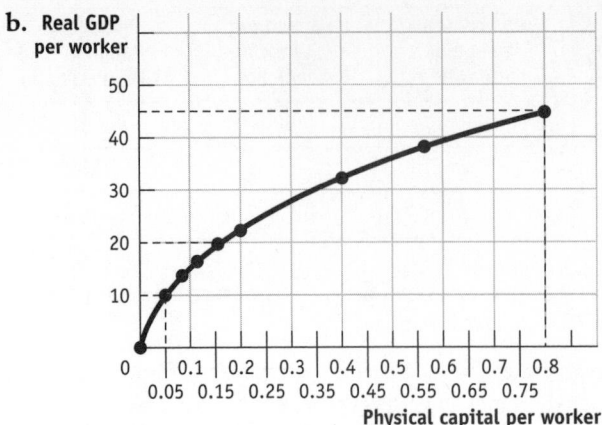

b. Real GDP per worker

Physical capital per worker

c. Real GDP per worker increases as physical capital per worker increases, but it increases at a diminishing rate. For example, if we hold the number of workers and all other variables constant, real GDP per worker increases by $4 when physical capital increases from $20 to $40, but real GDP per worker increases by $3.50 when physical capital increases from $40 to $60.

4. a. Macro States's aggregate production function will shift up relative to its initial position for every level of physical capital per worker. We can see this by recalculating output per worker, given the new aggregate production function.

K	K/L	Y/L
$0	$0	$0
20	0.20	12.00
40	0.28	16.80
60	0.35	21.00
80	0.40	24.00
100	0.45	27.00

b. Productivity is defined as output per worker. When physical capital equals $100, output per worker is initially $22.50, while, after the increase in human capital per worker and technology, output per worker increases to $27.00.

c. Increases in productivity are important because they indicate that each worker on average is now producing a greater level of output. This, in turn, makes it possible for people on average to experience higher standards of living.

5. a. Real GDP per capita in Macroland in 50 years will equal $(\$10,000)(1 + 0.02)^{50}$ or $26,916. Real GDP per capita in Pacifica in 50 years will equal $(\$15,000)(1 + 0.014)^{50}$, or $30,060.

b. Real GDP per capita in Macroland in 100 years will equal $(\$10,000)(1 + 0.02)^{100}$, or $72,446. Real GDP per capita in Pacifica in 100 years will equal $(\$15,000)(1 + 0.014)^{100}$, or $60,240.

c. In 50 years, the ratio of Macroland's real GDP per capita to Pacifica's real GDP per capita in percentage terms will be 89.5%, while in 100 years, it will be 120.3%.

6. Economists argue that vital resources, as they grow scarce, will command increasingly higher prices. These higher prices will cause people to conserve resources, and their scarcity will spur the development of alternatives to replace the scarce, but vital, resource.

7. Climate destruction arises from widespread economic growth, and this destruction is an example of a negative externality. Negative externalities arise when a market fails to include all the costs of producing a good in the calculation of the good's price. Many goods produced today also produce significant pollution, and the market does not internalize these costs of pollution. Without government intervention, firms and individuals do not have any incentive to reduce negative externalities. Reducing pollution and the climate destruction that accompanies it will require the cooperation of governments in the imposition of some form of market-based incentives: for example, both a "carbon tax" or a "cap and trade" system would reduce the amount of carbon emitted into the air.

Answers to Review Questions

1. **C.** Real GDP per capita is defined as the value of real GDP in a country divided by that country's population. Real GDP per capita may increase, decrease, or remain steady over time.

2. **C.** In 2012, the population in Macronesia increased by 5% as did real GDP. Since both population and real GDP increased by the same percentage amount, real GDP per capita is unaffected.

3. **E.** Answers (B) and (C) are factual statements from the text. Answer (A) is not true: an increase in population, other things equal, will reduce the average standard of living because the average standard of living is calculated as real GDP per capita. The increase in population increases the size of the denominator in this ratio while the numerator, or real GDP, stays constant.

4. **C.** This is a straightforward use of the definition of the Rule of 70, which states that an estimation of the number of years it takes for a variable to double is equal to 70 divided by the annual growth rate of the variable.

5. **A.** Sustained economic growth occurs only when an economy steadily increases the amount of output each worker produces. In other words, long-run economic growth depends upon rising labor productivity. Putting more people to work can increase output in the short run, but it does not result in sustained economic growth. Long-run economic growth is possible in relatively poor countries (for example, South Korea before 1970) and countries with low levels of resources (for example, Japan).

6. **D.** Each of these factors—physical capital, human capital, and technological advances—contributes to increases in productivity, or the ability to produce more output per worker.

7. **A.** Answer (A) provides a definition of the aggregate production function. In answers (B) and (C), we know there is a relationship between output per worker and the amount of human capital per worker or physical capital per worker. In both cases, an increase in either human or physical capital, holding everything else constant, will lead to an increase in output per worker.

8. **C.** This question focuses on the concept of diminishing returns to physical capital. Given an aggregate production function with a constant level of human capital per worker and state of technology, an increase in the quantity of physical capital per worker will lead the rate of productivity to fall while remaining positive. Thus, output per worker will increase but by smaller and smaller amounts.

9. **E.** Investment spending depends upon the availability of savings. An increase in investment spending is possible either by increasing the level of domestic savings or by borrowing foreign savings.

10. **D.** All of these statements are factual statements found in the text.

11. **D.** To find the growth rate of real GDP in Macroland between 2011 and 2012, use the following formula:
Growth rate of real GDP between 2011 and 2012 = {[(real GDP in 2008) − (real GDP in 2011)]/(real GDP in 2011)} × 100 = [(450 − 400)/(400)] × 100 = 12.5%

12. **A.** Infrastructure includes roads, power lines, ports, information networks, and basic public health measures. Countries lacking this infrastructure find it hard to maintain high rates of economic growth. Infrastructure is primarily provided by government, not private enterprise.

13. B. Long-run economic growth requires political stability and well-defined property rights. Long-run economic growth is hindered by bureaucratic restrictions and excessive government intervention in markets.

14. D. All of the statements are true: answers (A) and (B) are in the text. Answer (C) refers to the idea that technological innovation can result from relatively modest innovations and not just major innovations. The text provides the examples of flat-bottomed paper bags and Post-it® notes.

15. B. With fixed technology, labor, and human capital, an increase in physical capital per worker will eventually result in output per worker increasing at a decreasing rate due to diminishing returns to physical capital. The economy, despite its increased physical capital per worker, finds that each additional unit of this physical capital per worker results in smaller and smaller increases to output per worker because the fixed amount of labor cannot fully use the increases in physical capital per worker.

Notes

The Open Economy: International Trade and Finance

OVERVIEW

This section presents the key issues in open-economy macroeconomics: the determinants of a country's balance of payments, the factors affecting exchange rates, the different forms of exchange rate policy adopted by various countries, and the relationship between exchange rates and macroeconomic policy.

FEATURED MODEL/GRAPH: THE FOREIGN EXCHANGE MARKET

This section presents the foreign exchange market. A variation of the supply and demand model, the foreign exchange model uses the supply and demand for currency to determine the equilibrium exchange rate and quantity of currency exchanged.

MODULES IN THIS SECTION

Module 41: Capital Flows and the Balance of Payments

Module 42: The Foreign Exchange Market

Module 43: Exchange Rate Policy

Module 44: Exchange Rates and Macroeconomic Policy

Module 45: Putting It All Together

Module 41
Capital Flows and the Balance of Payments

Before You Read the MODULE

Summary

This module explains how economists keep track of international transactions using a different but related set of numbers, the balance of payments accounts.

Module Objectives

Review these objectives before you read the module. Place a "√" on the line when you understand each of the following:

_____**Objective 1.** The meaning of the **balance of payments accounts**

_____**Objective 2.** The determinants of international capital flows

While You Read the MODULE

Key Terms

Define these key terms as you read the module.

Balance of payments accounts

Balance of payments on the current account (current account)

Balance of payments on goods and services

Merchandise trade balance, or trade balance

Balance of payments on the financial account (financial account)

List questions or difficulties from your initial reading of the module.

After You Read the MODULE

Fill-in-the-Blanks

Fill in the blanks to complete the following statements. Terms may be used more than once. If you find your-self having difficulties, please refer to the appropriate section in the text.

- A country's transactions with other countries is summarized in the

  (1)_____ accounts. Transactions that don't create liabilities are

  considered part of the (2)_____ account. The most important

  part of the current account is the difference between the value of exports and the value of

  imports during a given period, known as the balance of payments on

  (3)_____. Transactions that involve the sale or purchase of

  assets that create future liabilities, for example, bonds are considered part of the

  (4)_____ account. Until a few years ago, economists often

  referred to the financial account as the capital account. The current account and the

  financial account must sum to (5)_____. The sale and purchase

  of assets is modeled using the market for (6)_____.

Module Review

The Rest of the World Has Been There All Along

In this section, we expand our study of the economy to include the rest of the world. But, "the rest of the world" has been there all along! We saw it when we studied comparative advantage, in the circular-flow model, and as "X" and "IM" as contributors to GDP. We live in an interconnected world, and it is impossible to study macroeconomics without considering the relationships between national economies. Today, all macroeconomics is "open-economy." So, while at the beginning we assumed away international trade and finance so that we could understand the simplified model, it is crucial that we now integrate the international sector into our understanding of the economy.

- The balance of payments shows the flow of money between national economies. It illustrates why the balance of payments on the current account must equal the balance of payments on the financial account. It illustrates the relationship in a domestic economy between the payments from the rest of the world for goods and services, factor income, and transfers, and payments to the rest of the world for goods and services, factor income, and transfers.

Module 42
The Foreign Exchange Market

Before You Read the MODULE

Summary

The financial account reflects the movement of capital and the current account reflects the movement of goods and services. The foreign exchange market ensures that the balance of payments offset each other. This module looks at how the exchange rate, determined in the foreign exchange market, ensures balance in the balance of payments.

Module Objectives

Review these objectives before you read the module. Place a "√" on the line when you understand each of the following:

_____**Objective 1.** The role of the **foreign exchange market** and the **exchange rate**

_____**Objective 2.** The importance of **real exchange rates** and their role in the current account

While You Read the MODULE

Key Terms

Define these key terms as you read the module.

Foreign exchange market

Exchange rates

Appreciates

Depreciates
_____

Equilibrium exchange rate
_____

Real exchange rates
_____

Purchasing power parity
_____

List questions or difficulties from your initial reading of the module.

After You Read the MODULE

Fill-in-the-Blanks

Fill in the blanks to complete the following statements. Terms may be used more than once. If you find yourself having difficulties, please refer to the appropriate section in the text.

- Currencies are exchanged for each other in the (1)_____ market.

  The price at which currencies trade is known as the (2)_____

  rate.

- The nominal exchange rate at which a given basket of goods and services would cost the

  same amount in each country is called (3)_____. This nominal

  exchange rate will change over time if countries have different rates of

  (4)_____.

Suppose Someone Says, "The U.S. Exchange Rate Is Up." What Does That Mean?

It isn't clear. Sometimes the exchange rate is measured as the price of a dollar in terms of foreign currency, sometimes as the price of foreign currency in terms of dollars. So the statement could mean either that the dollar appreciated or that it depreciated!

You have to be particularly careful when using published statistics. Most countries other than the United States express their exchange rates in terms of the price of a dollar in their domestic currency—for example, Mexican officials will say that the exchange rate is 10, meaning 10 pesos per dollar. But Britain, for historical reasons, usually states its exchange rate the other way. At 3:49 P.M. on September 13, 2008, US$1 was worth £0.55878, and £1 was worth US$1.7896. More often than not, this number is reported as an exchange rate of 1.7896. In fact, on occasion, professional economists and consultants embarrass themselves by getting the direction in which the pound is moving wrong!

By the way, U.S. citizens generally follow other countries' lead. We usually say that the exchange rate against Mexico is 10 pesos per dollar but that the exchange rate against Britain is 1.8 dollars per pound. But this rule isn't reliable; exchange rates against the euro are often stated both ways. So it's always important to check before using exchange rate data which way the exchange rate is being measured.

- An exchange rate is the price of one currency in terms of another currency. When a country's exchange rate increases, or appreciates, this makes its domestically produced goods relatively more expensive than goods produced by other economies. This will decrease exports and increase imports for the domestic economy. The balance of payments on the current account will decrease, while the balance of payments on the financial account will increase.

Module 43
Exchange Rate Policy

Before You Read the MODULE

Summary

This module looks at government policies, called exchange rate regimes, that have been adopted to influence exchange rates.

Module Objectives

Review these objectives before you read the module. Place a "√" on the line when you understand each of the following:

_____**Objective 1.** The difference between **fixed exchange rates** and **floating exchange rates**

_____**Objective 2.** Considerations that lead countries to choose different **exchange rate regimes**

While You Read the MODULE

Key Terms

Define these key terms as you read the module.

Exchange rate regimes

Fixed exchange rate

Floating exchange rate

Exchange market intervention

Foreign exchange reserves

Foreign exchange controls

List questions or difficulties from your initial reading of the module.

After You Read the MODULE

Fill-in-the-Blanks

Fill in the blanks to complete the following statements. Terms may be used more than once. If you find yourself having difficulties, please refer to the appropriate section in the text.

- A rule governing policy toward the exchange rate is known as an exchange rate

  (1)_____. When the government keeps the exchange rate against

  some other currency at or near a particular target it has a

  (2)_____. A country has a (3)_____

  exchange rate when the government lets the exchange rate go wherever the market takes it.

- Government purchases or sales of currency in the foreign exchange market are called

  exchange market (4)_____. Most countries maintain foreign

  exchange (5)_____, stocks of foreign currency that they can use

  to buy their own currency to support its price. A government can shift the supply and

  demand for its currency in the foreign exchange market by changing

  (6)_____ policy.

Fixed Versus Floating Exchange Rates

When countries use a floating exchange rate regime, the foreign exchange market determines the exchange rate. With a floating exchange rate, you can use the supply and demand model of a country's currency to analyze how changes in, for example, interest rates, affect exchange rates the same way you used the supply and demand model to analyze changes in markets for goods and services . Any change that affects a determinant of the demand or supply of a country's currency will shift the relevant curve and move the market to a new equilibrium. The determinants of the demand and supply of a country's currency are listed below.

Determinants of Demand and Supply in the Foreign Exchange Market Model

Supply	Demand
Domestic residents buying in other countries	Foreigners buying domestically
– Goods	– Goods
– Services	– Services
– Assets	– Assets

A change in a determinant of demand or supply will shift the demand or supply curve and lead to a new equilibrium exchange rate. In a fixed exchange rate regime, a country must respond anytime a change affects the foreign exchange market. Without a government response, a change in a determinant of demand or supply will shift the demand or supply curve and lead to a new equilibrium exchange rate. To keep the exchange rate fixed, the government must take an action to counteract the effect of any change that affects the equilibrium exchange rate in the market. In the case of either a floating or a fixed exchange rate regime, this model of the exchange rate has the same underlying principles as the supply and demand model of a market for a good or service.

- You should understand the distinction between fixed and floating exchange rate regimes and the advantages and disadvantages associated with either type.

Module 44
Exchange Rates and Macroeconomic Policy

Before You Read the MODULE

Summary

This module looks at three policy issues raised by open-economy macroeconomics: devaluation and revaluation of fixed exchange rates, monetary policy under floating exchange rates, and international business cycles.

Module Objectives

Review these objectives before you read the module. Place a "√" on the line when you understand each of the following:

_____**Objective 1.** The meaning and purpose of **devaluation** and **revaluation** of a currency under a fixed exchange rate regime

_____**Objective 2.** Why open-economy considerations affect macroeconomic policy under floating exchange rates

While You Read the MODULE

Key Terms

Define these key terms as you read the module.

Devaluation

Revaluation

List questions or difficulties from your initial reading of the module.

After You Read the MODULE

Fill-in-the-Blanks

Fill in the blanks to complete the following statements. Terms may be used more than once. If you find yourself having difficulties, please refer to the appropriate section in the text.

- A reduction in the value of a currency that is set under a fixed exchange rate regime is

  called (1)_____. We learned previously that

  (2)_____ is a downward move in a currency. The new term

  applies when the downward move is due to a revision in a fixed exchange rate target. An

  increase in the value of a currency is called (3)_____, and when

  it is set under a fixed exchange rate regime, it is called a

  (4)_____.

Module Review

Monetary Policy in an Open Economy

In this module, we learned that monetary policy will have effects in an open economy beyond those we saw in a closed economy. We already know that, in a closed economy, expansionary monetary policy involves lowering interest rates. This increases aggregate demand by increasing investment spending and interest-sensitive consumer spending. Contractionary monetary policy (in a closed economy) involves raising interest rates. This decreases aggregate demand by decreasing investment spending and interest-sensitive consumer spending. Now we need to understand how, under floating exchange rates, these effects are reinforced in an open economy.

In an open economy with a floating exchange rate, changes in interest rates also affect aggregate demand in another way. For example, when interest rates fall, the supply of the domestic currency increases as its citizens trade it for other currencies in order to invest where interest rates are higher. At the same time, the demand for the domestic currency decreases, as the incentive to invest in the country is lower when domestic interest rates are lower. The increase in the supply and the decrease in the demand for the domestic currency both lead the currency to depreciate. Depreciation, as we have seen, makes exports cheaper and imports more expensive, which increases exports and decreases imports, further increasing aggregate demand. An increase in interest rates has the opposite effects: it leads to an appreciation of the domestic currency, which increases imports and reduces exports. This reinforces the decrease in aggregate demand from the contractionary monetary policy. To fully analyze a change in monetary policy in an open economy, it is important to trace the chain of events through the international sector.

Module 45
Putting It All Together

Before You Read the MODULE

Summary

This module shows you how to use the models developed in the text to analyze different scenarios and evaluate alternative policy recommendations.

Module Objectives

Review these objectives before you read the module. Place a "√" on the line when you understand each of the following:

_____**Objective 1.** How to use macroeconomic models to conduct policy analysis

_____**Objective 2.** How to approach free-response macroeconomics questions

Module Review

When faced with analyzing the macroeconomy, we have seen how breaking a question up into its components (starting point, event, response, short-run effects, long-run effects) can make the task more manageable. Here are some other tips to make your analysis more efficient and effective.

What is the question?
We have seen that macroeconomic analysis can be very complex. It is easy to go off on tangents when you are thinking about all of the related issues. Make sure that you keep the question you are trying to answer at the front of your mind as you consider different scenarios. Pay close attention to exactly what is asked of you. Were you asked to draw a graph, identify, or explain? Were you asked a simple yes/no or increase/decrease question? Be sure you provide the answer to what was asked. And after you complete your analysis, check to make sure you have answered each of the specific questions that were asked. Also, there is no point to adding explanations or information that wasn't the focus of the scenario/questions. There are no bonus points for extraneous information, and adding it takes time and may confuse you or negate a correct answer you have given.

Use symbols and abbreviations
To save time and make your answer more concise, use common symbols and abbreviations. You can expect any economists evaluating your analysis to understand typical "economics shorthand." For example, an economists will know what GDP, C, or Q stand for. You can also use symbols to more quickly and clearly convey your analysis. For example, if you are asked to explain how an increase in the money supply will affect the aggregate demand curve, you could write out your answer:

An increase in the money supply causes the interest rate to fall, which results in an increase in investment, which leads to a rightward shift in the aggregate demand curve.

You could also answer using symbols and abbreviations: $\uparrow MS \rightarrow \downarrow i \rightarrow \uparrow I \rightarrow \uparrow AD$

Keep going

Analyzing a scenario involves several steps and there are a number of connections between the conclusion from one step and the analysis in the next step. It is not uncommon to become uncertain about whether you have made a mistake on a previous step. If you are unsure about your analysis at any step, don't just give up! Continue with your answer through the entire scenario. For example, you might be asked to determine what happens to the real interest rate in a situation and you answer that it will increase, but you aren't completely sure. You are then asked what will happen to investment if the real interest rate changes as you specified. Whether or not you are sure that the real interest rate increases, you can show you understand that *if* it increased, investment will fall. Always complete the analysis and answer every question. Even if you make a mistake early on, you will still have the opportunity to show that you understand other parts of the analysis.

BEFORE YOU TAKE THE TEST: section 8

Draw the Featured Model: The Foreign Exchange Market

Draw a graph of the markets for pesos and U.S. dollars. On your graph, show the initial equilibrium exchange rate and the effect in each market if U.S. investors decide to invest more in Mexico.

Peso Market

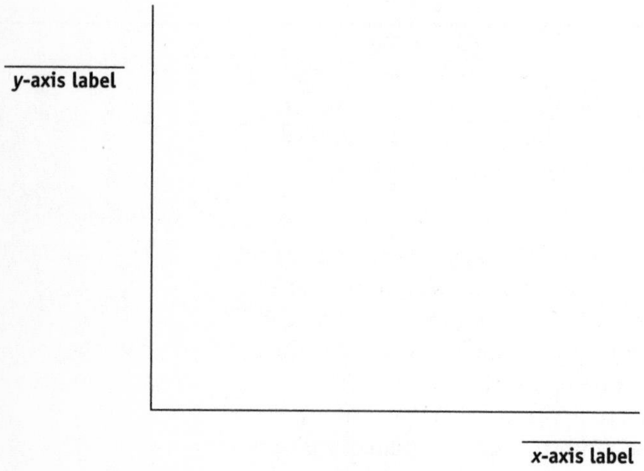

y-axis label

x-axis label

Dollar Market

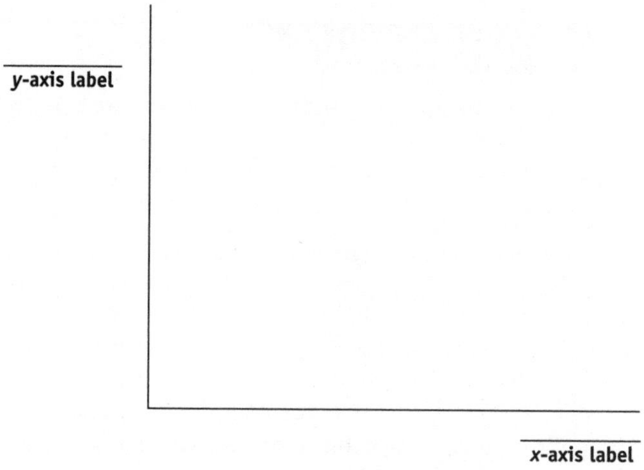

y-axis label

x-axis label

Complete the Exercise

Assume the United States and China are the only countries in the world. Given inflation and the change in the nominal exchange rate in each scenario, which country's goods become more attractive?

1. Inflation is 2% in China and 5% in the United States; the U.S dollar-Chinese yuan exchange rate stays the same.

2. Inflation is 3% in the United States and 8% in China; the price of the U.S. dollar falls from 6.25 to 5.15 Chinese yuan.

3. Inflation is 5% in the United States and 3% in China; the price of the yuan falls from $.15 to $.10.

4. Inflation is 5% in the United States and 4% in China; the price of Chinese yuan rises from $.10 to $.50.

Problems

1. Use the following table of information to answer this question.

	Payments from foreigners (millions of dollars)	Payments to foreigners (millions of dollars)	Sales of assets to foreigners (millions of dollars)	Purchases of assets from foreigners (millions of dollars)
Goods	$200	$80	—	—
Services	50	20	—	—
Factor income	70	10	—	—
Transfer payments	10	20	—	—
Official sales and purchases	—	—	$100	$300
Private sales and purchases	—	—	80	80

a. Provide a definition or an equation for each of the following items.
  (i.) Merchandise trade balance

  (ii.) Balance of payments on goods and services

  (iii.) Net international factor income

(iv.) Net international transfer payments

(v.) Balance of payments on the current account

(vi.) Balance of payments on the financial account

b. Given the previous information, compute the value of each of the terms given in part (a).

c. Explain why the sum of the balance of payments on the current account and the balance of payments on the financial account must equal zero.

2. The following graphs represent the loanable funds market in Macroland and Funland, the only two economies in the world.

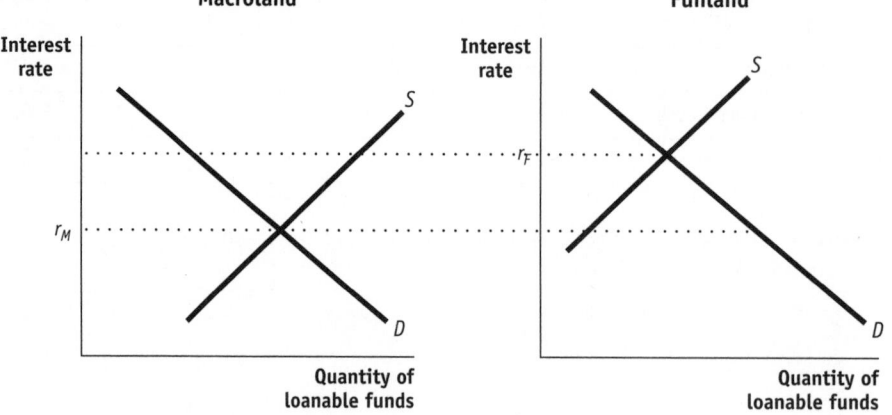

Residents in Macroland and Funland believe that foreign assets and liabilities are as good as domestic assets and liabilities.

a. Given the two graphs, which country is likely to attract capital? Why?

b. Given the Macroland graph, what do you predict will happen to the interest rate in Macroland over time? Explain your answer.

c. Given the Funland graph, what do you predict will happen to the interest rate in Funland over time? Explain your answer.

d. Briefly describe the capital flows between Macroland and Funland.

3. a. Calculate the missing values in the following table.

	U.S. dollars	Funland dollars	Macroland dollars
1 U.S. dollar exchanged for			1.05
1 Funland dollar exchanged for	0.005		
1 Macroland dollar exchanged for			

Suppose that the above exchange rates change as shown in the following table.

	U.S. dollars	Funland dollars	Macroland dollars
1 U.S. dollar exchanged for	1	210	
1 Funland dollar exchanged for		1	
1 Macroland dollar exchanged for	1.02		1

b. Fill in the missing values for this table.

c. Which currencies appreciated against the U.S. dollar?

d. Which currencies depreciated against the U.S. dollar?

e. Holding everything else constant, what do you expect will happen to the level of U.S. exports to Funland?

f. Holding everything else constant, what do you expect will happen to the level of U.S. exports to Macroland?

4. Suppose you are shown the information in the following table. Assume net international transfers and factor income equal zero for this problem.

Funland purchases of Macroland dollars in the foreign exchange market to buy Macroland goods and services	3.0 million Macroland dollars
Funland total purchases in the foreign exchange market of Macroland dollars	5.0 million Macroland dollars
Macroland sales of Macroland dollars in the foreign exchange market to buy Funland assets	1.5 million Macroland dollars
Macroland sales of Macroland dollars in the foreign exchange market to buy Funland goods and services	3.5 million Macroland dollars

a. Given the information in this table, compute the values in the following table.

Funland purchases of Macroland dollars in the foreign exchange market to buy Macroland assets	= _____
Total sales of Macroland dollars in the foreign exchange market	= _____
Macroland balance of payments on the current account	= _____
Macroland balance of payments on the financial account	= _____

Suppose capital flows to Macroland from Funland decrease and this causes Macroland's currency to depreciate against Funland's currency, holding everything else constant.

b. How will this affect the demand and supply of Macroland dollars in the foreign exchange market? Use the following graph to illustrate your answer.

**Exchange rate
(Funland dollars
per Macroland
dollar)**

**Quantity of
Macroland dollars**

c. How will this depreciation affect Macroland's balance of payments on the current account? Explain your answer.

d. How will this depreciation affect Macroland's balance of payments on the financial account? Explain your answer.

5. Suppose, initially, the nominal exchange rate is 20 Macroland dollars per 1 Funland dollar, and the aggregate price index in both countries has a value of 100.

   a. What is the real exchange rate expressed as Macroland dollars per Funland dollar?

   b. Suppose the real exchange rate increases to 25 Macroland dollars per Funland dollar when the aggregate price index in Funland increases to 150. Assuming the nominal exchange rate is unchanged, what is the aggregate price index in Macroland?

   c. Suppose the aggregate price index in Funland is 150 and the aggregate price index in Macroland is 125. If the nominal exchange rate increases to 25 Macroland dollars per Funland dollar, what is the real exchange rate?

   d. If the real exchange rate measured as Macroland dollars per Funland dollar increases, holding everything else constant, what happens to the level of exports and imports in Macroland?

6. Suppose that currently the cost of a standardized market basket in Macroland is 300 Macroland dollars, while the same market basket in Funland costs 150 Funland dollars.

   a. If purchasing power parity holds for the two countries, what must the nominal exchange rate be, expressed as Macroland dollars per Funland dollar? Explain your answer.

b. If the actual nominal exchange rate is 4 Macroland dollars per 1 Funland dollar, what do you expect will happen to the nominal exchange rate over the long run, holding everything else constant? Explain your answer.

7. Compare and contrast the advantages and disadvantages of a fixed exchange rate regime and a floating exchange rate regime.

8. Suppose Macroland has adopted a fixed exchange rate regime and wishes to target the exchange rate to U.S. $2.25 for each Macroland dollar.

   a. The following figure represents the current situation in Macroland.

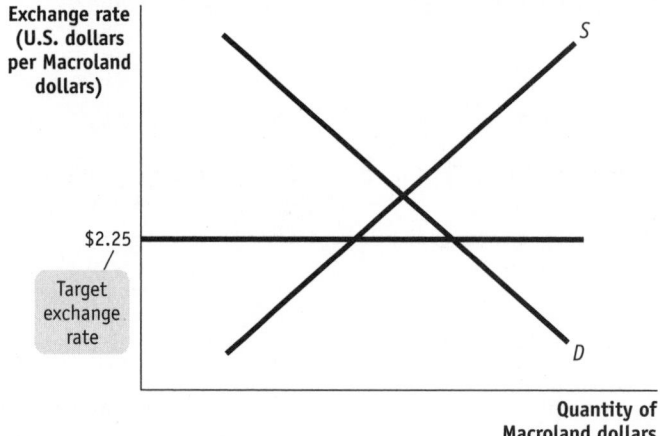

   Describe the situation depicted in this figure, given that Macroland would like to maintain a fixed exchange rate of U.S. $2.25.

   b. Given the graph in part (a), what policies are available to Macroland if it is determined to maintain the exchange rate at U.S. $2.25? Explain each option.

c. The following figure represents the situation in Macroland six months later.

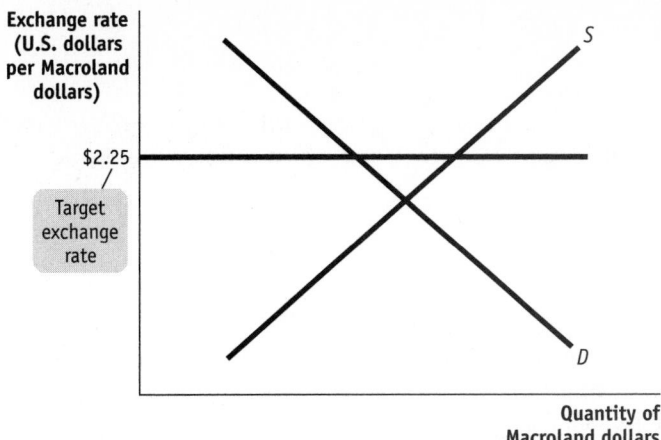

Describe the situation depicted in this graph, given that Macroland would like to maintain a fixed exchange rate of U.S. $2.25.

d. Given the graph in part (c), what policies are available to Macroland if it is determined to maintain the exchange rate at U.S. $2.25? Explain each option.

9. Suppose there are only two countries—Macrobia and Tacrobia—that investors view as being equally attractive for investment. Furthermore, suppose the loanable funds markets in these two countries can be described by the demand and supply equations given below:

   Demand for loanable funds in Macrobia: $r = 10 - (1/100)LF$

   Supply of loanable funds in Macrobia: $r = (1/100)LF$

   Demand for loanable funds in Tacrobia: $r = 10 - (1/200)LF$

   Supply of loanable funds in Tacrobia: $r = (1/300)LF$

In the above equations, r is the interest rate expressed as a percentage (e.g., if the interest rate is 10%, then that would be expressed as 10 in the above equation) and LF is the quantity of loanable funds measured in dollars. Currently, the two countries do not allow capital inflows or capital outflows.

a. What is the equilibrium interest rate and quantity of loanable funds in Macrobia?

b. What is the equilibrium interest rate and quantity of loanable funds in Tacrobia?

c. If these two countries decide to allow capital flows, what do you predict will happen? Which country will provide capital outflows and which country will provide capital inflows? Explain your answer.

d. Suppose that at every interest rate, Tacrobia provides $200 of loanable funds to Macrobia. What will be the effect of this on the supply of loanable funds curve in Tacrobia? Write the new supply of loanable funds curve equation for Tacrobia.

e. Given the new supply of loanable funds curve you computed in part (d), what will be the new equilibrium interest rate and quantity of loanable funds in Tacrobia?

f. Suppose that at every interest rate, Tacrobia provides $200 of loanable funds to Macrobia. What will be the effect of this on the supply of loanable funds curve in Macrobia? Write the new supply of loanable funds curve equation for Macrobia.

g. Given the new supply of loanable funds curve you computed in part (f), what will be the new equilibrium interest rate and quantity of loanable funds in Macrobia?

h. Given your answers in parts (e) and (g), what do you predict about capital flows between these two countries?

10. Consider each of the following transactions and identify how the transaction would be categorized in the U.S. balance of payments accounts. For each transaction, identify whether it would be counted as part of the balance of payments in the current account or the financial account. Lastly, identify whether the transaction will increase or decrease the relevant account.

a. A U.S. company purchases machinery produced in Germany by a German company.

b. A U.S. citizen donates money to the foreign group organizing an international sporting event in another country.

c. A French citizen purchases cheese produced in the United States.

d. A U.S. citizen purchases 100 shares of a Swiss company.

Review Questions

Circle the correct answer.

1. Which of the following statements is true?
   A. The balance of payments on goods and services is the difference between the value of imports and the value of exports during a given period.
   B. The merchandise trade balance includes the sale of goods as well as financial assets.
   C. A country's international transactions are tracked by the balance of payments accounts.
   D. Answers (A), (B), and (C)
   E. Answers (A) and (C)
   F. Answers (B) and (C)

2. For a hypothetical economy, if the balance of payments on the financial account equals −$100 million, then the balance of payments on the current account must
   A. equal −$100 million.
   B. be greater than −$100 million.
   C. be less than −$100 million.
   D. equal $100 million.

3. The balance of payments tracks the
   A. flow of payments into a country from the rest of the world, as well as the flow of payments from the country to the rest of the world.
   B. flow of payments for goods and services, factor income, and transfers in the balance of payments on the current account.
   C. flow of payments for assets in the balance of payments on the financial account.
   D. Answers (A), (B), and (C) are all correct.

4. Suppose there are two countries with open economies. If the interest rate in the loanable funds market in the first country is higher than the interest rate in the loanable funds market in the second country, we can expect that
   A. this interest rate differential will continue if citizens in both countries view their domestic assets as comparable to foreign assets.
   B. this interest rate differential will be eliminated due to the movement of international capital flows.
   C. the supply of loanable funds in the first country will increase while the supply of loanable funds in the second country will decrease.

D. the supply of loanable funds in the first country will decrease while the supply of loanable funds in the second country will increase.

E. Answers (B) and (C) are both correct.

F. Answers (B) and (D) are both correct.

5. An increase in capital inflows into a country, holding everything else constant, will

   A. result in an increase in net exports for the country.

   B. result in a decrease in net exports for the country.

   C. result in an increase in the balance on the financial account for the country and an equal and opposite reaction in the balance of payments on the current account.

   D. Answers (A) and (C) are both correct.

   E. Answers (B) and (C) are both correct.

Answer the next two questions using the following information: Suppose the aggregate price level for a given market basket of goods in Macroland is 125, while the aggregate price level for the same market basket of goods in Funland is 150. Suppose that the current exchange rate is 10 Macroland dollars for 1 Funland dollar.

6. Given the previous information, what is the real exchange rate initially?

   A. 10 Macroland dollars for 1 Funland dollar

   B. 1 Macroland dollar for 10 Funland dollars

   C. 1 Macroland dollar for 1 Funland dollar

   D. 10 Macroland dollars for 10 Funland dollars

   E. 12 Macroland dollars for 1 Funland dollar

7. If the aggregate price level of the market basket in Macroland increases to 150, what must the exchange rate be in order for the real exchange rate to be unchanged from its initial level?

   A. 10 Macroland dollars for 1 Funland dollar

   B. 1 Macroland dollar for 10 Funland dollars

   C. 1 Macroland dollar for 1 Funland dollar

   D. 10 Macroland dollars for 10 Funland dollars

   E. 12 Macroland dollars for 1 Funland dollar

8. Which of the following statements is true?

   A. When a country's currency undergoes a real depreciation, exports fall and imports rise.

   B. Nominal exchange rates almost always equal the purchasing power parity rate.

   C. The current account is affected by changes in the nominal exchange rate as well as the real exchange rate.

   D. None of the above is true.

9. If a government wishes to fix the value of a currency above its equilibrium value in the foreign exchange market, it can

   A. engage in monetary policy to reduce interest rates, thereby increasing capital flows into its country.

   B. reduce the supply of its currency by limiting the right of its citizens to buy foreign currencies.

   C. engage in selling its currency through exchange market intervention.

   D. Answers (A), (B), and (C) will all help the government to reduce the exchange rate to its desired level.

10. Suppose that in the foreign exchange market there is a shortage at the target exchange rate. We know that

   A. the supply of the country's currency is less than the demand for that country's currency.
   B. it is impossible to maintain the target exchange rate unless the government engages in exchange market intervention, changes monetary policy, adjusts foreign exchange controls, or pursues some combination of these three policies.
   C. maintaining a fixed exchange rate will limit the ability of the government to pursue stabilization policy.
   D. Answers (A), (B), and (C) are all true.

11. A fixed rate regime

   A. reduces uncertainty for businesses about the value of a currency.
   B. exposes a country to a potential bias toward inflationary policies.
   C. reduces the amount of foreign currency a country must hold.
   D. creates an incentive to pursue monetary policy to help stabilize the country's economy.

12. A devaluation of a currency, holding everything else constant,

   A. makes foreign-produced goods more attractive to purchase in the domestic economy and, therefore, leads to an increase in imports in the domestic economy.
   B. decreases the balance of payments on the current account.
   C. may be used as a macroeconomic policy tool because a devaluation stimulates aggregate demand.
   D. Answers (A), (B), and (C) are all true.
   E. Answers (A) and (C) are both correct.
   F. Answers (B) and (C) are both correct.

13. When a country pursues an expansionary monetary policy, this will

   A. increase the level of investment spending.
   B. decrease the demand for that country's currency in the foreign exchange market.
   C. increase the supply of that country's currency in the foreign exchange market.
   D. Answers (A), (B), and (C) are all correct.

14. Which of the following statements is true?

   A. Demand shocks may originate from outside the domestic economy.
   B. Business cycles in different countries often seem to be synchronized because changes in aggregate supply affect the demand for goods and services produced abroad as well as at home.
   C. A fixed exchange rate seems to lessen the impact of changes in aggregate demand in one country on the economic performance in other countries.
   D. Answers (A), (B), and (C) are all true.

15. Which of the following represents a payment from foreigners to the hypothetical economy called Macropedia?

   A. the dollar value of corn that Macropedia imports from Cornucopia
   B. the dollar value of bicycles that Macropedia exports to Pedal Land
   C. the fees engineering firms in Macropedia receive for bridge designs they provide to the foreign country of Islandville
   D. the fees companies in Macropedia pay to Islandville in compensation for the financial services Islandville provides
   E. Answers (A), (B), (C), and (D) all represent payments from foreigners to Macropedia.
   F. Answers (A) and (C) both represent payments from foreigners to Macropedia.
   G. Answers (A) and (D) both represent payments from foreigners to Macropedia.

16. Foreign exchange reserves are

    A. funds of one country's currency held by another country.

    B. funds of a country's currency that the government holds in case it needs money unexpectedly.

    C. are sometimes used by a country to maintain a fixed exchange rate.

    D. Answers (A) and (C) are both correct.

    E. Answers (B) and (C) are both correct.

17. Which of the following statements is true?

    I. The sum of the balance of payments on the current account *(CA)* and the balance of payments on the financial account *(FA)* must equal zero.

    II. The balance of payments accounts illustrate the concept that the flow of funds into a country's economy must equal the flow of funds out of that country's economy.

    III. A country that imports more than it exports must by definition have negative capital inflows.

    A. Statements I, II, and III are all true.   **C.** Statements I and III are both true.

    B. Statements I and II are both true.   **D.** Statements II and III are both true.

18. In 2007, which of the following statements were true?

    I. The United States had a substantial current account deficit.

    II. China had a substantial current account deficit.

    III. Middle Eastern countries had substantial current account surpluses.

    A. Statements I, II, and III are all true.

    B. Statements I and II are both true.

    C. Statements I and III are both true.

    D. Statements II and III are both true.

19. Suppose the loanable funds market in Macroland is currently in equilibrium. Holding everything else constant, if capital inflows increase to Macroland, this will cause the equilibrium interest rate

    A. to decrease while the equilibrium quantity of loanable funds will increase.

    B. to increase while the equilibrium quantity of loanable funds will decrease.

    C. and the equilibrium quantity of loanable funds to decrease.

    D. and the equilibrium quantity of loanable funds to increase.

20. Suppose the loanable funds market in Macroland is currently in equilibrium. Holding everything else constant, if businesses in Macroland increase the level of their investment spending that is financed by borrowing, this will cause a shift

    A. in the supply of loanable funds curve to the right and a movement along the demand for loanable funds curve.

    B. in the supply of loanable funds curve to the left and a movement along the demand for loanable funds curve.

    C. in the demand for loanable funds curve to the right and a movement along the supply of loanable funds curve.

    D. in the demand for loanable funds curve to the left and a movement along the supply of loanable funds curve.

21. Which of the following statements is true?
    I. Fast-growing economies often have greater demand for loanable funds than do slower-growing economies because these countries often have greater investment opportunities.
    II. The supply of loanable funds in any particular country is affected by the country's private savings rate; some countries have higher savings rates than others.
    III. Between 1996 and 2007, the United States provided huge capital outflows to much of the rest of the world.

   A. Statements I, II, and III are all true.
   B. Statements I and II are both true.
   C. Statements I and III are both true.
   D. Statements II and III are both true.

22. Holding everything else constant, an increase in political risk in a country will most likely cause capital inflows into that country to

   A. increase.   B. decrease.

23. Suppose that the current exchange rate is one U.S. dollar to 5 Mexican pesos. If the exchange rate changes to one U.S. dollar to 10 Mexican pesos, then the peso has

   A. appreciated against the dollar.
   B. depreciated against the dollar.

24. Suppose there are only two currencies in the world: the U.S. dollar and the Mexican peso. Furthermore, suppose that the foreign exchange market for U.S. dollars is initially in equilibrium. If the demand for U.S. dollars increases, holding everything else constant, this will result in a movement along the supply of U.S. dollars curve and

   A. an increase in the peso–U.S. dollar exchange rate.
   B. a decrease in the peso–U.S. dollar exchange rate.

25. Holding everything else constant, if the U.S. dollar rises against the Mexican peso, then

   A. U.S. goods will look cheaper to Mexico.
   B. U.S. goods will look more expensive to Mexico.
   C. Mexico's goods will look cheaper to the U.S.
   D. Mexico's goods will look more expensive to the U.S.
   E. Answers (A) and (D) are both correct.
   F. Answers (B) and (C) are both correct.

ANSWER KEY

Fill-in-the-Blanks

Module 41: (1) balance of payments, (2) current, (3) goods and services, (4) financial, (5) zero, (6) loanable funds

Module 42: (1) foreign exchange, (2) exchange, (3) purchasing power, (4) inflation

Module 43: (1) regime, (2) fixed exchange rate, (3) floating, (4) interventions, (5) reserves, (6) monetary

Module 44: (1) devaluation, (2) depreciation, (3) appreciation, (4) revaluation

Featured Graph

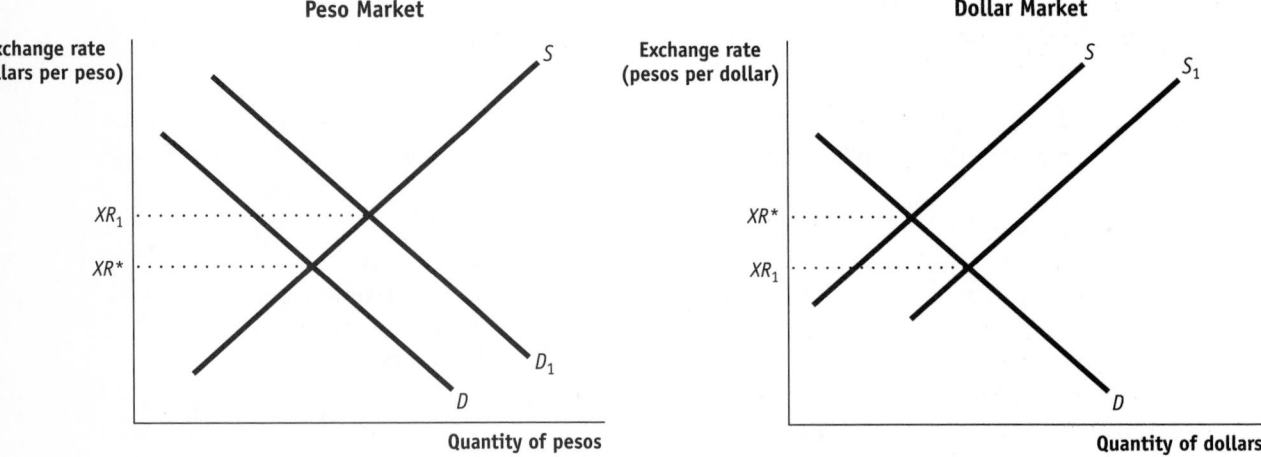

Exercise

1. China

2. United States

3. China

4. United States (The effect of depreciation outweighs the effect of inflation.)

Answers to Problems

1. **a.** (i.) Merchandise trade balance = (exports of goods) − (imports of goods) = (payments from foreigners for goods) − (payments to foreigners for goods)

   (ii.) Balance of payments on goods and services = (exports of goods and services) − (imports of goods and services) = (payments from foreigners for goods and services) − (payments to foreigners for goods and services)

   (iii.) Net international factor income = (factor income payments from foreigners) − (factor income payments to foreigners)

   (iv.) Net international transfer payments = (transfer payments from foreigners) − (transfer payments to foreigners)

   (v.) Balance of payments on the current account = (balance of payments on goods and services) + (net international transfer payments) + (net international factor income)

   (vi.) Balance of payments on the financial account = (sales of assets to foreigners) − (purchases of assets from foreigners)

b. (i.) Merchandise trade balance = $200 million – $80 million = $120 million

(ii.) Balance of payments on goods and services = $250 million – $100 million = $150 million

(iii.) Net international factor income = $70 million – $10 million = $60 million

(iv.) Net international transfer payments = $10 million – $20 million = – $10 million

(v.) Balance of payments on the current account = $150 million + (– $10 million) + ($60 million) = $200 million

(vi.) Balance of payments on the financial account = – $200 million

c. This reflects a basic rule of balance of payments accounting for any country: the flow of money into a country must equal the flow of money out of the country.

2. a. Funland will attract capital because its equilibrium interest rate is higher than the equilibrium interest rate in Macroland.

b. Over time, the interest rate in Macroland will rise due to capital outflows. Because Macroland initially has a lower equilibrium interest rate than Funland, some Macroland lenders will decide to send their funds to Funland to take advantage of the higher interest rate. Over time, this will cause the interest rate in the two countries to equalize.

c. Over time, the interest rate in Funland will fall due to capital inflows from Macroland. As funds from Macroland are attracted to Funland's loanable funds market, due to its initially higher equilibrium interest rate, the interest rate will fall in Funland. Eventually, the interest rates in the two countries will equalize.

d. Capital will flow out of Macroland and into Funland. Thus, Macroland will experience capital outflows, while Funland will experience capital inflows.

3. a.

	U.S. dollars	Funland dollars	Macroland dollars
1 U.S. dollar exchanged for	1	200	1.05
1 Funland dollar exchanged for	0.005	1	0.0047642
1 Macroland dollar exchanged for	0.952381	210	1

b.

	U.S. dollars	Funland dollars	Macroland dollars
1 U.S. dollar exchanged for	1	210	0.980392
1 Funland dollar exchanged for	0.004762	1	0.004669
1 Macroland dollar exchanged for	1.02	214.2	1

c. Macroland dollars appreciated against the U.S. dollar because in part (a), 1 Macroland dollar was worth 0.952381 U.S. dollar, and in part (b), 1 Macroland dollar was worth 1.02 U.S. dollars.

d. Funland dollars depreciated against the U.S. dollar because in part (a), 1 Funland dollar was worth 0.005 U.S. dollar, and in part (b), 1 Funland dollar was worth 0.004762 U.S. dollar.

e. U.S. exports to Funland, holding everything else constant, will fall because, as Funland's currency depreciates against the U.S. dollar, this makes U.S. products more expensive to the residents of Funland relative to Funland's products. Funland will export more to the United States and the United States will export less to Funland.

f. U.S. exports to Macroland, holding everything else constant, will increase because, as Macroland's currency appreciates against the U.S. dollar, this makes U.S. products cheaper to the residents of Macroland relative to Macroland's products. Macroland will export less to the United States and the United States will export more to Macroland.

4. a.

Funland purchases of Macroland dollars in the foreign exchange market to buy Macroland assets	= 2 million Macroland dollars
Total sales of Macroland dollars in the foreign exchange market	= 5.0 million Macroland dollars
Macroland balance of payments on the current account	= –0.5 million Macroland dollars
Macroland balance of payments on the financial account	= 0.5 million Macroland dollars

b. The depreciation of the Macroland currency against Funland's currency will cause the demand for Macroland dollars to decrease at every exchange rate (measured as Funland dollars per Macroland dollars). This will, for a given supply of Macroland dollars, cause the exchange rate to decrease. This is illustrated in the following figure.

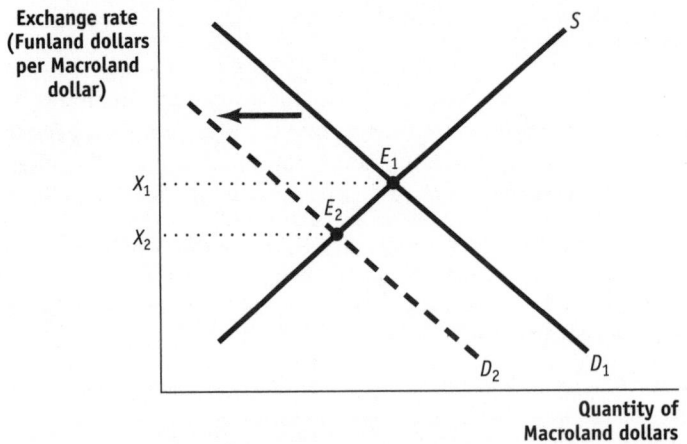

c. This depreciation of Macroland's currency against Funland's currency will cause Macroland's balance of payments on the current account to increase because Funland will now find Macroland goods and services relatively cheaper.

d. This depreciation of Macroland's currency against Funland's currency will cause Macroland's balance of payments on the financial account to decrease because any increase in Macroland's balance of payments on the current account must be offset by an equal and opposite reaction in the balance of payments on the financial account.

5. a. The real exchange rate in Macroland dollars per Funland dollar = (20 Macroland dollars per Funland dollar)(100/100) = 20 Macroland dollars per Funland dollar.

b. To answer this question, use the following equation:

Real exchange rate =
(nominal exchange rate)[(price index in Funland)/(price index in Macroland)]

Thus, 25 Macroland dollars per Funland dollar = (20 Macroland dollars per Funland dollar)[(150)/(price index in Macroland)], and solving for the price index in Macroland, we find that the price index in Macroland equals 120.

c. To answer this question, use the equation given in part (b):

Real exchange rate =
(nominal exchange rate)[(price index in Funland)/(price index in Macroland)]

Thus, the real exchange rate = (25 Macroland dollars per Funland dollar) [(150)/(125)], and solving this equation for the real exchange rate yields a real exchange rate of 30 Macroland dollars per Funland dollar.

d. When the real exchange rate increases, Macroland's currency appreciates, and this appreciation will make Macroland's products more expensive to foreigners. Macroland will export less and import more when the real exchange rate increases, holding everything else constant.

6. a. If purchasing power parity holds in the two countries, then the price of the market basket in the two countries is 300 Macroland dollars and 150 Funland dollars. This implies that the exchange rate must equal 2 Macroland dollars per Funland dollar or, equivalently, 1 Macroland dollar per 0.5 Funland dollar.

b. If the actual exchange rate is greater than the purchasing power parity exchange rate, one would anticipate that the exchange rate will fall over time because nominal exchange rates between countries at similar levels of economic development tend to fluctuate around levels that lead to similar costs for a given market basket.

7. A fixed exchange rate regime provides certainty about the value of a country's currency This certainty facilitates transactions between countries. In addition, adoption of a fixed exchange regime may help a country commit to not engaging in inflationary policies. But, adherence to a fixed exchange rate presents challenges as well as benefits to the country. In order to fix the exchange rate, the country will find that it must hold large amounts of foreign currency; this is typically a low-return investment for the country. In addition, a country with a fixed exchange rate will find that it can no longer use monetary policy to pursue macroeconomic goals such as output stabilization and inflation rate control. Finally, the adoption of a fixed exchange rate potentially distorts the incentives for importing and exporting goods and services.

A floating exchange rate regime neither requires the country to hold large amounts of foreign currency nor constrains the country with regard to monetary policy. It does, however, introduce uncertainty about the value of the country's currency, and that may hinder the level of international trade between the country and other countries. A floating exchange rate does provide very clear price incentives for the determination of the level of exports and imports at any particular point in time.

8. a. In the graph depicted in part (a), Macroland finds that there is a shortage of Macroland dollarsat the target exchange rate of U.S. $2.25 per Macroland dollar. That is, the quantity of Macroland dollars demanded exceeds the quantity of Macroland dollars supplied at the desired exchange rate.

b. When there is a shortage of Macroland dollars, the government of Macroland can intervene in the foreign exchange market and sell Macroland dollars and acquire U.S. dollars to add to its foreign exchange reserves. In addition, the government can act to reduce interest rates in order to increase the supply of Macroland dollars while reducing the demand for Macroland dollars. By reducing the interest rate, the government of Macroland will decrease capital flows into Macroland, thus reducing the demand for Macroland dollars, and increase capital flows out of Macroland, thereby increasing the supply of Macroland dollars. Finally, the government of Macroland can impose foreign exchange controls that limit the ability of Macroland residents to sell currency to foreigners. Each of these policies will reduce the value of the Macroland dollar.

c. In the graph depicted in part (c), Macroland finds that there is a surplus of Macroland dollars at the target exchange rate of U.S. $2.25 per Macroland dollar. That is, the quantity of Macroland dollars demanded is less than the quantity of Macroland dollars supplied at the desired exchange rate.

d. When there is a surplus of Macroland dollars, the government of Macroland can intervene in the foreign exchange market and buy Macroland dollars and sell U.S. dollars from its foreign exchange reserves. In addition, the government can act to increase interest rates in order to decrease the supply of Macroland dollars while increasing the demand for Macroland dollars. By increasing the interest rate, the government of Macroland will increase capital flows into Macroland, thus increasing the demand for Macroland dollars, and decrease capital flows out of Macroland, thereby decreasing the supply of Macroland dollars. Finally, the government of Macroland can impose foreign exchange controls that limit the ability of Macroland residents to buy foreign currency. Each of these policies will increase the value of the Macroland dollar.

9. **a.** To find the equilibrium interest rate and quantity of loanable funds in Macrobia, you need tofind the intersection of the demand and supply curves. Thus, the equilibrium interest rate is 5% and the equilibrium quantity of loanable funds is $500.

b. To find the equilibrium interest rate and quantity of loanable funds in Tacrobia, you need to find the intersection of the demand and supply curves. Thus, the equilibrium interest rate is 4% and the equilibrium quantity of loanable funds is $1,200.

c. Because the interest rate is higher in Macrobia than in Tacrobia, you would expect loanable funds to be attracted to the higher interest rate. + Tacrobia will have capital outflows and Macrobia will have capital inflows until the interest rates in the two countries are equalized.

d. If Tacrobia has capital outflows of $200 to Macrobia, this will cause the supply of loanable funds curve in Tacrobia to shift to the left by 200. This shift will be a parallel shift of the loanable funds supply curve because it is a constant amount of capital outflows irrespective of the interest rate. The new loanable funds curve is $r = (1/300)LF + (2/3)$.

e. With the new loanable funds supply curve and the original loanable funds demand curve, we can solve for the new equilibrium interest rate and quantity of loanable funds in Tacrobia. This new equilibrium is at an interest rate of 4.4% and a quantity of loanable funds of $1,120.

f. If Tacrobia provides Macrobia with $200 of capital inflows, this will cause the supply of loanable funds curve in Macrobia to shift to the right by 200. This shift will be a parallel shift of the loanable funds supply curve because it is a constant amount of capital inflows irrespective of the interest rate. The new loanable funds curve is $r = (1/100)LF - 2$.

g. With the new loanable funds supply curve and the original loanable funds demand curve, we can solve for the new equilibrium interest rate and quantity of loanable funds in Macrobia. This new equilibrium is at an interest rate of 4% and a quantity of loanable funds of $600.

h. Since the interest rates in the two countries are still different, you would expect capital flows to continue between the two countries until these interest rates are equalized. Thus, Tacrobia will increase its capital outflows and Macrobia will have higher capital inflows.

10. **a.** When the U.S. company purchases machinery produced in Germany by a German company, this transaction enters the U.S. balance of payments current account as an import. This transaction will reduce the balance of payments on the U.S. current account.

b. When the U.S. citizen donates money to the foreign group organizing an international sporting event, this enters the current account as a transfer payment to a foreigner. This transaction will reduce the balance on the U.S. current account.

c. When a French citizen purchases cheese produced in the United States, this transaction enters the U.S. balance of payments on the current account as an export. This transaction will increase the balance of payments on the U.S. current account.

d. When the U.S. citizen purchases 100 shares of a Swiss company, this transaction is categorized as part of the U.S. balance of payments on the financial account. The balance of payments on the U.S. financial account will fall.

Answers to Review Questions

1. **C.** The balance of payments on goods and services is the difference between the value of exports and the value of imports during a given period. The merchandise trade balance does not include the sale of financial assets but does include the sale of goods. The balance of payments accounts provide a set of numbers that describe a country's international transactions.

2. **D.** The sum of the balance of payments on the current account and the balance of payments on the financial account must sum to zero. Thus, if the balance of payments on the

financial account is − $100 million, then the balance of payments on the current account must be $100 million.

3. **D.** Figure 41-1 in your text reviews this concept: the balance of payments tracks flows of goods and services, factor income, transfers, and assets between a country and the rest of the world. Transactions involving goods and services, factor income, and transfers are measured in the balance of payments on the current account, while transactions involving assets are measured in the balance of payments on the financial account.

4. **E.** If two countries are open to trade and allow capital to flow freely between them, then an interest rate differential in their loanable funds market will disappear quickly due to capital flows between the two countries. Capital will tend to flow into the country with the relatively higher interest rate and out of the country with the relatively lower interest rate. Thus, the supply of loanable funds in the market with the higher interest rate will increase, while the supply of loanable funds in the market with the lower interest rate will decrease. This will cause the interest rate to fall in the first country and to rise in the second country until the interest rate differential is eliminated.

5. **E.** When a country has an increase in capital inflows, the exchange rate increases, leading to an appreciation of that country's currency. With this appreciation of its currency, the country will find that its goods and services become relatively more expensive and, therefore, its net exports will decrease. Furthermore, the increase in capital inflows will cause the balance on the financial account to increase, and this increase will be met by an equal, but opposite, reaction in the balance of payments on the current account.

6. **E.** To find the real exchange rate, we need to know the nominal exchange rate (in this case, 10 Macroland dollars per 1 Funland dollar) and the aggregate price level in the two countries. We can plug them into Equation 42–1 from your text: real exchange rate equals (10 Macroland dollars/Funland dollars)(150/125) = 12 Macroland dollars per 1 Funland dollar.

7. **E.** To find the exchange rate, we need to know the real exchange rate (in this case, 12 Macroland dollars per 1 Funland dollar) and the aggregate price level in the two countries. We can plug them into Equation 42–1 for your text: 12 Macroland dollars per 1 Funland dollar equals (the exchange rate)(150/150). Solving for the exchange rate yields an exchange rate of 12 Macroland dollars per 1 Funland dollar.

8. **D.** When a country's currency undergoes a real depreciation, exports rise and imports fall because the depreciation reduces the price of the country's goods and services relative to the prices for goods and services produced in other countries. Nominal exchange rates almost always differ from purchasing power parity rates. The nominal rate tends to fluctuate around the purchasing power parity rate. The current account responds only to changes in the real exchange rate, not the nominal exchange rate: it is a change in the real exchange rate that alters the relative cost of domestic goods and services in comparison to foreign produced goods and services.

9. **B.** When the government wishes to fix the exchange rate to a rate above its equilibrium value in the foreign exchange market, it must deal with the fact that there is a surplus of its currency at that desired exchange rate. The government can eliminate this surplus by buying its currency through an exchange market intervention; by pursuing monetary policy that raises its interest rate relative to the interest rates of other economies, thus increasing capital flows into its country (and increasing the demand for its currency); or by reducing the supply of its currency to the foreign exchange market through the imposition of foreign exchange controls.

10. **D.** When there is a shortage at the target exchange rate, this indicates that the demand for the country's currency is greater than the supply. A government will find that it can maintain the target exchange rate only if it is willing to give up its use of monetary policy for stabilization purposes and instead use monetary policy, exchange market intervention, and foreign exchange controls to pursue its target exchange rate.

11. A. A fixed rate regime benefits businesses by eliminating uncertainty about the value of a currency while reducing the ability of the government to use monetary policy as a means of stabilizing the economy. A fixed rate regime reduces, in some cases, a country's bias toward inflationary policies because it can send a signal to the foreign exchange market about the country's commitment to a stable exchange rate and decision to pursue noninflationary policies in the future.

12. C. A devaluation of a currency is a reduction in the value of a currency that previously had a fixed exchange rate. This devaluation makes domestic goods cheaper in terms of foreign currency and will, therefore, increase the level of exports and decrease the level of imports in the domestic economy. This will stimulate aggregate demand in the domestic economy. The effect of these changes is to increase the balance of payments on the current account.

13. D. When a country pursues expansionary monetary policy, the interest rate decreases, which makes investment spending more attractive. In addition, the decrease in the interest rate also affects the foreign exchange market. The demand for the domestic currency will decrease because the domestic economy is now offering a relatively lower rate of return on their loans, and the supply of the domestic currency will increase because there is now a greater incentive to move funds abroad, since the rate of return on loans in the domestic economy has fallen.

14. A. Business cycles in different countries often seem to be synchronized because changes in aggregate demand in one country often have an effect on the level of aggregate demand in other countries. Adherence to a floating exchange rate regime helps insulate countries from recessions originating from outside their economies because the movement in the exchange rate limits the level of change in aggregate demand.

15. F. Payments to Macropedia from foreigners are represented by dollars that flow into Macropedia. For example, the farmers in Macropedia will receive compensation from abroad if they export their agricultural commodity to another country, or the providers of a service will receive compensation from abroad if they provide their service to people residing in another country. Thus, answers (B) and (D) both represent flows of funds into Macropedia, while answers (A) and (C) represent flows of funds out of Macropedia.

16. D. Foreign exchange reserves entail the holding of one country's currency by another country. For example, China and the major oil-exporting countries in 2007 held U.S. dollars. These dollars are sometimes used to help maintain a fixed exchange rate. For instance, if the exchange rate is depreciating, the country can buy some of its own currency, using its foreign exchange reserves to keep the exchange rate from falling.

17. B. Statements I and II state the same idea: if the sum of the balance of payments on the current account *(CA)* and the balance of payments on the financial account *(FA)* equal zero, the flow of funds into a country's economy must equal the flow of funds out of that country's economy. If a country is importing more than it is exporting, its balance of payments on the current account is negative and, therefore, its balance of payments on the financial account is positive. When the balance of payments on the financial account is positive, the country has positive capital inflows.

18. C. The facts underlying this question are discussed in the module's Global Comparison discussion of "Current Account Surpluses and Deficit." This data is noteworthy because of the financial crisis that occurred during this period and the effect of this financial crisis on countries throughout the world.

19. A. An increase in capital inflows will cause the supply of loanable funds curve to shift to the right. This shift will cause a movement along the demand for loanable funds curve and result in a decrease in the equilibrium interest rate and an increase in the quantity of loanable funds.

20. C. An increase in the level of investment spending that is financed through borrowing will cause the demand curve to shift to the right because at every interest rate there is now greater demand for loanable funds. This shift will cause a movement along the supply of loanable funds curve as the interest rate rises in response to the increase in the demand for loanable funds.

21. **B.** Fast-growing countries typically offer many attractive investment opportunities because of their rapid growth rates. The supply of loanable funds curve for any particular country is affected by that country's private savings rate. Some countries have much higher savings rates than others. Between 1996 and 2007, the United States was the recipient of huge capital inflows from much of the rest of the world, including China, Japan, and many Middle Eastern countries.

22. **B.** When a country experiences an increase in political risk, this makes the country a less attractive place for foreign investors to spend their wealth. An increase in political risk may entail the possibility that the government will seize foreign property, and that possibility lessens the attractiveness of the country to foreign investors. When political risk increases, capital inflows decrease.

23. **B.** Five pesos originally are worth 1 U.S. dollar, but when the exchange rate changes, five pesos are worth only 0.50 in U.S. dollars. The value of the peso in terms of U.S. dollars has fallen and, thus, the peso has depreciated against the U.S. dollar.

24. **A.** When there is an increase in the demand for U.S. dollars, the demand curve for dollars shifts to the right. The subsequent move along the supply of U.S. dollars curve will cause the equilibrium exchange rate of pesos to U.S. dollars to increase.

25. **F.** If the U.S. dollar rises against the Mexican peso, it takes more pesos to buy a U.S. dollar. U.S. goods are now relatively more expensive to Mexico than they were before the dollar rose against the peso. If U.S. goods are now relatively more expensive to Mexico, then Mexico's goods are now relatively cheaper to those of the United States.

Notes

Preparing for the AP Macroeconomics Exam

I.   Overview

II.   Sample Schedule

III.   The AP Course Outline

IV.   Exam Format

V.   Planning Your Test Preparation and Review

VI.   Reviewing for the AP Macroeconomic Exam

VII.   Test-taking Tips

VIII.   Practice Tests

I. Overview

As the grand finale of your macroeconomics class, you will take the AP Macroeconomics exam in early May. There are a number of benefits that come from doing well on the exam. The benefits include, but are not limited to, becoming eligible to receive college credit for all of your hard work. Keep in mind that your AP scores will become part of your academic record. Receiving AP credit at a university is the same as completing the university's introductory macroeconomics course. The credit means that you are one course closer to graduation, you don't have to pay tuition for the course, you are eligible to take courses for which introductory macroeconomics is a prerequisite, and you gain credit hours that advance your academic standing and move you up the priority list for things like course registration. So, for these and a variety of other reasons, make sure you do your best on the AP exam. Doing your best requires that you have a plan to prepare and review for the exam. The material that follows is designed to help you as you prepare for and take the AP Macroeconomics exam.

Every year the number of students attempting the AP Macroeconomics exam grows. As of 2010, more than 70,000 bright, nerdy kids took the AP Macroeconomics exam. The majority of test-takers were high school seniors, but this is not a requirement for taking the exam. A little more than 1/2 of those taking the exam scored a 3 or higher. According to the College Board, AP test scores carry the following recommendations:

AP SCORE	QUALIFICATION	OUR TRANSLATION
5	Extremely well qualified	Oh yeah!
4	Well qualified	most likely college credit
3	Qualified	maybe college credit
2	Possibly qualified	hmmm . . . probably not
1	No recommendation	ugh!

Maximizing your performance on any AP exam requires a well thought out preparation and review plan. Below is a suggested schedule for preparing for your AP Macroeconomics exam. Keep in mind that this suggested schedule will need to be modified to fit your individual circumstances. In particular, you will need to adjust the schedule based on any other AP exams and activities that you will also have during this very busy time of year!

II. Sample Schedule

What follows is a general guide for creating a plan to prepare and review for the AP Macroeconomics exam. While each student's approach will differ, consider these suggestions for creating your own plan to maximize your performance on the exam!

1. *At the start of your AP Macroeconomic course*

   During the first few weeks of your class, take some time to familiarize yourself with the course outline and AP exam information. It will be helpful to have a general idea about the topics you will study and the format of the AP exam. AP Economics exams are not the same as AP exams in other disciplines; be aware of the differences so that your approach to the class best prepares you to succeed on the exam. The AP course outline and format of the exam are presented in the following sections. Additional information about AP exams is available on the College Board's AP Central website.

2. *During your AP Macroeconomics course*

   As you progress through each section of material, periodically refer to sample AP exam questions to get an idea of course expectations. It is important to understand the level at which the material will be tested and to see how questions testing that material are typically written. You can find sample exam questions in the sections that follow and on the College Board's AP Central website.

3. *Six weeks before the exam*

   Approximately six weeks before the exam, you should begin planning for your exam preparation and review. Depending on what other exams and commitments you have, you may need to start your preparation right away or you may wait until the exam date is closer. Remember that AP exams for all subjects are given over a two-week period. The economics exams are given during the second week. So, if you are taking other AP exams, you will need to complete your exam preparations before AP exams begin, more than a week before the AP Macroeconomics exam is scheduled.

4. Five weeks before the exam

About five weeks before your exam (at the end of March or the beginning of April), you should use the diagnostic test provided in the following section to determine how much additional studying you will need and what specific areas you should emphasize as you allocate your additional study time. Follow the instructions provided to take the diagnostic test, and use the score sheet and guidelines to help you determine your study and review schedule. At this point, there will still be several weeks of class left and therefore some content will still need to be covered in class. Make sure that your plan includes this material and allows time for you to learn, practice, and review it.

5. The week before the exam

During the week preceding the AP Macroeconomics exam (the last week in April), you should be finished studying for the exam and spend your available time reviewing. At this stage, you should be reminding yourself of things you have already learned and reviewing the topics that you had the most trouble mastering or remembering. The study sheets included in the following sections are a great way to review the most important models, formulas, and graphs you will need to understand for the exam. At this point, you can use one of the practice tests included below to help you get used to the exam process and format.

6. A night or two before the exam

Schedule time for one last review of the course material to make sure it is fresh in your mind. You may want to use the second practice test at this point. You can take the practice test as another mock exam, use it to review, or work through it with a study group. Your final review session should not be too long or intense. (You have already done the hardest work!) Make sure you arrange to get a good night's sleep the night before the exam, have a good breakfast the morning of the exam, have everything you need to take to the exam with you, and get to your exam site early on the day of your exam!

III. The AP Course Outline

The course outline for AP Macroeconomics is provided below. This outline shows the content areas covered in the course and the percentage of the course/exam devoted to that material.

Content area (Percentage of the exam—Multiple-Choice section)

I. **Basic Economic Concepts (8–12%)**

    A. Scarcity, choice, and opportunity costs

    B. Production possibilities curve

    C. Comparative advantage, absolute advantage, specialization, and exchange

    D. Demand, supply, and market equilibrium

    E. Macroeconomic issues: business cycle, unemployment, inflation, growth

II. **Measurement of Economic Performance (12–16%)**

    A. National income accounts

    B. Inflation measurement and adjustment

    C. Unemployment

III. **National Income and Price Determination (10–15%)**

    A. Aggregate demand

    B. Aggregate supply

    C. Macroeconomic equilibrium

IV. **Financial Sector** (15–20%)

    A. Money, banking, and financial markets

    B. The central bank and control of the money supply

V. **Inflation, Unemployment, and Stabilization Policies** (20–30%)

    A. Fiscal and monetary policies

    B. Inflation and unemployment

VI. **Economic Growth and Productivity** (5–10%)

    A. Investment in human capital

    B. Investment in physical capital

    C. Research and development, and technological progress

    D. Growth policy

VII. **The Open Economy: International Trade and Finance** (10–15%)

    A. Balance of payments accounts

    B. The foreign exchange market

    C. Links to financial and goods markets

IV. Exam Format

The AP Macroeconomics test is divided into two sections. The first section is composed of 60 multiple-choice questions, and the second is composed of three free-response questions. The multiple-choice section counts for two-thirds of the overall exam score. The free-response section counts for one-third of the overall exam score. The number of questions you will be asked from each section of the course outline corresponds to the percentages provided in the course outline. For example, "VI. Economic Growth and Productivity (5–10%)" means that anywhere from three to six questions on this topic will be asked on the multiple-choice section.

Multiple-Choice

You will have 70 minutes to complete the 60 questions on the multiple-choice section of the exam. Each multiple-choice question has five answer choices, only one of which is correct. The 70 minutes you are allotted to complete the multiple-choice section translates to 70 seconds per question. For each question answered correctly, you earn one point. Beginning with the 2011 exam, no deductions are made for an incorrect response. This means that if you are unsure about the answer to a question, then your best strategy is to make an educated guess. This is a major departure from previous years in which students would often omit questions of which they were unsure in order to avoid a 1/4 point deduction. Since this is a change from how the test was scored in the past, take note and make sure you answer all of the questions. You are trying to rack up as many points as possible. So when in doubt, give it your best shot and guess; you just might get lucky. The worst thing that can happen is that no point will be earned.

Unlike tests that you might take in a class, the AP exams do not use "all of the above," "none of the above" or "true/false" questions. Instead, the multiple-choice questions you will encounter will come in five different formats. The most common question type asks you to either define or classify concepts learned in macroeconomics. The next most common question type is best described as cause-and-effect. Far less common are questions that ask you to calculate an answer or interpret a graph. The least common question type is the I, II, III style.

Free-Response

The second section of the AP Macroeconomics exam is made up of three free-response questions. The time allotted to the free-response section is broken down into two parts: a planning period and a writing period. The free-response section of the exam begins with a ten-minute planning period in which you can read over the questions and map out your response. At the end of the planning period, you are allowed 50 minutes to answer the free-response questions in the answer book.

The first free-response question is the longest and most comprehensive, and you should allocate roughly half of your time, about 25 minutes, to answering it. The second and third free-response questions are shorter and typically test a particular area of the course outline. You should allocate roughly a quarter of the time available, about 12–13 minutes, to each of the shorter questions. Allocate and monitor your time carefully so that you are able to provide at least a basic response to each question.

V. Planning Your Test Preparation and Review

The following test is designed to help you assess the strengths and weaknesses in your knowledge of AP Macroeconomics. The test is composed of 60 multiple-choice questions, each with 5 answer choices. This test is for diagnostic purposes and does not include free-response questions. Allow yourself 70 minutes to take this diagnostic test. The use of a calculator is not permitted on the AP exam, so do not use one on this test either. If you are uncertain of the correct answer, make an educated guess.

The answers, along with explanations, are provided below. In addition, the answer key correlates each question with a section on the AP Course Outline. When you are finished, take time to review the answers to the questions you missed and assess which areas of the course outline you have mastered and which you need to review. Use your results to allocate your study time before the AP exam. Good luck!

Diagnostic Test

1. Which fiscal policy would be most appropriate for combating inflation?

   A. increase taxes and transfer payments
   B. raise the reserve requirement
   C. the open-market purchase of treasury securities by the Federal Reserve
   D. increase taxes and decrease government spending
   E. decrease taxes and decrease government spending

2. If the government increases its defense spending, the opportunity cost is

   A. zero.
   B. irrelevant.
   C. the dollar amount of the spending increase.
   D. the next best alternative use for the money spent on defense.
   E. the dollar amount by which taxes are increased to pay for defense spending.

3. Appreciation of the Indian rupee in the foreign exchange market could be caused by a decrease in which of the following?

   A. India's imports from China
   B. the U.S. price level
   C. demand for the Indian rupee by U.S. investors
   D. India's real interest rate
   E. India's exports to Australia

4. Economic growth is best illustrated by which of the following? A

   A. leftward shift in the production possibilities curve.
   B. rightward shift of the short run Phillips curve.
   C. rightward shift of the aggregate demand curve.
   D. rightward shift of the long-run aggregate supply curve.
   E. decrease in the slope of the money demand curve.

5. If the combination of goods or services being produced in an economy lies on the production possibility curve, then

   A. any increase in the production of one of the goods or services incurs an opportunity cost in terms of the other good or service.
   B. the combination of goods or services produced is not productively efficient.
   C. a tariff would increase the capacity of the economy to produce efficiently.
   D. available resources are idle.
   E. the combination must be allocatively efficient.

6. Which group or groups are most likely harmed by unanticipated inflation?

      I. Borrowers paying fixed-interest rates
     II. Savers earning fixed-interest rates
    III. Financial institutions that issue long-term fixed-interest rate loans

   A. I only
   B. II only
   C. I, II, and III
   D. I and II only
   E. II and III only

7. If the money supply is constant, then an increase in money demand will result in which of the following?

	Nominal Interest Rate	Quantity of Money
A.	Increase	Decrease
B.	Decrease	Increase
C.	No change	No change
D.	Increase	No change
E.	Increase	Increase

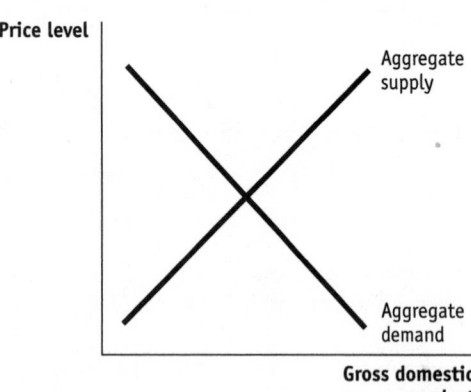

8. According to the graph on the previous page, an increase in input prices will most likely cause the price level and employment to change in which of the following ways?

	Price Level	Employment
A.	Increase	Increase
B.	Decrease	Increase
C.	Decrease	Decrease
D.	Increase	No change
E.	Increase	Decrease

9. Which type of unemployment would not exist if fiscal and monetary policy effectively eliminated the business cycle?

   A. Frictional
   B. Cyclical
   C. Seasonal
   D. Structural
   E. Part-time

10. If the average propensity to consume is greater than one, then

    A. households are saving all of their income.
    B. the marginal propensity to save must be zero.
    C. households are dissaving.
    D. the spending multiplier is negative.
    E. banks hold additional excess reserves.

11. If an economy is operating below the natural rate of unemployment, an appropriate stabilizing monetary policy would be to

    A. lower the required reserve ratio.
    B. raise taxes.
    C. lower taxes.
    D. purchase bonds on the open market.
    E. raise the discount rate.

12. Which of the following combinations of fiscal and monetary policy would effectively reduce capital investment while not reducing output?

	Fiscal Policy	Monetary Policy
A.	Expansionary	Contractionary
B.	Expansionary	Expansionary
C.	Contractionary	No change
D.	Contractionary	Contractionary
E.	Contractionary	Expansionary

13. If the real interest rate in the United States increased relative to the real interest rate in Belgium while domestic prices remained unchanged, then the U.S. dollar would

    A. appreciate, making Belgian exports to the United States more expensive.
    B. appreciate, making United States imports from Belgium more expensive.
    C. appreciate, making Belgian imports from the United States cheaper.
    D. appreciate, making United States imports from Belgium cheaper.
    E. depreciate, making United States exports to Belgium cheaper.

14. If an economy is experiencing a significant recession, which of the following will cause employment to increase and interest rates to decrease?

    A. The Federal Reserve raises the discount rate.
    B. The government reduces spending while raising taxes.
    C. The Federal Reserve buys treasury securities on the open market.
    D. The Federal Reserve raises the reserve requirement.
    E. The government increases spending and reduces taxes.

15. An increase in which of the following would most likely hinder economic growth?

    A. personal savings
    B. gross private investment
    C. the government's budget deficit
    D. capital formation
    E. bond purchases by the Federal Reserve

16. Money is classified as inconvertible fiat when

    A. it is not backed by a valuable commodity.
    B. it is backed by gold.
    C. it acts as a source of intrinsic value.
    D. it lacks portability.
    E. it does not function as a medium of exchange.

17. A criticism of expansionary fiscal policy to stimulate the economy and contractionary monetary policy to restrict the economy is that they

    A. lead to demand-pull inflation.
    B. result in lower interest rates.
    C. create cost-push inflation.
    D. lead to higher interest rates.
    E. result in permanent increases in the money supply.

18. In the long run, increases in the money supply result in which of the following changes in the price level and unemployment?

	Price Level	Employment
A.	Increase	Increase
B.	Increase	Decrease
C.	Decrease	No change
D.	Increase	No change
E.	No change	Increase

19. Crowding out is best described as

    A. an increase in capital investment at the expense of government spending.
    B. a decrease in net exports resulting from appreciation of the currency.
    C. an increase in both inflation and unemployment.
    D. a decrease in gross private investment resulting from government borrowing.
    E. a rightward shift of the money supply.

20. If the real interest rate in China increases relative to that of the rest of the world, capital flow and currency should change in which of the following ways?

	Capital Flow	Currency
A.	Out	Appreciate
B.	In	Appreciate
C.	In	Depreciate
D.	Out	Depreciate
E.	No change	No change

21. Which of the following is a combination of fiscal and monetary policy designed to offset the effects of a recession in an economy?

    A. increase taxes and reduce government spending
    B. lower the discount rate and buy treasury bonds
    C. reduce taxes and buy treasury bonds
    D. decrease government spending and the required reserve ratio
    E. increase taxes and sell treasury bonds

22. Which of the following groups would be included in the labor force?

    I. People classified as part-time employees
    II. People who want a job and are thinking about filling out job applications next month
    III. Recently terminated factory workers who are actively seeking employment in the service sector

    A. I and III only
    B. II only
    C. II and III only
    D. I, II, and III
    E. III only

23. Which of the following best describes the sequence of events that occurs when the Federal Reserve sells treasury securities on the open market?

    A. Money supply increases, interest rates decrease, consumption and investment increase, aggregate demand increases, and output and price level increases.
    B. Money supply increases, interest rates decrease, consumption and investment decrease, aggregate demand decreases, and output and price level decreases.
    C. Money supply decreases, interest rates increase, consumption and investment decrease, aggregate demand decreases, and output and price level decreases.
    D. Money supply decreases, interest rates decrease, consumption and investment decrease, aggregate demand decreases, and output and price level decreases.
    E. Money supply decreases, interest rates increase, consumption and investment increase, aggregate demand increases, and output and price level increases.

24. Assume that autonomous consumption is $500 and that the marginal propensity to consume is 0.9. If disposable income increases by $1000, then saving will increase by how much?

    A. $450
    B. $900
    C. $1500
    D. $50
    E. $100

25. Assume that all input prices are flexible. A decrease in labor productivity will have which of the following effects on output, price level, and real wages?

	Output	Price Level	Real Wages
A.	Increase	Increase	Increase
B.	Decrease	Decrease	Increase
C.	Decrease	Increase	Increase
D.	Decrease	Increase	Decrease
E.	Decrease	Decrease	Decrease

26. If the money supply increases by 5 percent, then which of the following must also increase by 5 percent for the real gross domestic product to remain unchanged?

    A. nominal interest rates
    B. real interest rates
    C. nominal exchange rates
    D. the average price level
    E. the income velocity of money

27. Which of the following will occur in a competitive market if the price exceeds the equilibrium price?

    A. The price will increase to eliminate the surplus.
    B. The price will decrease to eliminate the surplus.
    C. The price will decrease to eliminate the shortage.
    D. Demand will decrease.
    E. Supply will decrease.

28. The inverse relationship between price level and real gross domestic product is shown by the

    A. aggregate demand curve.
    B. demand for loanable funds.
    C. short-run Phillips curve.
    D. short-run aggregate supply curve.
    E. production possibilities curve.

29. If consumers spend $0.90 for each extra $1.00 of disposable income, then a $50 billion increase in government spending financed by a $50 billion increase in taxes will have which of the following effects on the economy? Aggregate demand will

    A. increase by $500 billion.
    B. decrease by $500 billion.
    C. increase by $450 billion.
    D. decrease by $450 billion.
    E. increase by $50 billion.

30. A decrease in the government's budget surplus will most likely result in which of the following?

    A. increased tax revenues
    B. decreased government spending
    C. higher interest rates
    D. a decrease in the international value of the dollar
    E. an increase in unemployment

31. Which of the following would cause the Japanese yen to appreciate relative to the euro?

    A. increase in Japanese household income
    B. decrease in Japanese interest rates relative to European interest rates
    C. increase in Japan's average price level
    D. decrease in Japanese household income
    E. decrease in European household income

32. Demand-pull inflation is caused by which of the following?

    A. increased short-run aggregate supply
    B. decreased short-run aggregate supply
    C. increased aggregate demand
    D. decreased aggregate demand
    E. rightward shift of the short-run Phillips curve

33. Which of the following is true if the nominal interest rate is 5 percent and inflation unexpectedly increases from 2 percent to 3 percent?

    A. The nominal interest rate of 5% benefits savers at the expense of borrowers.
    B. The nominal interest rate of 5% is now too high.
    C. The real interest rate has increased from 7% to 8%.
    D. The real interest rate benefits fixed-rate borrowers at the expense of fixed-rate lenders.
    E. The real interest rate remains unchanged.

34. Which of the following would lead to an increase in the U.S. average price level?

    A. Personal income taxes increase.
    B. Banks lend out less of their excess reserves.
    C. Full-time employees are reclassified as part-time employees according to a new government definition.
    D. Households increase their savings.
    E. A significant tax is placed on all capital investment.

35. An increase in labor productivity will cause the

    A. aggregate demand curve to shift left.
    B. aggregate demand curve to shift right.
    C. long-run aggregate supply curve to shift left.
    D. long-run aggregate supply curve to shift right.
    E. short-run aggregate supply curve to shift left.

36. Which is most likely to occur if the Federal Reserve acts to combat recession with open-market operations?

    A. The discount rate will increase.
    B. Aggregate demand will shift to the left.
    C. Bond prices will increase.
    D. The money supply will decrease.
    E. Government spending will decrease.

37. Which action by the government will shift the short-run aggregate supply curve to the left?

    A. the open-market sale of bonds by the Federal Reserve
    B. an increase in the discount rate
    C. a decrease in personal income taxes
    D. an increase in government spending
    E. an increase in business taxes

38. Assume that the Federal Reserve buys $100 billion worth of treasury securities on the open market. If the required reserve ratio is 20 percent, what is the maximum amount of new loans the banking system can create?

    A. $20 billion
    B. $80 billion
    C. $100 billion
    D. $400 billion
    E. $500 billion

Questions 39–41 are based on the diagram below, which shows the choices in production of two countries, Orville and Huey, producing two goods, airplanes and helicopters. Both countries have the same amount of resources and are using all of their available resources.

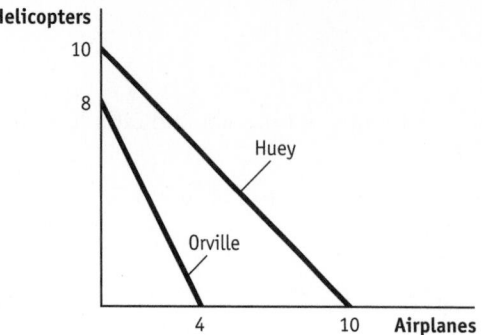

39. Before specialization and trade, the opportunity cost of producing one helicopter in Huey and Orville is which of the following?

	Huey	Orville
A.	1 airplane	10 airplanes
B.	8 airplanes	2 airplanes
C.	1 airplane	0.5 airplane
D.	0.5 airplane	2 airplanes
E.	1 airplane	2 airplanes

40. Which of the following statements best describes absolute advantage or comparative advantage for these two countries?

A. Huey has a comparative advantage in helicopters, and Orville has a comparative advantage in airplanes

B. Huey has a comparative advantage in helicopters, and Orville has an absolute advantage in helicopters.

C. Huey has absolute and comparative advantages in both airplanes and helicopters.

D. Huey has a comparative advantage in airplanes, and Orville has absolute disadvantages in both.

E. Huey has an absolute advantage in both, and Orville has a comparative advantage in airplanes.

41. According to the theory of comparative advantage, Orville would find it advantageous to

A. export airplanes and import helicopters.

B. import both helicopters and airplanes.

C. export both airplanes and helicopters.

D. import airplanes and export helicopters.

E. not trade because Huey has absolute advantages in both airplanes and helicopters.

42. A decrease in personal income taxes will most likely cause aggregate demand and short-run aggregate supply to change in which of the following ways?

	Aggregate Demand	Short-run Aggregate Supply
A.	Increase	No change
B.	Increase	Decrease
C.	Decrease	Increase
D.	Decrease	No change
E.	Decrease	Decrease

Disposable income = $9 trillion
Imports = $3 trillion
Household savings = $1 trillion
Government expenditures = $3 trillion
Exports = $2 trillion
Gross private investment = $2 trillion

43. Based on the information in the table above, how much is gross domestic product?

    A. $20 trillion

    B. $14 trillion

    C. $16 trillion

    D. $12 trillion

    E. $5 trillion

44. If firms face increased per unit production costs, then the short-run aggregate supply curve, short-run Phillips curve, and inflation will change in which of the following ways?

	Short-run Aggregate Supply Curve	Short-run Phillips Curve	Inflation
A.	Shift to the right	Shift to the right	Increase
B.	Shift to the right	Shift to the left	Decrease
C.	Shift to the right	No change	Increase
D.	Shift to the left	Shift to the left	Decrease
E.	Shift to the left	Shift to the right	Increase

45. Aggregate demand and aggregate supply would simultaneously decrease because of an increase in which of the following?

    A. household savings

    B. the M2

    C. business taxes

    D. disposable income

    E. inflation expectations

46. An increase in the government's budget deficit will have which of the following effects on the exchange rate and net exports?

	Exchange Rate	Net Exports
A.	Appreciate	Decrease
B.	Appreciate	Increase
C.	Appreciate	No change
D.	Depreciate	Increase
E.	Depreciate	Decrease

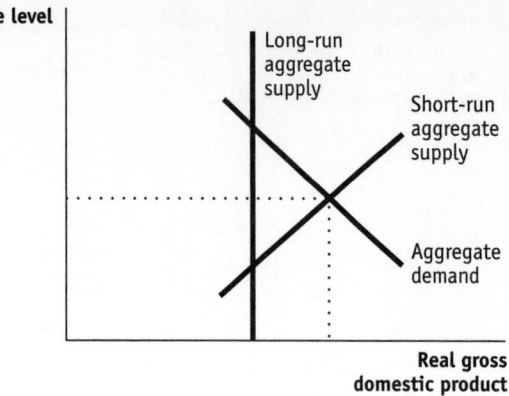

Price level

Long-run aggregate supply

Short-run aggregate supply

Aggregate demand

Real gross domestic product

47. According to the graph above, which of the following is true about this economy in the long run?

   A. Expansionary monetary policy will restore this economy to its long-run equilibrium.
   B. The long-run aggregate supply curve will shift to the left to restore the long-run equilibrium.
   C. The economy depicted is currently in a long-run equilibrium.
   D. A combination of increased government spending and an increase in the money supply could shift aggregate demand to the right and restore long-run equilibrium.
   E. Wages will increase as they adjust to the new price level and the short-run aggregate supply curve will shift to the left and restore long-run equilibrium.

48. Assuming that input prices are flexible, an economy in recession will experience which of the following changes in output and price level in the long run?

	Output	Price Level
A.	Increase	Increase
B.	No change	Increase
C.	Increase	No change
D.	Increase	Decrease
E.	Decrease	Increase

49. Assuming a system of flexible exchange rates, an open-market sale of bonds by the Federal Reserve while other countries do nothing will most likely have which of the following effects on the rate of inflation and the international value of the U.S. dollar?

	Inflation Rate	International Value of the U.S. Dollar
A.	Decrease	Appreciate
B.	Decrease	Depreciate
C.	Increase	Appreciate
D.	Increase	Depreciate
E.	Increase	No change

50. The discount rate is the

    A. interest rate the Federal Reserve charges member banks for overnight loans.
    B. interest rate banks charge their best commercial customers.
    C. interest rate banks charge other banks for overnight loans.
    D. percentage of demand deposits that banks may not lend to customers.
    E. difference between the nominal interest rate and the real interest rate.

Labor Market in Kumbiktu (in thousands of persons)	
Population	240
Labor Force	200
Employed	180

51. According to the information in the table above, what is the unemployment rate for Kumbiktu?

    A. 25%
    B. 30%
    C. 10%
    D. 8.3%
    E. 11.1%

52. An increase in taxes combined with an open-market purchase of bonds will result in a(n)

    A. increase in real gross domestic product and an increase in the interest rate.
    B. increase in unemployment and an indeterminate change in the interest rate.
    C. indeterminate change in real gross domestic product and a decrease in the interest rate.
    D. decrease in real gross domestic product and a decrease in the interest rate.
    E. decrease in unemployment and an increase in the inflation rate.

53. If the marginal propensity to save is 0.2, then a $40 billion decrease in taxes could cause a maximum increase in output of how much?

    A. $8 billion
    B. $32 billion
    C. $200 billion
    D. $160 billion
    E. $250 billion

54. An increase in labor productivity will shift the

    A. short-run aggregate supply to the left.
    B. short-run aggregate supply to the right.
    C. aggregate demand to the right.
    D. aggregate demand to the left.
    E. long-run aggregate supply to the left.

55. In the long run, decreases in aggregate demand lead to which of the following changes in unemployment and price level?

	Unemployment	Price Level
A.	No change	Decrease
B.	Decrease	No change
C.	Decrease	Decrease
D.	Increase	Increase
E.	Increase	No change

56. Assume that the required reserve ratio is 10 percent. If Jumanja deposits $50 in cash into her checking account, what is the maximum change in demand deposits possible in the banking system?

   A. $45
   B. $50
   C. $500
   D. $450
   E. $5

57. If the U.S. rate of economic growth increases relative to its trading partners and if exchanged rates are fixed, then the U.S. imports and exports will most likely change in which of the following ways?

	Imports	Exports
A.	Increase	Decrease
B.	Decrease	Decrease
C.	Decrease	Increase
D.	Increase	Increase
E.	No change	No change

58. Which of the following would be counted as part of gross domestic product?

   A. the purchase of corporate stock
   B. the sale of a treasury bond
   C. the purchase of a new domestically produced tractor
   D. daycare services provided by stay-at-home fathers for their own children
   E. the purchase of a twenty-year-old house

59. A shift in the aggregate demand curve corresponds to

   A. a shift in the long-run Phillips curve.
   B. a shift in the short-run Phillips curve.
   C. a decrease in the slope of the short-run Phillips curve.
   D. movement along an existing short-run Phillips curve.
   E. an increase in the slope of the short-run Phillips curve.

60. Which of the following would cause a leftward shift in the short-run aggregate supply curve? A(n)

   A. increase in the expected price level
   B. increase in the available capital stock
   C. decrease in interest rates
   D. decrease in the nominal wage rate
   E. increase in the exchange rate

Place a "√" by the questions you answered correctly.

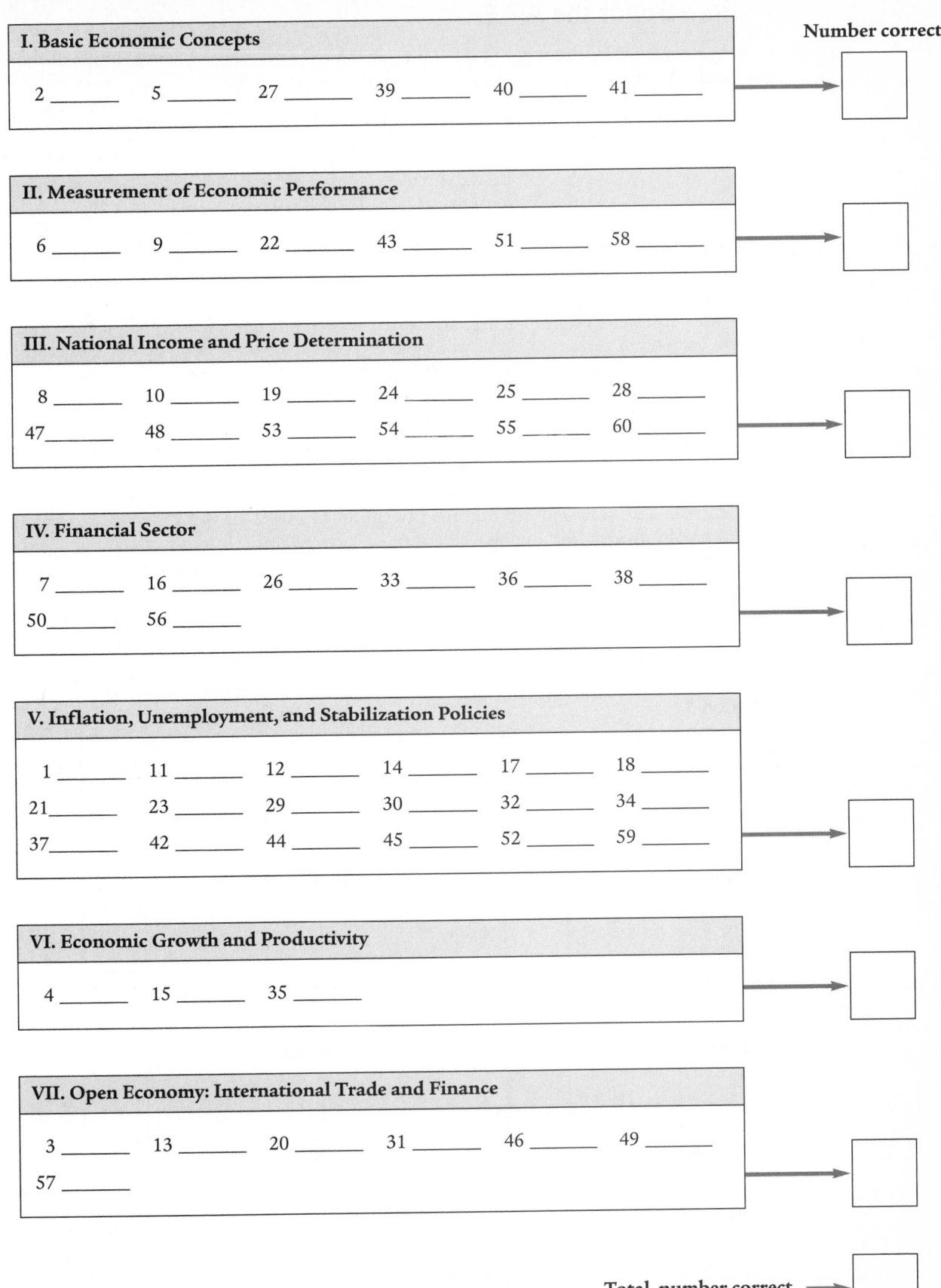

I. Basic Economic Concepts

Number correct

2 _____   5 _____   27 _____   39 _____   40 _____   41 _____

II. Measurement of Economic Performance

6 _____   9 _____   22 _____   43 _____   51 _____   58 _____

III. National Income and Price Determination

8 _____   10 _____   19 _____   24 _____   25 _____   28 _____
47 _____   48 _____   53 _____   54 _____   55 _____   60 _____

IV. Financial Sector

7 _____   16 _____   26 _____   33 _____   36 _____   38 _____
50 _____   56 _____

V. Inflation, Unemployment, and Stabilization Policies

1 _____   11 _____   12 _____   14 _____   17 _____   18 _____
21 _____   23 _____   29 _____   30 _____   32 _____   34 _____
37 _____   42 _____   44 _____   45 _____   52 _____   59 _____

VI. Economic Growth and Productivity

4 _____   15 _____   35 _____

VII. Open Economy: International Trade and Finance

3 _____   13 _____   20 _____   31 _____   46 _____   49 _____
57 _____

Total number correct

Use Your Scores on the Diagnostic Test to Determine How to Prepare for the AP Exam

Start by determining the percent of questions you answered correctly. Your total number correct divided by 60 is the percent of questions you answered correctly:

$$\boxed{} \div 60 = \boxed{}$$

Total # correct   **Total % correct**

To get an idea of how much you will need to study for your AP Macroeconomics exam, you can compare your performance to students who took the most recently released AP Macroeconomics exam. Of the students who scored a "3" on the AP Macroeconomics exam (the minimum score to receive college credit), 80% scored between 31 and 60 on the multiple choice section. Sixty-seven percent of those scoring a "3" scored between 31 and 36 on the multiple choice section. So if your score was below 50% on this diagnostic test, you need to allocate additional time to studying for the AP exam, beyond the review time that all students need to spend in order to do well on the exam. If you scored above 50%, you should still plan to spend time studying the sections for which you most need to improve your performance, as well as taking time to review all of the sections in the week leading up to the exam.

Next, determine how to allocate your study time to each section of material by evaluating your scores in each section. First, find the percent of the questions you answered correctly in each section by dividing the number you answered correctly by the number of questions in the section. Spend more time studying the material in those sections for which the percent you answered correctly is less than your total percent correct and less time studying the sections for which the percent you answered correctly is greater than your total percent correct. Next, look at how much each section is weighted on the AP exam. Spend more time studying those sections that are given more weight on the exam.

Section 1:

$$\boxed{} \div 6 = \boxed{} \quad \textbf{10\%}$$

Sec. 1 # correct

Section 2:

$$\boxed{} \div 6 = \boxed{} \quad \textbf{14\%}$$

Sec. 2 # correct

Section 3:

$$\boxed{} \div 12 = \boxed{} \quad \textbf{13\%}$$

Sec. 3 # correct

Section 4:

$$\boxed{} \div 8 = \boxed{} \quad \textbf{17\%}$$

Sec. 4 # correct

Section 5:

$$\boxed{} \div 18 = \boxed{} \quad \textbf{25\%}$$

Sec. 5 # correct

Section 6:

$$\boxed{} \div 3 = \boxed{} \quad \textbf{8\%}$$

Sec. 6 # correct

Section 7:

$$\boxed{} \div 7 = \boxed{} \quad \textbf{13\%}$$

Sec. 7 # correct

Answers and Explanations

(The section on the course outline is indicated in parentheses.)

1. **D.** Increasing taxes and decreasing government spending reduces aggregate demand and therefore the price level and inflation (V.)

2. **D.** Opportunity cost is the next best alternative use of a resource (I.)

3. **A.** As India imports less from China, the supply of the rupee decreases, causing it to appreciate (VII.)

4. **D.** Economic growth is illustrated by either an increase in the production possibilities curve or the long-run aggregate supply (VI.)

5. **A.** If an economy is producing at the production possibilities curve, then outside of economic growth, any increase in the production of one good comes at the cost of a decrease in the production of the alternative good (I.)

6. **E.** Savers and lenders at fixed rates are harmed by unanticipated inflation because the interest rate they are earning does not reflect the additional cost of the higher inflation (II.)

7. **D.** An increase in money demand increases the nominal interest rate, but because the money supply curve is vertical, no change to the quantity of money occurs (IV.)

8. **E.** An increase in input prices causes the short-run aggregate supply curve to shift left, resulting in an equilibrium at a higher price level and a lower level of output, and thus employment (III.)

9. **B.** Cyclical unemployment is associated with downturns in the business cycle (II.)

10. **C.** Dissaving occurs when consumption exceeds disposable income (III.)

11. **E.** Raising the discount rate is the appropriate monetary policy response to an inflationary gap in the economy (V.)

12. **A.** Expansionary fiscal and contractionary monetary policies result in higher interest rates without necessarily reducing output (V.)

13. **D.** A higher real interest rate creates demand for the dollar, causing it to appreciate and making foreign goods relatively less expensive (VII.)

14. **C.** When the Federal Reserve buys bonds on the open market, banks are left with more excess reserves, which can be lent. This results in lower interest rates and more investment and interest-sensitive consumption, which increases aggregate demand and therefore employment (V.)

15. **C.** An increase in the government's budget deficit would increase the demand for loanable funds and therefore the real interest rate, which would in turn reduce investment in capital (VI.)

16. **A.** Inconvertible fiat means that money's value derives from government mandate and people's willingness to accept it (IV.)

17. **D.** Over the business cycle, if expansionary fiscal policy is used during recessions and contractionary monetary policy is used to offset inflation, then over time, interest rates will "ratchet" upward (V.)

18. **D.** In the long run an increase in the money supply increases only the price level and has no impact on real output or unemployment (VII.)

19. **D.** Crowding out refers to the decrease in gross private investment that results from deficit-induced higher interest rates (III.)

20. **B.** The higher interest rate attracts foreign savings and creates a demand for the currency (VII.)

21. **C.** Reducing taxes is the fiscal policy that increases disposable income and consumption, while buying treasury bonds is the open-market operation that leads to lower interest rates and hence more investment and interest-sensitive consumption (V.)

22. **A.** The labor force is composed of those people classified as either employed or unemployed (II.)

23. **C.** The sale of treasury bonds reduces the money supply, which results in a higher interest rate. This results in lower levels of consumption and investment, and therefore aggregate demand decreases, leading to a lower level of output and a lower price level (V.)

24. **E.** Given the marginal propensity to consume of 0.9, the marginal propensity to save is 0.1. If disposable income increases by $1000, then 10%, or $100, of this change will be saved (III.)

25. **D.** Decreases in labor productivity result in a decrease in the short-run aggregate supply, which leads to less output, a higher price level, and therefore lower real wages (III.)

26. **D.** Using the monetary equation of exchange (MV = PQ), a 5% increase in the money supply, holding velocity (V) and real gross domestic product (Q) constant, must result in a 5% increase in price level (P). (IV.)

27. **B.** A price above the market equilibrium induces competitive sellers to reduce prices, and as prices fall, consumers respond by purchasing more, thus clearing the surplus (I.)

28. **A.** The aggregate demand curve is the inverse relationship between price level and real GDP (III.)

29. **E.** Spending financed by an equal amount of taxation results in a balanced budget multiplier of 1 (III.)

30. **C.** A decrease in government's budget surplus reduces the overall supply of loanable funds, which results in a higher equilibrium real interest rate (III.)

31. **D.** A decrease in Japan's household income would result in fewer yen being supplied in foreign exchange as Japanese households imported fewer European goods, causing the yen to appreciate (VII.)

32. **C.** Demand pull inflation occurs when aggregate demand shifts to the right (V.)

33. **D.** The real interest rate would fall from 3% to 2%, benefitting borrowers and harming lenders (IV.)

34. **E.** A tax on capital investment in technology would reduce productivity, and therefore short-run aggregate supply, which would lead to a higher price level (V.)

35. **D.** Increased productivity has the effect of increasing the long-run aggregate supply

36. **C.** The Federal Reserve will engage in the open-market purchase of bonds, which would result in an increase in demand for bonds, driving up their price (IV.)

37. **E.** An increase in business taxes raises the unit cost of production for business and reduces the short-run aggregate supply curve (V.)

38. **D.** $400 billion in new loans are capable of being created as the $80 billion dollar increase in excess reserves is multiplied by the reciprocal of the required reserve ratio of 20% (IV.)

39. **C.** Huey gives up 1 airplane for each helicopter produced, while Orville gives up 0.5 airplane for each helicopter produced (I.)

40. **D.** Huey has a comparative advantage in airplanes because the opportunity cost is 1 helicopter, as opposed to 2 for Orville. Orville has absolute disadvantages in both because Huey is capable of producing more airplanes and helicopters (I.)

41. **D.** Orville has a comparative advantage in helicopters and would benefit by specializing in their production and importing airplanes from Huey (I.)

42. **A.** A decrease in personal income taxes would increase households' disposable income, resulting in more consumption and leading to an increase in aggregate demand (V.)

43. **D.** Real GDP = Consumption + Investment + Government Spending + Net Exports. Consumption = Disposable income − Savings. Net exports = Exports − Imports, so . . . [DI ($9 trillion) − S($1 trillion)] + Ig($3 trillion) + G($3 trillion) + [X($2 trillion) − M($3 trillion)] = $12 trillion (II.)

44. **E.** Increased production costs result in a leftward shift in short-run aggregate supply, a rightward shift in the short-run Phillips curve, and an increase in inflation (V.)

45. **C.** Increased business taxes would increase unit production cost and also reduce the incentive to invest, which would result in decreases in short-run aggregate supply and aggregate demand (V.)

46. **A.** Increased deficits increase the demand for loanable funds, resulting in higher real interest rates, which attracts foreign saving, resulting in appreciation of the currency, which drives down net exports as exports become relatively more expensive and imports become relatively cheap (VII.)

47. **E.** In the long run, output above full employment results in higher nominal wages, which reduces short-run aggregate supply (III.)

48. **D.** In the long run, a recession results in lower input prices, which leads to an increase in short-run aggregate supply, reducing the price level while increasing output (III.)

49. **A.** The sale of bonds decreases the money supply, resulting in a higher interest rate, which leads to appreciation of the currency (VII.)

50. **A.** The discount rate is the interest rate the Fed charges member banks for borrowing reserves overnight (IV.)

51. **C.** The unemployment rate is equal to the number of unemployed persons divided by the labor force. The number of unemployed persons equals the labor force minus the employed. 20 unemployed divided by 200 in the labor force equals 10% unemployment (II.)

52. **C.** One policy is contractionary while the other is expansionary; however, both result in lower interest rates (V.)

53. **D.** The tax multiplier = mpc/mps = 0.8 / 0.2 = 4. 4 × $40 billion = $160 billion (III.)

54. **B.** Increased labor productivity results in lower unit production costs, thus increasing short- run aggregate supply (III.)

55. **A.** In the long run, AD intersects LRAS at a lower price level at full employment output (III.)

56. **C.** $50 cash originally converted into demand deposit + $450 in loans created and redeposited = $500 in new demand deposits (IV.)

57. **A.** Assuming exchange rates are fixed, imports increase and exports decrease as the faster growing economy consumes more foreign and domestic production (VII.)

58. **C.** The tractor is the only thing listed that is a new, final, domestically produced good for which a market transaction took place (II.)

59. **D.** Shifts in aggregate demand result in a trade-off between inflation and unemployment, which is illustrated by the short-run Phillips curve (V.)

60. **A.** An increase in the expected price level results in higher unit production costs, which reduces short-run aggregate supply (III.)

VI. Reviewing for the AP Macroeconomic Exam

The AP Macroeconomics exam includes both multiple-choice and free-response questions that require calculations. For example, you may be required to calculate GDP, the unemployment rate, or any of the multipliers you have studied. To answer calculation questions, you must remember and understand some important formulas. The key macroeconomic formulas are listed below.

One of the best ways to prepare for the AP exam is to work released free-response questions and practice answering as many examples of multiple-choice questions as you can. As you begin, keep this list of key macroeconomic formulas handy and use it as a guide. With practice, you will discover that these formulas become planted in your memory. Make sure that you practice and review enough that you can recall and apply these formulas without a guide on the AP exam.

The Formulas of Macro

Expenditure Approach to Real GDP

- Real GDP = consumption + investment + government spending + net exports

  $$RGDP = C + I_G + G + X_N$$

Income Approach to Real GDP

- Real GDP = Rent + Wages + Interest + Profits

  $$RGDP = r + w + i + p$$

Labor Force

- LF = # Employed + # Unemployed

  $$LF = E + U$$

Labor Force Participation Rate

- Labor force participation rate $= \dfrac{\text{Labor Force}}{\text{Working Age Population}}$

  $$LFPR = \dfrac{LF}{pop}$$

Unemployment Rate

- $UR = \dfrac{\text{\#Unemployed}}{\text{Labor Force}}$

  $$UR = \dfrac{U}{LF}$$

Inflation Rate (CPI is Consumer Price Index)

- $\text{Infl } R = \left(\dfrac{\text{New } CPI - \text{Old } CPI}{\text{Old } CPI}\right) \times 100$

GDP Deflator

- $GDP\,\text{Defl} = \left(\dfrac{\text{Nominal } GDP}{\text{Real } GDP}\right) \times 100$

Converting Nominal GDP to Real GDP

- $RGDP = \left(\dfrac{\text{Nominal } GDP}{CPI}\right) \times 100$

Real Interest Rate

- Real interest rate = Nominal interest rate − Inflation rate

  $$r\% = i\% - \pi\%$$

Nominal Interest Rate

- Nominal interest rate = Real interest rate + Expected inflation rate

$$i\% = r\% + \pi^{exp}\%$$

Marginal Propensity to Save

- $MPS = \dfrac{\text{Change in saving}}{\text{Change in disposable income}}$

Marginal Propensity to Consume

- $MPC = \dfrac{\text{Change in consumption}}{\text{Change in disposable income}}$

Spending Multiplier

- $Mult_{spend} = \dfrac{1}{1 - MPC}$ or $\dfrac{1}{MPS}$

Tax Multiplier

- $Mult_{tax} = \dfrac{-1\,PC}{1 - MPC}$ or $\dfrac{-MPC}{MPS}$

Money Multiplier

- $Mult_m = \dfrac{1}{\text{required reserve ratio}}$

Multiple Deposit Expansion

- Required reserve = amount of deposit × required reserve ratio

- Maximum amount a single bank can loan = change in excess reserves caused by a deposit

- Change in loans throughout banking system = initial change in excess reserves × Multiplier money

- Change in money supply = change in loans throughout banking system + $ amount of any OMOs

Monetary Equation of Exchange

- Money Stock × Income Velocity of Money = Nominal GDP

- Money Stock × Income Velocity of Money = Price Level × Real GDP

- $MV = PQ$ $MV = PY$

Graphs

The AP Macroeconomics exam requires you to understand and correctly draw the important graphs you have studied throughout the course. The following pages are designed to help you learn the various graphs that you will be required to use to answer questions on the exam. You should be comfortable and confident drawing each of them and using them to answer questions. Correct labeling of axes is especially important. Also, be sure that you understand what causes changes in the various diagrams and the resulting effects on the variables represented on both the vertical and horizontal axes of each graph. Rest assured that you will be required to draw and analyze at least four different graphs on the free-response section of the exam.

To prepare for the AP Macroeconomics exam, practice answering free-response questions that require you to draw graphs. You can find sample free-response questions on previous exams released by the College Board and in your textbook. Make sure that you also look at answer keys and scoring guidelines provided to make sure you are answering correctly and that you understand how your AP exam is scored. You should also get into the habit of using graphs to help you answer questions even when a graph is not required. For example, drawing a supply and demand graph can often help you answer multiple-choice questions that involve the supply and demand model. And a graph can often be used to help explain an answer to a free-response question, even if a graph is not explicitly required. Remember, a picture can be worth a thousand words!

Understanding how to use economic models is central to any economics course and therefore it is central to the AP Macroeconomic exam. So, if you understand and can apply the models presented in this section, then you will have gone a long way in striving for a five!

The Production Possibilities Curve

The production possibilities curve illustrates trade-offs and opportunity cost incurred as a result of scarce factors of production.

The concave shape indicates that the opportunity cost of producing more consumer/capital goods is ever increasing.

In the graph on top, an economy that is fully employing all of its available resources by currently producing at point A and that wishes to produce instead at point B must sacrifice 2 units of capital goods in order to gain about 1 1/2 units of consumer goods.

The bottom graph illustrates the effect of an increase in available factors of production, the quality of those factors of production, increased technology, or increased productivity.

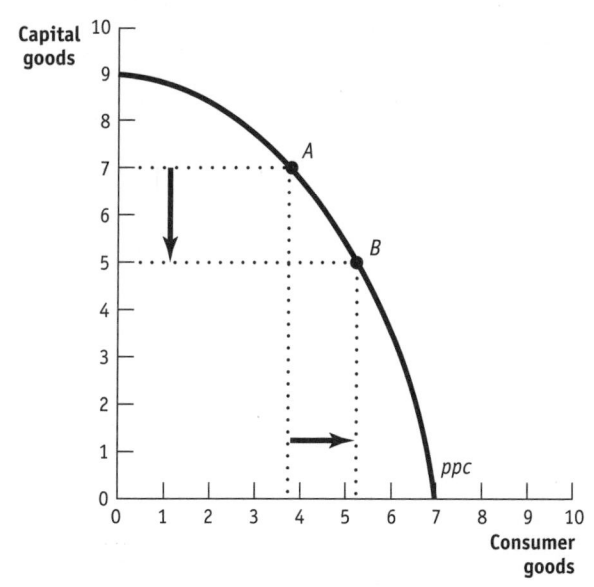

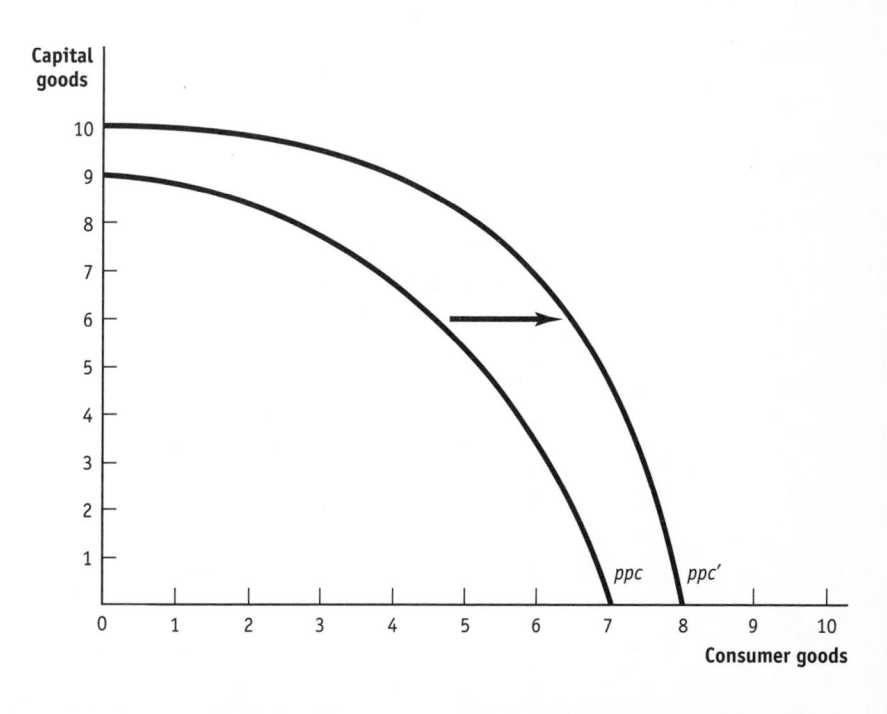

Supply and Demand

The supply and demand model illustrates producers' willingness and ability to produce a good or service (supply) combined with consumers' willingness and ability to consume a good or service (demand). The intersection of these two functions determines the equilibrium price and equilibrium quantity.

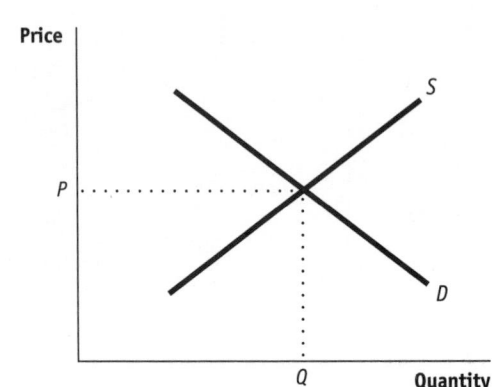

Changes in Demand

Δ in *M.E.R.I.T.*:

ΔD.: ΔP & ΔQ

   D right .: $P\uparrow$ & $Q\uparrow$

   D left .: $P\downarrow$ & $Q\downarrow$

Changes in Supply

Δ in *N.I.C.E.J.A.G.T.*:

ΔS.: ΔP & ΔQ

   S right .: $P\downarrow$ & $Q\uparrow$

   S left .: $P\uparrow$ & $Q\downarrow$

Demand Shifters

M.E.R.I.T.

M — market size

E — expected prices

R — related prices (complements and substitutes)

I — income

T — tastes

Supply Shifters

N.I.C.E.J.A.G.T.

as in, "Nice Jag, T!"

N — natural phenomenon

I — input prices

C — competition

E — expected prices

J — joint production prices (think beef and leather)

A — alternate production prices (think corn and wheat)

G — government taxes and subsidies

T — technology

Foreign Exchange Market

Market which brings together people who need to buy or sell one currency in exchange for the currency of another country.

The equilibrium price is referred to as an exchange rate and is denoted as (*e*).

The graph to the right illustrates the market for the E.U. euro in terms of the U.S. dollar.

Exchange rates are determined by

Relative S.T.R.I.N.G.

Relative Speculation

Relative Tastes

Relative Rates (interest)

Relative Inflation

Relative Net Exports

Relative Growth

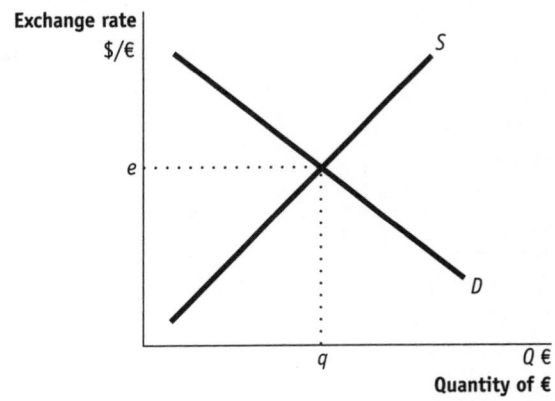

Loanable Funds Market

Market which brings together savers and borrowers. Savers supply loanable funds and borrowers demand them.

The equilibrium price which equates savings to borrowing is the real interest rate (*r*%).

Saving and borrowing go by different names, depending on which sector of the economy is doing the saving and borrowing.

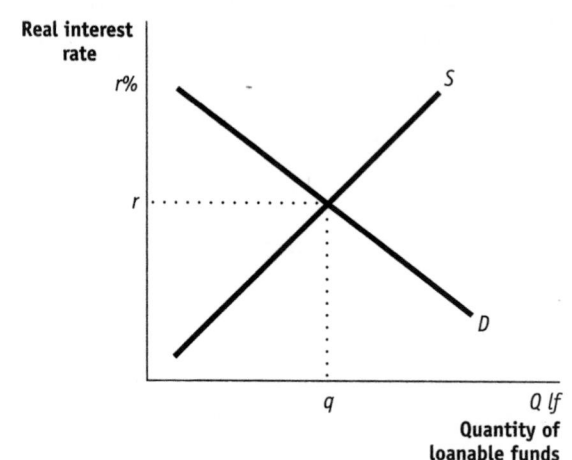

Δ Saving = Δ *S*

Δ *S* .: Δ *r*% & Δ *Qlf*

    S right .: *r*% $\downarrow$ & *Qlf* $\uparrow$

    S left .: *r*% $\uparrow$ & *Qlf* $\downarrow$

Households – Saving

Business – Retained Earnings

Government – Budget Surplus

Foreign Sector –

    Capital inflows (+)

    Capital outflows (–)

Δ Borrowing = Δ *D*

Δ *D* .: Δ *r*% & Δ *Qlf*

    D right .: *r*% $\uparrow$ & *Qlf* $\uparrow$

    D left .: *r*% $\downarrow$ & *Qlf* $\downarrow$

Households – Borrowing

Businesses – Capital Investment

Government – Budget Deficit

Foreign Sector – Foreign borrowing

Money Market

Market which brings together the central bank (the Fed) and everybody else in the economy.

The Fed supplies money (M1) and everyone else demands it.

The equilibrium price, which equates the supply of money with the demand for money, is the nominal interest rate (*i*%).

The supply is vertical because the central bank issues the money independent of the interest rate, so that at any point in time, the supply of money is the stock of money available.

The demand for money reflects the economy's liquidity preference or willingness to hold cash at various interest rates. The demand for money is never zero because there is always transaction demand regardless of the interest rate.

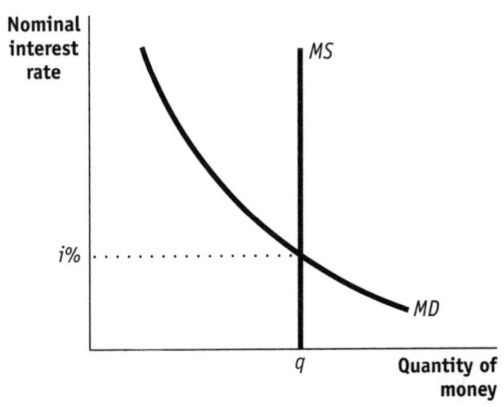

Δ Federal Reserve Policy = Δ *MS*

Δ *MS* .: Δ *i*% & Δ *QM*

   MS right .: *i*% ↓ & *QM* ↑

     S left .: *i*% ↑ & *QM* ↓

Δ Nominal GDP = Δ *MD*

Δ *MD* .: Δ *i*% & *NO* Δ in *QM*

   MD right .: *i*% ↑

     D left .: *i*% ↓

Aggregate Supply and Aggregate Demand

The aggregate supply and aggregate demand model illustrates the economy as a whole. Aggregate supply represents producers' willingness and ability to produce all of the output of the nation at various price levels. Aggregate demand reflects the private, public, and foreign sectors' willingness and ability to purchase the output at various price levels.

Notice in the graph that there are two aggregate supply curves. *SRAS* refers to the short-run aggregate supply. *LRAS* refers to long-run aggregate supply. In the short run, firms willingly produce more output as price level changes because inflexible input prices allow firms to experience profits. In the long run, input prices adjust to change in the price level so firms have no incentive to vary output as price level changes.

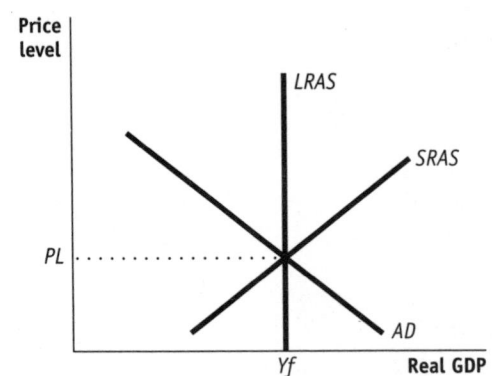

Δ *P.I.L.E.* = Δ *SRAS*

Δ *SRAS* .: Δ *PL* & Δ *RGDP*

   SRAS right .: *PL* $\downarrow$ & *RGGP* $\uparrow$

   SRAS left .: *PL* $\uparrow$ & *RGDP* $\downarrow$

P.I.L.E. = things that change firms' unit production costs

P — productivity

I — input prices

L — laws, regulations, taxes, and subsidies on businesses

E — expected inflation

Δ *C.Ig.G.Xn* = Δ *AD*

Δ *AD* .: Δ *PL* & Δ *RGDP*

   AD right .: *PL* $\uparrow$ & *RGDP* $\uparrow$

   AD left .: *PL* $\downarrow$ & *RGDP* $\downarrow$

C.Ig.G.Xn = the spending that comes from the different sectors of the economy

C — consumption (household spending)

Ig — investment (business spending)

G — government spending

Xn — net exports (net foreign spending)

The Phillips Curve

The Phillips curve can be further divided into short-run and long-run versions. The short-run Phillips curve shows the trade-off that exists between inflation (π%) and unemployment (u%) in the short run.

The long-run Phillips curve exists at an economy's natural rate of unemployment (natural u%) and shows that no relationship exists between inflation rates and unemployment rates in the long run.

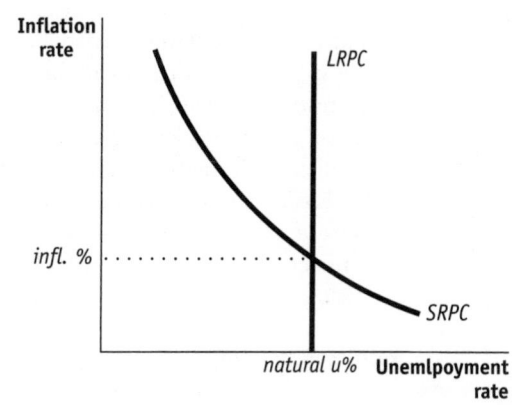

Δ SRAS $= -\Delta$ SRPC

Think of SRAS and SRPC as mirror images.

Δ SRAS .: $-\Delta$ SRPC

    SRAS right .: SRPC left

        .: π% $\downarrow$ & u% $\downarrow$

    SRAS left .: SRPC right

        .: π% $\uparrow$ & u% $\uparrow$

Δ natural u% .: Δ LRPC

natural u% increase = LRPC right

natural u% decrease = LRPC left

Δ AD = movement along SRPC

Δ AD .: slide along SRPC

    .: Δ π% & Δ u%

    AD right .: slide up SRPC

        π% $\uparrow$ & u% $\downarrow$

    AD left .: slide down SRPC

        π% $\downarrow$ & u% $\uparrow$

VII. Test-Taking Tips

Once you have mastered all of the course material, you are ready to begin reviewing for the AP Macroeconomics exam. Below is a description of the types of questions you will find on the exam, as well as tips and suggestions for how to answer these types of questions.

The Multiple-Choice Section

When you are taking the multiple-choice section of the exam, be careful that you do not spend too much time on any one question. You have only 70 minutes to answer 60 questions, so don't get stuck on any one question. Skip and return to a difficult question, or make a guess if you have no idea how to answer it. Also, be very careful that you fill in the correct bubble for your answer (be especially careful if you do skip a question) and that each bubble is filled in neatly.

Unlike tests that you might take in a class, the AP exams do not use "all of the above," "none of the above" or "true/false" type questions. Instead, the multiple choice questions you will encounter will come in five different formats. The most common question type asks you to either define or classify concepts learned in macroeconomics. The next most common question type is best described as cause and effect format. Far less common are questions that ask you to calculate an answer or interpret a graph. The least common question type is the I, II, III style, described below.

Define/Classify Format

This format asks you to simply identify or classify information. These are often the simplest questions and require that you have read and understood the material. Read through each question carefully, and then analyze the answer choices. Some of the answer choices will contain "correct" information , but they may not be relevant to the question being asked, so avoid the temptation to skim the question and look for the first "true thing you see. Make sure the answer matches the question being asked.

Question: Which of the following would be classified as a debit to the current account in the balance of payments?

A. The purchase of real estate in Hawaii by Japanese investors

B. $20 million in medicine is exported from U.S. pharmaceutical manufacturers to private hospitals in Australia

C. Argentine investors purchase $5 million worth of U.S. Treasury securities.

D. U.S. corporations pay $400 million in dividends to foreign shareholders

E. U.S. gasoline producers import $1 billion worth of crude oil from foreign producers

Cause-and-Effect Format

The cause-and-effect format questions are quite popular on the AP Macroeconomics exam and can be a real challenge unless you have a strategy. The strategy that works well for many successful students is to analyze a single column and see what possible answers you can eliminate. For example, in the question below you are asked to determine which answer best corresponds to a contractionary policy by the Fed. If you know that contractionary means interest rates go up, then you can immediately eliminate answer choices B, C, and D. If you also know that selling bonds is contractionary, then you have your answer and you did not even look at the other columns.

Question: Which of the following is most likely to occur if the Federal Reserve conducts a contractionary monetary policy?

	Open-Market Operation	Nominal Interest Rate	$Exchange Rate	Unemployment
A.	Sell bonds	Increase	$ Appreciates	Increase
B.	Sell bonds	Decrease	$ Depreciates	Decrease
C.	Buy bonds	Decrease	$ Depreciates	Decrease
D.	Buy bonds	Decrease	$ Appreciates	Decrease
E.	Buy bonds	Increase	$ Depreciates	Increase

Calculation

When answering calculation questions, make sure to read all the answers carefully for clues to the right answer. One thing that might help is to do some quick math and calculate some other information. When given information about marginal propensity to consume, as in the question below, also calculate the marginal propensity to save, the spending multiplier, and the tax multiplier, and jot them down on the test. That way you can "test" each answer until you find the correct one.

Question: If consumers have a marginal propensity to consume of 0.8, then which of the following is true?

   A. A $4 billion increase in private investment will lead to a maximum economic expansion of $40 billion

   B. An increase in income of $400 billion will result in an increase in $80 billion in savings.*

   C. An increase in income of $400 billion will result in a decrease in consumption of $320 billion.

   D. The spending multiplier is 4.

   E. The tax multiplier is –3.

Graphic Interpretation

AP economics exams will frequently ask you to refer to a graph to answer questions. These questions require you to understand what is shown on the graph provided. Pay close attention to the specific information provided on the graph, especially the labels on the axes of the graph, as you determine your answer.

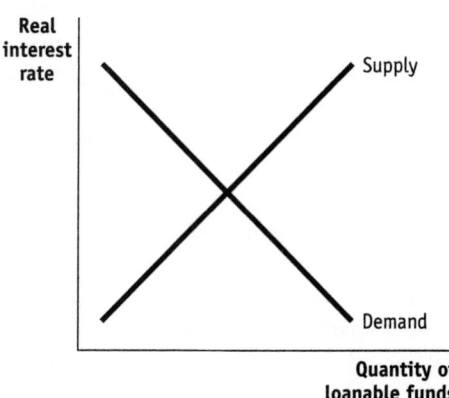

Question: Refer to the loanable funds diagram above, an increase in private borrowing is best shown as

   A. an increased demand for loanable funds.*

   B. an increased supply of loanable funds.

   C. a decreased demand for loanable funds.

   D. a decreased supply of loanable funds.

   E. no change in the loanable funds market.

I, II, III Format

This format is very rare and may or may not appear on your test. If it does, do not fret. This format is nothing more than a true-false question. In the example below, you are asked to determine who benefits from unexpected inflation. Go through each choice and if it is false, then cross it out. What you are left with is the right answer! Go ahead and try it on the example below.

Question: An unexpected increase in inflation will most likely benefit which of the following?

    I. Households with significant savings earning a fixed interest rate

    II. Borrowers with fixed-rate mortgage loans

    III. Governments experiencing large amounts of debt

  A. I only

  B. II only

  C. I, II, and III

  D. I and III

  E. II and III*

The Free-Response Section

The second section of the AP Macroeconomics exam is made up of free response questions. The time allotted to the free-response section is broken down into two parts: a planning period and a writing period. The free-response section of the exam begins with a ten-minute planning period during which you can read over the questions and map out your response in the **question** booklet. Note: the readers scoring your free-response answers will not see anything written on the questions sheet. During the mandatory 10-minute "reading" period, you should carefully read the questions. Use this time to plan your response by underlining the verbs in the questions. At the end of the planning period, you are then allowed 50 minutes to answer the free-response questions in the **answer** booklet. Make sure you use your time wisely by outlining your answers during the planning period and using graphs, symbols, and abbreviations where applicable. Note: only answers written in the answer book will be scored (i.e., answers written on the question sheet will not be graded).

Remember that someone will eventually read and score the answers that you write. The easier it is to find and follow your answers, the easier it is to give you points! Practice writing clear, concise, organized answers. Clearly label the question number in the box on the top of the answer booklet page. Denote which part of the question you are answering as you write your answer. Provide a clear, organized answer to each part of the question. Use the scoring guides provided for the practice tests below as an example of a clear, complete, concise, organized response, and strive to use a similar format for your answer. But don't be concerned if you must answer questions out of order, cross out an answer and start again, include extraneous information, etc. Exam readers will do their best to award you the points that you deserve It is just in your best interest to make that as easy as possible for them!

You should also make sure that you answer each part of each question to the best of your ability. Even if you are unsure of the correct answer, write something. You may actually know more than you think. Also, make sure that you answer each part of the question even when you think your answer on an earlier part may not be correct. Each part of a free-response question is scored independently, so an incorrect answer on one part of a question does not mean you can't receive points for a subsequent part.

The free-response section is divided into three separate questions. The first question is the longest and most comprehensive, and you should allocate roughly half of your time, about 25 minutes, to answering it. The second and third free response questions are shorter and typically test a particular area of the course outline. You should allocate roughly a quarter of the time available, or about 12–13 minutes, to each of the shorter questions. Allocate and monitor your time carefully so that you are able to provide at least a basic response to each question. Each question usually has parts that require a simple "coin-flip" response, e.g., yes/no or increase/decrease. Make sure you take the time to at least answer these parts of every question. Under no circumstances should you leave a free-response question unanswered. Omission is a guarantee of no points and therefore you will probably not receive a five.

On the free-response section, read each question carefully. Pay close attention to what each question is specifically asking. Remember those verbs you underlined during the planning period? As you answer each part of each question, cross out the corresponding verb so that you make sure you answer each part of the question. According to the experts, i.e., those who score your responses, one of the best ways to make sure you receive maximum points for your answer is to read the question and do *exactly* what it says. Below are examples of some of the phrases and terms used in free-response questions and the responses that should go with them.

"Draw a correctly labeled graph" — Draw the required diagram and *correctly label* the axes and curves on the graph!

> *Question:* Draw a correctly labeled diagram of the short-run Phillips curve, label the curve SRPC

> *Response:*

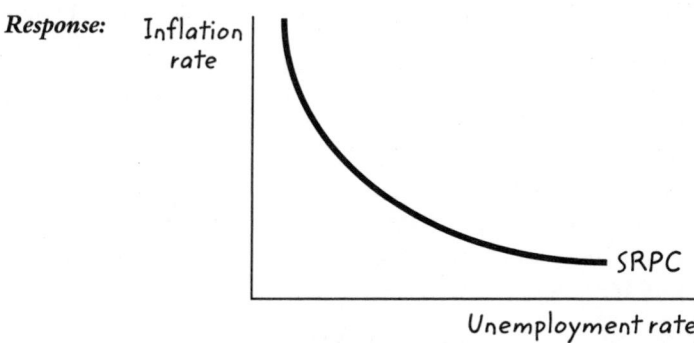

"Show" — Go back to a graph that you have previously drawn and clearly show changes on that graph.

> *Question:* Show the effect of an increase in inflationary expectations on the short-run Phillips curve from part a (i).

> *Response:*

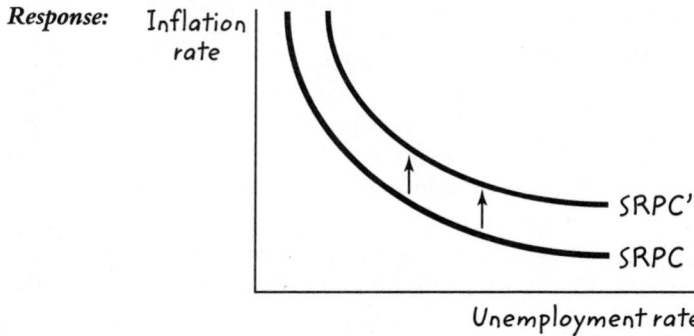

"Identify" — Make an assertion based on the information given in the question.

> *Question:* Identify the effect of a decrease in consumption on output.

> *Response:* Output Decreases

"Explain" — Go beyond the assertion, and describe why the assertion you made would happen.

Question: Identify the effect of a decrease in consumption on output. Explain.

Response: Output decreases because aggregate demand decreased . . .

"List" — Make a bulleted list of items.

Question: List three actions the Federal Reserve can undertake to change the money supply.

Response: Buy or sell treasury securities

Change the reserve requirement

Change the discount rate

"Define" — Write a definition.

Question: Define discount rate.

Response: The discount rate is the interest rate charged when member banks borrow reserves from the Fed overnight.

"Calculate" — Do some math and find a numerical answer.

Question: Assume that the required reserve ratio is 10% and that banks hold no excess reserves. The Federal Reserve purchases $50 million in treasury securities on the open market Calculate the maximum possible change in loans throughout the banking system.

Response: Change in loans = Amt. single bank can lend X money multiplier

$50 million deposit - (10% X $50 million) = $45 million

$45 million X (1/10%) = $450 million <— ANSWER!!!

VIII. Practice Tests

You should use the following sample tests to help you prepare for your AP Macroeconomics exam. Allow yourself 70 minutes to complete the multiple-choice section without using a calculator or any outside resources. Starting in 2011, there is no penalty for guessing, so attempt each question. After you have completed the multiple-choice section, give yourself 10 minutes to plan your response to the three free-response questions. After your 10-minute planning period, you should complete the free-response questions within 50 minutes. For the multiple-choice section you are required to fill in the answer blanks on the answer document using a #2 pencil.

Answers and explanations along with scoring guidelines for the free-response section are at the end of this section.

Practice Test 1

Multiple-Choice Questions

1. Which monetary policy would be most appropriate for combating inflation?

   A. increase taxes and transfer payments
   B. raise the reserve requirement
   C. the open market purchase of treasury securities by the Federal Reserve
   D. increase taxes and decrease government spending
   E. decrease taxes and decrease government spending

2. If the resources used in making consumer goods can be perfectly substituted for making capital goods, then the opportunity cost is

   A. increasing.
   B. zero.
   C. decreasing.
   D. constant.
   E. diminishing.

3. Depreciation of the U.S. dollar in the foreign exchange market could be caused by a decrease in which of the following?

   A. U.S. imports from Japan
   B. the U.S. price level
   C. demand for the British pound by U.S. investors
   D. the U.S. real interest rate
   E. Mexican exports to the United States

4. Assuming a system of flexible exchange rates, an open market purchase of bonds by the United States Federal Reserve while other countries do nothing will most likely affect the rate of inflation and the international value of the United States dollar in which of the following ways?

	Inflation Rate	**International Value of the United Sates Dollar**
A.	Decrease	Appreciate
B.	Decrease	Depreciate
C.	Increase	Appreciate
D.	Increase	Depreciate
E.	Increase	No change

5. The federal funds rate is

   A. the interest rate the Federal Reserve charges member banks for overnight loans.
   B. the interest rate banks charge their best commercial customers.
   C. the interest rate banks charge other banks for overnight loans.
   D. the percentage of demand deposits that banks may not lend to customers.
   E. the difference between the nominal interest rate and the real interest rate.

Labor Market in Parlin (in thousands of persons)	
Population	250
Labor Force	200
Employed	160

6. Study the information in the table on the previous page. If 20,000 discouraged workers are now reclassified as unemployed, what would be the new unemployment rate for Parlin?

   A. 20%
   B. 36%
   C. 18.2%
   D. 27.3%
   E. 40%

7. An increase in government spending combined with an open-market purchase of bonds will result in

   A. an increase in real gross domestic product and an increase in the interest rate.
   B. an increase in real gross domestic product and an indeterminate change in the interest rate.
   C. an indeterminate change in real gross domestic product and a decrease in the interest rate.
   D. a decrease in real gross domestic product and a decrease in the interest rate.
   E. a decrease in unemployment and an increase in the interest rate.

8. If a $50 billion increase in government spending results in a $200 billion increase in real output, then which of the following would be the marginal propensity to consume?

   A. 0.90
   B. 0.80
   C. 0.75
   D. 0.50
   E. 0.25

9. Money, as measured by M1 functions primarily as a

   A. unit of account.
   B. store of value.
   C. medium of exchange.
   D. source of divisibility.
   E. source of durability.

10. A sudden increase in energy prices will most likely trigger

    A. cost-push inflation.
    B. demand-pull inflation.
    C. lower interest rates.
    D. a decrease in the money supply.
    E. an immediate decrease in inventory.

11. Simultaneous increases in the rates of inflation and unemployment are best associated with which of the following?

    A. a leftward shift of the money demand curve
    B. a leftward shift of the aggregate demand curve
    C. a rightward shift of the short-run Phillips curve
    D. a rightward shift of the long-run Phillips curve
    E. a rightward shift of the short-run aggregate supply curve

12. Which is most likely to occur if the Federal Reserve increases the reserve requirement on demand deposits?

    A. Banks will be able to lend more excess reserves.
    B. Interest rates will decrease.
    C. The money supply will decrease.
    D. The discount rate will decrease.
    E. Investment will definitely increase.

13. Which monetary policy action by the Federal Reserve will shift aggregate demand to the right?

   A. the open-market sale of bonds by the Federal Reserve
   B. a decrease in the discount rate
   C. a decrease in taxes
   D. an increase in government spending
   E. an increase in the reserve requirement

14. The net export effect is best described as

   A. an increase in capital investment at the expense of government spending.
   B. a decrease in net exports resulting from appreciation of the currency.
   C. an increase in both inflation and unemployment.
   D. a decrease in gross private investment resulting from government borrowing.
   E. a rightward shift of the money supply.

15. If the real interest rate in France decreases relative to that of the rest of the world, capital flow and currency should change in which of the following ways?

	Capital Flow	Currency
A.	Out	Appreciate
B.	In	Appreciate
C.	In	Depreciate
D.	Out	Depreciate
E.	No change	No change

16. Which of the following policies would be appropriate for reducing inflation?

   I. Decrease the money supply
   II. Decrease taxes
   III. Decrease government spending

   A. I only
   B. II only
   C. II and III only
   D. I and III only
   E. I, II, and III

17. Which of the following best exemplifies frictional unemployment?

   A. Skilled workers are replaced by robots.
   B. Economic recession forces companies to lay off many workers.
   C. Workers lack the necessary skills to gain employment in the semiconductor industry.
   D. College graduates enter the labor force and seek employment.
   E. Men and women quit working to take care of their young children.

18. Which of the following best describes the sequence of events that occurs when the Federal Reserve buys treasury securities on the open market?

   A. Money supply increases, interest rates decrease, consumption and investment increase, aggregate demand increases, and output and price level increases.
   B. Money supply increases, interest rates decrease, consumption and investment decrease, aggregate demand decreases, and output and price level decreases.
   C. Money supply decreases, interest rates increase, consumption and investment decrease, aggregate demand decreases, and output and price level decreases.
   D. Money supply decreases, interest rates decrease, consumption and investment decrease, aggregate demand decreases, and output and price level decreases.
   E. Money supply decreases, interest rates increase, consumption and investment increase, aggregate demand increases, and output and price level increases.

19. Assume that autonomous consumption is $500 and that the marginal propensity to save is 0.25. If disposable income increases by $1000, then consumption spending will increase by

    A. $250.
    B. $125.
    C. $1250.
    D. $750.
    E. $375.

20. Assume that all input prices are inflexible. An increase in the money supply will have which of the following effects on output, price level, and real wages?

	Output	Price Level	Real Wages
A.	Increase	Increase	Increase
B.	Increase	Decrease	Increase
C.	Decrease	Increase	Increase
D.	Increase	Increase	Decrease
E.	Increase	Decrease	Decrease

21. Assuming the income velocity of money is constant, if the Federal Reserve wants the real economy to grow at a rate of 3% per year without creating inflation, then the money supply must

    A. grow at a rate of 2%.
    B. decrease by 3% in order to eliminate inflation.
    C. increase by 4% to offset the effect of inflation.
    D. increase by exactly 3%.
    E. increase by more than 4%.

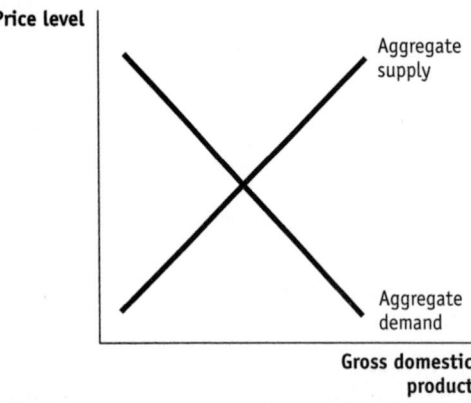

22. According to the graph above, an increase in consumers' wealth will most likely cause income and unemployment to change in which of the following ways?

	Income	Unemployment
A.	Increase	Increase
B.	Decrease	Increase
C.	Decrease	Decrease
D.	Increase	No change
E.	Increase	Decrease

23. If the price level in the United States increased relative to the price level in Belgium, then the United States dollar would

    A. appreciate, making Belgian exports to the United States more expensive.
    B. depreciate, making U.S. imports from Belgium more expensive.
    C. appreciate, making Belgian imports from the United States cheaper.
    D. appreciate, making U.S. imports from Belgium cheaper.
    E. depreciate, making U.S. exports to Belgium cheaper.

24. If an economy is currently operating below the natural rate of unemployment, then which of the following will cause unemployment to increase and interest rates to increase?

  A. The Federal Reserve raises the discount rate.
  B. The government reduces spending while raising taxes.
  C. The Federal Reserve buys treasury securities on the open market.
  D. The Federal Reserve lowers the reserve requirement.
  E. The government increases spending and reduces taxes.

25. A decrease in which of the following would most likely lead to economic growth?

  A. personal savings
  B. gross private investment
  C. the real interest rate
  D. capital formation
  E. bond purchases by the Federal Reserve

26. Which of the following will occur in a competitive market when a surplus exists?

  A. Surpluses are impossible.
  B. The price and the quantity in the market will decrease.
  C. The price will decrease and the quantity supplied will increase.
  D. The price will increase and the quantity demanded will decrease.
  E. The price will decrease and the quantity demanded will increase.

27. The inverse relationship between the real interest rate and the quantity of funds available for borrowing is shown by the

  A. the aggregate demand curve.
  B. the demand for loanable funds.
  C. the short-run Phillips curve.
  D. the supply of loanable funds.
  E. the production possibilities curve.

28. A $10 billion increase in government spending funded by a $10 billion increase in taxes will have which of the following effects on aggregate demand?

  A. increase aggregate demand by an amount greater than $10 billion
  B. increase aggregate demand by an amount of $10 billion
  C. no change in aggregate demand
  D. decrease aggregate demand by an amount greater than $9 billion
  E. decrease aggregate demand by an amount of $9 billion

29. An increase in the government's budget deficit will most likely result in

  A. increased tax revenues.
  B. decreased government spending.
  C. higher interest rates.
  D. a decrease in the international value of the dollar.
  E. an increase in unemployment.

30. Which of the following would cause the Canadian dollar to depreciate relative to the Mexican peso?

  A. an increase in Canadian household income
  B. a decrease in Mexican interest rates relative to Canadian interest rates
  C. an increase in Mexico's average price level
  D. a decrease in Canada's average price level
  E. an increase in Mexican household income

31. Deflation is caused by

    A. an increase in the money supply.
    B. a decreased short run aggregate supply.
    C. an increased aggregate demand.
    D. a decreased aggregate demand.
    E. a rightward shift of the short-run Phillips curve.

32. If the nominal interest rate increases from 6 percent to 8 percent while the real interest rate remains unchanged, then

    A. expected inflation remains unchanged.
    B. expected inflation decreases 2%.
    C. expected deflation increases 2%.
    D. disinflation occurs.
    E. expected inflation increases 2%.

33. Which of the following would lead to a decrease in the U.S. gross domestic product in the short run?

    A. Personal income taxes decrease.
    B. Banks lend out all excess reserves.
    C. Households increase their savings.
    D. Businesses increase their investment in new capital.
    E. Government increases defense spending.

34. An improvement in the population's educational attainment will cause the

    A. aggregate demand curve to shift left.
    B. aggregate demand curve to shift right.
    C. long run aggregate supply curve to shift left.
    D. long run aggregate supply curve to shift right.
    E. short run aggregate supply curve to shift left.

35. Assume that private investors buy $100 billion worth of treasury securities on the open market from the Federal Reserve. If the required reserve ratio is 25 percent, the maximum increase in the money supply is

    A. $25 billion.
    B. $75 billion.
    C. $300 billion.
    D. $400 billion.
    E. $500 billion.

Questions 36–38 are based on the diagram below, which shows the choices in production of two countries, Zumbulu and Costa Del Rey, producing two goods, bananas and cocoa, using all of their available resources.

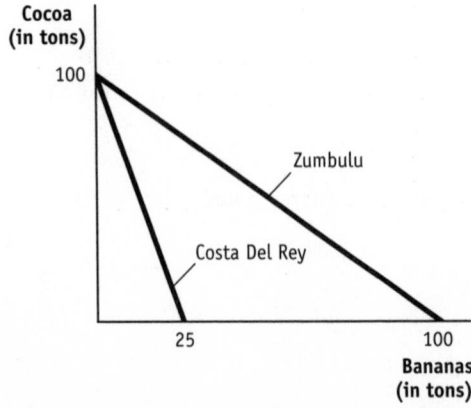

36. Before specialization and trade, the opportunity cost of producing 1 ton of bananas in Zumbulu and in Costa Del Rey is which of the following?

Zumbulu	Costa Del Rey
A. 4 tons of cocoa	1 ton of cocoa
B. 1 ton of cocoa	1 ton of cocoa
C. 1 ton of cocoa	0.25 ton of cocoa
D. 1 ton of cocoa	4 tons of cocoa
E. 0.25 ton of cocoa	4 tons of cocoa

37. Which of the following statements best describes the absolute advantage or comparative advantage that each country has?

   A. Zumbulu has an absolute advantage in bananas, while Costa Del Rey has a comparative advantage in bananas.
   B. Neither has an absolute advantage in cocoa, while Costa Del Rey has a comparative advantage in bananas.
   C. Zumbulu has a comparative advantage in bananas, while Costa Del Rey has a comparative advantage in cocoa.
   D. Zumbulu has a comparative disadvantage in bananas, while Costa Del Rey has an absolute advantage in bananas.
   E. Neither has a comparative advantage in cocoa, while Zumbulu has a comparative advantage in bananas.

38. If Zumbulu and Costa Del Rey were to specialize according to their comparative advantage and trade, then which of the following terms of trade between tons of bananas (B) and tons of cocoa (C) would both countries find mutually advantageous?

   A. $1B = 0.5C$
   B. $1B = 5C$
   C. $1B = 3C$
   D. $1B = 6C$
   E. $1B = 0.2C$

39. A decrease in government spending will most likely cause aggregate demand and short-run aggregate supply to change in which of the following ways?

Aggregate Demand	Short-run aggregate supply
A. Increase	Increase
B. Increase	Not change
C. Decrease	Increase
D. Decrease	No change
E. Decrease	Decrease

40. Which type of unemployment would decrease if computer-based social networking reduced the amount of time it took for job seekers to find jobs?

   A. Frictional
   B. Cyclical
   C. Seasonal
   D. Structural
   E. Part-time

41. The marginal propensity to save is

   A. always equal to the marginal propensity to consume.
   B. equal to the tax multiplier.
   C. the percentage of the change in disposable income that is spent.
   D. used to calculate the money multiplier.
   E. equal to one minus the marginal propensity to consume.

42. If an economy is operating above full-employment, an appropriate monetary policy would be to

    A. lower the required reserve ratio.
    B. raise taxes.
    C. lower taxes.
    D. sell bonds on the open market.
    E. lower the discount rate.

43. Which of the following combinations of fiscal and monetary policy would effectively increase capital investment while not increasing the price level?

	Fiscal Policy	Monetary Policy
A.	Expansionary	Contractionary
B.	Expansionary	Expansionary
C.	Contractionary	Expansionary
D.	Contractionary	Contractionary
E.	Contractionary	No change

This Year's Production	Last Year's Price	This Year's Price
100 consumer goods	$2 per good	$3 per good
50 capital goods	$10 per good	$10 per good
200 Services	$1.50 per service	$2 per good

44. Based on the information in the table above, calculate this year's nominal gross domestic product (GDP) and the rate of inflation that occurred between last year and this year assuming that actual production did not change.

	This Year's Nominal GDP	Inflation Rate
A.	$1000	50%
B.	$1000	20%
C.	$1200	20%
D.	$1200	10%
E.	$750	10%

45. If firms are able to reduce their per-unit production costs through increased productivity, then the short-run aggregate supply curve, short-run Phillips curve, and inflation will change in which of the following ways?

	Short-run Aggregate Supply Curve	Short-run Phillips Curve	Inflation
A.	Shift to the right	Shift to the right	Increase
B.	Shift to the right	Shift to the left	Decrease
C.	Shift to the right	Not change	Increase
D.	Shift to the left	Shift to the left	Decrease
E.	Shift to the left	Shift to the right	Increase

46. Assuming that input prices are flexible, an economy operating above full employment will experience which of the following changes in output and price level in the long run?

	Output	Price Level
A.	Increase	Increase
B.	No change	Increase
C.	Increase	No change
D.	Increase	Decrease
E.	Decrease	Increase

47. In the long-run, increases in the money supply result in which of the following changes in the nominal and real gross domestic product (GDP)?

	Nominal GDP	Real GDP
A.	Increase	Increase
B.	Increase	Decrease
C.	Decrease	No change
D.	Increase	No change
E.	No change	Increase

48. An increase in resource prices will shift the

A. short run aggregate supply to the left.
B. short run aggregate supply to the right.
C. aggregate demand to the right
D. aggregate demand to the left.
E. long-run aggregate supply to the right.

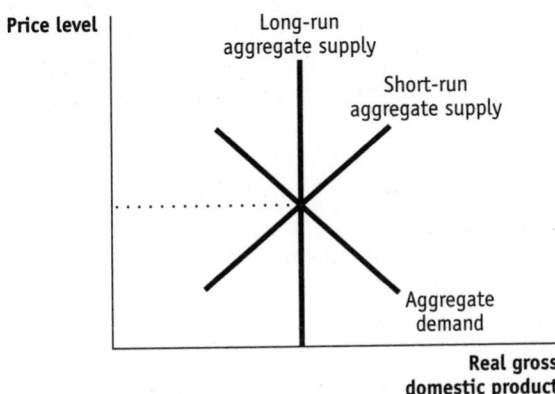

49. According to the graph above, which of the following is true about this economy in the long run?

A. Contractionary monetary policy will restore this economy to its long-run equilibrium.
B. The long-run aggregate supply curve will shift to the left in order to restore the long-run Equilibrium.
C. The economy depicted is currently in a long-run equilibrium.
D. A combination of increased government spending and an increase in the money supply could shift aggregate demand to the right and restore long-run equilibrium.
E. Wages will increase as they adjust to the new price level and the short-run aggregate supply curve will shift to the left and restore long-run equilibrium.

50. In the long run, decreases in aggregate demand lead to which of the following changes in nominal and real gross domestic product (GDP)?

	Nominal GDP	Real GDP
A.	No change	Decrease
B.	Decrease	No change
C.	Decrease	Decrease
D.	Increase	Increase
E.	Increase	No change

51. Assume that the required reserve ratio is 5 percent and that the bank keeps an additional 5 percent in reserve. If Shayne deposits $100 in cash into her checking account, the amount this bank will lend from this deposit is

   A. $10.
   B. $2000.
   C. $90.
   D. $900.
   E. $5.

52. If the U.S. dollar appreciates relative to the euro, then United States' imports and exports will most likely change in which of the following ways?

	Imports	Exports
A.	Increase	Decrease
B.	Decrease	Decrease
C.	Decrease	Increase
D.	Increase	Increase
E.	No change	No change

53. Which of the following would be included as current year consumption in calculating gross domestic product?

   A. The purchase of stock
   B. The sale of a treasury bond
   C. A professional manicure
   D. The purchase of a new construction crane by a corporation
   E. Wages paid to employees for work performed this year

54. A shift in the short-run Phillips curve corresponds to

   A. a shift in long-run aggregate supply.
   B. a shift in short-run aggregate supply.
   C. a shift in aggregate demand.
   D. a shift in the long-run Phillips curve.
   E. an increase in the slope of the short-run aggregate supply curve.

55. Which of the following would cause a rightward shift in the aggregate demand curve?

   A. an increase in household saving
   B. an increase in expected profits
   C. an increase in interest rates
   D. an increase in the exchange rate
   E. an increase in taxes

56. Decreased business taxes would increase real gross domestic product by increasing which of the following?

   A. unemployment
   B. the M2
   C. aggregate supply only
   D. aggregate demand only
   E. aggregate supply and aggregate demand

57. An increase in the supply of loanable funds will have which of the following effects on the exchange rate and net exports?

	Exchange Rate	Net Exports
A.	Appreciate	Decrease
B.	Appreciate	Increase
C.	Appreciate	No change
D.	Depreciate	Increase
E.	Depreciate	Decrease

58. A point lying inside the production possibilities curve indicates that the combination of goods or services being produced is

  A. not possible, given the available resources.
  B. both productively and allocatively efficient.
  C. the result of reduced trade barriers.
  D. an indication that resources are not being fully employed.
  E. desirable if economic efficiency is a primary economic goal.

59. Which would most likely gain from unanticipated inflation?

  A. Renters who rent on a month-to-month basis
  B. Banks that have issued many long-term loans at fixed interest rates
  C. Individuals living on fixed-pensions
  D. Governments running a budget deficit
  E. Employees who have already agreed to a long-term wage contract

60. If the money supply is constant, then a decrease in nominal gross domestic product will result in which of the following?

	Nominal Interest Rate	Quantity of Money
A.	Increase	Decrease
B.	Decrease	Increase
C.	Decrease	Not change
D.	Increase	Not change
E.	Increase	Increase

Free Response Questions

On the actual AP exam you are given a 10 minute period to plan your response to the three free response questions. After the planning period, you have 50 minutes to complete all three questions. The College Board requires that all free responses be completed in blue or black ink. Although you should definitely plan your response on the question sheet during the 10 minute planning period, note that only answers written in the provided answer document will be scored.

1. The unemployment rate in Krugopolis is less than the natural rate of unemployment.

  (a) Using a correctly labeled graph of the aggregate demand and aggregate supply, show the current real gross domestic product and price level in Krugopolis.

  (b) Identify an open-market operation that would restore the economy to full employment output.

  (c) Using a correctly labeled graph of the money market, show the effect of the open market operation identified in (b) on

    (i) the nominal interest rate

    (ii) the quantity of money

  (d) Show on the graph in (a) the effect of the change in the nominal interest rate identified in (c)(i) on the price level and real gross domestic product.

(e) Explain how the change in the nominal interest rate you identified in (c)(i) will affect gross private investment.

(f) Assume that input prices are flexible. In the absence of any monetary or fiscal policy, explain what will happen to the following:

    (i) short run aggregate supply

    (ii) price level

2. Assume the United States Federal Reserve requires banks to keep reserves of 10 percent against demand deposits only.

(a) Roberto deposits $500 cash into his checking account. Calculate the following:

    (i) The initial amount his bank can lend

    (ii) The maximum possible change in the money supply from his deposit

(b) Instead of depositing $500 cash into his checking account, Roberto deposits the cash into his savings account. Calculate the following:

    (i) The amount his bank must maintain as required reserve

    (ii) The value of the money multiplier on time deposits

(c) Explain why banks may try to avoid the required reserve ratio by temporarily treating demand deposits as time deposits.

3. Assume that the real interest rate in Brazil increases from 2 percent to 6 percent while the real interest rate in the United States has stayed at 2 percent.

(a) Using a correctly labeled graph of the foreign exchange market for the U.S. dollar, show the effect of the increase in Brazil's real interest rate on the following:

    (i) The supply of the U.S. dollar. Explain.

    (ii) The value of the U.S. dollar.

(b) Using a correctly labeled graph of the loanable funds market in the United States, show how the increase in Brazil's real interest rate affects the real interest rate in the United States.

Answers to Multiple-Choice Questions with Explanations

1. **B.** Raising the reserve requirement leads to higher interest rates and less consumption, investment and exports.

2. **D.** Opportunity cost is constant when resources are perfectly substitutable.

3. **D.** A decrease in the real interest rate in the United States would decrease the demand for the dollar, resulting in its depreciation.

4. **D.** If the Fed purchases bonds, interest rates fall and investment increases, leading to more aggregate demand. Also, the decrease in interest rates either reduces the demand for the dollar or induces an increase in the supply of the dollar in the foreign exchange market, leading to its depreciation.

5. **C.** The fed funds rate is the interest rate banks charge each other for borrowing reserves overnight.

6. **D.** The reclassification of discouraged workers to unemployed workers results in an increase in the number of officially unemployed persons and the labor force. To solve for the unemployment rate, you must divide 60 by 220 in order to arrive at the unemployment rate of 27.3%.

7. **B.** Both policies are expansionary, but have opposite effects on interest rates.

8. **C.** $200 billion/$50 billion results in a multiplier of 4. This means that the marginal propensity to save must be 0.25 and therefore the marginal propensity to consume must be 0.75.

9. **C.** The M1 includes cash, coin, and demand deposits, which are all used primarily for buying and selling.

10. **A.** Increased energy prices increase the costs of production, which results in a decrease in short-run aggregate supply, a.k.a., cost-push inflation.

11. **C.** A rightward shift of the short run Phillips curve is consistent with an increase in both unemployment and inflation.

12. **C.** The money supply will decrease as a result of banks having fewer excess reserves to lend.

13. **B.** Decreasing the discount rate provides an incentive for banks to borrow reserves and make more loans which results in lower interest rates and more consumption and investment.

14. **B.** Changes in interest rates directly affect the international value of the currency, leading to a change in net exports.

15. **D.** A decrease in French interest rates results in more euros being supplied in foreign exchange, leading to its depreciation.

16. **D.** Decreasing the money supply raises interest rates and discourages investment and consumption. The decrease in government spending, combined with the above policy, results in a decrease in aggregate demand and therefore inflation.

17. **D.** Frictional unemployment is associated with voluntary unemployment, which results from entering the labor force in order to find work.

18. **A.** When the Federal Reserve buys bonds, banks have more excess reserves and the money supply increases.

19. **D.** If the marginal propensity to save is 0.25, then the marginal propensity to consume is 0.75. If disposable income increases by $1000, then consumers will spend 75% of this, or $750.

20. **D.** Increases in the money supply reduce the interest rate, resulting in more investment and consumption, which further leads to an increase in aggregate demand. An increase in aggregate demand leads to a higher price level and output. Real wages decrease in the short run as input prices are inflexible and do not adjust to the change in the price level.

21. **D.** If the money supply grows by exactly 3%, then 3% growth is accommodated without inducing inflation.

22. E. Increased consumer wealth results in greater consumption and hence aggregate demand. Increases in aggregate demand lead to greater income and lower unemployment in the short run.

23. B. A higher price level in the United States results in the dollar depreciating, making imported goods relatively more expensive.

24. A. The increased discount rate results in higher interest rates and less investment, which leads to less aggregate demand and higher unemployment.

25. C. A decrease in the real interest rate encourages more investment in capital.

26. E. The presence of a surplus leads to competition among producers to lower prices.

27. B. The demand for loanable funds shows an inverse relationship between the real interest rate and the quantity of loanable funds.

28. B. The equal size increases in spending and taxes results in a balanced budget multiplier of 1.

29. C. Increases in the government's budget deficit increase the demand for loanable funds and thus the real interest rate.

30. A. Increased Canadian household income results in more imports by Canadian consumers, leading to the Canadian dollar depreciating.

31. D. Decreases in aggregate demand result in a decrease in the price level or deflation.

32. E. Nominal interest rate = real interest rate + expected inflation. If nominal rates increase by 2 percent while real interest rates remain unchanged, then expected inflation must have also increased by 2 percent.

33. C. Increased savings comes at the expense of consumption which results in less aggregate demand in the short run.

34. D. Increased educational attainment increases the productivity of labor, resulting in an increase in the long-run aggregate supply.

35. C. $100 billion in new deposits, $75 billion in new excess reserves. Given a reserve ratio of 25 percent, the multiplier is 4. $75 billion in excess reserves × 4 = $300 billion in new loans and money supply. Because the transaction was private, the change in loans equals the change in the money supply.

36. D. Zumbulu faces an opportunity cost of 100 tons of cocoa for 100 tons of bananas produced, thus Zumbulu produces 1 ton of cocoa for each ton of bananas sacrificed. Costa Del Rey faces an opportunity cost of 100 tons of cocoa for each 25 tons of bananas produced, thus each ton of bananas costs Costa Del Rey 4 tons of cocoa.

37. C. Zumbulu has the comparative advantage in bananas and Costa Del Rey has the comparative advantage in cocoa (See explanation to question 36.).

38. C. 1B = 3C benefits Zumbulu because they now gain an additional 2 tons of cocoa for each ton of bananas produced. 1B = 3C benefits Costa Del Rey as well because they now have to sacrifice only 3 tons of cocoa to gain a ton of bananas through trade, as opposed to 4 tons of cocoa for each ton of bananas when they are self-sufficient.

39. D. Decreases in government spending result in a decrease in aggregate demand and no change in the short-run aggregate supply.

40. A. Frictional unemployment is associated with voluntary job search.

41. E. The marginal propensity to save is equal to one minus the marginal propensity to consume.

42. **D.** Selling bonds on the open market reduces output and price level by decreasing the money supply, raising interest rates, discouraging investment and therefore reducing aggregate demand.

43. **C.** This combination results in lower interest rates, which encourages capital investment but has offsetting effects on the price level.

44. **C.** The nominal gross domestic product for this year is calculated by multiplying the amount of production by this year's prices and summing the results. The rate of inflation is calculated by finding the difference between last year and this year's nominal GDP and dividing by last year's nominal GDP.

45. **B.** Reduced production costs result in an increase in short-run aggregate supply, which decreases the price level and expected inflation, causing a leftward shift in the short-run Phillips curve and a decrease in inflation.

46. **E.** In the long run, output above full employment forces nominal wages up, resulting in a leftward shift in the short run aggregate supply curve.

47. **D.** Increases in the money supply drive up the price level in only the long run, therefore nominal GDP increases while real GDP remains unchanged.

48. **A.** Increases in the price of resources causes an increase in the unit cost of production that firms face, resulting in a decrease in the short-run aggregate supply.

49. **C.** This economy is in long-run equilibrium because the short-run aggregate supply and aggregate demand intersect at full employment output.

50. **B.** Decreases in aggregate demand in the long run result in a lower price level at full employment, therefore nominal GDP is decreased while real GDP remains unchanged.

51. **C.** The banks effectively keeps 10% reserves against demand deposits, resulting in $90 of excess reserves that the bank will lend.

52. **A.** Dollar appreciation results in American goods being relatively more expensive and European goods being relatively cheaper.

53. **C.** A professional manicure is a service counted as consumption.

54. **B.** Shifts in short-run aggregate supply are mirrored shifts of the short-run Phillips curve.

55. **B.** An increase in expected profits would increase firms' incentive to invest in new capital, resulting in an increase in aggregate demand.

56. **E.** Decreased business taxes not only reduce the unit cost of production but also provide an incentive to increase their investment in capital.

57. **D.** Increases in the supply of loanable funds decrease the real interest rate, which either decreases the demand for the currency or an increase in the supply of the currency, leading to the currency's depreciation. The depreciated currency induces an increase in net exports as exports become relatively cheaper and imports become relatively more expensive.

58. **D.** Points inside the production possibilities curve occur when resources are not being fully employed.

59. **D.** Governments running a budget deficit gain from unanticipated inflation because it effectively reduces the real value of their debt.

60. **C.** A Decrease in nominal GDP with no change in the money supply results in a lower money demand and thus a lower nominal interest rate.

Scoring Guidelines for Free Response Questions

Question 1 (10 points)

Part (a) 3 points

 1 pt. correctly labeled AS/AD diagram
 1 pt. vertical LRAS at full employment
 1 pt. current output and price level above full employment

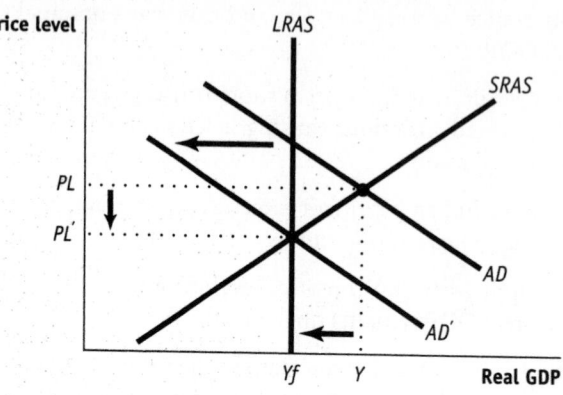

Part (b) 1 point

 1 pt. - sell bonds

Part (c) 2 points

 1 pt. - correctly labeled graph of the money market
 1 pt. - decrease in the money supply and quantity of money, and increase in the nominal interest rate

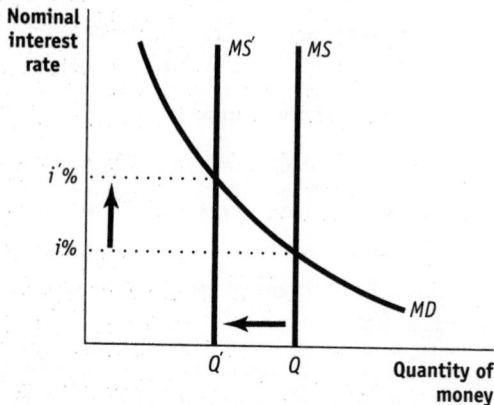

Part (d) 1 point

 1 pt. - decrease in AD, causing decreases in GDP and PL as shown in graph on part (a)

Part (e) 1 point

 1 pt. - gross private investment decreases as fewer investments remain possible at the higher nominal interest rate

Part (f) 2 points

 1 pt. - short run aggregate supply decreases as wages or input prices increase
 1 pt. - price level increases as a result of the decrease in SRAS

Question 2 (5 points)

Part (a) 2 points
        1 pt. - (i) $450
        1 pt. - (ii) $4500

Part (b) 2 points
        1 pt. - (i) 0
        1 pt. - (ii) undefined or infinite

Part (c) 1 point
        1 pt. - Banks profit by lending as much of their reserves as possible.

Question 3 (5 points)

Part (a) 3 points
        1 pt. - correctly labeled foreign exchange graph for the U.S. dollar
        1 pt. - increase in the supply of the dollar because U.S. investors seek higher Brazilian
            returns
        1 pt. - U.S. dollar depreciates

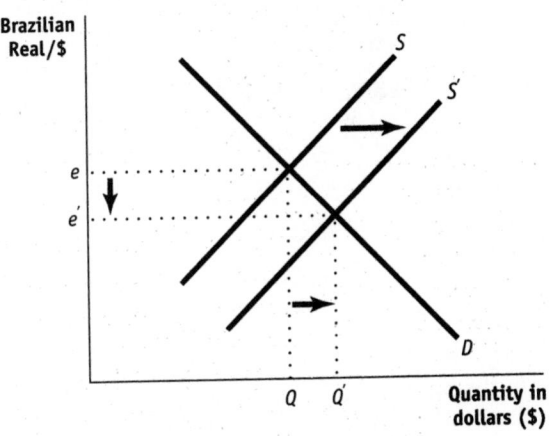

Part (b) 2 points
        1 pt. - correctly labeled loanable funds graph
        1 pt. - decrease in supply of loanable funds and increase in the real interest rate

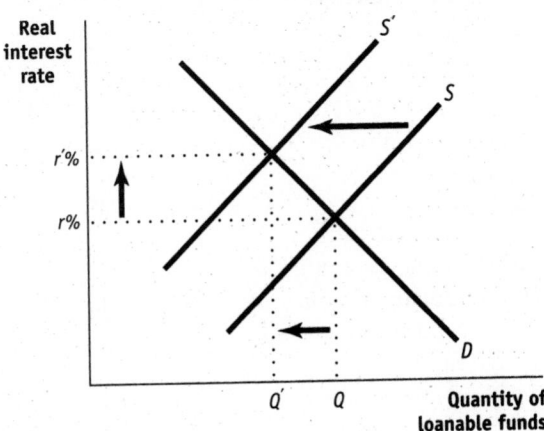

Practice Test 2

Multiple-Choice Questions

1. Which of the following is included in both the M1 and M2?

   A. time deposits
   B. demand deposits
   C. overnight eurodollars
   D. money market mutual funds
   E. Everything included in the M2 is also included in the M1.

2. An increase in government spending while the economy is fully employed will most likely result in

   A. cost-push inflation.
   B. Stagflation.
   C. demand-pull inflation.
   D. lower interest rates.
   E. a decrease in the money supply.

3. In the long-run, increases in the money supply result in which of the following changes in aggregate demand and the long-run aggregate supply?

	Aggregate Demand	Long-run Aggregate Supply
A.	Increase	Increase
B.	Increase	Decrease
C.	Decrease	No change
D.	Increase	No change
E.	No change	Increase

4. A decrease in resource prices will shift the

   A. short-run aggregate supply to the left.
   B. short-run aggregate supply to the right.
   C. aggregate demand to the right.
   D. aggregate demand to the left.
   E. long-run aggregate supply to the left.

5. In the long run, decreases in aggregate demand lead to which of the following changes in the nominal gross domestic product (GDP) and the price level?

	Nominal GDP	Price Level
A.	No change	Decrease
B.	Decrease	No change
C.	Decrease	Decrease
D.	Increase	Increase
E.	Increase	No change

6. Assume that the required reserve ratio is 20 percent. If Coriander deposits $100 in cash into her checking account, the maximum dollar amount in new loans the banking system can create is

   A. $20.
   B. $80.
   C. $400.
   D. $500.
   E. $5.

7. If exchange rates are fixed and the U.S. rate of inflation decreases relative to its trade partners, then U.S. imports and exports will most likely change in which of the following ways?

	Imports	Exports
A.	Increase	Decrease
B.	Decrease	Decrease
C.	Decrease	Increase
D.	Increase	Increase
E.	No change	No change

8. Which of the following would be counted toward gross private investment in this year's gross domestic product?

   A. the purchase of corporate stock
   B. the sale of a treasury bond
   C. the purchase of inventory
   D. the purchase of a new car
   E. the purchase of a college education

9. Movement along an existing short-run Phillips curve corresponds to

   A. a shift in long-run aggregate supply.
   B. a shift in short-run aggregate supply.
   C. a shift in aggregate demand.
   D. a shift in the long-run Phillips curve.
   E. an increase in the slope of the short-run aggregate supply curve.

10. Which of the following would cause a leftward shift in the aggregate demand curve?

   A. an increase in the expected price level
   B. a decrease in interest rates
   C. a decrease in the exchange rate
   D. a decrease in consumer confidence
   E. an increase in household wealth

11. Increased business taxes would decrease real gross domestic product by decreasing which of the following?

   A. unemployment
   B. the M2
   C. aggregate supply only
   D. aggregate demand only
   E. aggregate supply and aggregate demand

12. An increase in the demand for loanable funds will have which of the following effects on the exchange rate and net exports?

	Exchange Rate	Net Exports
A.	Appreciate	Decrease
B.	Appreciate	Increase
C.	Appreciate	No change
D.	Depreciate	Increase
E.	Depreciate	Decrease

13. A production possibility curve with a constant slope indicates which of the following?

   A. Increasing opportunity cost is present.
   B. The combination of goods and services that lies on the production possibilities curve is unattainable given the current technology.
   C. The opportunity cost of production is decreasing.
   D. The opportunity cost of producing the first unit is the same as the opportunity cost of producing each successive unit.
   E. Resources are being used at a slower rate than they were in the past.

14. Which would most likely be harmed by unanticipated inflation?

    A. property owners who rent to occupants on a month to month basis
    B. a bank that has made many long-term loans at fixed interest rates
    C. an individual whose main source of income is stock dividends
    D. governments running a budget deficit
    E. an employer whose labor force is locked into a long-term wage contract

15. An increase in banks' willingness and ability to lend excess reserves will most likely result in which of the following?

	Nominal Interest Rate	Quantity of Money
A.	Increase	Decrease
B.	Decrease	Increase
C.	No change	No change
D.	Increase	No change
E.	Increase	Increase

16. An increase in personal income taxes will most likely cause output and unemployment to change in which of the following ways?

	Output	Unemployment
A.	Increase	Increase
B.	Decrease	Increase
C.	Decrease	Decrease
D.	Increase	No change
E.	Increase	Decrease

17. If the real interest rate in France decreased relative to the real interest rate in the United States while domestic prices remained unchanged then the euro would

    A. depreciate, making French exports to the United States more expensive.
    B. appreciate, making U.S. imports from France more expensive.
    C. depreciate, making French imports from the United States cheaper.
    D. depreciate, making U.S. imports from France cheaper.
    E. appreciate, making French exports to the United States more expensive.

18. If an economy is experiencing a significant recession, which of the following will cause employment and interest rates to increase?

    A. The Federal Reserve raises the discount rate.
    B. The government reduces spending while raising taxes.
    C. The Federal Reserve buys treasury securities on the open market.
    D. The Federal Reserve lowers the reserve requirement.
    E. The government increases spending and reduces taxes.

19. Which best describes the mechanism by which interest rates influence economic growth?

    A. Lower interest rates encourage increased consumption, which results in economic growth
    B. Higher interest rates discourage private investment, which results in economic growth
    C. Decreases in net investment and increases in depreciation, which results in economic growth
    D. Lower interest rates encourage gross private investment, capital formation, and economic growth
    E. Increased interest rates result in the currency appreciating, which leads to economic growth

20. Which combination of monetary and fiscal policies would be appropriate for an economy experiencing a recession?

   A. The Federal Reserve purchases securities on the open market while government spending increases.
   B. The Federal Reserve purchases securities on the open market while government increases taxes.
   C. The Federal Reserve sells securities on the open market while government increases spending.
   D. The Federal Reserve sells securities on the open market while government increases taxes.
   E. The Federal Reserve lowers the discount rate while the government simultaneously decreases spending and raises taxes.

21. If an economy can produce more consumer goods without giving up capital goods, which of the following are true?

   I. The opportunity cost of producing an additional consumer good is zero.
   II. The economy is operating within its production possibilities frontier.
   III. The economy is productively efficient.

   A. I only
   B. II only
   C. I, II, and III
   D. I and II only
   E. I and III only

22. Depreciation of the Japanese yen in the foreign exchange market could be caused by an increase in which of the following?

   A. U.S. imports from Japan
   B. the U.S. price level
   C. demand for the Japanese yen by U.S. investors
   D. the U.S. real interest rate
   E. Japanese exports to Mexico

23. Decreased employment and increased price level are best associated with

   A. a leftward shift of the short-run Phillips curve.
   B. a leftward shift of the aggregate demand curve.
   C. a leftward shift of the short-run aggregate supply curve.
   D. a rightward shift of the long-run Phillips curve.
   E. a rightward shift of the investment demand curve.

24. Which of the following is a combination of fiscal and monetary policy designed to reduce inflation in an economy?

   A. increase taxes and reduce government spending
   B. raise the discount rate and sell treasury bonds
   C. sell treasury bonds and reduce taxes
   D. decrease both government spending and the required reserve ratio
   E. increase taxes and sell treasury bonds

25. Which of the following would cause an increase in the official unemployment rate?

   A. People quit working in order to attend school full-time.
   B. People working in the service industry are reclassified from full-time to part-time.
   C. College students begin actively applying for employment.
   D. People who were employed by the government start their own consulting businesses.
   E. People retire from their jobs and perform volunteer work for charitable organizations.

26. Which of the following best describes the sequence of events that occurs when the Federal Reserve increases the required reserve ratio?

   A. Money supply increases, interest rates decrease, consumption and investment increase, aggregate demand increases, and output and price level increases
   B. Money supply increases, interest rates decrease, consumption and investment decrease, aggregate demand decreases, and output and price level decreases
   C. Money supply decreases, interest rates increase, consumption and investment decrease, aggregate demand decreases, and output and price level decreases
   D. Money supply decreases, interest rates decrease, consumption and investment decrease, aggregate demand decreases, and output and price level decreases
   E. Money supply decreases, interest rates increase, consumption and investment increase, aggregate demand increases, and output and price level increases

27. Assume that autonomous consumption is $500 and that the marginal propensity to save is 0.05. An increase in disposable income of $2000 from $0.00 will result in total consumption of

   A. $100
   B. $25
   C. $600
   D. $2400
   E. $2575

28. Assume that all input prices are flexible. An increase in labor productivity will have which of the following effects on output, price level, and real wages?

	Output	Price Level	Real Wages
A.	Increase	Increase	Increase
B.	Increase	Decrease	Increase
C.	Decrease	Increase	Increase
D.	Decrease	Increase	Decrease
E.	Increase	Decrease	Decrease

29. If the average price level is 1.1, the real gross domestic product is $10 trillion and the income velocity of money is 2, then the money supply equals

   A. $11 trillion.
   B. $10 trillion.
   C. $20 trillion.
   D. $5 trillion.
   E. $5.5 trillion.

30. Which of the following will occur in a competitive market when a shortage exists?

   A. Nothing; shortages occur at the market equilibrium price.
   B. The price and the quantity in the market will decrease.
   C. The price and the quantity in the market will increase.
   D. The price will increase and the quantity demanded will decrease.
   E. The price will decrease and the quantity supplied will decrease.

31. The inverse relationship between inflation and unemployment is shown by the

   A. aggregate demand curve.
   B. demand for loanable funds.
   C. short run Phillips curve.
   D. long run Phillips curve.
   E. production possibilities curve.

32. If the government wants to increase spending by $100 billion without increasing the price level, then

    A. taxes must increase by exactly $100 billion.
    B. taxes must increase by more than $100 billion.
    C. taxes must decrease by exactly $100 billion.
    D. taxes must decrease by more than $100 billion.
    E. taxes must remain constant.

33. An increase in the government's budget surplus will most likely result in

    A. decreased tax revenues.
    B. increased government spending.
    C. higher interest rates.
    D. a decrease in the international value of the dollar.
    E. an increase in inflation.

34. Assume that the United States has a balance of trade deficit with China. What action by Chinese policy makers would offset the effects of the trade deficit on China's currency?

    A. increase exports to the United States
    B. decrease imports from the United States
    C. increase Chinese interest rates
    D. increase the purchase of U.S. real and financial assets
    E. decrease the purchase of United States' real and financial assets

35. Cost-push inflation results in

    A. increased short-run aggregate supply.
    B. decreased short-run aggregate supply.
    C. increased aggregate demand.
    D. decreased aggregate demand.
    E. leftward shift of the short-run Phillips curve.

36. If the real interest rate is 4 percent and expected inflation is 3 percent, then the nominal interest rate is

    A. 1%.
    B. −1%.
    C. 3%.
    D. 7%.
    E. 12%.

37. Which of the following would lead to an increase in the United States' gross domestic product in the short run?

    A. Personal income taxes increase.
    B. Banks lend out fewer excess reserves.
    C. Full-time employees are reclassified as part-time employees according to a new government definition.
    D. Households begin saving less of their disposable income.
    E. A significant tax is placed on all capital investment in new technology.

38. A decrease in available technology will cause the

    A. aggregate demand curve to shift left.
    B. aggregate demand curve to shift right.
    C. long run aggregate supply curve to shift left.
    D. long run aggregate supply curve to shift right.
    E. short run aggregate supply curve to shift right.

39. Assume that the Federal Reserve buys $1 billion worth of treasury securities from a primary security dealer. If the required reserve ratio is 25 percent, the initial change in excess reserves is

  A. $250 million.
  B. $750 million.
  C. $3 billion.
  D. $4 billion.
  E. $4.25 billion.

Questions 40–42 are based on the diagram below, which shows the choices in production of two countries, Ostrichalia and New Zebrand, producing two goods, cotton shirts and wool sweaters, using all of their available resources.

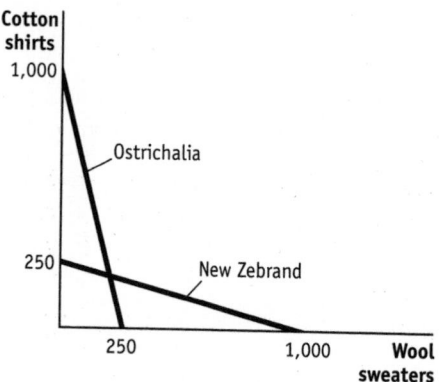

40. According to the theory of comparative advantage, Ostrichalia would find it advantageous to

  A. export cotton shirts and import wool sweaters.
  B. import both wool sweaters and cotton shirts.
  C. export both wool sweaters and cotton shirts.
  D. import cotton shirts and export wool sweaters.
  E. trade 1000 cotton shirts for 200 wool sweaters.

41. Which of the following statements best describes the conditions for specialization in either Ostrichalia or New Zebrand?

  A. Ostrichalia should specialize in wool sweaters, according to their absolute advantage in them.
  B. Ostrichalia should specialize in wool sweaters, according to their comparative advantage in them.
  C. New Zebrand should specialize in wool sweaters, according to their absolute advantage in them.
  D. New Zebrand should specialize in wool sweaters, according to their comparative advantage in them.
  E. Neither country should specialize, but instead should avoid trade and become self-sufficient.

42. Which of the following terms of trade would be advantageous for Ostrichalia but not for New Zebrand?

  A. 1 cotton shirt for 1 wool sweater
  B. 500 cotton shirts for 100 wool sweaters
  C. 200 cotton shirts for 900 wool sweaters
  D. 200 cotton shirts for 775 wool sweaters
  E. 1000 cotton shirts for 1000 wool sweaters

43. Which is most likely to occur if the Federal Reserve sells treasury bonds on the open market?

 A. Interest rates will decrease.
 B. The money supply will increase.
 C. Net exports will increase.
 D. Excess reserves in the banking system will decrease.
 E. Aggregate demand will increase.

44. Which fiscal policy action by government will shift aggregate demand to the left?

 A. the open market sale of bonds by the Federal Reserve
 B. an increase in the discount rate
 C. an increase in taxes
 D. an increase in government spending
 E. an increase in the reserve requirement

45. Cost-push inflation occurs when there is

 A. an increase in capital investment at the expense of government spending.
 B. a decrease in net exports resulting from appreciation of the currency.
 C. an increase in both inflation and unemployment.
 D. a decrease in gross private investment resulting from government borrowing.
 E. a rightward shift of the money supply.

46. If the real interest rate in Argentina has increased from 5% to 6% and the real interest rate in Brazil has increased from 4% to 6%, Brazilian capital flow and currency should change in which of the following ways?

	Capital Flow	Currency
A.	Out	Appreciates
B.	In	Appreciates
C.	In	Depreciates
D.	Out	Depreciates
E.	No change	No change

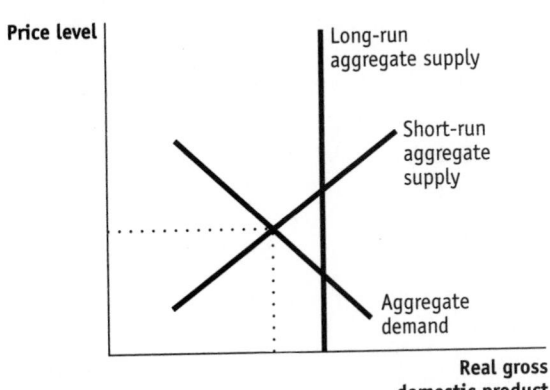

47. According to the graph above, which of the following is true about this economy in the long-run?

 A. Contractionary monetary policy will restore this economy to its long-run equilibrium.
 B. The long-run aggregate supply curve will shift to the left in order to restore the long-run Equilibrium.
 C. The economy depicted is currently in a long-run equilibrium.
 D. A combination of increased government spending and an increase in the money supply could shift aggregate demand to the right and restore long-run equilibrium.
 E. Wages will increase as they adjust to the new price level and the short-run aggregate supply curve will shift to the left and restore long-run equilibrium.

48. An increase in government spending, combined with a decrease in personal income taxes, will most likely cause aggregate demand and short-run aggregate supply to change in which of the following ways?

Aggregate Demand	Short-run Aggregate Supply
A. Increase	Decrease
B. Increase	No change
C. Decrease	Increase
D. Decrease	Not change
E. Decrease	Decrease

49. Which type of unemployment would increase if robot technology were widely adopted in manufacturing?

A. Frictional
B. Cyclical
C. Seasonal
D. Structural
E. Part-time

50. The spending multiplier increases as

A. the tax multiplier decreases.
B. the marginal propensity to save increases.
C. the average propensity to consume decreases.
D. the balanced budget multiplier increases.
E. the marginal propensity to consume increases.

51. If an economy is operating above the natural rate of unemployment, an appropriate stabilizing monetary policy would be to

A. lower the required reserve ratio.
B. raise taxes.
C. lower taxes.
D. sell bonds on the open market.
E. increase government spending.

52. Which of the following combinations of fiscal and monetary policy would effectively reduce net exports and capital investment?

Fiscal Policy	Monetary Policy
A. Expansionary	Contractionary
B. Expansionary	Expansionary
C. Contractionary	No change
D. Contractionary	Contractionary
E. Contractionary	Expansionary

Last Year's and This Year's Production	Last Year's Price	This Year's Price
100 Consumer Goods	$2 per good	$2 per good
50 Capital Goods	$10 per good	$10 per good
200 Services	$0.50 per service	$1.50 per service

53. Based on the information in the table above, if this year is chosen as the base year for the GDP deflator (GDP price index), what was the GDP deflator for last year?

A. 75
B. 80
C. 100
D. 120
E. 125

54. If households experience an increase in disposable income, then aggregate demand, the short-run Phillips curve, and unemployment will change in which of the following ways in the short run?

	Aggregate Demand Curve	Short-run Phillips Curve	Unemployment
A.	Shift to the right	Shift to the right	Increase
B.	Shift to the right	Shift to the left	Decrease
C.	Shift to the right	No change	Decrease
D.	Shift to the left	No change	Decrease
E.	Shift to the left	Shift to the right	Increase

55. Assuming that input prices are flexible, an economy operating above the natural rate of unemployment will experience which of the following changes in output and price level in the long run?

	Output	Price Level
A.	Increase	Increase
B.	No change	Increase
C.	Increase	No change
D.	Increase	Decrease
E.	Decrease	Increase

56. Assuming a system of flexible exchange rates, an open-market purchase of bonds by the United States Federal Reserve while Japan does nothing will most likely affect the U.S. rate of inflation and the international value of the Japanese yen in which of the following ways?

	Inflation Rate	International Value of the Japanese Yen
A.	Decreases	Appreciates
B.	Decreases	Depreciates
C.	Increases	Appreciates
D.	Increases	Depreciates
E.	Increases	No change

57. In order to increase the federal funds rate, the Federal Reserve

A. raises the discount rate.
B. raises the reserve requirement.
C. lowers the reserve requirement.
D. buys bonds on the open market.
E. sells bonds on the open market.

Labor Market in Burpia (in thousands of persons)	
Population	300
Labor Force	240
Employed	230

58. Based on the information in the table above how many unemployed persons are there in Burpia?

    A. 70 thousand
    B. 40 thousand
    C. 10 thousand
    D. 470 thousand
    E. Not enough information is present to determine the number of unemployed persons.

59. A decrease in taxes with an increase in the required reserve ratio will result in

    A. an increase in real gross domestic product and an increase in the interest rate.
    B. an increase in unemployment and an indeterminate change in the interest rate.
    C. an indeterminate change in real gross domestic product and an increase in the interest rate.
    D. a decrease in real gross domestic product and a decrease in the interest rate.
    E. a decrease in unemployment and an increase in the inflation rate.

60. If the marginal propensity to consume is 0.8, then a $50 billion increase in government spending could cause a maximum increase in output of

    A. $10 billion.
    B. $40 billion.
    C. $200 billion.
    D. $160 billion.
    E. $250 billion.

Free-Response Questions

On the actual AP exam, you are given a 10-minute period to plan your response to the three free-response questions. After the planning period, you have 50 minutes to complete all three questions. The College Board requires that all free responses be completed in blue or black ink. Although you should definitely plan your response on the question sheet during the 10-minute planning period, note that only answers written in the provided answer document will be scored.

1. Assume that the U.S. economy is currently experiencing a recession.

    (a) Draw a correctly labeled graph of aggregate demand and aggregate supply for the United States showing each of the following:

        (i) Current output and price level

        (ii) Full employment output

    (b) Identify an appropriate fiscal policy to restore the U.S. economy to full employment.

    (c) Show on the graph in (a) the effect of the fiscal policy you identified in (b) on

        (i) output.

        (ii) price level.

    (d) Using a correctly labeled graph of the money market, show the effect of the change in output and price level on the nominal interest rate.

    (e) Identify an appropriate open-market operation that would offset the change in the nominal interest rate you identified in (d).

    (f) Define the nominal interest rate.

2. Assume that households increase their savings.

(a) Using a correctly labeled graph of the loanable funds market, show how the increase in savings affects the real interest rate.

(b) Indicate how the change in the real interest rate you identified in part (a) will affect gross private investment.

(c) Explain how the change in investment you identified in (b) will affect the rate of economic growth.

3. Because of political turmoil in Europe, foreign investors have been purchasing financial assets in the United States.

(a) Using a correctly labeled graph of the U.S. dollar, show the effect of the increase in the purchase of U.S. financial assets on the following:

(i) the demand for the dollar

(ii) the international value of the dollar

(b) Explain how the change in the international value of the dollar you identified in (a)(ii) will affect United States net exports.

(c) Using a correctly labeled graph of the short run Phillips curve with a point labeled 'A' on the curve, show how the change in net exports you identified in (b) will affect the following:

(i) inflation

(ii) unemployment

Answers to Multiple-Choice Questions with Explanations

1. **B.** Demand deposits are the only thing listed that are part of the M1 as well as the M2.

2. **C.** Demand pull inflation is caused by an increase in aggregate demand.

3. **D.** An increase in the money supply increases aggregate demand but has no effect on the long-run aggregate supply.

4. **B.** Decreased resource prices reduce the unit cost of production for firms, resulting in an increase in short-run aggregate supply.

5. **C.** A decrease in aggregate demand reduces both the nominal GDP and price level in the long run.

6. **C.** $400 in new loans are created. $100 deposit −$20 required reserve = $80 in excess reserves. $80 in excess reserves * (1 / 20%) = $400.

7. **C.** A decrease in inflation in the United States results in less foreign substitution by U.S. citizens and more by U.S. trade partners.

8. **C.** Inventory investment is a component of gross private investment.

9. **C.** A shift in aggregate demand corresponds to movement along an existing short-run Phillips curve.

10. **D.** Decreases in consumer confidence result in less consumption and therefore less aggregate demand.

11. **E.** Increases in business taxes result in higher costs of production, so firms both produce and invest less.

12. **A.** An increase in the demand for loanable funds results in higher interest rates, which induces an inflow of financial capital causing the currency to appreciate. The appreciated currency causes exports to be relatively more expensive and/or imports to be relatively cheaper, resulting in an overall decrease in net exports.

13. **D.** A production possibilities curve with a constant slope indicates that the opportunity cost of production does not change.

14. **B.** Banks that have extended many long-term fixed-rate loans will be harmed by inflation because the nominal interest rate they are earning does not reflect the increase in inflation.

15. **B.** An increase in banks willingness to lend results in an increase in the money supply, which leads to a lower nominal interest rate and an increase in the quantity of money.

16. **B.** An increase in personal income taxes results in lower disposable income and therefore less consumption and hence aggregate demand. The lower aggregate demand reduces output which increases the rate of unemployment.

17. **D.** The lower real interest rate in France reduces the demand for the euro, thus leading to its depreciation. The depreciated euro makes French goods relatively less expensive for U.S. consumers.

18. **E.** An increase in government spending coupled with a decrease in taxes results in higher aggregate demand and more employment. The combination of spending increases and tax decreases also moves the government's budget towards deficit, which results in higher interest rates.

19. **D.** Investment in capital is the key to economic growth.

20. **A.** Need expansionary policies to combat a recession.

21. **D.** This economy is within its production possibilities curve and can increase the production of consumer goods by employing more resources without having to sacrifice capital goods production.

22. **D.** An increase in the U.S. real interest rate induces an outflow of financial capital from Japan, and so the supply of yen in the foreign exchange market increases.

23. **C.** A decrease in the short-run aggregate supply decreases real GDP and therefore employment, while also causing an increase in the price level.

24. **E.** Increasing taxes is the appropriate fiscal policy response, while selling treasury bonds is the appropriate monetary policy response to inflation.

25. **C.** New entrants into the labor force results in a higher unemployment rate.

26. **C.** An increase in the required reserve ratio reduces the ability of banks to lend excess reserves and results in a decrease in the money supply.

27. **D.** $2000 − $100 in savings = $1900 in new consumption. $1900 in new consumption + $500 in autonomous consumption = $2400 in total consumption.

28. **B.** Increased labor productivity leads to an increase in short-run aggregate supply. Increases in short-run aggregate supply result in increased output and a decreased price level, which in turn leads to an increase in real wages.

29. **E.** $5.5 trillion. Using the monetary equation of exchange $MV = PQ$, solve for M. $M = PQ/V$, $M = (1.1)(\$10 \text{ trillion}) / 2 = \$5.5$ trillion.

30. **D.** When a shortage exists, the price is lower than the market equilibrium price, this results in consumers bidding up the price and reducing the quantity.

31. **C.** The downward sloping short run Phillips curve illustrates the trade-off between inflation and unemployment.

32. **B.** Taxes must increase by more than $100 billion in order to offset the increase in aggregate demand caused by the government spending increase.

33. **D.** As the government budget surplus increases, the supply of loanable funds increases, which results in a decrease in the real interest rate. Domestic savers seek higher rates of return abroad, which leads to an increase in the supply of dollars in the foreign exchange market.

34. **D.** If Chinese policymakers increased the purchase of U.S. real and financial assets, this would offset the appreciation of the yuan as more yuan would be supplied in foreign exchange.

35. **B.** Decreases in short run aggregate result from an increase in producer prices.

36. **D.** Nominal interest rate = real interest rate + expected inflation, therefore the nominal interest rate = 4% + 3% = 7%.

37. **D.** As households save less of their disposable income, then they are necessarily consuming More, which leads to an increase in aggregate demand and so the gross domestic product.

38. **C.** Decreases in technology reduce the capacity of the economy to produce and lead to a decrease in the long run aggregate supply.

39. **B.** $1 billion deposit − $250 million required reserves = $750 million in excess reserves.

40. **A.** Ostrichalia produces cotton shirts at a lower opportunity cost and would benefit from exporting shirts in exchange for sweaters, which New Zebrand produces at a lower opportunity cost.

41. **D.** Specialization is based on comparative advantage.

42. **C.** At 200 cotton shirts for 900 wool sweaters, Ostrichalia benefits by an additional 850 wool sweaters while New Zebrand is sacrificing an additional 100 wool sweaters to acquire the same number of shirts that they could produce on their own at a lower opportunity cost.

43. D. Excess reserves decrease because as the Fed sells bonds, checks and cash are used to purchase the bonds which results in a depletion of bank reserves.

44. C. An increase in taxes reduces disposable income and consumption, and as a result, aggregate demand.

45. C. Cost push inflation involves a decrease in short run aggregate supply, which increases the price level and inflation, while simultaneously decreasing output thus increasing unemployment.

46. E. No change occurs because the real interest rates in both countries are now equal and no incentives exist for capital to flow in or out based on the interest rate.

47. D. An economy in recession as depicted could return to full employment with a combination of expansionary fiscal and monetary policy.

48. B. Increased spending and decreased taxes spur consumption and as a result aggregate demand.

49. D. Structural unemployment is associated with permanent employment caused by technology, resource immobility, government incentives, and skill mismatch.

50. E. As the marginal propensity to consume increases, the marginal propensity to save decreases. The multiplier = 1 / *MPS*, so decreases in mps make the multiplier larger.

51. A. If the economy is in recession, a.k.a. operating above the natural rate of unemployment, then the appropriate *monetary* policy is lower than the required reserve ratio, which results in an increase in the money supply, lower nominal interest rate, increases in investment and consumption, an increase in aggregate demand, and a decrease in unemployment.

52. A. This combination results in higher interest rates as the fiscal policy results in an increase in the demand for loanable funds and the demand for money, while the contractionary monetary policy results in a decrease in the money supply.

53. B. To calculate the price index, divide last year's cost by this year's cost and multiply the answer by 100.

54. C. Increases in disposable income lead to an increase in consumption and aggregate demand. Increases in aggregate demand do not cause the short-run Phillips curve to shift, but instead reflect an increase in inflation and decrease in unemployment on an existing short-run Phillips curve.

55. D. Given flexible input prices, a recession ultimately resolves as wages decrease, short-run aggregate supply increases, and price level decreases.

56. C. An open-market purchase of bonds leads to lower interest rates, increased investment, increased aggregate demand, and an increase in the price level. The lower interest rates and higher price level lead to the dollar depreciating and the yen appreciating as consumers Import more Japanese products and as domestic savers seek higher Japanese returns.

57. E. Open-market operations are used to target the federal funds rate that the Fed wants to achieve. Buying bonds lowers the federal funds rate, while selling bonds raises it.

58. C. 10 thousand unemployed persons = 240 thousand in labor force − 230 thousand employed persons.

59. C. Decreasing taxes is expansionary, while increasing the reserve ratio is contractionary, so the effect on GDP is uncertain; however, both actions lead to a higher interest rate as the demand for loanable funds and the demand for money increase from the tax decrease, while the increased reserve ratio decreases the money supply.

60. E. $250 billion. If the marginal propensity to consume is 0.8, then the multiplier equals $1 / (1 - 0.8) = 1 / 0.2$, which $= 5.5 \times \$50$ billion $= \$250$ billion.

Scoring Guidelines for Free-Response Questions

Question 1 (10 points)

Part (a) 3 points
  1 pt.- correctly labeled AS/AD diagram
  1 pt.- current output and price level below full employment
  1 pt.- vertical LRAS at full employment

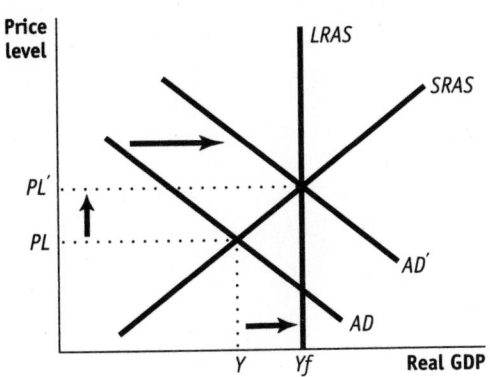

Part (b) 1 point
  1 pt.- decrease taxes and/or increase government spending

Part (c) 2 points
  1 pt. increase in aggregate demand (See graph in part (a).)
  1 pt. increase in output and price level (See graph in part (a).)

Part (d) 2 points
  1 pt. correctly labeled graph of the money market
  1 pt. increase in money demand, resulting in an increase in the nominal interest rate

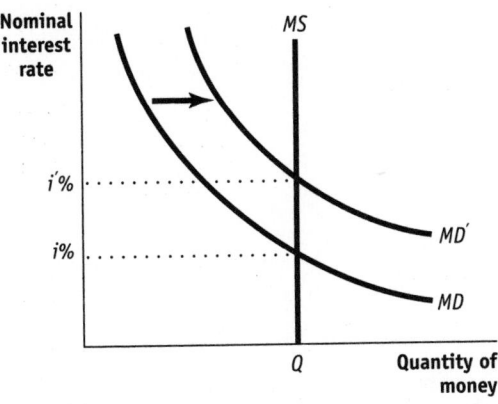

Part (e) 1 point
  1 pt.- buy bonds

Part (f) 1 point
  1 pt.- the nominal interest rate is the real interest rate plus expected inflation or $i\% = r\% + \pi^e\%$

Question 2 (5 points)

Part (a) 2 points

    1 pt.- correctly labeled graph of the loanable funds market

    1 pt.- increase in supply of loanable funds, resulting in a decrease in the real interest rate

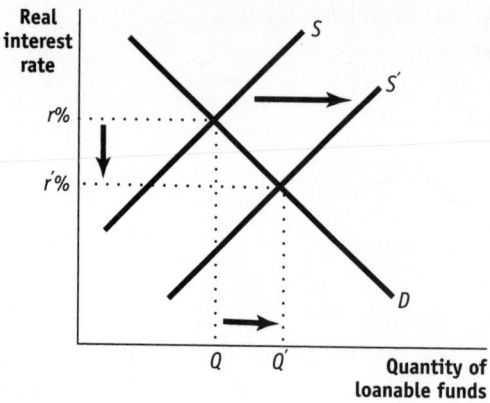

Part (b) 1 point

    1 pt.- gross private investment increases

Part (c) 2 points

    1 pt. -Economic growth increases.

    1 pt.- Capital increases.

Question 3 (5 points)

Part (a) 2 points

    1 pt. - correctly labeled foreign exchange graph for the U.S. dollar

    1 pt.- Increased demand for the dollar causes the international value of the dollar to appreciate.

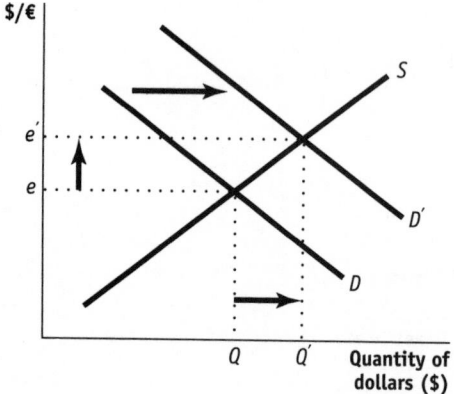

Part (b) 1 point

    1 pt.- An increase in the value of the dollar makes U.S. exports relatively more expensive and/or makes European imports relatively less expensive, causing a decrease in exports and an increase in imports, which leads to an overall decrease in net exports.

Part (c) 2 points

    1 pt-. correctly labeled graph of the short-run Phillips curve

    1 pt.- increase in inflation and decrease in unemployment shown on the graph

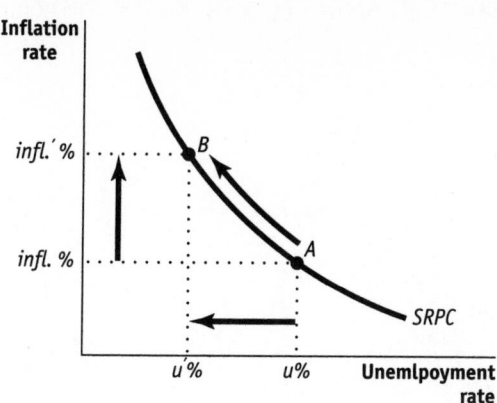